Intimate Partner and Family Abuse

John Hamel, LCSW, acquired both his BA in psychology (1986) and master's in social welfare (1988) from the University of California at Los Angeles and was licensed as an LCSW (LCS 15194) in November 1990. Since 1991, he has been director of John Hamel & Associates, with offices in Walnut Creek, Berkeley, and Greenbrae, California. Mr. Hamel and his associates provide a wide range of clinical, consultation, and training services. His areas of expertise are in the assessment and treatment of anger management and family violence, as well as substance abuse and codependency. Specialized clinical services include a substance-abuse relapse prevention group, family violence assessments (including specialized assessments in disputed child-custody cases), victim services and advocacy (including victim support groups), and treatment programs for angry and violent men, women, couples, parents, and teens. Although many of his clients are voluntary participants, many are referred from family court or child protective services or are mandated by the courts to participate in either a batterer treatment program or a parenting program.

Mr. Hamel has provided consultation and training for mental health professionals, batterer intervention providers, shelter workers and victim advocates, court mediators and evaluators, teachers, attorneys, and law enforcement and has spoken on family violence at a number of events, including the California Department of Social Services 10th Annual Family Strengths Training Institute, the 2006 Training Conference of the California Association of Family and Conciliation Courts, and the 2007 University of New Hampshire Family Violence Conference in Portsmouth, New Hampshire; he has presented regularly at the IVAT (formerly Family Violence & Sexual Assault Institute) International Conferences on Family Violence. Mr. Hamel is a pioneer in the development of the gender-inclusive approach to domestic violence, a newly emerging, empirically based model of research and treatment. His trainings have been praised both for their innovative look at theory and policy and for their abundance of practical, hands-on intervention tools. Mr. Hamel has also served as an expert court witness on the subject of family violence and has testified before the California legislature on domestic violence public policy.

His first book, *Gender-Inclusive Treatment of Intimate Partner Abuse: A Comprehensive Approach,* was published in 2005 by Springer Publishing. His second book, co-edited with Tonia Nicholls, PhD, is *Family Interventions in Domestic Violence: A Handbook of Gender-Inclusive Theory and Treatment* (2007) and includes contributions from the most respected experts in the field. Mr. Hamel is a founding member of the Family Violence Treatment and Education Association (www.FAVTEA.com), as well as the National Family Violence Legislative Resource Center (www.NFVLRC.org). He is married and lives with his wife, Judi, and their twins, Jacob and Aviva, in San Rafael, California.

Intimate Partner and Family Abuse

A Casebook of Gender-Inclusive Therapy

JOHN HAMEL, LCSW, Editor

SPRINGER PUBLISHING COMPANY

New York

Springer Publishing Company, LLC
11 West 42nd Street
New York, NY 10036
www.springerpub.com

Acquisitions Editor: Jennifer Perillo
Production Editor: Julia Rosen
Cover design: Joanne E. Honigman
Composition: Apex Publishing, LLC

08 09 10 11/ 5 4 3 2 1

Library of Congress Cataloging-in-Publication Data

Intimate partner and family abuse : a casebook of gender inclusive therapy / [edited by] John Hamel.
    p. ; cm.
  Includes bibliographical references and index.
  ISBN 978–0–8261–2135–6 (alk. paper)
  1. Family violence—Treatment.   2. Marital violence—Treatment.   I. Hamel, John.
  [DNLM: 1. Domestic Violence—psychology—Case Reports.
2. Family Therapy—methods—Case Reports.   3. Domestic Violence—prevention & control—Case Reports.   4. Family Relations—Case Reports. WM 55 I612 2008]

RC569.5.F3I5775 2008
362.82'9286—dc22   2008016041

Printed in the United States of America by Victor Graphics.

This book is dedicated to my wife, Judi, and my children, Jacob and Aviva.

Contents

Contributors

Melissa C. Anderson, PhD, MA, MFT, was an elder abuse specialist at the Institute on Aging, working with seniors traumatized by physical, psychological, emotional, and financial abuse. Her background in therapy includes work with domestic violence and sexual assault as a founder of the Rape Crisis Intervention Program at Mt. Sinai Hospital, New York City. Melissa received her doctorate in neurobiology from Mt. Sinai School of Medicine in 1988 and a master's degree in clinical psychology from New College of California in 2001. She presented in 2003 on substance abuse, mental illness, and family violence at the Eighth International Conference on Family Violence in San Diego and in 2005, through the American Society on Aging, on multidisciplinary teamwork in geriatrics. She has taught statewide for Adult Protective Service on ethics and elder abuse in California. Her research on the biochemical aspects of anxiety and trauma has been published in *Brain Research Bulletin* and the *European Journal of Pharmacology*. Melissa is in private practice in Oakland and also sees clients through the Institute for Labor & Mental Health.

Derek Ball, PhD, is the senior therapist and director of the Hiebert Institute at Marriage and Family Counseling Service in Rock Island, Illinois. As a licensed marriage and family therapist, he has worked in the Prevention of Abuse program and has supervised interns on the prevention approach for over 10 years. He earned both his MA and PhD in marriage and family therapy at Purdue University. Dr. Ball has coauthored several book chapters, including chapters on the following topics: four predivorce marital typologies that aid in clinical assessment (with William Hiebert), couples facing divorce (with Peter Kivisto), and research in family therapy (with Doug Sprenkle). Dr. Ball also coauthored an article with Fred Piercy and Gary Bischof titled "Externalizing the Problem Through Cartoons: A Case Example."

Lori Bloom has been a licensed marriage and family therapist for 27 years. Along with her private practice, which includes facilitating stress-reduction workshops in the United States and abroad, she has been the director of the People's Alternatives to Violence (PAV), a court-certified anger management program, for 19 years. She works with both female and male offenders. She has studied strategic family therapy with Jay Haley and Cloe Madanes and has trained with and been a trainer for John Grinder in neurolinguistic programming. Lori has also worked with drug- and alcohol-addicted adults and teenagers as hospital psychodramatist and was the substance abuse counselor/coordinator for the Mendocino County Health Department. She was also the director of a "court to community" program that transitioned children from foster care back to their parents. As a school counselor, Lori worked with children who came from violent homes. She also does family and divorce mediation. Lori believes that her work over the years has shown her that the one thing we all must learn to acknowledge is that fear and anger will come up in all of our lives. It is only when we can separate our true selves from the feelings of fear and the stories that we tell ourselves that keep the fear alive that we truly begin to live as compassionate and authentic human beings.

Ellen L. Bowen began her master's degree in social work at the University of Iowa and completed it at San Diego State University in 1979. She has over 34 years of clinical experience—initially in private, nonprofit settings and the last 23 years in private practice in Santa Rosa, California. She is a past board member and fellow in the California Society for Clinical Social Work. Ten years ago she cofounded Non-Violent Alternatives (NOVA), a certified domestic violence treatment program. Through NOVA, she facilitates groups for male and female domestic violence offenders. She also coteaches a continuing education class for therapists titled "Understanding and Treating Intimate Partner Abuse." She is in the process of writing a book tentatively titled *Domestic Violence Treatment for Abusive Women: A Step-by-Step Approach*.

Wendy Bunston is a senior social worker, has a master's degree in family therapy, and has undertaken further postgraduate studies in organizational development. She is manager of the national award-winning Community Group Program (CGP) and Addressing Family Violence Programs (AFVP) within Melbourne, Australia's Royal Children's Hospital Mental Health Service (RCH MHS). She has specialized in working with children, adolescents, and families considered at high risk and within the areas of sexual violence and family violence. She has published work in the area of child protection, childhood trauma, child/adolescent sex-offending, and group work. Most recently she has coauthored *The Therapeutic Use of Games in Group Work* and coedited the book *Addressing Family Violence Programs: Group Work Interventions for Infants, Children and Their Families.* Wendy has codeveloped specialist group-work programs for children and their parents affected by family violence called PARKAS, as well as the Peek a Boo Club, for infants and mothers.

Tom Caplan received his MSW from McGill University and an MA in counseling psychology from the Adler School of Professional Psychology. He is an adjunct professor at the McGill University School of Social Work and director and supervisor of the McGill Domestic Violence Clinic. He is a designated expert in domestic violence for the Quebec court system. Tom is on the editorial board of Social Work With Groups and is a certified marriage and family therapist and supervisor (A.A.M.F.T.). He has published many articles on therapeutic techniques, the treatment of domestic violence, and the comorbidity of substance abuse and domestic violence. His recently published book is *Needs ABC: A Needs Acquisition and Behavior Change Model for Group Work and Other Psychotherapies* (2007).

Mirna E. Carranza works as an assistant professor at the School of Social Work, McMaster University. She is a social worker and a registered marriage and family therapist. She is a clinical member of AAMFT and a member of AFTA. Her experience includes working with individuals, couples, and families within a clinical setting and the development of community initiatives aiming at social change regarding the social inclusion of disadvantaged populations such as women and children, particularly looking at the intersection of gender, race, ethnicity, and sexual orientation. Her theoretical standpoint is a liberationist perspective with strong commitment to social justice and human rights issues.

Karen Cohen has been a licensed marriage and family therapist since 1987. She is certified in chemical dependency counseling as well as in the use of cognitive behavioral therapy and group psychotherapy. From 1999 to the present, she has presented workshops and trainings on intergenerational, multicultural multiple-family group therapy. Since 1988, Karen has supervised graduate practicum students and registered California marriage and family therapy interns. She has been an adjunct professor at Mount Saint Mary's College graduate programs in marriage and family therapy and at the University of La Verne. Karen previously served as clinical program director for Santa Anita Family Services' Pathways Program, an outpatient drug and alcohol treatment in Monrovia, California, from 1985 to 2002. She has also served as clinical director of counseling services for Project SISTER, a counseling program for male and female adults and adolescent survivors of rape trauma and childhood sexual molestation and their families in Pomona, California.

Kimberly Flemke, PhD, is an assistant professor at Drexel University in the graduate programs of couple and family therapy. She is a trained couple and family therapist and clinically works at Council for Relationships in Philadelphia, where she evaluates and treats women with rage and trauma. Dr. Flemke previously worked as a forensic family therapist in a Philadelphia prison, frequently treating incarcerated women on past issues of rage, violence, and trauma. She also worked as a BIS treatment provider for Bucks County Adult Probation and Parole Department for women arrested for domestic violence. Dr. Flemke's primary research interest is in understanding women's use of violence and rage in their intimate relationships, having recently completed a study of incarcerated women's experiences of rage toward their intimate partners. She has published and presented on her findings both nationally and locally.

Bo Gunnehill has worked for almost 20 years in Sweden as a social worker, family therapist, and couples counselor and most recently also as a family therapy supervisor. He has previously worked in the field of child and adolescent psychiatry, as well as in the field of adult psychiatry, and has maintained a private practice.

Currently, he provides clinical services to troubled families in Helsingborg, in partnership with Martin Söderquist and three other therapists. His articles, all published in Swedish, include "Focus På Familjen, nr 4, 2004" (Universitetsforlaget, Oslo) and "Handledning-ett kreativt samspel."

K. Kerstin Gutierrez, PhD, is a licensed clinical psychologist in private practice in San Ramon, California. She provides psychotherapy and psychological assessment services to adults, children, and families and specializes in co-parenting counseling, mediation, parent–child reunification, and other services related to helping families cope with separation and divorce. She also is a member of the Contra Costa Collaborative Practice Group, providing mental health services within a collaborative team approach to families going through divorce. She worked for several years as a mediator for both the Alameda and Contra Costa County superior courts, where she also taught the high-conflict parenting program. She has taught graduate-level courses on child, adolescent, and adult development and has given presentations abroad and in California on mediation, co-parenting counseling, and report writing for the court and has published articles on the impact on children of domestic violence and on the transmission of violent coping from parent to child.

Alison Heru is a graduate of Glasgow University Medical School in Scotland and has completed psychiatric residencies in Edinburgh, Scotland, and Brown University in Providence, Rhode Island. Dr. Heru is an associate professor in the Department of Medicine at National Jewish Medical and Research Center and in the Department of Psychiatry at the University of Colorado at Denver and Health Sciences Center. Dr. Heru is a member of the family committee of the Group for the Advancement of Psychiatry and the American Psychiatric Association. She is the secretary and treasurer of the Association of Family Psychiatrists. Dr. Heru has published articles on family psychiatry and coauthored a book titled *Working With Families of Psychiatric Inpatients.* She has conducted and published research on caregiver burden in chronic mental illness, gender differences in supervision, and intimate partner violence. Most recently she has conducted pilot research in couples therapy where one partner has major depression and where there is comorbid intimate partner violence. The case described in this book is an example from this study.

William J. Hiebert, DMin, is the executive director of marriage and family counseling service in Rock Island, IL. Dr. Hiebert has worked with previolent families for 40 years, is a licensed marriage and family therapist, and was instrumental in forming the Prevention of Abuse program in 1989. He earned his STM from Andover Newton Theological School and a DMin in marriage and family therapy from the Graduate Theological Foundation. Dr. Hiebert has coauthored two books: *Dynamic Assessment in Couple Therapy* (with Robert Stahmann and Joseph Gillespie) and *Premarital and Remarital Counseling* (with Robert Stahmann). He recently published a book chapter titled "Four Predivorce Marital Typologies That Aid in Clinical Assessment" (with Derek Ball).

Jodi Klugman-Rabb is a marriage and family therapist working in private practice in San Rafael, California. Jodi received her master's degree in counseling psychology from Dominican University and initially interned with the San Rafael Police Department's Youth Services Bureau, meeting with families of first-offender juveniles. Later she went on to become the anger management program manager for a local nonprofit agency specializing in multifamily groups for adolescents with anger problems and probation cases. Jodi uses the 7 years of expertise in the field of anger management to work in the unique multifamily format and tailor treatment programs for juvenile or adult probation and child protective services clients. Along with appearing as a guest lecturer at Sonoma State University, Jodi has also appeared on local cable programming, *Recovery Station*, to discuss the effects of anger and violence in conjunction with substance abuse. Please visit www.jkrabb.com for a more complete explanation of her specialties and contact information.

Catherine Lieb, LCSW, is a graduate of Santa Clara University and earned her master's in social work at California State University, Sacramento. Her foundation in family therapy began at an Asilomar training by David Freeman, DSW, in multigenerational family therapy to heal emotional pain. For many years she has worked with families who have histories of child abuse and want to heal and change their family's aggressive patterns. She is certified as a Gestalt therapist with the Sierra Institute for Contemporary Gestalt Therapy, where she has served as adjunct faculty and on the advisory council. She currently works as a psychotherapist for Veterans Affairs.

Michael Mesmer, MFT, has been a licensed marriage and family therapist since 2000 and a certified grief counselor since 1995. Michael has over 30 years of experience in empowering groups, having led inner-city teens on survival courses and in street theater classes; men, women, and children in drumming circles and support groups; and children and therapists in theater improvisation. Michael is also the cofounder and codirector of Building Better Families, Inc. (www.bbf marin.com), which provides weekly groups aimed at reducing anger and ending family violence for men, women, and teens in Marin County and surrounding communities. He also maintains a private practice in San Rafael, California, where he treats adults, couples, families, teens, and children in individual, couples, and family therapy. Michael can be reached at 415-601-7497; PO Box 2711, San Rafael, CA 94912; or mjm@therapyalternatives.org. His Web site is at www .therapyalternatives.org.

Darlene Pratt, MFT, graduated from San Diego State University with an MS degree in counseling and family therapy in May 1992 and obtained her LMFT license (MFC 36349) in February 2000. She has worked with John Hamel & Associates since 1994. A certified domestic violence counselor and an approved batterer intervention program provider in Contra Costa and Alameda counties, Ms. Pratt facilitates anger management and batterer intervention groups for both male and female offenders. She facilitates the teen anger management group, as well as the 26- to 52-week high-conflict family violence program, and provides counseling and psychotherapy to high-conflict families, including child victims of family violence. For many years, she has also conducted specialized family violence assessments on behalf of the family court in Contra Costa County. Ms. Pratt has spoken on the subject of family violence at numerous events, including the 2002 ACAD Training Conference and the Family Violence Treatment and Education Association 2003 Training Conference, and before the California Association of Marriage and Family Therapists. Recently, her article on high-conflict family-violence parent programs was included in the anthology *Family Interventions in Domestic Violence* (2007), edited by J. Hamel and T. Nicholls. In addition to her work in family violence, Ms. Pratt has expertise in the field of sexual addiction. She is also trained in EMDR.

Martin Söderquist is a licensed psychologist and family therapist, with a private clinical practice in Helsingborg, located in the south of Sweden. For the past 18 years, he has worked in the field of child and adolescent psychiatry and with drug and alcohol addicts. He has been a therapist, supervisor, and project head in several treatment and research projects focused on addicts and their families, sexually abused children and their parents, and obese children and their parents and has conducted assessment with families referred from child protection services. Over the years, Martin has provided training and supervision in family therapy and, in particular, solution-focused brief therapy. He has published several articles and five books in Swedish and several articles in English. His Web site is www.martin-utbildning.nu.

Arlene Vetere and Jan Cooper are codirectors of Reading Safer Families—an assessment and therapeutic service for both victims and perpetrators of violence in the family. They have published extensively about their work, and in 2005 they published the book *Domestic Violence and Family Safety: Working Systemically With Family Violence.* They are both UKCP-registered family therapists. Jan is also a trained social worker and has her own independent practice. Arlene is an academic and clinical psychologist, based at the University of Surrey, UK.

Laura Dreuth Zeman is licensed as a clinical social worker in Tennessee and is a tenured associate professor in social work and women's studies at Southern Illinois University, Carbondale. She earned a bachelor's degree in sociology emphasizing women's studies at Indiana University in Bloomington and later earned an MSW from the Jane Addams College of Social Work at the University of Illinois at Chicago, with a concentration in mental health. She earned a PhD from Vanderbilt University, Peabody College of Education and Human Development, in policy development and program evaluation. She completed her 2 years of post-master's clinical training at an acute and residential treatment psychiatric facility in Nashville, Tennessee. Her practice incorporated recovery and psychotherapeutic care for individuals and families recovering from sexual assault, mental illness, and substance abuse. Her research seeks to enhance consumer self-determination and well-being through improved understanding and policy across school, hospital, and community care settings.

Foreword

The publication of this casebook represents an achievement of extraordinary scope in which John Hamel brings gender-neutral treatment of domestic violence out of the closet. This book provides readers with the opportunity to learn how experienced therapists are actually using a systemic perspective in responding to domestic violence. To provide understanding of how innovative this book is, I begin with my own story.

From 1982 to 1985, while I was working on my doctorate in marriage and family therapy, I facilitated a support group for victims of domestic violence at the local shelter. The women at the shelter made the research I was reading for my dissertation on police response to domestic violence come alive. I learned from these women about the terror in which they lived and the myriad ways their partners controlled and terrorized them. Even though I was preparing to become a marriage and family therapist and a faculty member in a marriage and family therapy program, it seemed clear to me that the primary way we (i.e., marriage and family therapists) could be useful clinically in these situations was to support victims (female) in their efforts to get out of violent homes and to support them in rediscovering their strengths and resiliencies. I taught an undergraduate course in domestic violence in the early 1980s and remember saying, "Once a batterer, always a batterer." I did not see couples therapy as a potentially useful resource. In fact, I thought couples therapy for domestic violence was a dangerous practice advocated only by people who did not know what I knew from my work with terrorized victims.

I remember being surprised when I read Dan O'Leary and his colleagues' 1989 paper that indicated that the trajectory of violence is not consistent and that some offenders use violence in one period of their relationship, but not again. This research was the first that I remember making me wonder if the beliefs I firmly held about the dynamics of domestic violence (e.g., once a batterer, always a batterer) were accurate. In 1990, in an effort to encourage my students at Virginia Tech to use data collected by our family therapy clinic to inform their work, we sought to create a profile of presenting problems, compared with problems that were revealed by the end of treatment. Students went through all of our clinical files and came up with percentages of each category of problem. Even though I thought we did not treat couples who were experiencing domestic violence, I was surprised to find that at intake, 10% of the couples who came to our clinic indicated that there had been some violence in their relationships. Even more surprising was that a thorough review of our files indicated that in 40% of the couples we saw, physical violence was, or had been, an issue in their relationships (Stith, Rosen, Barasch, & Wilson, 1991). Articles appeared by Dan O'Leary and also by Amy Holtzworth-Munroe indicating that with careful screening, family therapy clinics were seeing even higher numbers of violent couples. It soon became clear to me that even though family therapists may think they do not treat violent couples, they do. As much as I preferred to stay out of this controversial arena, I began to think that the ethically responsible approach for family therapists to take was to carefully measure the safety and effectiveness of the treatment we provide for violent couples. In 1997 my colleagues Eric McCollum and Karen Rosen and I sought and received funding from the National Institutes of Health (NIH) to develop and pilot a treatment program for couples in which violence had occurred. In 2000 we began speaking about our work, and in 2004 we published our first outcome report from this work (Stith, Rosen, McCollum, & Thomsen, 2004).

Everywhere we went within the United States and Canada, Europe, and South America to present our clinical work with violent couples, family therapists spoke with us about how affirming both our research and our speaking out about our work was to them. They often whispered to us that they were also doing this work but did not want people to know they were doing it because they might think they were doing something unethical. As we continued to hear the same message, we were reminded of the early family therapists who bravely experimented with interviewing multiple members of a family in the same room at the same time. This type of clinical work was a direct challenge to the prevailing ideology that suggested that a therapist's contact with anyone in the family other than his or her own patient broke the critical patient–therapist confidentiality and was unethical (Goldenberg & Goldenberg, 2004). When the first family therapists met and began to share the experimental work they were doing, the family therapy movement blossomed and grew.

Hamel, in this book, has brought the systemic work with domestic violence that is being practiced all over the world out for public view. His earlier groundbreaking book, *Family Interventions in Domestic Violence,* provided important empirical support for the importance of taking a more systemic, gender-inclusive, and client-focused approach to working with domestic violence. This book furthers the dialogue and offers more detailed case examples of ways experienced clinicians are intervening systemically with clients. Some of the work described in this book really resonated with me and has challenged me to think about ways to adapt what we are doing to incorporate ideas shared by these practitioners. I would not have made the choices some of the authors made in working with violent families. But regardless of whether I agree with the choices made by some of the authors, I applaud their courage in being willing to put their work up for scrutiny. Sharing our work and being willing to talk about what we do is the first step in improving the way we work with domestic violence. My bias is that the next step is to carefully measure the effectiveness of our work as clinicians and to increase the number of empirically valid outcome studies. When we are facing ideological pressure against working systemically with domestic violence, it is crucial that we be able to document the effectiveness of our work. I applaud Hamel's effort to bring systemic, gender-inclusive treatment of domestic violence out of the closet and into the mainstream!

Sandra M. Stith, PhD, LCMFT
Professor and Program Director
Marriage and Family Therapy, Kansas State University

REFERENCES

Goldenberg, I., & Goldenberg, H. (2004). *Family therapy: An overview.* Pacific Grove, CA: Brooks/Cole.

O'Leary, K. D., Barling, J., Arias, I., & Rosenbaum, A. (1989). Prevalence and stability of physical aggression between spouses: A longitudinal analysis. *Journal of Consulting and Clinical Psychology, 57,* 263–268.

Stith, S. M., Rosen, K. H., Barasch, S. G., & Wilson, S. M. (1991). Clinical research as a training opportunity: Bridging the gap between theory and practice. *Journal of Marital and Family Therapy, 17,* 349–353.

Stith, S. M., Rosen, K. H., McCollum, E. E., & Thomsen, C. J. (2004). Treating intimate partner violence within intact couple relationships: Outcomes of multi-couple versus individual couple therapy. *Journal of Marital and Family Therapy, 30*(3), 305–318.

Introduction

JOHN HAMEL

In *Family Interventions in Domestic Violence: A Handbook of Gender-Inclusive Theory and Treatment* (2007), my recent volume coedited with Tonia Nicholls, we featured a number of treatment approaches to intimate partner and family violence that challenge the current policy and intervention paradigm. Unlike traditional models of treatment, limited primarily to psychoeducational groups for male offenders, many of them rooted in feminist theories of patriarchy, these alternative approaches are more broadly evidence based and are reflective of a systemic and *gender-inclusive* orientation that recognizes that males and females can be victims or perpetrators or both.

Also, whereas traditional groups are often facilitated by peer counselors and others with limited or no training in the mental health fields, paradigm-alternative treatment can be conducted only by licensed mental health professionals who have the requisite knowledge in child and human development, psychopathology, and interpersonal and family-systems issues to address the wide range of risk factors and issues associated with intimate partner and family violence and to work in the various modalities of individual, couples, and family therapy. This is not to suggest that psychoeducational groups are of no value; properly conducted, they can be an integral and effective part of an overall treatment strategy and, for some clients (e.g., partner has left or is uncooperative), the most sensible treatment option.

It is the purpose of this book to showcase these and other paradigm-alternative approaches through extended, detailed case examples. The book is primarily intended for clinicians who work with either court-mandated or voluntary domestic violence cases and for students taking graduate-level classes in the mental health fields, but it may also be of value to anyone concerned with domestic violence public policy, prevention, and intervention.

Chapter contributors were solicited from nationwide e-mail lists of batterer intervention providers and attendees at a major domestic violence conference, as well as members of the Family Therapy Academy across the United States and Canada. Additional contributors were recruited from classified ads placed in publications of three major mental health professional organizations—National Association of Social Workers, California Association of Marriage and Family Therapists, and the American Psychological Association. The British, Australian, and Swedish contributions came from my own personal contacts.

CONTRIBUTOR GUIDELINES

Potential contributors were required to be licensed mental health professionals and to have substantial clinical experience and training in the field of family violence. This training could be formal (e.g., classes, extensive supervision, certification) or "on the job," the clinician having worked with numerous family violence cases and having obtained additional information by reading books and articles, going to conferences and workshops, and so on. They were required to eschew a rigid gender-paradigm perspective, acknowledge that family violence is a complex phenomenon in which both males and females, parents and children, can be perpetrators or victims, and regardless of the theory or theories guiding their clinical interventions, provide treatment based on a sound assessment and "where the client is."

I asked of the clinicians that they write about a case involving partner violence or other family violence, preferably one in which they saw more than one family member for at least part of the time. Although looking primarily for treatment successes, I welcomed examples of treatment failures, so long as the cases were inherently interesting and other clinicians could learn from them. Diversity of cases was also sought, in terms of presenting problem, ethnic and socioeconomic status, sexual orientation, extent and type of abuse, types of stressors and mental health issues, and whether the clients were voluntary or referred through the criminal justice system.

Each chapter was required to include an introductory section containing information on the clinician's agency or practice and theoretical orientation, including research references; a description of the client(s) and family; assessment procedure; treatment goals and reasons for selecting a particular approach, with a particular consideration of client safety; and an account of the course of treatment. To protect client privacy and confidentiality, the authors were asked to not use real names and to not give any information that would clearly reveal client identities.

STRUCTURE OF THE BOOK AND OVERVIEW OF THE CHAPTERS

The book is divided into five parts. In the introductory chapter, I review the research literature and make the case for paradigm-alternative approaches to treatment. The subsequent sections, containing the extended case examples, are "Work With Individuals and Couples," "Work With Families," "Multicultural Aspects in Partner Violence," and the last chapter and section, "Supervision in Domestic Violence Casework," by Vetere and Cooper, which should be of particular interest to individuals working in agency settings.

Altogether, the chapters reflect a wide range of family violence cases. The focus in two of the chapters is on abuse between a parent and child (an adolescent in one case, an adult in the other); all the others involve abuse between intimate partners, and in a majority of the cases there are multiple perpetrators and victims, crossing generational lines. Except for a few cases in which the violence is severe and chronic, most of the cases involve mild to moderate levels of violence and mutual abuse, and the numbers of male and female perpetrators are roughly equivalent, reflective of known prevalence rates in Western industrialized countries.

Five of the chapters come from outside of the United States (two from Canada; the others from the UK, Sweden, and Australia). A total of 20 authors or coauthors contributed; they are clinicians in private practice or employed by various agencies, with some also holding teaching positions at a university. Eight are marriage and family therapists, and there are six licensed clinical social workers, five clinical psychologists, and one MD psychiatrist. A number of the authors have been previously published, and for others their contribution to this casebook represents their first opportunity to see their work in print. Couples and family therapy are the modalities most frequently written about, although a number of clinicians also saw clients individually, and two worked with the client within a psychoeducational group format. In many chapters, more than one modality was utilized, and the group format was sometimes a precursor to, or used in conjunction with, individual and conjoint sessions. Other than the absence of African Americans, there is diversity in terms of ethnic background and socioeconomic status. I was also unable to find a suitable case of same-sex abuse.

A reference guide to the chapters can be found in Table I.1, with summarized information on each, including agency or practice location, client background, type of abuse, other issues and risk factors, modality of treatment, and theoretical perspectives. A set of questions can be found at the end of each chapter, intended to stimulate discussion and deepen the reader's critical understanding of the cases described. In reading this casebook, the reader is also advised to answer the following general questions:

1 Did the author(s) adhere to the suggested guidelines?
2 Did their treatment include safety precautions for victims?
3 Was treatment based on an understanding of the family violence literature and what the literature suggests would be promising approaches?
4 Was treatment effective in eliminating or reducing the abuse?
5 To what extent did the treatment contribute to an amelioration of the underlying issues involved?

Intimate partner and family violence is a significant social problem, and current research indicates that the prevailing domestic violence paradigm is seriously flawed, its core concepts unsupported by research and the treatment models based on them limited in their effectiveness. The contributing authors of this casebook make a compelling argument for evidence-based, gender-inclusive, multimodal, and systemic approaches. It is my hope that in reading these cases, you will be inspired to utilize these techniques in your own practice. In doing so, you will have done more than expand your treatment options—you will also be able to take satisfaction in knowing that you are not alone, that the work you are doing reflects a growing, historic trend in the field, a trend that is at once exciting and rich with promise.

Table I.1

GUIDE TO CHAPTERS

			PART II: WORK WITH INDIVIDUALS AND COUPLES			
Author	Location	Clients' Background	Abuse Type	Other Issues, Risk Factors	Client(s) Seen? Modalities	Clinicians' Theoretical Perspectives
Ball, Derek; Hiebert, William	Rock Island, IL, USA	White, upper middle-class couple	Husband emotionally abusive	Financial problems	Conjoint; individual with husband	Family systems, psychoeducational
Caplan, Tom	Montreal, Canada	White, blue-collar couple with children	Husband physically abusive; wife verbally abusive	Alcohol abuse; acting-out by young children	Conjoint; husband in perpetrator group	Cognitive-behavioral, motivational, narrative, emotion-focused
Flemke, Kimberly	Philadelphia, PA, USA	White, upper middle-class couple	Female physically abusive; mutual emotional abuse		Individual	Bowenian, family systems, object relations, feminist, experiential
Heru, Alison	Providence, RI, USA	White, blue-collar couple	Mutual physical and emotional abuse	Alcohol abuse; depression	Conjoint	Problem-centered systems therapy

(Continued)

Table I.1 (Continued)

GUIDE TO CHAPTERS

			PART II: WORK WITH INDIVIDUALS AND COUPLES			
Author	Location	Clients' Background	Abuse Type	Other Issues, Risk Factors	Who Seen? Modalities	Clinicians' Theoretical Perspectives
Mesmer, Michael	Northern California, USA	White, middle-class couple	Female physically and emotionally abusive		Group, couples	Motivational, cognitive-behavioral, attachment
Zeman, Laura Dreuth	Nashville, TN, USA	White, blue-collar couple with child	Female physically abusive; male physically, sexually, and emotionally abusive	Financial concerns; alcohol and drug abuse; custody issues	Conjoint and individual with female	Family systems (Satir), cognitive-behavioral
			PART III: WORK WITH FAMILIES			
Bowen, Ellen L.	Santa Rosa, CA, USA	White, middle-class fundamentalist Christian couple with children	Husband physically abusive; mutual emotional abuse; child abuse	Daughter's depression; husband's drinking, use of pornography; son's school problems	Conjoint with couple; individual with daughter, wife, and husband	Family systems, psychoeducational, insight-oriented, cognitive behavioral
Bunston, Wendy	Melbourne, Australia	White, middle-class couple with infant daughter	Wife physically and verbally abusive toward husband; threatening toward infant daughter	Unemployment	Mother, child in separate groups; conjoint with mother and father	Systems, attachment

Author	Location	Clients' Background	Abuse Type	Other Issues, Risk Factors	Who Seen? Modalities	Clinicians' Theoretical Perspectives
Cohen, Karen	Southern California, USA	Latino, blue-collar couple with son	Mutual physical abuse	Alcohol abuse; child welfare issues	Multifamily couples group	Intergenerational; structural family therapy; cognitive-behavioral
Gutierrez, K. Kerstin	Northern California, USA	White and Mexican American middle-class couple	Physical abuse mostly by male partner; mutual emotional abuse	High-conflict divorce; drug abuse	Co-parenting conjoint counseling	Attachment, psychoneurobiological, family systems
Lieb, Catherine	Sacramento, CA, USA	White, middle-class couple with children	Husband physically abusive; mutual emotional abuse; mutual abuse between parents and children	Sibling molestation; husband's health, depression, and use of pornography; wife's depression; son's ADD, PDD	Family therapy; conjoint with husband and wife; individual with son, mother	Bowenian intergenerational, family systems, experiential (Gestalt), psychoeducational, feminist
PART IV: MULTICULTURAL ASPECTS IN PARTNER VIOLENCE						
Author	Location	Clients' Background	Abuse Type	Other Issues, Risk Factors	Who Seen? Modalities	Clinicians' Theoretical Perspectives
Anderson, Melissa C.	San Francisco, CA, USA	Middle-class, East Indian immigrant family	Elder abuse; mutual emotional abuse	Mother's physical health, property dispute	Conjoint; individual with mother, daughter, and son-in-law	Intergenerational, family systems, insight oriented

(Continued)

Table I.1 *(Continued)*

GUIDE TO CHAPTERS

		PART IV: MULTICULTURAL ASPECTS IN PARTNER VIOLENCE				
Author	Location	Clients' Background	Abuse Type	Other Issues, Risk Factors	Who Seen? Modalities	Clinicians' Theoretical Perspectives
Bloom, Lori	Mendocino, CA, USA	White and Native American, blue-collar couple with son	Physical abuse by female; emotional abuse by male	Alcohol and drug abuse; custody dispute	Domestic violence perpetrator group	Family systems, pyschoeducational, humanistic, experiential (Gestalt/ psychodrama)
Carranza, Mirna E.	Ontario, Canada	Sudanese Muslim; blue-collar couple with children	Husband physically abusive to first wife; first wife abusive to children; second wife abusive to husband	Immigration adjustments	Conjoint with husband and first wife; conjoint with husband and second wife	Family systems, motivational, narrative
Klugman-Rabb, Jodi	Northern California, USA	Middle-class couple of Swedish and Armenian descent with child	Husband physically and emotionally abusive toward wife and son	Son's juvenile justice problems; husband's ADD diagnosis	Family therapy	Intergenerational, structural family therapy, cognitive-behavioral

Pratt, Darlene	Berkeley, California, USA	Middle-class White and Hawaiian/Japanese couple with child	Wife physically and emotionally abusive toward husband; wife verbally abusive to daughter; husband abusive to wife	Alcohol abuse; presence of younger child	Domestic violence perpetrator group for wife; individual counseling for each family member	Psychoeducational, family systems, insight-oriented
Söderquist, Martin; Gunnehill, Bo	Sweden	White, Swedish mother and son	Mutual physical abuse by mother and son	Alcohol abuse; juvenile justice problems	Conjoint with mother and son	Motivational, solution-focused, family systems

PART V: SUPERVISION IN DOMESTIC VIOLENCE CASEWORK

Vetere, Arlene; Cooper, Jan	UK	White, British, blue-collar woman and children	Female physically and emotionally abused	Financial concerns; presence of young children; alcohol and drug abuse	Consultation to social services working on case	Family systems, feminist

Introduction

1 Beyond Ideology: Alternative Therapies for Domestic Violence

JOHN HAMEL

THE POLITICS OF ABUSE

Domestic violence, also known as intimate partner abuse or intimate partner violence (IPV), has been recognized as a major public health problem, addressed through the collective efforts of national and state policy makers, law enforcement and the courts, social service organizations, and mental health professionals. The emphasis has been on a vigorous law-enforcement response with rigid distinctions between perpetrators, who are viewed as solely responsible for their actions, and victims, who are regarded as blameless and deserving of protection and assistance. Arrested perpetrators, overwhelmingly male, are incarcerated or mandated to complete a batterer treatment program, usually consisting of a same-sex psychoeducational group and often based on theories of patriarchy (e.g., the Duluth model; Pence & Paymar, 1993); their female victims are referred to shelters and other organizations where they obtain refuge, counseling, legal help, and other services.

This public policy approach has not been entirely effective. Although one source of IPV statistics, the National Crime Survey conducted by the U.S. Department of Justice, indicates that domestic violence assaults have dropped sharply since the early 1990s (Rennison, 2003), the decline has paralleled that of overall assaults in the United States (Davis, 2008). Furthermore, the preferred modality of offender treatment, same-sex group batterer intervention programs, or BIPs, has not been found to be significantly more effective in reducing rates of recidivism than arrest and monitoring by probation (Babcock, Canady, Graham, & Schart, 2007).

Recently, some family violence scholars and clinicians have explained this public policy failure as a consequence of what has become known as the *patriarchal paradigm,* or *gender paradigm,* a set of beliefs derived from feminist sociopolitical theory that has dominated the field for the past three decades and driven public policy and treatment as well as research, education, training, and primary prevention (Dutton, 2006, 2007; Dutton & Nicholls, 2005; Hamel & Nicholls, 2007). The paradigm justifies high rates of male arrests because domestic violence is assumed to be rooted in patriarchal social structures that presumably support and encourage individual men to maintain their status and privilege in the home through dominance and, when necessary, emotional and physical abuse. Thus, BIPs became the preferred intervention option, in contrast to traditional individual or family therapy, because both intrapsychic and relationship- or family-level systemic factors were dismissed as etiologically irrelevant, and the task of "reeducating" violent men to abandon their sexist ways could be more efficiently accomplished in the group setting. Indeed, there has been a consistent trend, driven primarily by coalitions of battered-women advocates and BIPs, toward institutionalizing the same-sex group format into the standards regulating batterer intervention in the various states (Austin & Dankwort, 1999; Maiuro, Hagar, Lin, & Olson, 2001).

From a mental health standpoint, the pervasiveness of the paradigm in the research literature and most professional trainings has stymied the efforts of family violence therapists to provide evidence-based treatment, including those working with cases involving clients not referred through the criminal justice system, cases in which the clinician is not legally restricted to the one-size-fits-all group model. A 1994 op-ed article in *Social Work,* the premier journal for social workers, was subtitled "The Case Against Couple Counseling in Domestic Abuse" and concluded rather tersely with the view, now thoroughly discredited, that "arresting batterers is actually the most effective 'therapeutic' intervention yet discovered" (Golden & Frank, 1994, p. 637). Restricted in their choice of techniques and modalities, it is not surprising that many clinicians find themselves reluctant to comfortably proceed with treatment and refer to paradigm-bound BIPs.

Still, mental health professionals should be aware that couples counseling and family counseling are not universally prohibited. A recent

Internet search by this author of batterer intervention standards nation-wide, with a sample of 41 states, found that although couples counseling is permitted as part of a comprehensive court-mandated batterer inter-vention program in only 15 states (36.6%), it is allowed as an adjunct, or implied as an adjunct, to BIPs in 11 states (26.8%) and is allowed after completion of group session in 15 states (36.6%).

Paradigms and Pioneers

Policies and interventions based on the patriarchal paradigm are doomed to fail because the paradigm is first and foremost an ideology; empirical findings that might disconfirm its tenets are ignored, explained away, or sometimes cited as evidence of a "backlash" by apostates who are seen at best as dangerously ignorant or at worst as actively seeking to undermine the rights of women (Dutton & Corvo, 2007). Recent works by Felson (2002), Mills (2003), Hamel and Nicholls (2007), and Dutton (2006) have called attention to this neglected body of research findings.

From the early years of the battered women's shelter movement, evidence has been amassing in challenge to the patriarchal paradigm, particularly the large-scale population surveys conducted by Murray Straus and his team at the University of New Hampshire Family Vio-lence Research Laboratory (Straus, Gelles, & Steinmetz, 1980) and the work of Erin Pizzey, founder of the battered women's shelter movement (Pizzey, 1974, 1982). Straus and his colleagues found equal rates of ver-bal and physical assaults between intimate partners and determined that domestic violence is a complex phenomenon, with multiple etiological explanations, primary among them the dysfunctional and abusive pat-terns of behavior learned in one's childhood of origin (they also found much higher rates of physical injuries to female victims, which current research estimates to be at a ratio of approximately 2:1 over men—and higher for injuries requiring medical attention; Archer, 2000; Tjaden & Thoennes, 2000). Pizzey, who in her women's refuge in England took in some of the most severe abuse cases, observed that half of these women had their own problems with rage and had been violent to their hus-bands, their children, or both.

Treatment models soon emerged that would take these and similar findings into account. Saunders (1977) challenged the theory of cathar-sis, at that time the prevailing view of aggression derived from psycho-analytic writings, as disempowering to the offender and endorsed both a social learning and systemic view. Recognizing the complexity and heterogeneous nature of IPV, he wrote, "Each case of marital violence needs to be assessed separately. No simple, recurring pattern emerges from case material on the development of intramarital violence, and it is likely that none exists" (p. 45). Saunders stressed the importance of a proper assessment to determine levels of dangerousness. Therapy goals with abusive couples included teaching problem-solving and communication skills, increasing awareness of anger cues, and changing the consequences of violence (e.g., calling the police). Curiously, despite offering research evidence and even a case example of female-perpetrated abuse, the author succumbed to the prevailing view at the time, that victims are nearly always women.

Deschner (1984) favored a phased approach in working with abusive couples, in which the partners were relegated to separate same-sex groups prior to coming together in skills-building, multi-couples groups. Neidig and Friedman (1984) also advocated a skills-building approach and the use of a multi-couples format. More importantly, they drew from theories of family therapy and called attention to systemic factors in IPV and the phenomenon of circular causality, eschewing rigid perpetrator–victim distinctions. In their view, labeling either partner a victim is to disempower that person and tacitly support efforts to seek retribution, thus guaranteeing a continuation of the abuse cycle.

"Blaming the abuser," wrote Flemons (1989), "is perhaps a more morally defensible position than blaming the abused, but it keeps us caught in the same dichotomous, either/or logic of attribution" (p. 5). Comparing domestic abuse to a manufacturing plant that dumps toxic waste into its community water supply, the author pointed out that it is easy to blame the offender and fine it, but the company is then likely to simply increase the cost of its product to offset the fines, a cost that is passed on to the consumer, and in the meantime the company finds other ways to save to the detriment of consumer safety. Ultimately, everyone pays.

> Who is responsible? We all are. We all benefit from the short-term benefits of industries which exploit the environment. . . . By affixing blame on a single company or on industry in general we obfuscate the cybernetic nature of systemic relations and allow the exploitation to continue. However, if we take the notion of "responsibility" not as an opportunity to blame but rather as a call to action, we enable ourselves to awake from the passing stupor engendered by the label "victim." (p. 7)

Margolin (1979) highlighted the reciprocal nature of domestic violence, noting that abuse by one partner, according to social learning principles, often produces compliance in the other. Furthermore, if abuse "works" for one partner, it can work for the other. Margolin correctly understood IPV as consisting of both physical and psychological components:

> Careful exploration of a couple's history with violence may reveal that both spouses have contributed to the escalation of anger with one spouse being the more verbally assaultive while the other is the more physically abusive. This places each partner in the role of both abuser and victim. The therapist can use this information to acknowledge each partner's pain and confusion as a victim as well as to help each partner accept responsibility for any actions that accelerated the abusiveness. The therapist can also reattribute the violence as a mutual problem rather than the fault of one partner. The goal of this reattribution is not to relieve either partner of responsibility for what has happened but to elicit both spouses' cooperation in seeing that the abusiveness is stopped. (p. 16)

Like Saunders (1977), Margolin was equally concerned about safety and understood the limits of the conjoint format. However, she did not seek to minimize female-perpetrated IPV. Her treatment for couples, remarkably sophisticated and progressive for its time, comprised a multipronged, comprehensive approach consisting of identifying the cues that contribute to angry exchanges, developing a plan of action to interrupt the conflict pattern, de-cuing the victim (making victims aware of how their responses help maintain the abuse), modifying faulty cognitions regarding relationship functioning (e.g., unrealistic expectations), developing problem-solving skills, and improving the general tone of the relationship.

Feminist Critiques

Feminists were quick to criticize the couples format and systemic theories. According to Taggart (1985), for instance, systems theories do not adequately address issues of concern to women, such as battering, rape, and incest. James and McIntyre (1983) make the salient point that although family therapists were right in identifying the limitations of psychodynamic theories that studied the individual outside of the context of his intimate relationships, they made the same mistake in failing to acknowledge the broader context beyond the family system (i.e., the influence of the broader society and specifically its patriarchal structures that sanction male violence against women). "Systems theory," they wrote, "is a theory about the maintenance of problems—it is not a theory of causation" (p. 123).

Similar objections to systemic theory, reviewed in Hamel (2005, 2007), include Hansen and Harway's (1995) observation that family systems approaches too easily pathologize women by not taking social roles into account (e.g., the normal role of mothering is regarded as "overinvolvement") and Bograd's (1984) assertion that systems conceptualization and language fail to capture the human dimension of abuse (e.g., women do not stay in abusive relationships because of the "needs of the system," but rather out of fear and lack of resources).

Despite the chilling effect that the patriarchal paradigm has had in the field of domestic violence, feminist critiques of systems theory should not be readily dismissed. Many critiques, such as those just discussed, are quite reasonable and have helped further the growth of the family therapy field, especially when integrated into more comprehensive, evidence-based models.

Cook and Cook (1984), for instance, saw no contradiction between the feminist position that a battering husband is entirely responsible for his violence and the systemic view of the couple locked into a pattern of dysfunctional dynamics, in a recurrent cycle that serves to maintain the violence. They shared feminist concerns about safety risks when the therapist assigns equal blame to both partners in cases of unilateral male battering. Echoing the precautions put forth by Saunders (1977) and Margolin (1979), the authors offered this perspective:

> While there is experiential evidence to support this concern, we do not feel that the problem lies in the systemic approach to couple counseling *per se.* But there is a need for marital and family therapists to become aware of the special nature of battering problems and the necessity in most such cases to separate the couple for individual or segregated group treatment in the initial phases. (p. 84)

Evolving Research

What, then, exactly is the "special nature of battering problems"? From interviews with severely battered women, Walker (1979, 1983) identified a three-phase cycle of abuse in which the male batterer experiences a period of mounting internal tension (the first phase), eventually to explode in a verbal or physical assault upon the victim (the second phase). In the third phase, the male batterer experiences remorse, the abuse stops, and a period of reconciliation ensues, until the next cycle. Because the abuse is thought to be driven exclusively by factors internal to the batterer, rather than through a process of mutually escalating conflict, those factors would have to be addressed right from the outset. The question as to whether this work should be done concurrent to any couples or family sessions, or at some point later in the treatment, should be made on a case-by-case basis, and the therapist should be guided not only by considerations of physical and emotional safety but also by practical considerations—for example, can the batterer realistically attend to systemic factors and general relationship issues while identifying, accepting, controlling, and working through his or her rage and violence?

Issues of Patriarchy

According to the patriarchal paradigm, what drives these men is a need to dominate out of gender privilege. However, research suggests that although this may be the case for some men, battering, characterized by a chronic pattern of physical violence leading to injury in combination with the use of controlling and emotionally abusive behaviors, is essentially a product of disordered personality. Typology research (e.g., Holtzworth-Munroe & Stuart, 1994) has identified these men as either depressed with borderline features or having antisocial tendencies, and a growing number of studies of female batterers have yielded a similar profile (Babcock, Miller, & Siard, 2003; Henning, Jones, & Holdford, 2003; Simmons, Lehmann, Cobb, & Fowler, 2005). Sexist male attitudes *have* been linked to male-perpetrated IPV, but mostly in countries where the status of women is economically and politically low relative to men (Archer, 2006). Patriarchal factors and sexist male attitudes do not distinguish male IPV perpetrators from other men (Sugarman & Frankel, 1996), and there is no support for the view that most men endorse the use of IPV (Simon et al., 2001). In fact society is significantly more supportive of female-perpetrated IPV (Arias & Johnson, 1989; Straus, Kaufman-Kantor, & Moore, 1997).

Straus and Yodanis (1996) found that hostile attitudes toward the opposite sex were significantly correlated with female-perpetrated IPV but not with male-perpetrated IPV. Results of the International Dating Survey (Straus, 2006) indicate that there is a significant correlation between attitudes of dominance (e.g., "My partner needs to know that I am in charge") and partner violence for both males and females; the National Family Violence Survey found correlations between relationship dominance (measured as who has the final say in important family decisions) and IPV for husbands and for wives (Coleman & Straus, 1990); and a reanalysis of the National Violence Against Women Survey found that controlling behaviors predict physical assault equally for men and women (Felson & Outlaw, 2007)—these findings suggesting that it is the need to dominate and control, not patriarchy or male sexist ideology, that is at issue. Even in the most patriarchal countries, there is evidence of high levels of female violence, perpetrated for a variety of reasons, especially sexual jealousy (Archer, 2006; Pandey, 2007). This is because institutional power does not necessarily translate to personal power in any given home, because personal power is derived from the strength of one's personality and is not therefore gender-bound, and because dominance is also related to relationship power, or the extent to which one party is dependent (e.g., economically, emotionally) on the other (Felson, 2002). Indeed, the numbers of male and female perpetrators who engage in both controlling behaviors and physical violence upon their partners—one definition of battering and also known as *intimate terrorism* (Johnson, 2000; Johnson & Leone, 2005)—are comparable (Felson & Outlaw, 2007; Graham-Kevan, 2007).

Clearly, same-sex batterer groups may be an appropriate treatment choice for some of these personality-disordered, dominant batterers, but many would benefit from intensive individual psychotherapy in lieu of, or in addition to, the group work. Partner-violent adults who have been raised in abusive homes carry within them feelings of shame, which they experience as anger and rage, and in their relationships they are as insecurely attached to their intimate partners as they were to their primary caregivers. Research by Follingstad, Bradley, Helff, and Laughlin (2002) suggests that intimate partner anger is related to anxious attachment and that aggressive males and females alike use coercive tactics as a means of preventing abandonment. For some individuals, the healing process of overcoming shame and building secure attachments can be accomplished only in the safety and security of the therapeutic relationship (Sonkin & Dutton, 2003).

Are societal factors therefore irrelevant? Research has documented the correlation, for instance, between perpetration of IPV and poverty (Hotaling & Sugarman, 1986; Straus & Gelles, 1990) and attitudes that support the use of violence (Sugarman & Frankel, 1996). Traditional attitudes may not distinguish abusive men from nonabusive men, but these attitudes have not entirely gone away. Abusers are driven primarily by personal characteristics, but some may *justify* their violence on the basis of gender. This is the case both for men, who may expect of their spouses unlimited quantities of "feminine" patience, love, and understanding, and for women, who may excuse their violence on the grounds that "he should be able to take it" (Cook, 1997; Fiebert & Gonzalez, 1997). These conditions cannot be understood simply through an individual-level or family analysis. Expanding on the work of Bronfenbrenner and Belsky, Dutton (2006) has provided mental health professionals a useful description of the multiple etiological roots of IPV. In this ecological model, the risk factors relevant to IPV for any particular individual can be found at different levels (see Table 1.1).

The work of Bronfenbrenner and Belsky (Belsky, 1980; Dutton, 2006) has paralleled a reformist trend in the field of family therapy, advanced by a number of reform-minded researchers and practitioners; consequently, mental health professionals are today less preoccupied solely with the immediate family system and are free to fashion more sophisticated and effective interventions (Carlson, Sperry, & Lewis, 2005).

Interpersonal Dynamics: The Complexities of IPV

In determining the "special nature of battering problems," one must pay special attention to the microsystem because it is at this level where

Table 1.1

ECOLOGICAL MODEL OF IPV

- *Macrosystem* (broader society)—Cultural beliefs supportive of violence and IPV; empowerment of women relative to men

- *Exosystem* (environment, neighborhood)—Job, life stress; undereducated, unemployed, lack of positive support systems, negative peer influence

- *Microsystem* (the relationship and family)—Either partner dominates; high conflict and relationship dissatisfaction; substance abuse; spiraling negative interactions

- *Ontogenetic Level* (the individual)—Need to dominate partner; pro-violent beliefs; insecurely attached; had violent role models, was shamed by parents; has poor impulse control, poor conflict-resolution skills; jealous and suspicious of other's motives

abusive relationships play themselves out. The most commonly recognized battering dynamic is the three-phase cycle postulated by Lenore Walker (1979, 1983). However, it is hardly the only battering dynamic. Batterers with antisocial tendencies, for example—what Jacobsen and Gottman (1998) called *cobras* (in contrast to the equally dangerous *pit bulls*)—do not experience tension release upon assaulting their partner or contrition. Furthermore, Jacobsen and Gottman found that in some abusive relationships, which they called "Bonnie and Clyde couples," both partners engage in serious, repetitive abuse, with no clear victim or perpetrator. In the typology put forth by sociologist Michael Johnson (2000), these couples would fall in the category of *mutual violence control,* indicating that both perpetrate serious physical violence on the other, as well as high levels of controlling and emotionally abusive behaviors. This type of mutual battering can be found not only in the general population but also to a large extent among couples where the man has been court-ordered to complete a BIP (Stacey, Hazelwood, & Shupe, 1994).

Johnson (2000) postulated another IPV category, *common couple violence,* referring to abuse that occurs within the context of a mutually escalating conflict, does not lead to serious injuries, and does not involve high levels of emotional abuse and control. This constitutes by far the greater proportion of IPV and is the type of abuse most amenable to systemic interventions involving the couple or family. As useful as these distinctions may be, however, they are hardly clear-cut. For instance, Simpson, Doss, Wheeler, and Christensen (2007) interviewed 273 couples seeking marital therapy and found empirical support for a two-category typology consisting of a low-level violence and physical injury group and a moderate-to-severe violence and physical injury group, roughly comparable to Johnson's intimate partner terrorism and common couple violence. They also found in the low-level violence group a number of highly emotionally abusive couples who really fit a batterer profile and in the moderate-to-severe violence group many couples who infrequently engaged in emotional abuse and would fit more closely into the category of common couple violence.

Unlike Walker, whose three-phase battering cycle was derived exclusively from interviews with victimized women, other researchers during the 1990s found evidence of other cycles, some from self-report questionnaires and interviews with both the male and the female partner (e.g., Cascardi & Vivian, 1995) and others from observations of high-conflict and abusive couples in the laboratory. From this research we know, for example, that marital aggression typically reflects "an outgrowth of conflict between both partners" (Cascardi & Vivian, 1995, p. 265), and that couples engage in *negative reciprocity*, characterized by attack–defend cycles in which insults and criticisms are met with a similar response (Burman, John, & Margolin, 1992), or by demand–withdraw cycles in which demands by either partner result in the other's withdrawal, thereby fostering resentments and guaranteeing a continuation of the power struggle (Babcock, Waltz, Jacobsen, & Gottman, 1993). A study by Jacobsen et al. (1994), whose sample of couples was selected for the existence of a battering husband, found that husbands are more domineering, but wives are more angry, belligerent, and contemptuous, and many of them would qualify for batterer treatment themselves.

It may be presumed that when conflict escalates to high levels, the female partner is more vulnerable to physical harm because of her usually (but not always) lesser strength and the possibility that the man's rage might overwhelm whatever chivalry and self-control he may have. There is evidence that at high levels of conflict, the woman is more likely than the man to withdraw (Ridley & Feldman, 2003), and at least one study (Jacobsen et al., 1994) found that once the man becomes violent, there is little that the woman can do to stop it. Nevertheless, a recent large-scale national survey found that in reciprocally violent relationships, men actually incur somewhat higher rates of physical injuries in comparison to women (25.3% vs. 20.0%; Whitaker, Haileyesus, Swahn, & Saltzman, 2007).

An exhaustive self-report study of 153 partner-violent women by Ridley and Feldman (2003) concluded,

> The results reported here largely confirm that conflict-based communication responses and outcomes contribute to female domestic violence as well as male domestic violence (Feldman & Ridley, 2000). . . . Results regarding mutual verbal aggression are consistent with the findings of observational studies of domestic violence which suggest that attack-counterattack interactional sequences appear to be far more emotionally and behaviorally escalating than other types of negative communication sequences (Burman et al., 1992, 1993; Cordova et al., 1993; Sabourin, 1995). Research suggests that verbal aggression may escalate into physical aggression because (a) couples tend to "lock in" to dominant reciprocal response patterns, such as crosscomplaining and invalidation loops, contempt, defensiveness, and stonewalling (Gottman, 1979, 1994); (b) arguments tend to progress through three levels of escalation, the issue level, the personality level and the relationship level, each more difficult to address and contain (Stuart, 1980); (c) there is a high probability of retaliation in order to save face and

prevent future attacks, particularly when the receiver believes the initial attack was intentional and illegitimate (Infante, et al., 1990; Roloff, 1996); and (d) the negative physiological and affective arousal of one partner, generated in verbally aggressive interactions, becomes mirrored in the other partner (Levinson & Gottman, 1983). (p. 167)

Furthermore, the Burman et al. study (1992), as well as prior research (e.g., Telch & Lindquist, 1984), determined that the dynamics and communication styles of distressed, high-conflict couples are more similar to physically violent couples than they are to nondistressed, nonviolent ones, with low levels of self-esteem, poor communication and problem-solving skills, and high relationship conflict and dissatisfaction. In separate research, marital discord and underlying relationship issues were found to be the most accurate predictors of IPV within a couple (Pan, Neidig, & O'Leary, 1994). Combined, these findings blur the distinctions between perpetrator and victim and between battering and common couple violence and support the use of a systemic approach and conjoint treatment in a wider variety of cases than previously thought.

IPV and Family Violence

From her work with battered women and their children, Erin Pizzey (1982) offered the following observation:

> Instead of flowing with the warmth and the love of a happy family, children born into violent homes have had to survive against the violent and often incestuous onslaughts of their parents. Violent and incestuous families do not let each other go. The parents take little pleasure in each other's company, and use one or all of the children in the highly complex emotional theatre and battleground of the family. Betrayal is the key word in these families. Betrayed parents in turn betray their children. They rob them of their childhoods. They exploit them physically. They exploit them emotionally. They keep them on edge in a jealous rage for attention. Then when the children do finally break away, the rest of their lives are spent in reaction against their parents. (p. 161)

Recent research has supported this conception of domestic violence as an intergenerational, human, and family problem (Hines & Malley-Morrison, 2004). Children who have witnessed their parents physically abuse one another are at higher risk than other children for experiencing emotional and conduct disturbance, deterioration in peer and family relations, and poor school performance (Wolak & Finkelhor, 1998), and they incur these problems regardless of the parent's gender (English, Marshall, & Stewart, 2003; Fergusson & Horwood, 1998; Johnston & Roseby, 1997; Mahoney, Donnelly, Boxer, & Lewis, 2003). They are at equal, or greater, risk for becoming depressed, engaging in substance abuse, and themselves perpetrating intimate partner abuse as adults regardless of whether the mother or the father was the abuser (Kaura & Allen, 2004; Langhinrichsen-Rohling, Neidig, & Thorn, 1995; Sommer, 1994; Straus, 1992). Other research has found a high correlation between perpetration of spousal abuse and child abuse for both genders (Appel & Holden, 1998; Margolin & Gordis, 2003; Straus & Smith, 1990). The overall impact on children of having witnessed interparental violence and the impact of having been physically abused are comparable (Kitzmann, Gaylord, Holt, & Kenny, 2003), but verbal and emotional abuse directed by a parent against a child may cause the greatest damage, both in the short run (English et al., 2003; Moore & Pepler, 1998) and in the long run (Dutton, 1998).

Family violence is a complex phenomenon. Although the most common pattern involves violence by the parents, against both each other and the children (Slep & O'Leary, 2005), abuse can take a variety of possible pathways (Appel & Holden, 1998; Davies & Sturge-Apple, 2007). Family violence is often reciprocal (Ullman & Straus, 2003) and sometimes initiated by the children, upon their parents and each other (Caffaro & Con-Caffaro, 1998; Lynch & Cicchetti, 1998; Moretti, Penney, Obsuth, & Odgers, 2007; Sheehan, 1997; Straus & Gelles, 1990). The one common element appears to be the role of stress in maintaining the various dysfunctional and abusive interactions (Margolin & Gordis, 2003; Salzinger et al., 2002).

CURRENT MODELS

Over the past decade, mainstream domestic violence experts, including feminists, have acknowledged the usefulness of couples and family therapy (Greenspun, 2000; Potter-Efron, 2005; Stuart & Holtzworth-Munroe, 1995). From an assessment and treatment standpoint, the clinician benefits greatly from seeing multiple family members. Children can be a more reliable source of information about prevalence of abuse, and the clinician is better able to identify the factors that maintain the abuse, such as family beliefs about anger and violence, family structure (including organization, boundaries, hierarchies, and accessibility to outside influences), and the function of each person's behavior in the family context (Hamel, 2007).

Harris (2006) summarizes the case for utilizing conjoint therapy in cases of domestic violence.

1   Perpetrators who are violent only in their families, rather than generally, and do not have serious psychopathology, are more amenable to couples work.
2   Many couples engage in reciprocal violence, which needs to be addressed to eliminate the relationship violence in general.
3   When women engage in IPV, they are at higher risk for being severely injured by their partners.
4   BIPs do not address the underlying relationship dynamics that cause and maintain relationship violence.
5   Many individuals in abusive relationships are too ashamed or afraid of seeking help on their own and find the couples therapy label more appealing.
6   In the conjoint format, clients have the opportunity to practice with each other the anger management and communication skills they otherwise would learn separately.

In addressing the underlying relationship dynamics, the couples therapist also has the opportunity to address important childhood-of-origin issues and in doing so to identify how these issues become projected by one partner onto the other (Goldner, 1998). Research on adult attachment has determined that abusive couples are at a higher risk for violence when both partners are insecurely attached and especially when an anxiously attached partner with a fear of abandonment is paired with a dismissive partner who has a fear of intimacy (Bartholomew, Henderson, & Dutton, 2001; Bookwala, 2002; Roberts & Noller, 1998). In addressing this dynamic, akin to the attack–defend cycle previously discussed, and mechanisms such as projection, the couples therapist helps in the healing process of the individual parties while helping the couple correct their abusive dynamics.

Multimodal Treatment

Clinicians with a systemic perspective do not need to be limited to any particular modality or approach. Thinking systemically, as Bograd (1984) pointed out, does not mandate working with the partners together. Recent books by Hamel (2005), Hamel and Nicholls (2007), and Potter-Efron (2005) argue for a flexible, multimodal, and comprehensive approach, and Hamel (2005, 2007) stresses the importance of using a phased approach, regardless of modality, in which the abuse is addressed first prior to a more intensive, potentially stressful and emotionally dangerous exploration of trauma and childhood-of-origin issues.

Individual therapy, as previously noted, is appropriate for clients with serious psychopathology, for whom overcoming their violence requires far more than the acquisition of prosocial skills. Its advantages are primarily in the flexibility of fashioning a treatment plan suited to the client's individual needs. Murphy and Eckhardt (2006) argue that individual treatment can hold batterers more accountable in comparison to group treatment, particularly those groups that are too large or led by poorly trained facilitators who are unable to prevent negative role modeling and reinforcement.

Group is the ideal modality for offenders no longer with their partner and for those who remain violent and dangerous and require the acquisition of prosocial skills. Maiuro and colleagues (2001) lament the rigidity of one-size-fits-all intervention policies but argue that there are advantages to group format, such as helping the batterer feel understood among peers and overcome not only denial but also feelings of shame and thus motivating him or her to stay in treatment. There are a number of alternatives to the anachronistic Duluth model that eschew confrontational tactics and are not based exclusively on patriarchal ideology, including those based in cognitive-behavioral approaches, collectively known as CBT (Price & Rosenbaum, 2007; Sonkin & Durphy, 1997). When tailored to the needs of the client, such groups may be more efficacious than the outcome research would indicate (Babcock et al., 2007). Among these are homogeneous, culturally specific groups, for Native Americans (Kiyoshk, 2003), Asians (Mun Wah, 1998), Latinos (Carrillo & Zarza, unpublished), and African Americans (Williams, 1994); groups for parents who have abused their children as well as each other (Pratt & Chapman, 2007); and groups for at-risk, partner-violent, and family-violent adolescents (Langhinrichsen-Rohling, Turner, & McGowan, 2007). And finally, given that a disproportionately high number of batters come from populations with low socioeconomic status (SES), group is still the most economical modality.

Working in the modalities of couples or family, the clinician may see any number of individuals, in various combinations. This may involve the couple, either as a dyad (Coleman, 2007; Goldner, 1998; O'Leary & Cohen, 2007; Vetere & Cooper, 2007) or in group (Geffner & Mantooth, 2000; O'Leary, Heyman, & Neidig, 1999), the entire family, or selected members (Downey, 1997; Hamel, 2005, 2007; Potter-Efron, 2005; Thomas, 2007).

Outcome research on family therapy for IPV is essentially nonexistent; however, family therapy has consistently been found to be more effective in preventing relapse among substance abusers (Stanton & Shadish, 1997), an "acting out" population that shares many personality and behavior characteristics with partner-violent individuals (Potter-Efron, 2007). When compared to traditional BIP groups, couples counseling with low- to moderate-level IPV is as effective and just as safe (Dunford, 2000; O'Leary et al., 1999)—and significantly more effective for batterers who also have a substance abuse problem (Brannen & Rubin, 1996). Preliminary research suggests that traditional systems-oriented couples therapy of various schools (e.g., structural, strategic, narrative, solution-focused, emotion-focused) is as effective as a psychoeducational, skills-building approach to couples counseling (LaTaillade, Epstein, & Werlinich, 2006). However, the couples group format, which emphasizes skills-building, has been found in one study be somewhat more effective in reducing IPV recidivism and significantly more effective in changing pro-violent attitudes (Stith, Rosen, & McCollum, 2004) than the conjoint format.

In summary, current treatment programs as a whole have failed to significantly reduce domestic violence. As the research literature suggests, such programs have failed because they are based fundamentally on ideology rather than the body of empirical evidence. Alternative forms of treatment, reflective of a gender-inclusive, systemic, and multimodal perspective, have reemerged to challenge the dominant paradigm. Although these alternative approaches have only recently begun to be tested under experimental conditions, they are fundamentally rooted in the research data and would seem to hold much promise for intimate partner and family violence treatment in this new millennium.

REFERENCES

Appel, A., & Holden, G. (1998). The co-occurrence of spouse and physical child abuse: A review and appraisal. *Journal of Family Psychology, 12*(4), 578–599.

Archer, J. (2000). Sex differences in aggression between heterosexual partners: A meta-analytic review. *Psychological Bulletin, 126*(5), 651–680.

Archer, J. (2006). Cross-cultural differences in physical aggression between partners: A social-role analysis. *Personality and Social Psychology Review, 10*(2), 133–153.

Arias, I., & Johnson, P. (1989). Evaluations of physical aggression among intimate dyads. *Journal of Interpersonal Violence, 4*(3), 298–307.

Austin, J., & Dankwort, J. (1999). Standards for batterer programs. *Journal of Interpersonal Violence, 14*(2), 152–168.

Babcock, J., Canady, B., Graham, K., & Schart, L. (2007). The evolution of battering interventions: From the dark ages into the scientific age. In J. Hamel & T. Nicholls (Eds.), *Family interventions in domestic violence: A handbook of gender-inclusive theory and treatment* (pp. 215–244). New York: Springer Publishing.

Babcock, J., Miller, S., & Siard, C. (2003). Toward a typology of abusive women: Differences between partner-only and generally violent women in the use of violence. *Psychology of Women Quarterly, 13,* 46–59.

Babcock, J., Waltz, J., Jacobsen, N., & Gottman, J. (1993). Power and violence: The relation between communication patterns, power discrepancies, and domestic violence. *Journal of Consulting and Clinical Psychology, 61*(1), 40–50.

Bartholomew, K., Henderson, A., & Dutton, D. (2001). Insecure attachment and abusive intimate relationships. In C. Culow (Ed.), *Adult attachment and couple psychotherapy* (pp. 43–61). New York: Brunner-Routledge.

Belsky, J. (1980). Child maltreatment: An ecological integration. *American Psychologist, 35*(4), 320–325.

Bograd, M. (1984). Family systems approaches to wife battering: A feminist critique. *American Journal of Orthopsychiatry, 54,* 558–568.

Bookwala, J. (2002). Adult attachment styles and aggressive behaviors in dating relationships. *Journal of Social and Personal Relationships, 15,* 175–190.

Brannen, S., & Rubin, A. (1996). Comparing the effectiveness of gender-specific and couples groups in a court-mandated spouse abuse treatment program. *Research on Social Work Practice, 6*(4), 405–424.

Burman, B., John, R., & Margolin, G. (1992). Observed patterns of conflict in violent, nonviolent, and nondistressed couples. *Behavioral Assessment, 14,* 15–37.

Caffaro, J., & Conn-Caffaro, A. (1998). *Sibling abuse trauma: Assessment and intervention strategies for children, families and adults.* Binghamton, NY: Haworth Maltreatment & Trauma Press.

Carlson, J., Sperry, L., & Lewis, J. (2005). *Family therapy techniques.* New York: Routledge.

Carrillo, R., & Zarza, M. (unpublished). *An intervention model for Latino perpetrators of intimate partner violence: El hombre noble buscando balance.* Unpublished manuscript, available from the author at mzarza@ucla.edu

Cascardi, M., & Vivian, D. (1995). Context for specific episodes of marital violence: Gender and severity of violence differences. *Journal of Family Violence, 10*(3), 265–293.

Coleman, D., & Straus, M. (1990). Marital power, conflict and violence in a nationally representative sample of American couples. In M. Straus & R. Gelles (Eds.), *Physical violence in American families.* New Brunswick, NJ: Transaction.

Coleman, V. (2007). Dangerous dances: Treatment of domestic violence in same-sex couples. In J. Hamel & T. Nicholls (Eds.), *Family interventions in domestic violence: A handbook of gender-inclusive theory and treatment* (pp. 397–416). New York: Springer Publishing.

Cook, D., & Cook, A. (1984). A systemic treatment approach to wife battering. *Journal of Marital and Family Therapy, 10*(1), 83–93.

Cook, P. (1997). *Abused men: The hidden side of domestic violence.* Westport, CT: Praeger.

Davies, P., & Sturge-Apple, M. (2007). The impact of domestic violence on children's development. In J. Hamel & T. Nicholls (Eds.), *Family interventions in domestic violence: A handbook of gender-inclusive theory and treatment* (pp. 165–190). New York: Springer.

Davis, R. (2008). *Domestic violence: Intervention, policies and solutions.* New York: Taylor Francis CRC Press.

Deschner, F. (1984). *The hitting habit: Anger control for battering couples.* New York: Simon & Schuster.

Downey, L. (1997). Adolescent violence: A systemic and feminist perspective. *Australian & New Zealand Journal of Family Therapy, 18*(2), 70–79.

Dunford, F. (2000). The San Diego navy experiment: An assessment of interventions for men who assault their wives. *Journal of Consulting and Clinical Psychology, 68*(3), 468–476.

Dutton, D. (1998). *The abusive personality.* New York: Guilford.

Dutton, D. (2006). *Domestic violence reexamined.* Vancouver: University of British Columbia Press.

Dutton, D. (2007). Thinking outside the box: Gender and court-mandated therapy. In J. Hamel & T. Nicholls (Eds.), *Family interventions in domestic violence: A handbook of gender-inclusive theory and treatment* (pp. 27–58). New York: Springer Publishing.

Dutton, D. G., & Corvo, K. C. (2007). The Duluth model: A data-impervious paradigm and a flawed strategy. *Aggression and Violent Behavior, 12*, 658–667.

Dutton, D., & Nicholls, T. (2005). A critical review of the gender paradigm in domestic violence research and theory: Part I—Theory and data. *Aggression and Violent Behavior, 10*, 680–714.

English, D., Marshall, D., & Stewart, A. (2003). Effects of family violence on child behavior and health during early childhood. *Journal of Family Violence, 18*(1), 43–57.

Felson, R. (2002). *Violence & gender reexamined.* Washington, DC: American Psychological Association.

Felson, R., & Outlaw, M. (2007). The control motive and marital violence. *Violence and Victims, 22*(4), 387–407.

Fergusson, D., & Horwood, J. (1998). Exposure to interparental violence childhood and psychosocial adjustment in young adulthood. *Child Abuse & Neglect, 22*(5), 339–357.

Fiebert, M., & Gonzalez, D. (1997). Women who initiate assaults: The reasons offered for such behavior. *Psychological Reports, 80*, 583–590.

Flemons, D. (1989). An ecosystemic view of family violence. *Family Therapy, 16*(1), 1–10.

Follingstad, D., Bradley, R., Helff, C., & Laughlin, J. (2002). A model for predicting dating violence: Anxious attachment, angry temperament and a need for relationship control. *Violence and Victims, 17*(1), 35–47.

Geffner, R., & Mantooth, C. (2000). *Ending spouse/partner abuse: A psychoeducational approach for individuals and couples.* New York: Springer Publishing.

Golden, G., & Frank, P. (1994). When 50-50 isn't fair: The case against couple counseling in domestic abuse. *Social Work, 39*(6), 636–637.

Goldner, V. (1998). The treatment of violence and victimization in intimate relationships. *Family Process, 37*(3), 263–286.

Graham-Kevan, N. (2007). Power and control in relationship aggression. In J. Hamel & T. Nicholls (Eds.), *Family interventions in domestic violence: A handbook of gender-inclusive theory and treatment* (pp. 87–108). New York: Springer Publishing.

Greenspun, W. (2000). Embracing the controversy: A metasystemic approach to the treatment of domestic violence. In P. Papp (Ed.), *Couples on the fault line: New directions for therapists* (pp. 154–179). New York: Guilford.

Hamel, J. (2005). *Gender-inclusive treatment of intimate partner abuse: A comprehensive approach.* New York: Springer Publishing.

Hamel, J. (2007). Gender inclusive family interventions in domestic violence: An overview. In J. Hamel & T. Nicholls (Eds.), *Family interventions in domestic violence: A handbook of gender-inclusive theory and treatment* (pp. 247–274). New York: Springer Publishing.

Hamel, J., & Nicholls, T. (2007). *Family interventions in domestic violence: A handbook of gender-inclusive theory and treatment.* New York: Springer Publishing.

Hansen, M., & Harway, M. (1995). Intervening with violent families: Directions for future generations of therapists. In M. Hansen & M. Harway (Eds.), *Battering and family therapy* (pp. 227–251). Newbury Park, NJ: Sage.

Harris, G. (2006). Conjoint therapy and domestic violence: Treating the individuals and the relationship. *Counseling Psychology Quarterly, 19*(4), 373–379.

Henning, K., Jones, A., & Holdford, R. (2003). Treatment needs of women arrested for domestic violence: A comparison with male offenders. *Journal of Interpersonal Violence, 18*(8), 839–856.

Hines, D., & Malley-Morrison, K. (2004). *Family violence in the United States: Defining, understanding, and combating abuse.* Thousand Oaks, CA: Sage.

Holtzworth-Munroe, A., & Stuart, G. (1994). Typologies of male batterers. *Psychological Bulletin, 116*(3), 476–497.

Hotaling, G. T., & Sugarman, D. B. (1986). An analysis of risk markers in husband to wife violence. *Violence and Victims, 1*(2), 101–124.

Jacobsen, N., & Gottman, J. (1998). *When men batter women.* New York: Simon & Schuster.

Jacobsen, N., Gottman, J., Waltz, J., Rushe, R., Babcock, J., & Holtzworth-Munroe, A. (1994). Affect, verbal content, and psychophysiology in the arguments of couples with a violent husband. *Journal of Consulting and Clinical Psychology, 62*(5), 982–988.

James, K., & McIntyre, D. (1983). The reproduction of families: The social role of family therapy? *Journal of Marital and Family Therapy, 9*(2), 119–129.

Johnson, M. (2000). *Conflict and control: Symmetry and asymmetry in domestic violence.* Paper prepared for the National Institute of Justice Gender Symmetry Workshop, Arlington, VA. Available by contacting author at mpj@psu.edu

Johnson, M., & Leone, J. (2005). The differential effects of intimate terrorism and situational couple violence: Findings from the National Violence Against Women Survey. *Journal of Family Issues, 26*(3), 322–349.

Johnston, J., & Roseby, V. (1997). *In the name of the child.* New York: Free Press.

Kaura, S., & Allen, C. (2004). Dissatisfaction with relationship power and dating violence perpetration by men and women. *Journal of Interpersonal Violence, 19*(5), 576–588.

Kitzmann, K., Gaylord, N., Holt, A., & Kenny, E. (2003). Child witnesses to domestic violence: A meta-analytic review. *Journal of Consulting and Clinical Psychology, 71*(2), 339–352.

Kiyoshk, R. (2003). Integrating spirituality and domestic violence treatment: Treatment of Aboriginal men. In D. Dutton & D. Sonkin (Eds.), *Intimate violence: Contemporary treatment innovations* (pp. 237–256). New York: Haworth Press.

Langhinrichsen-Rohling, J., Neidig, P., & Thorn, G. (1995). Violent marriages: Gender differences in levels of current violence and past abuse. *Journal of Family Violence, 10*(2), 159–175.

Langhinrichsen-Rohling, J., Turner, L., & McGowan, M. (2007). Family therapy and interpersonal violence: Targeting at-risk adolescent mothers. In J. Hamel & T. Nicholls (Eds.), *Family interventions in domestic violence: A handbook of gender-inclusive theory and treatment* (pp. 477–498). New York: Springer Publishing.

LaTaillade, J., Epstein, N., & Werlinich, C. (2006). Conjoint treatment of partner violence: A cognitive behavioral approach. *Journal of Cognitive Psychotherapy, 20*(4), 393–410.

Lynch, M., & Ciccheti, D. (1998). An ecological-transactional analysis of children and contexts. *Developmental Psychopathology, 10*, 235–257.

Mahoney, A., Donnelly, W., Boxer, P., & Lewis, T. (2003). Marital and severe parent-to-adolescent physical aggression in clinic-referred families: Mother and adolescent reports on co-occurrence and links to child behavior problems. *Journal of Family Psychology, 17*(1), 3–19.

Maiuro, R., Hagar, T., Lin, H., & Olson, N. (2001). Are current state standards for domestic violence perpetrator treatment adequately informed by research? A question of questions. *Journal of Aggression, Maltreatment & Trauma, 5*(2), 21–44.

Margolin, G. (1979). Conjoint marital therapy to enhance anger management and reduce spouse abuse. *American Journal of Family Therapy, 7*(2), 13–23.

Margolin, G., & Gordis, E. (2003). Co-occurrence between marital aggression and parent's child abuse potential: The impact of cumulative stress. *Violence & Victims, 18*, 243–258.

Mills, L. (2003). *Insult to injury: Rethinking our responses to intimate abuse.* Princeton, NJ: Princeton University Press.

Moore, T., & Pepler, D. (1998). Correlates of adjustment in children at risk. In G. Holden, R. Geffner, & E. Jouriles (Eds.), *Children exposed to domestic violence* (pp. 157–184). Washington, DC: American Psychological Association.

Moretti, M., Penney, S., Obsuth, I., & Odgers, C. (2007). Family lessons in attachment and aggression. In J. Hamel & T. Nicholls (Eds.), *Family approaches to domestic violence: A guide to gender-inclusive research and treatment* (pp. 191–214). New York: Springer Publishing.

Mun Wah, L. (1998). Asian men and violence. In R. Carrillo & J. Tello (Eds.), *Family violence and men of color* (pp. 128–146). New York: Springer Publishing.

Murphy, C., & Eckhardt, C. (2006). *Treating the abusive partner: An individualized cognitive-behavioral approach.* New York: Guilford.

Neidig, P., & Friedman, D. (1984). *Spouse abuse: A treatment program for couples.* Champaign, IL: Research Press.

O'Leary, K., & Cohen, S. (2007). Treatment of psychological and physical abuse in a couples context. In J. Hamel & T. Nicholls (Eds.), *Family interventions in domestic violence: A handbook of gender-inclusive theory and treatment* (pp. 363–380). New York: Springer Publishing.

O'Leary, K., Heyman, R., & Neidig, P. (1999). Treatment of wife abuse: A comparison of gender-specific and conjoint approaches. *Behavior Therapy, 30,* 475–505.

Pan, H., Neidig, P., & O'Leary, K. (1994). Predicting mild and severe husband-to-wife physical aggression. *Journal of Consulting and Clinical Psychology, 62,* 975–981.

Pandey, V. (2007, September 20). Spouse abuse: It's the husband's turn now. *Daily News & Analysis.* Retrieved November 19, 2007, from http://www.dnaindia.com/dnaprint.asp?newsid=1122392

Pence, E., & Paymar, M. (1993). *Education groups for men who batter: The Duluth model.* New York: Springer Publishing.

Pizzey, E. (1974). *Scream quietly or the neighbours will hear you.* Harmondsworth, England: Penguin.

Pizzey, E. (1982). *Prone to violence.* London: Hamlyn Press.

Potter-Efron, R. (2005). *Handbook of anger management: Individual, couple, family, and group approaches.* New York: Haworth Press.

Potter-Efron, R. (2007). Anger, aggression, domestic violence and substance abuse. In J. Hamel & T. Nicholls (Eds.), *Family interventions in domestic violence: A handbook of gender-inclusive theory and treatment* (pp. 437–456). New York: Springer Publishing.

Pratt, D., & Chapman, T. (2007). Family violence parent groups. In J. Hamel & T. Nicholls (Eds.), *Family interventions in domestic violence: A handbook of gender-inclusive theory and treatment.* New York: Springer Publishing.

Price, B., & Rosenbaum, A. (2007, July). *National survey of batterer intervention programs.* Presented at the International Family Violence and Child Victimization Research conference.

Rennison, C. (2003, February). *Intimate partner violence.* NCJ 197838. Washington, DC: U.S. Department of Justice/Office of Justice Programs. Retrieved November 2, 2005, from www.ojp.usdoj.gov/bjs/pub/pdf/ipv01.pdf

Ridley, C., & Feldman, C. (2003). Female domestic violence toward male partners: Exploring conflict responses and outcomes. *Journal of Family Violence, 18*(3), 157–170.

Roberts, N., & Noller, P. (1998). The association between adult attachment and couple violence. In J. Simpson & W. Rholes (Eds.), *Attachment theory and close relationships* (pp. 317–350). New York: Guilford.

Salzinger, S., Feldman, R., Ing-mak, D., Mojica, E., Stockhammer, T., & Rosario, M. (2002). Effects of partner violence and physical child abuse on child behavior: A study of abused and comparison children. *Journal of Family Violence, 17*(1), 23–52.

Saunders, D. (1977). Marital violence: Dimensions of the problem and modes of intervention. *Journal of Marriage and Family Counseling, 3,* 43–49.

Sheehan, M. (1997). Adolescent violence: Strategies, outcomes and dilemmas in working with young people and their families. *Australian and New Zealand Journal of Family Therapy, 18*(2), 80–91.

Simmons, C., Lehmann, P., Cobb, N., & Fowler, C. (2005). Personality profiles of women and men arrested for domestic violence: An analysis of similarities and differences. *Journal of Offender Rehabilitation, 41*(4) 63–81.

Simon, T., Anderson, M., Thompson, M., Crosby, A., Shelley, G., & Sacks, J. (2001). Attitudinal acceptance of intimate partner violence among U.S. adults. *Violence and Victims, 16*(2), 115–126.

Simpson, L., Doss, B., Wheeler, J., & Christensen, A. (2007). Relationship violence among couples seeking therapy: Common couple violence or battering? *Journal of Marital and Family Therapy, 33*(2), 270–283.

Slep, A., & O'Leary, S. G. (2005). Parent and partner violence in families with young children: Rates, patterns, and connections. *Journal of Consulting and Clinical Psychology, 73*(3), 435–444.

Sommer, R. (1994). *Male and female perpetrated partner abuse.* Doctoral dissertation, University of Manitoba. University Microfilms International, ISBN-0-315-99064-3.

Sonkin, D., & Durphy, M. (1997). *Learning to live without violence.* Volcano, CA: Volcano Press.

Sonkin, D., & Dutton, D. (2003). Treating assaultive men from an attachment perspective. In D. Sonkin & D. Dutton (Eds.), *Intimate violence: Contemporary treatment innovations* (pp. 105–133). New York: Haworth Maltreatment & Trauma Press.

Stacey, W., Hazelwood, L., & Shupe, A. (1994). *The violent couple.* Westport, CT: Praeger.

Stanton, M., & Shadish, W. (1997). Outcome, attrition, and family-couples treatment for drug abuse: A meta-analysis and review of the controlled, comparative studies. *Psychological Bulletin, 122*(2), 170–191.

Stith, S., Rosen, K., & McCollum, E. (2004). Treating intimate partner violence within intact couple relationships: Outcomes of multi-couple versus individual couple therapy. *Journal of Marital and Family Therapy, 30*(3), 305–318.

Straus, M. (1992, September). *Children as witnesses to marital violence: A risk factor for lifelong problems among a nationally representative sample of American men and women.* Twenty-third Ross Roundtable on Critical Approaches to Common Pediatric Problems, M5796.

Straus, M. (2006, May). *Dominance and symmetry in partner violence by male and female university students in 32 nations.* Paper presented at conference on Trends in Intimate Violence Intervention, New York University.

Straus, M., & Gelles, R. (1990). *Physical violence in American families.* New Brunswick, NJ: Transaction.

Straus, M., Gelles, R., & Steinmetz, S. (1980). *Behind closed doors: Violence in the American family.* Newbury Park, CA: Sage.

Straus, M., Kaufman-Kantor, G., & Moore, D. (1997). Change in cultural norms approving marital violence from 1968 to 1994. In G. Kaufman-Kantor & J. Jasinski (Eds.), *Out of the darkness: Contemporary perspectives on family violence* (pp. 3–16). Thousand Oaks, CA: Sage.

Straus, M., & Smith, C. (1990). Family patterns and child abuse. In M. Straus & R. Gelles (Eds.), *Physical violence in American families* (pp. 245–262). New Brunswick, NJ: Transaction.

Straus, M., & Yodanis, C. (1996, August). *Gender hostility and violence against dating partners.* Paper presented at the XII World Meeting of the International Society for Research on Aggression, Strasbourg, France.

Stuart, G., & Holtzworth-Munroe, A. (1995). Identifying subtypes of maritally violent men: Descriptive dimensions, correlates and causes of violence, and treatment implications. In S. M. Stith & M. A. Straus (Eds.), *Understanding partner violence: Prevalence, causes, consequences, and solutions* (pp. 162–172). Minneapolis, MN: National Council on Family Relations.

Sugarman, D., & Frankel, S. (1996). Patriarchal ideology and wife-assault: A meta-analytic review. *Journal of Family Violence, 11*(1), 13–39.

Taggart, M. (1985). The feminist critique in epistemological perspective: Questions of context in family therapy. *Journal of Marital and Family Therapy, 11*(2), 113–126.

Telch, C., & Lindquist, C. (1984). Violent vs. non-violent couples. *Psychotherapy, 21*(2), 242–248.

Thomas, M. (2007). Treatment of family violence: A systemic perspective. In J. Hamel & T. Nicholls (Eds.), *Family interventions in domestic violence: A handbook of gender-inclusive theory and treatment* (pp. 417–436). New York: Springer Publishing.

Tjaden, P., & Thoennes, N. (2000). *Extent, nature, and consequences of intimate partner violence.* NCJ 181867. Washington, DC: National Institute of Justice.

Ullman, A., & Straus, M. (2003). Violence by children against mothers in relation to violence between parents and corporal punishment by parents. *Journal of Comparative Family Studies, 34,* 41–60.

Vetere, A., & Cooper, J. (2007). Couple violence and couple safety: A systemic and attachment-oriented approach to working with complexity and uncertainty. In J. Hamel & T. Nicholls (Eds.), *Family interventions in domestic violence: A handbook of gender-inclusive theory and treatment* (pp. 381–396). New York: Springer Publishing.

Walker L. (1979). *The battered woman.* New York: Harper & Row.

Walker, L. (1983). *The battered woman syndrome.* New York: Springer Publishing.

Whitaker, J., Haileyesus, T., Swahn, M., & Saltzman, L. (2007). Differences in frequency of violence and reported injury between relationships with reciprocal and nonreciprocal intimate partner violence. *American Journal of Public Health, 97*(5), 941–947.

Williams, O. (1994). Group work with African American men who batter: Toward more ethnically sensitive practice. *Journal of Comparative Family Studies, 25*(1), 91–101.

Wolak, J., & Finkelhor, D. (1998). Children exposed to partner violence. In J. Jasinski & L. Williams (Eds.), *Partner violence: A comprehensive review of 20 years of research* (pp. 184–209). Thousand Oaks, CA: Sage.

Work With Individuals and Couples

2

An Ounce of Prevention: Stopping Violence Before It Begins

DEREK BALL AND WILLIAM J. HIEBERT

Marriage and Family Counseling Service was founded in 1967 in Rock Island, Illinois, and was the first marriage and family therapy institute in either Illinois or Iowa. The agency was a direct result of the consultation of: two pioneers in the then-new field of marriage and family therapy in the 1960s: Emily Mudd and Aaron Rutledge. Mudd had organized the marriage council of Philadelphia, the first marriage-counseling program in the United States, in 1928, and Rutledge headed the first doctoral program in marriage and family therapy at the Merrill Palmer School in Detroit, Michigan.

Funding for the new agency was a three-way special 5-year grant provided by the John Deere Foundation, the Moline Foundation, and the United Way of the Quad City Area. In an effort to serve clients across the socioeconomic spectrum, the founding board was determined to have an agency that functioned on a sliding fee scale in order to accommodate all income levels. Since its inception, licensed marriage and family therapists have become part of the third-party payor system, thus making insurance benefits possible for those who carry health insurance. Today, the agency operates both with a sliding fee scale for non-insurance clients and with health insurance and EAPs for those who have such benefits.

The agency staff is made up of two doctoral-level full-time therapists/supervisors, one to two doctoral interns in marriage and family therapy, and three to five part-time licensed marriage and family therapists.

29

PREVENTION OF ABUSE PROGRAM

The prevention program seeks to identify families at highest risk for abuse and battering and bring them into treatment using specialized systems-based couple and family therapy. The goal is to identify the dysfunctional dynamics that result in an escalation of anger and conflict and then to intervene in the dysfunctional patterns through a variety of strategies.

Pre-abusive couples tend to have a clearly defined recurring abusive cycle: growing tension that leads to either coercion or blow-ups, which are then followed by a period of contrition and a honeymoon phase before the cycle repeats itself. Although a variety of stressors can cause conflict to escalate, factors such as school failure, rebellious teenagers, alcohol or other substance abuse, death, divorce, sudden illness or unemployment, low self-esteem, and lack of anger control seem to be primary factors that aggravate the abusive cycle.

The program uses many techniques that have been found effective in lowering the potential for violence or stopping beginning abuse, including genograms (looking at anger control in families of origin), mapping arguments (looking for triggers), time-outs (helping couples successfully step out of a battle), behavioral contracts (making commitments to halt escalating conflict), and in-house/out-house separations (developing a healing separation before a reuniting).

Before couples are released from treatment, they are taught to look for the warning signs of all possible future abuse, including repetitive put-downs, alcohol and drug abuse, extreme jealousy, sexist values, expression of intense anger, and a pattern of holding frustrations in and then blowing up.

Outcome Research

The outcome research the agency conducts consists of a two-part evaluation process. Clients complete a client satisfaction survey (CSS) at the fourth and eighth sessions. Clients also complete a preclinical test and then repeat the same test before the eighth session, or approximately 2 months after treatment onset.

The pre- and post-test employed is the OQ45.2, an outcome instrument tested with over 10,000 clients by its designers, Dr. Michael Lambert and Dr. Gary Burlingame. After five years of testing, the designers have determined that an agency using this test needs to use it only with

15% of its randomly selected clients to test an agency's successfulness. In 2006 over 61% of our clients completed eight sessions and completed both pre- and post-tests. Another 11% completed the post-test between the fourth and seventh sessions when they concluded therapy early. The OQ45.2 was chosen because it was a clinically significant instrument, meaning that if an individual's score moves down more than 9 points, actual or real change has occurred. In the 3 years of usage, our average scores have moved significantly beyond the scientifically established clinically significant change score of 9 points. The average pre-test score for our Prevention of Abuse clients was 63.19; the average post-test score was 50.66.

Clients are also encouraged to provide feedback regarding their therapy experience. The most frequent statement written on our client satisfaction survey by Prevention of Abuse clients was that they appreciated learning specific skills that help them to de-escalate conflict. Other comments included "feeling cared for" and "feeling respected" by the therapist.

DEFINING THE AT-RISK COUPLE

Despite vast media attention and the growing number of studies examining spousal battering, there are major conceptual gaps. O'Leary (1993) suggests there are two forms of domestic violence: (a) Mild-moderate (e.g., restraining, grabbing, and pushing) and (b) severe (e.g., choking, beating, and use of weapons). The process by which batterers move from pre-abusive or mild forms to severe forms of violence remains unclear. Perez and Rasmussen (1997) note that a lack of longitudinal and process-oriented research has left preventionists groping in the dark.

Research has failed to examine the temporal relationships between spousal battering and characteristics correlated with it, note Perez and Rasmussen (1997); thus it cannot be established whether correlates are risk factors or merely consequences of abuse (Sedlak, 1988). Perez and Rasmussen note that until there is more empirical evidence and clearer, conceptual frameworks, we must assume that spouses who move from psychological aggression (e.g., intimidation, humiliation, and threats) to mild physical violence are at risk for inflicting more severe acts.

Spousal relationships refers to any couple, self-identified, whether married, cohabiting, or recently separated. A couple is diagnosed "at-risk" when at least one of two criteria is met: (a) a pattern of aggressive arguments, coercion, humiliation, intimidation, or threatening statements and (b) a pattern of using mild forms of violence characterized by throwing objects, pushing, shoving, or restraining.

Factors Associated With Partner Battering

Empirical research delineating the correlates of spousal battering is inconclusive and offers limited guidance for clinicians working with at-risk couples. Perez and Rasmussen (1997) indicate that predictive models for at-risk men and couples do not exist in the therapy literature. Clinical observation and research suggests, however, that battering couples often experience one or more associated factors. In reviewing the factors, Perez and Rasmussen discovered the following: alcohol or other drug abuse (Gelles, 1993; Kantor & Straus, 1987; Miller, Downs, & Gondole, 1989; Neff, Holamon, & Schluter, 1995), financial stress (Fagan, Barnett, & Patton, 1988; Gelles & Straus, 1988), marital stress (Gelles, 1974; Leonard & Blane, 1992; Rounsavile, 1978; Steinmetz, 1978), low sex-role egalitarianism (Crossman, Stith, & Bender, 1990; Yllo, 1993), beliefs that violence in relationships is acceptable (Crossman et al., 1990; Stith, 1990), and observed domestic violence as a child or adolescent (Arias, 1984; Rosenbaum & O'Leary, 1982; Rouse, 1984; Telch & Lindquist, 1984).

CASE STUDY: GREG AND GINA

The couple discussed in this chapter is outwardly happy and "normal." The husband, Greg, is a successful lawyer in his family's firm. At 36, he is attractive, outgoing, and community-minded. He was raised in a family with a high profile in the community. He shares that his family instilled in him a drive to succeed and to give back to his community. As a result, he is active in the chamber of commerce and volunteers regularly with Habitat for Humanity and at his small Lutheran church. As junior partner in the law firm, he feels a lot of pressure to perform well so as not to embarrass his father, who is senior partner. With a broad smile and firm handshake, he is the picture of confidence and success.

The wife, Gina, is equally successful and engaging. She is 34 and works at a local marketing firm. She is also attractive and outgoing and has just recently gone back to work after taking 8 years off to stay at home with her children, ages 8 and 6. She sees one of her primary goals in life as being the best mom she can be. She takes pride in her involvement in her children's school and has made many new friends through her volunteer work there and in her new job. She reports that the job she started 6 months ago has brought her renewed energy and satisfaction—satisfaction she is not receiving in her marriage.

Greg and Gina's marriage of 11 years was best described by Greg, who said that it was "high profile, high income, high stress." Their desire to maintain appearances and give their kids everything has led them to live at the very outer edge of their means. Their mortgage payments and private-school tuitions leave little left of their incomes. Her return to work, although personally enriching, was also required given their mounting bills and some very poor investment decisions. Finances are the primary source of conflict for Greg and Gina: they fight with every new bill that arrives in the mail.

Their relationship history was, by most standards, fairly normal. They met at a large Midwestern university. She was a cheerleader, and he was the team mascot. Their dating life was filled with fraternity parties, dances, and sporting events. They reported that they never fought, except for one big blow-up over his drinking. This did not dissuade them from marriage.

Their conflict really did not begin until they had children, 3 years later. Around the same time their first child was born, Greg got a promotion in the law firm. Although these changes were positive, they still brought stress, which led to conflict. Their fights were small (they called them "spats") and tended to blow over quickly.

By all appearances, Greg and Gina had everything: good jobs, a beautiful spouse, and beautiful children. They seemed happy and successful, and many people who knew them probably would have described them as having the perfect life. By the time Greg and Gina reached therapy, however, they felt quite differently. In fact, they reported that they were in a crisis. They had seen their intensity of conflict escalate at an alarming rate, and they did not feel that they had the relational skills to manage it.

From a therapist's standpoint, Greg and Gina had a moderate to poor relational skill set. The intense drive that yielded them both such success in their jobs led them to be competitive and driven to "win" every conflict at home. Both were skilled at articulating the things that made them unhappy, but neither was able to listen to the other's complaints without defensiveness or engaging in rebuttal.

Neither Greg nor Gina had good models for conflict management in their families of origin. Greg's parents fought tooth and nail: he grew up feeling that this style was the way all families had discussions. He witnessed some violence in his parents' marriage, primarily perpetrated by his father toward his mother. He also reported that his father drank every evening and that this was the source of many of their arguments. Gina reported a revulsion toward her in-laws' style of relating; early in therapy she shared a story of coming home by herself from a family vacation because she was overwhelmed by the profanity-laced tirades of Greg's parents.

Gina's family, however, did not pass along many positive skills for dealing with conflict either. Her family could best be described as conflict-avoidant. Gina reported with some pride that she never heard her parents argue. When her father was upset, he would grow silent. When her mother was upset, she would clean things. Greg reported that, on trips to visit her family, the silence could be deafening. Both Gina and Greg felt that their respective family was healthy and that their spouse's family was dysfunctional. In truth, neither family had modeled how to work through conflict together in a respectful, loving manner.

Another contributor to the level of conflict in Gina and Greg's relationship was her recent return to the workplace. Her job required her to spend evenings away from home on occasion, which meant that the couple had even less time to nurture their already tenuous marriage.

Warning Signs

In our Prevention of Abuse program, therapists are trained to notice the warning signs of violence—the subtle signs that the relationship is moving beyond normal conflict and toward something more destructive. Greg and Gina showed a number of these signs when they presented for therapy. Each of these behaviors moved the couple closer to violence with each occurrence.

Greg showed three warning-sign behaviors prior to therapy. The first was his jealousy. Greg was very jealous of Gina's contact with other men. At first, this trait seemed sweet to Gina because she saw it as evidence of his affection for her. Eventually, however, his jealousy felt very controlling to her, especially when she began her new job.

The second warning sign grew out of Greg's jealousy and insecurity. When he felt these feelings, he would interrogate Gina about her daily schedule and what was said, word for word, during her interactions with other men. These interrogations could sometimes last until the wee hours of the morning.

Finally, Greg would have explosive outbursts. Sometimes, they would be directed at Gina (name-calling or exclamations about a mistake she had made), but often they were about seemingly unimportant things like a poor play by his favorite sports team or the lawnmower not starting. Again, none of these explosive outbursts led to violence toward Gina or the children. They did, however, increase in number over the years.

Gina showed two important warning-sign behaviors as well. First, she would avoid bringing up topics or lie about information to avoid an angry outburst from Greg. Her deceitful behavior also increased over the years and ranged from lying about her schedule to lying about how much money she had spent to even lying about her children's schedules.

The second warning sign was her refusal to let Greg leave during a conflict. Ironically for a person raised to be conflict-avoidant, Gina felt that to take a time-out was the equivalent of rejection. She believed that, if two people truly loved one another, they would discuss a problem until a solution was reached. What she did not realize was that denying Greg the opportunity to leave actually resulted in escalating the argument.

The thing to recognize about these warning signs is that they are tied together. The more Greg would interrogate Gina about every detail of her day, the more she would lie and cover up. The more she lied to him, the more he would explode. Both Gina and Greg were contributing to the escalation of the negative intensity in their marriage. However, if you talked to either of them about their contribution to the negative cycle, they would easily point out how they were justified in their behavior by their partner's negative behavior. This would be a challenge with this couple.

Presenting Issue

Greg and Gina presented for therapy at the recommendation of a friend of hers who had come to counseling with me and had seen positive results. When Gina shared with her friend the following story, her friend gave Gina my business card.

Gina had a work party to attend, hosted by her boss at his house for all of the employees of the marketing firm and their significant others. Given the recent stress in their marriage and wanting to save money on a babysitter, Gina decided to go to the party alone while Greg stayed home with the children. This decision left Greg feeling very insecure and jealous, especially given that he suspected an inappropriate relationship on Gina's part with her coworker Alex.

When Gina arrived at the party, she wanted to have fun and leave some of her troubles behind. Therefore, she left her cell phone in her car. This move to avoid Greg's harassing "check in" phone calls led to much larger problems.

Given his paranoia about Alex and previous lies he had uncovered about some of Gina's spending behavior, Greg did not believe that she was actually going to a work function. He decided to call her to confirm. When he called, he got her voice mail. He left a message and waited. And then he called again. And again. By the end of the party, Greg had left 27 increasingly angry voice mails on Gina's cell phone.

When Gina got back into her car at two o'clock in the morning, she discovered the hostile messages. She didn't bother checking them or calling him back because she did not feel like dealing with one of his explosive rants. When she returned home, she found him pacing. She came home not only to an angry husband but also to a house full of broken phones. Apparently, as Greg's frustration increased, he took it out on the phone he was using. In all, Greg broke the receivers on all four phones that they had in the house as well as his cell phone.

After Gina shared this information in our first session, Greg was careful to point out that, even though he had broken every phone in the house, he had "never laid a finger on Gina." Although technically correct, this piece of information did not give me much confidence that this couple could keep violence out of their relationship or the parenting of their children. Therefore, they were good candidates for the Prevention of Abuse program.

TREATMENT

Greg and Gina represent an example of a "marital violence only" couple. There was never any violence directed at the children throughout the therapist's work with them, and any yelling or conflict seemed to center on the marital relationship. There was no physical violence perpetrated by either of the spouses toward the other; however, the intense conflict and property destruction, although pre-violent behavior in our criteria, may be considered a form of violent behavior and was certainly "abusive."

After doing a brief assessment with the couple, the first step in treatment was to build some basic skills in managing conflict effectively. One way of viewing Prevention of Abuse clients is to see them as old steam radiators with no knob. They cannot turn down (or turn off) the heat.

The therapist's first goal is to give the couple some tools that will help them "lower the temperature" and regain control over the heat in the relationship.

Our treatment model has been refined over the years through feedback from our clients. In data collected over the last five years, 73% of our clients in the Prevention of Abuse program indicated that therapy was "very helpful" or "helpful" in helping them reduce explosive arguments, intimidating statements, and threatening behaviors. Further, clients have indicated that skill-based interventions have the most immediate impact. Of those surveyed, 68% indicated that learning skills such as time-outs and communication skills helped them to reduce the symptoms just mentioned. As compared to clients in our family counseling (no report of escalating conflict) program, the Prevention of Abuse clients were more likely to say that problems were "almost resolved." We think that this comparison is related to the fact that clients in our Prevention of Abuse program have more immediate, concrete issues (i.e., escalating conflict) than our family counseling program clients.

Time-Outs

The first skill the therapist works on with a Prevention of Abuse couple is the time-out. In Greg and Gina's case, the therapist spoke with them about the importance of managing intensity by walking away from a conflict when they felt the intensity moving beyond their control. The therapist spent an entire session helping them establish their "intensity thermometers," where they indicate what they are thinking, feeling, and doing when their intensity is a 1 out of 10, 3 out of 10, 5 out of 10, 7 out of 10, and 10 out of 10. The therapist and clients talked about how, as intensity increases, intelligence decreases. Therefore, it was important to call the time-out early so that they would have their wits about them and could call it appropriately. At the end of that session, the therapist emphasized the importance of calling the time-out when they were no higher than a 3 out of 10. The therapist had them recognize what they would be thinking, feeling, and doing that would tell them that they needed to call a time-out. The therapist also emphasized the importance of calling the time-out in a self-responsible way ("I need to reduce my intensity" instead of "I need to get away from you") and discussed the importance of setting a reconciliation time so that their partner understood that they would come back and finish the discussion after they had reduced their intensity.

The concrete nature of the anger thermometer was especially help-ful to Greg. Rather than focusing on emotion, he could notice his behav-ior (for Greg, he tended to raise his hands in emphatic gestures as his intensity rose) and call the time-out before he lost control. In the session after discussing the time-out, Greg returned and said, "I saw my hands and asked for a time-out." Gina also felt more comfortable with Greg's calling a time-out than she did with his simply leaving and was more able to back away from him when he asked for a time-out. In that session, they reported that that had been their only conflict.

Meta-Communication

A second, skills-based intervention done with Prevention of Abuse cou-ples is meta-communication. Many couples focus on the content of their conflict and do not think to comment on the process of their conflict pat-terns. During therapy with Greg and Gina, conflicts they had had were dissected, and patterns to their conflict were identified. The therapist then taught them how to step out of their conflict and comment on their in-terpretations of their partner's behavior and ask for clarification. By being able to meta-communicate, they were able to let their partner know how they were experiencing each other and gain clarity on what their partner was thinking and feeling. This helped Greg and Gina avoid conflict that would have been based on misinterpretations of each other's behavior.

In addition to building skills, we hope to help our couples become informed observers of their own relationship. We encourage them to "think like a therapist" so that they can intervene at home rather than waiting for a session in which the therapist can intervene with them. As mentioned previously, one of the ways in which we attempt to help couples do this is to have them process with us a recent conflict. We talk about "unpacking an argument" with a couple, and like unpacking a suitcase full of clothes and sorting through what needs to be washed, ironed, or hung up, we help them look at the parts of a recent conflict and differentiate how each part contributed to the escalation.

Greg and Gina identified the following cycle to their conflict. Greg would typically initiate, sometimes confronting Gina. Gina would re-spond by avoiding the topic Greg had raised. Greg would then inten-sify his confrontation, and Gina would shut down. At this point, Greg would explode. Understanding that their own behavior tended to hook or intensify their partner's behavior, Gina and Greg were able to share responsibility for the cycle.

Behavioral "Off-Ramps"

Once the cycle had been identified in the second session, a brainstorming session was held in the third. In this session, Gina and Greg were allowed to brainstorm "off-ramps" of the cycle for their own behavior (not their partner's behavior; this helps to avoid other-oriented advice giving). The therapist encouraged Greg and Gina to list as many off-ramps as possible, from the ridiculous to the sublime, and to avoid evaluation. With this freedom, they were able to list several ideas that, later in the session, they evaluated and prioritized.

The several off-ramps that Greg came up with included communicating vulnerable feelings when he felt like making demands, going and working out when he felt Gina's avoidance, and writing down his issue rather than confronting her verbally. Gina's off-ramps included using meta-communication to help clarify what she saw as controlling behavior, calling for a time-out rather than avoiding, and bringing up issues of her own more frequently so that it was not just Greg bringing up issues.

In the fourth session, Greg and Gina evaluated and refined each of these off-ramps to help them make the ideas even more usable. They rehearsed these in session, and the therapist gave them homework to have "practice conflict" at home so that they could become accustomed to their off-ramps.

Relationship History

The third intervention we use with our Prevention of Abuse couples is more historical in nature. In addition to building skills and helping them unpack the cycle of current conflicts, we want our couples to understand the historical roots of their escalating conflict. In order to accomplish this task, we do both a relational and a familial history.

In our relationship history, called the structured initial interview (Hiebert, Gillespie, & Stahmann, 1993), we help the clients identify the relationship patterns that set the context for the presenting problem. In Greg and Gina's relationship history, we identified three patterns. The first pattern was predictable. Over the course of their relationship history, their conflict had gotten more and more intense. The cycle described earlier had remained the same, but the conflict had gotten more intense and more frequent over the years.

The second pattern was one of intolerance. Both felt that their family's way of doing things (whether it be conflict, parenting, or opening

Christmas presents) was "right." This meant that if the other's way was different, he or she was also "wrong."

Finally, we noticed how having children had affected Gina and Greg's relationship. By looking at the history, the impact of pregnancy and child-rearing came into stark relief for them. We concluded this three-session relationship history with a wrap-up in which the therapist discussed each of these patterns.

In the familial history, the therapist used genograms to look at the impact of family patterns on the way they experienced conflict. The therapist spent one session on Greg's family and one session on Gina's. In each session, the client whose family was being discussed led the discussion. The spouse took notes and was encouraged to give feedback at the close of the session.

In Greg's family, there was a pattern of coercion. With both his mother and his father, there was a great competition to influence both each other and other family members. Typically, this coercion was done verbally and cognitively, trying to convince one another by using logic to poke holes in the other person's arguments, but there was also an emotional component to the coercion wherein one person would use put-downs or humiliation to "defeat" the other person's argument. While Gina was silently taking notes, Greg was free to comment openly on how he thought he had been affected negatively as a child (rather than spending time defending his family as he had in the first session). This opened the door for him to realize how their manipulation and coercion had affected his self-esteem. It also helped him have greater empathy for how his similar behavior had negatively affected Gina.

In Gina's family, there was a pattern of avoidance. She had a much greater difficulty looking objectively at her family, even with Greg staying silent. Her father, especially, was beyond reproach. She was, however, able to identify how her complaints were not taken seriously because they were avoided and how she had not liked this. She was also able to build empathy toward Greg to a degree and see how her avoidance had led him to feel ignored. Her defensiveness, however, was palpable in the session. Where she had been very energized in the prior sessions, she seemed reluctant and aloof in this one. Unfortunately, this 10th session was to be her last.

After 10 sessions, Greg and Gina stopped coming to therapy. Three months later, Greg returned to therapy alone. He reported that, following that 10th session, Gina had moved out of the house and begun an open relationship with the coworker with whom Greg had suspected she had been having an affair. His fears confirmed, Greg filed for divorce. He returned for therapy because he did not want to repeat the problems he had experienced with Gina in future relationships. In another five sessions, we explored his family of origin, worked on building his intensity-management skills, and helped him deal with the grief over the loss of his relationship.

OUTCOMES AND CONCLUSION

Assessing outcome in a case such as Greg and Gina's is not always easy. On the surface, the outcome could look poor given their decision to divorce. However, it is important to evaluate the case based on the goals set when Gina and Greg began therapy. The couple wanted to reduce the frequency of conflict, learn more effective means of managing their intensity, and improve their relationship. The Prevention of Abuse Program also has the mission to prevent violence from occurring before it starts. We think that there are three important outcomes to consider in evaluating Greg and Gina.

First, the couple was able to implement some basic relationship skills in order to reduce any further damage. By using meta-communication and time-outs, they were able to manage their intensity more effectively (their second goal). This allowed them to get through more of the content of their interactions, which reduced the number of their conflicts (their first goal). Giving couples like Gina and Greg some basic skills seems to help them keep from escalating into full-blown violence.

Second, Gina and Greg increased their awareness of the cycle of conflict and were able to identify some creative off-ramps for exiting this negative cycle. In fact, it was Gina who commented in the fifth session that, in using some of these off-ramps, they were able to "get off the anger highway for a change." Many couples that enter into the Prevention of Abuse Program see only one or two options for responding to their spouse, especially when conflict occurs. The therapist's job with these couples is to help encourage curiosity and creativity in the clients when doing so feels too dangerous to the couple.

Finally, Greg began some individual work, which continued even after the relationship was on its way to divorce. He focused on his family of origin and set some personal goals of not repeating those patterns with his own children and with another partner. Greg's work speaks to the importance we place on the historical patterns in the Prevention of

Abuse Program. Only by inspecting where he has come from did Greg become able to change where he is going.

So we would evaluate the outcome of this couple as positive, even though the marriage ended in divorce. Sometimes there has been too much damage, too much scar tissue prior to counseling, for the marriage to be rescued. Clearly, their goal of improving the marriage was not attained. Still, Greg and Gina were able, during the course of therapy, to learn some new skills and gain some basic understanding that prevented physical violence from erupting in the relationship and that will hopefully help them prevent it from occurring in their future relationships as well.

REFERENCES

Arias, I. (1984). *A social learning theory explication of the intergenerational transmission of physical aggression in intimate heterosexual relationships.* Unpublished doctoral dissertation, State University of New York at Stony Brook.

Crossman, R., Stith, S., & Bender, M. (1990). Sex role egalitarianism and marital violence. *Sex Roles, 22,* 293–303.

Fagan, R., Barnett, O., & Patton, J. (1988). Reasons for alcohol use in maritally violent men. *American Journal of Drug and Alcohol Abuse, 14,* 371–392.

Gelles, R. J. (1974). Child abuse as psychopathology: A sociological critique and reformation. In S. Steinmetz & M. Straus (Eds.), *Violence in the family* (pp. 190–204). New York: Dodd, Mead.

Gelles, R. J. (1993). Alcohol and other drugs are associated with violence: They are not its cause. In R. J. Gelles & D. R. Loseke (Eds.), *Current controversies on family violence* (pp. 182–196). Newbury Park, CA: Sage.

Gelles, R. J., & Straus, M. A. (1988). *Intimate violence: The causes and consequences of abuse in the American family.* New York: Simon & Schuster.

Hiebert, W., Gillespie, J., & Stahmann, R. (1993). *Dynamic assessment in couple therapy.* New York: Lexington Books.

Kantor, G. K., & Straus, M. A. (1987). The "drunken bum" theory of wife beating. *Social Problems, 34,* 213–230.

Leonard, K. E., & Blane, H. T. (1992). Alcohol and marital aggression in a national sample of young men. *Journal of Interpersonal Violence, 7,* 19–30.

Miller, B. A., Downs, W. R., & Gondole, D. M. (1989). Spousal violence among alcoholic women as compared to a random household sample of women. *Journal of Studies on Alcoholism, 50,* 533–540.

Neff, J. A., Holamon, B., & Schluter, T. D. (1995). Spousal violence among Anglos, Blacks, and Mexican Americans: The role of demographic variables, psychosocial predictors and alcohol consumption. *Journal of Family Violence, 10,* 1–21.

O'Leary, K. D. (1993). Through a psychological lens: Personality traits, personality disorders, and level of violence. In R. Gelles & D. Loseke (Eds.), *Current controversies on family violence* (pp. 7–30). Newbury Park, CA: Sage.

Perez, P., & Rasmussen, K. (1997). An ounce of prevention: A model for working with couples at-risk for battering. *Contemporary Family Therapy, 19,* 229–251.

Rosenbaum, A., & O'Leary, K. (1982). Marital violence: Characteristics of abusive couples. *Journal of Consulting Clinical Psychology, 49,* 63–71.

Rounsavile, B. J. (1978). Battered wives: Barriers to identification and treatment. *American Journal of Orthopsychiatry, 48,* 487–494.

Rouse, L. (1984). Models, self-esteem, and locus of control as factors contributing to spouse abuse. *Victimology, 9,* 130–141.

Sedlak, A. J. (1988). Prevention of wife abuse. In V. B. Van Hasselt, R. L. Morrison, A. S. Bellack, & M. Hersen (Eds.), *Handbook of family violence* (pp. 725–766). New York: Plenum.

Steinmetz, S. K. (1978). The battered husband syndrome. *Victimology, 2,* 499–509.

Stith, S. M. (1990). Police response to domestic violence: The influence of individual and familial factors. *Violence and Victimization, 5,* 37–49.

Telch, C., & Lindquist, C. (1984). Violent versus non-violent couples: A comparison of patterns. *Psychotherapy, 21,* 242–248.

Yllo, K. A. (1993). Through the feminist lens: Gender, power, and violence. In R. J. Gelles & D. R. Loseke (Eds.), *Current controversies on family violence* (pp. 47–62). Newbury Park, CA: Sage.

QUESTIONS FOR REFLECTION AND DISCUSSION

1   What would you say was Greg and Gina's primary abuse dynamic? In what ways does it support a systemic view of domestic violence?

2   How did Greg's family-of-origin experiences impact on his relationship with Gina? Identify the connections between childhood experience, self-esteem, jealousy, and possessive control. How common do you think this is in cases of male-perpetrated intimate partner abuse? In cases of female-perpetrated abuse?

3   The therapist employs a very direct, concrete approach with this couple. Do you think this approach works better in some phases of treatment than others? Why or why not? Would you have used the same approach throughout the treatment?

After the Fall: Using the Needs ABC Model With Couples Affected by Domestic Violence

TOM CAPLAN

I originally developed the Needs ABC model at the McGill Domestic Violence Clinic, where I am director, and I have also implemented it in my work as director of the Montreal Anger Management Centre, as well as in my work with individuals, couples, and families in private practice. I am an adjunct professor in the McGill School of Social Work, responsible for four master's-level interns at the McGill Domestic Clinic where the model is in use. The model uses an integrated therapeutic approach combining observation and elucidation of client and couple process, using concepts also described in cognitive-behavioral (Ellis, 1997; Jacobson & Gurman, 1995), motivational (Miller & Rollnick, 1991), narrative (Myers-Avis, 2004; White & Epston, 1990), and emotion-focused (Greenberg & Johnson, 1988; Greenberg & Pavio, 1997) models.

The Needs ABC approach emphasizes the relational needs behind maladaptive behaviors, rather than the behaviors themselves, and is very flexible in terms of application to clients in a range of settings. Specifically, this approach helps clients understand the reasons behind maladaptive behaviors, express the associated feelings, comprehend the underlying emotions, and strive to develop better mechanisms for processing difficult emotional states. Once relational needs have been ascertained, a plan for meeting them can be readily established. A fundamental premise is that it is the need that drives the emotion and the emotion that

45

drives the behavior. Having identified client needs through an examination of client process (Caplan, 2005; Shulman, 1992), with the help of a list of "relational needs" (Caplan & Thomas, 2004), therapist and client collaboratively arrive at possibilities for problem solving.

CHARACTERISTICS OF THE NEEDS ABC MODEL

One of the primary characteristics of the Needs ABC model is to provide a safe environment. The therapeutic environment should provide a supportive framework ensuring emotional safety (Anderson & Stewart, 1983) from the initial contact (often over the phone) and through the screening process, as well as from the clients' first session to the termination of treatment (Caplan, 2006b). Needs ABC therapists strive for a positive working relationship by appreciating that client comfort will vary (Caplan & Thomas, 1995; Wessler, 1993) and by employing interventions that interpret relational meta-messages in clients' narratives. Because the "uncomfortable" feeling experienced when a relational need is not being met precipitates a strategy to try and relieve it, the client must understand what is missing in the relationship in order to consider new, more appropriate strategies.

Crucially, the therapist should focus on the client's needs rather than the client's behavior. Maintaining focus on behavior may enforce shame or misgivings. The question that has to be answered is, "what matters so much to the clients that when they do not get it, they will try almost anything to acquire it?" Although the therapist should gently guide the couple in the choice-making process, supporting and validating their positive work, it is the individual client's responsibility to consider new problem-solving strategies. The therapist should help the couple endure the anxiety created during their examination of options, helping them become more resilient and in charge of their treatment process.

The Needs ABC model promotes client-paced work (Caplan & Thomas, 1998; Weinberger, 1993). When the therapist collaborates with the couple in uncovering a number of problem-solving possibilities and supports them in choosing one (Miller & Rollnick, 1991), their self-efficacy and assimilation of problem-solving strategies (Bandura, 1997) will improve. The therapist should always ally with client's emotion and not with the client's behavior. Interventions should be made as observations or invitations to try new approaches. The Needs ABC model moves clients away from what they have done "wrong" to what they can do to make things "right," giving them an understanding of what they have been looking for and examining the strategies that they have been using.

Because the need drives the emotion, and the emotion drives the behavior, it is important to examine the origin and development of relational needs. We try to remain in relationships with those who seem to meet our needs, and when these needs are no longer being met, we attempt to reacquire them. The more important they seem, the more effort we invest. In adulthood, we often resort to strategies similar to those employed successfully in childhood. Meeting a need through appropriate behavior will result in extinguishing the inappropriate behavior. "The Needs ABC Law of Relationships" states, whenever you use a dysfunctional behavior to solve a problem, you always get exactly what you *don't* want! Functional problem-solving strategies will become curative.

Although the needs, exactly as described in the model, do not necessarily represent *all* the emotional possibilities available, the concept of focusing on easily identifiable, and identified with, needs is key. These needs are universal insofar as everyone can relate to them (therapist and client alike). They are emotionally (rather than rationally) based and often express the unresolved issues "left over" from the client's earlier stages of development (Caplan, 2006b). They seem to express the way the client sees the world in general (Caplan, 2006a) and particularly what is lacking in the client's relationships. They describe fears as well as relational needs. Although the descriptors listed in Table 3.1 are universally recognized, they do not necessarily represent all the issues that may be brought to bear in the therapeutic context.

Although there is usually one predominant client need, there are often several possibilities for what the client is lacking in the couple relationship. As treatment progresses, the issue of which needs are the most powerful, as described in the "universal need" construct, will become clear. Relational problem-solving strategies usually include an expression of the client's emotional (feeling) state. Usually, there are a number of possible emotions. Because clients often inadequately describe how they feel, understanding which emotions are more useful in dealing with relational issues helps with understanding needs. Sometimes, a less useful emotion is presented because it is more culturally acceptable and more easily expressed, although it may actually worsen the predicament. Less useful emotions tend to drive problematic behaviors (Caplan & Thomas,

Table 3.1

FEAR/THEMES/NEEDS PARADIGMS

PRIMARY	SECONDARY
Reliability (Availability) FEAR: abandonment—"Here today and gone tomorrow" THEME: lonely NEED: emotional connection, constancy (consistency), and predictability	**Intimacy (Closeness/Distance/Trust)** FEAR: too much or too little emotional/physical space THEME: suffocated, disconnected NEED: closeness or distance
Loyalty (Trust) FEAR: being taken advantage of THEME: betrayal NEED: trust, unconditional support	**Power (To Get Needs Met)** FEAR: loss of control, powerlessness THEME: helpless, hopeless NEED: control of one's environment
Respect (Self-Worth) FEAR: being unimportant or marginalized THEME: invisible, unimportant, objectified NEED: acknowledgement, value	**Responsibility (For the Problem)** FEAR: blame, culpability THEME: environmental control NEED: safety, security
Competence (Self-Efficacy) FEAR: not being good enough, failing THEME: inadequacy, incapable NEED: adequacy, proficiency	**Grief/Loss (A "Time-Out")** FEAR: change, acknowledgement THEME: paralyzed, stuck NEED: acceptance, recognition

2002; Greenberg & Pavio, 1997). More useful emotions tend to expose more appropriate options for satisfying unmet needs. When more useful emotional states are accessed, problematic ways of coping with them will gradually be discontinued.

CASE STUDY: JOHN AND BETTY

John Jones's performance at work had been poor for several weeks. One morning, when he clocked in late for the sixth time, his foreman "chewed him out" in front of the 12 other workers on the shift. When quitting time came at 3:30, John stomped out and went to his local bar, where he usually only went on Friday evenings, with every intention of staying until he was thrown out. Drinking heavily, however, was not a new behavior. John had started drinking steadily at home about 6 months ago.

Betty, John's wife, was upset about her husband's new drinking habits but felt there was little she could say to him. She knew that something was bothering him, but she did not know what. Besides, she was busy with the kids, who were occupying more and more of her time as they grew up. Betty had worked as a manicurist before her marriage and was now doing temp work as a clerk at Wal-Mart. Goodness knew they needed some help when the holidays came around. The three kids were close in age, and taking care of them demanded a lot of attention. While Betty was working, the two little ones attended a day care center. Jonathan, the oldest, let himself in with a key and waited an hour or so until his mom got home. In the meantime, John started coming home from work a couple of hours late on a regular basis. "At least," Betty thought to herself, "he's out with friends and able to let off steam about the tensions I know he is feeling. I'd like to get out more often myself."

Shortly before the violent incident that finally brought Betty and John into therapy, John "calmed down" after work with three beers and then put away a couple of boilermakers when his crowd showed up after 5 p.m.; he had left work an hour and a half early after yet another warning from his supervisor. One thing led to another and one drink to another. At 10 p.m., John finally headed home.

At home in their two-bedroom apartment, Betty had no time to worry about John or the dinner getting cold on the table. Their three children needed all her attention and patience. It had been their bedtime a few hours ago, but this had been one of those days. Stacey, 3, was in bed at last, but still crying and feverish, with a sore throat. Betty was afraid that she might also be coming down with chicken pox—it was going around the school—but had not had time to check for spots. Jonathan, 11, had been glued to the television since coming home from school and at least claimed to have done his homework.

But the real problem was Mark, who was 6. Betty could no longer control him. Stacey acted spoiled, and Jonathan was turning into a surly teenager, but Mark seemed to be completely out of control. When John came in, Mark was sitting on the floor, banging his head against his blocks and screaming, as he had been for the last hour. He had soiled his trousers but had refused to let Betty do anything about it. Nothing she said or did could calm him down, and she was afraid to restrain him physically in case she might hurt him. The day care center where the two smaller kids spent their afternoons had called that day and asked Betty to come and take Mark home. He was fighting with the other kids and had been caught scribbling on the walls in the boys' bathroom. Betty got permission to leave early from work and had been trying to deal with Mark ever since. She was terrified she might lose her job. The teachers in school—the day care center was attached to the local grade school— could not control Mark any better than Betty could, and she knew that they might refuse to take him. The guidance counselor had suggested in May that Betty have him tested or get counseling before first grade started in September. She suggested that he might have ADHD. John had refused. Nothing was wrong with his son, John declared. Besides, testing would cost money they did not have, and ADHD was just a scam dreamed up to sell drugs.

It took a minute before Betty heard John's pounding at the door over the noise of the television, Mark's screaming, and Stacey's crying. When Betty opened the door at last, one word led to another. Betty told John that he was a poor excuse for a man; John retorted that if she did her job and kept the kids under control, he'd be more inclined to come home early. Betty said she should have married Shane Willis when she had a chance. He had his own shop now, and she was sure he was nice to his wife and kids.

That was the final straw. John had yelled at Betty before; he had even shoved her once. This time, however, he pushed her up against the wall with his hands around her throat and dug his knee into her belly. Somehow Betty managed to free herself and lock herself in the bathroom, where she called 911 on her cell phone. The police came and took John to jail, where he spent the night. He was charged by the police with domestic assault and told he could not have any form of contact with Betty for the time being. During his hearing, the judge mandated him to undergo domestic violence treatment. At the same time, the couple was strongly encouraged to attend counseling following John's domestic violence treatment by the court social worker.

ASSESSMENT AND TREATMENT PLAN

During the intake (screening) interview with the therapist, John admitted to what he had done. He stated, "I'll never drink again! It's that goddamn booze that screwed things up. It wasn't really me who hit Betty; it was the guy I become when I drink. I don't know why I have to take your stupid course. All I ever needed to do was stop drinking!"

Even though there is no rationale for the use of violence as a problem-solving strategy, John's drinking and violent behavior are only symptoms of his unmet relational needs, needs that he has been unable to express in a mature and coherent manner. As well, it is universally understood that alcohol is not the cause of violence, though it does have a disinhibiting effect on the ability to set appropriate limits—in John's case, his ability to become frustrated or angry without acting out in a destructive manner. It appears evident that John has been unable to feel adequate (*competence*) at work in meeting the expectations of his foreman and, as a father and husband, unable to help guide his children toward more productive behaviors and to support his family adequately. When he faced the possibility of losing his job, John started to feel that he is not a "real man." In addition, John was probably thinking something such as the following: "If I can't do better than this, I will never gain my family's respect, and Betty will have an affair and leave me" (*abandonment*).

For her part, Betty was probably feeling betrayed by John's drinking and the accompanying problematic behavior (*loyalty*) and feeling marginalized (*respect*) with regard to her needs for John to help care for three young children, who need attention.

For John and Betty, couple work could be used to illuminate the couple's unmet relational needs; then treatment planning could be done around the appropriate acquisition of these "needs-deficits." For example, by abstaining from, or controlling, his drinking, as well as taking concomitant anger-management treatment, John could demonstrate loyalty and respect toward Betty. Betty, on the other hand, could work more collaboratively with John, on parenting their children as well as on examining options to deal with their financial situation. In this way, she would be saying, "I can't do this alone, and I need your help," an affirmation that he can be a capable father and husband and that Betty respects and values his input. Overall, what is important in all couples work is an understanding of what each can do to help the other feel connected and supported in their relationship.

TREATMENT

As we have seen, the Needs ABC model is strongly focused on the universality of experience, the fact that the emotional landscape can be described using a vocabulary that allows every listener to tap into the issues being discussed. In practical terms this means that, rather than only examining individual client needs, the counselor's role is to involve the couple in discussing the unmet needs of each, to relate to their experience, and to collaborate in finding ways that may enable them to break out of the loop that they have been stuck in for once and for all.

In the case of John and Betty, John needs to find a more effective way of meeting his need to feel competent, respected, and acknowledged. Although John's treatment relating to domestic violence is mandated, the couple is provided with a couples therapist's information—mine—and asked to make contact. At this point, John is living on a temporary basis in a hostel, but he and Betty are once more on speaking terms. John asks Betty to make the call because she is "better at that sort of thing."

When Betty rings and confirms that John has made sufficient progress in his own therapy to proceed with couple work, I affirm her courage by saying that I know it takes guts to decide to make things change: "You and John are both taking a big step forward, and that can only be a good thing." We agree to meet in the evenings, when John has finished work and when the children can be left with a neighbor for an hour or so.

Practice Techniques

The Needs ABC model relies on the following practice techniques that are essential to supporting participants in a successful therapeutic experience and that combine the approaches listed previously to create a therapeutic environment tailored to the peculiar needs of each given individual client or couple:

1   The awareness of client needs as described in the themes embedded in their respective narratives
2   The identification and exploration of these theme-based needs, which are descriptive of missing relational needs for the individual as well as for the couple as a whole
3   The recognition of the emotional components of a client's narrative
4   The illumination of the most effective of these expressed emotions in addressing client and couple needs
5   The interpretations formulated from these techniques, reflected back to the couple, to support the development of possibilities for them to meet their therapeutic goals

6   The organization of strategies to help needs acquisition, both within and beyond the therapeutic setting

When applied respectfully, these skills can become the "royal road" (Freud, 1913) to the identification and acquisition of client and couple relational needs.

Finally, by focusing on client and couple needs, rather than behaviors, the Needs ABC therapeutic process provides a vehicle whereby social skills and appropriate behaviors in relationships are modeled and assimilated (Garvin, 1985). The Needs ABC model suggests that, in all forms of therapy, a clinician is expected to be a participant, observer, mentor, and teacher. Implicit in this model is that challenging clients' maladaptive behaviors should be considered a goal rather than a technique. The aim is for the counselor to support the couple in challenging ineffective attempts to meet their relational needs by presenting objective observations about the themes and emotions perceived in their narrative. Knowing what emotional needs are lacking, the counselor can encourage the couple to collaboratively problem-solve around possibilities for meeting these emotional needs. If the couple is able to act toward appropriately changing how they are attempting to meet their unmet needs, maladaptive behaviors will gradually be extinguished.

First Session

John and Betty came regularly on a once-weekly basis for seven sessions. In the first session both were quite subdued, almost accepting of the possibility that things would never be the same again, that their relationship had been destroyed forever. Both seemed to agree that John's drinking was problematic, but John seemed to have a bit of trouble "owning" his responsibility entirely for what he had done. He would say, "I know my drinking was out of control, and I shouldn't have hit her, but when I drink, I lose control," as if to say that the alcohol might have been responsible for his violence against Betty.

Rather than challenge John at this time about this difficulty, I did not focus on the behavior at first. Instead, we undertook an examination of individual relational needs with regard to their relationship. The first session, therefore, illuminated John's need to feel connected to his wife unconditionally (*reliability*), as well as his need to feel adequate (*competence*) as a husband and father. Betty felt that John did not value her role in the family (*respect*) and that he chose alcohol and his friends over Betty even though he had promised her time and time again that he would be there for her (*loyalty*). Both felt encouraged by the first session because it seemed to clarify what was causing them to operate as they had.

Second Session: Family History

In the second session, we examined their developmental history, specifically with regard to how they saw their relationships with their parents. In John's case, I helped him to uncover the origins of his destructive behavior. John had grown up as the youngest child in a large family. His parents had both worked outside the home, and he had felt that he never got any consistent attention from them, loving or otherwise. Because he was by far the smallest, he got the sense that he was "holding everybody back." His older brothers and sisters were usually charged with the tasks of getting him washed and dressed every day and "out of his mother's hair." John had never really done anything for himself, not because he was not encouraged to be independent, but because it would take longer than if his siblings just did it for him. John always felt that nobody really believed that he could do anything on his own. To make matters worse, John's parents both drank and seemed to become inaccessible emotionally when they did. "They changed," he said, "into zombies."

Betty's father, on the other hand, had left her family home for the first time when she was just 5 years old. Over the course of the next 10 years, he had "come and gone" as he pleased. Her mother, Sandra, was an unskilled woman who had had her first child before turning 16. Because she felt that she had little to offer prospective employers, she had never looked for serious work and had put up with whatever her errant husband dished out, feeling that she had no choice. Betty had resolved as a child that she would never put up with this sort of thing. She had trained as a manicurist, feeling that this was a good, flexible profession in which she could earn relatively good money. Most of all, she had always longed for a man on whom she could depend for love and practical and emotional support. When John failed to live up to his side of the bargain on which she felt they had agreed, she felt bitterly betrayed and very disinclined to trust him again because, she said, "that's what Mom did, and look where that got her!" When Betty understood with greater clarity her own and John's needs, she was able to appreciate that by asking for his help and advice with the children, she was validating him as a father. At the same time, by making it clear that drinking to excess and being abusive was not acceptable, she was able to meet her own need to insist on reliability from her partner.

In this session Betty and John were able to get a clearer understanding of where they learned to do what they did with regard to "survival" in their relationship. As well, they appeared to more clearly understand how their relational needs developed. John seemed to understand that he had always been fearful of "never making the grade" and acknowledged that Betty's taking over because of his drinking only exacerbated his fears. Betty realized that she, almost without thinking, would take charge of her family whenever she felt abandoned by John. She admitted that her anger at John prevented her from including him in her decision making.

Third Session

In the third session the couple's individual challenges to improve their relationship were discussed. John had to remain reliable and available and demonstrate that he valued what Betty did for him and the family. Betty had to try her best to include John in decisions that she made as long as he was doing his part. As well, she was encouraged to validate his successes. Toward the end of the session, John still appeared to have difficulty with the concept that alcohol was not an excuse for his behavior, so I suggested that they each log their negative emotions and report back with regard to their perceived successes and failures in dealing with difficult feelings in their relationship.

Fourth Session

The fourth session began with an examination of their "behavior/ emotion" log. Betty acknowledged that, even though he was never threatening, there were a few dicey moments when John appeared to be "taking things for granted." Rather than alienating him as she had done in the past, she was able to discuss this with him (as she was encouraged to do when the logging began). John admitted that he had thoughts about drinking at times and admitted that he had become quite angry at Betty on one occasion, when she told him that "he didn't know what he was talking about." With this incident the therapist was able to convince John that alcohol was not the issue, but his unmet relational needs were. John stated that he understood that his anger was generally not about Betty, but about feelings from his childhood that came up for him when Betty did certain things. As well, though he agreed that alcohol did exacerbate the potential for him to lose control, he admitted that earlier on in their relationship, he had "lost it" without alcohol being in the picture.

Final Sessions

In the fifth, sixth, and seventh sessions, the couple continued to examine how their emotions were affected by unmet relational needs on a day-to-day basis. They continued to use the logs, and even though I suggested treatment could be terminated after the sixth session, they stated that they wanted to have just one more session in about 4 weeks, just to be sure they were able to continue successfully without the therapist.

The seventh and final session proved to be positive. By this point they were able to describe how their development impacted on their negative emotions without a therapeutic interpretation. John stated that understanding where his needs came from made it easier for him to examine his behavior more objectively. He also stated that understanding how Betty's behavior was impacted by her own history made him more sensitive and motivated to meet her needs.

OUTCOMES AND CONCLUSION

Overall, John worked hard at getting his drinking under control and also learned some strategies that he could use in seeking to obtain the validation that he needed, at home and at work. On completion of the domestic violence management course he had been mandated to take, he was allowed to move back home. Although it looked as though alcohol was always going to be a temptation for him—most of his social life revolved around going to the bar with his friends—he did become able to accept that he had been responsible for his violent behavior and that he had the power to choose not to engage in it. Betty was encouraged to look for the support and reliability she needed not just from John but also by widening her circle of friends. She joined a local mothers' group and became involved in the community regeneration committee.

Mark continued to be a difficult child, and indeed, his teachers continued to insist that he had ADHD. However, with more consistent parenting, he became easier to manage and talk to, and the most destructive elements of his behavior came under control. Therapy for the whole family, or at least the parents and the two older children, would probably be helpful at this point, but because John and Betty are still struggling financially, this seems unlikely to occur at the present time.

REFERENCES

Anderson, C., & Stewart, S. (1983). *Mastering resistance: A practical guide to family therapy.* New York: Guilford.

Bandura, A. (1997). *Self-efficacy: The exercise of control.* New York: Freeman.

Caplan, T. (2005). Active or passive interventions in groups: The group leader's dilemma. *Group Work, 15*(1), 25–42.

Caplan, T. (2006a). Seeing the forest for the trees: An integrated approach to formulating group work interventions. *Social Work With Groups, 29*(1), 63–77.

Caplan, T. (2006b). "First impressions": Treatment considerations from first contact to first group. *Group Work, 15*(3), 44–57.

Caplan, T., & Thomas, H. (1995). Safety and comfort, content and process: Facilitating open group work for men who batter. *Social Work With Groups, 18* (2–3), 33–51.

Caplan, T., & Thomas, H. (1998). "Don't worry, it's just a stage he's going through": A reappraisal of the stage theory of group work as applied to an open treatment group for men who abuse women. *Group Work, 10*(3), 231–250.

Caplan, T., & Thomas, H. (2002). The forgotten moment: Therapeutic resilience and its promotion in social work with groups. *Social Work With Groups, 24*(2), 5–26.

Caplan, T., & Thomas, H. (2004). If we are all in the same canoe, why are we using different paddles? The effective use of common themes in diverse group situations. *Social Work With Groups, 27*(1), 53–73.

Ellis, A. (1997). *The practice of rational emotive behavior therapy.* New York: Springer Publishing.

Freud, S. (1913). *The interpretation of dreams* (A. A. Brill, Trans.). New York: Macmillan. (Original work published 1900)

Garvin, C. (1985). Group process: Usage and uses in social work practice. In M. Sundell, P. Glasser, R. Sari, & R. Vinter (Eds.), *Individual change through small groups* (pp. 203–225). New York: The Free Press.

Greenberg, L., & Johnson, S. (1988). *Emotionally focused couples therapy.* New York: Guilford.

Greenberg, L., & Pavio, S. C. (1997). *Working with emotions in psychotherapy.* New York: Guilford.

Jacobson, N. S., & Gurman, A. S. (Eds.). (1995). *Clinical handbook of couple therapy* (2nd ed.). New York: Guilford.

Miller, W., & Rollnick, S. (1991). *Motivational interviewing: Preparing people to change addictive behavior.* New York: Guilford.

Myers-Avis, J. (2004, November 5). *Narrative ideas in clinical practice.* Workshop given at the University of Guelph.

Shulman, L. (1992). *The skills of helping: Individuals, families and groups.* Itasca, IL: F. E. Peacock.

Weinberger, J. (1993). Common factors in psychotherapy. In G. Stricker & J. R. Gold (Eds.), *Comprehensive handbook of psychotherapy integration* (pp. 43–56). New York: Plenum Press.

Wessler, R. (1993). Groups. In G. Stricker & J. R. Gold (Eds.), *Comprehensive handbook of psychotherapy integration* (pp. 453–464). New York: Plenum.

White, M., & Epston, D. (1990). *Narrative means to therapeutic ends.* New York: Norton.

QUESTIONS FOR REFLECTION AND DISCUSSION

1   Do you agree with the author's contention that by initially focusing on a client's unmet needs and the emotions they provoke, he or she can be encouraged to take appropriate responsibility for his or her behavior? Why or why not?

2   How would you contrast the ABC Needs approach with the well-known Duluth model? Which model do you think would work better in this case?

3   John and Betty began conjoint sessions as soon as the couples therapist had contacted John's domestic violence program and it was confirmed that the client had made "sufficient progress." How would you define "sufficient progress," and at what point would you begin couples work with a client who had perpetrated domestic violence?

4   This case study illustrates how a victim's codependent behavior can unwittingly maintain an abusive relationship. Does the couple's therapist address this issue? Do you think, ultimately, that all parties took responsibility without blaming the victim for the abuse? Why or why not?

Examining Women's Rage in Intimate Partner Violence

KIMBERLY FLEMKE

4

The discussion of women initiating violence in their intimate relationships has historically generated great controversy, unlike other areas of domestic violence exploration. Early studies that introduced the idea of women being violent in their intimate relationships (Steinmetz, 1977–1978; Straus & Gelles, 1988) elicited intense reactions within the field. Subsequent studies over the past 30 years have reported similar findings of mutual perpetration of intimate partner violence (IPV; Archer, 2000; Busch & Rosenberg, 2003; Chen & White, 2004). As a result, the dialogue surrounding women's perpetration of IPV has slowly started to shift; research is now exploring women's motives for using violence (Emery & Lloyd, 1994; Holtzworth-Munroe, 2005; Swan & Snow, 2002). As a result, the narrowly defined and historically designated victim role is broadening, as the assumed motive of self-defense becomes reconsidered and expanded (Dutton & Nicholls, 2005).

Such expansions are illuminating complexities formerly overlooked within women's experience of intimate violence. The long-standing perception of fear and terror that many women continue to experience in IPV (Walker, 1983) is becoming challenged and subsequently rethought as simply being one possible experience among other possibilities. McHugh and colleagues (McHugh, Livingston, & Ford, 2005) reject understanding the issue of IPV with the polarizing lens of gender dichotomies; it does not seem to provide the complex conceptualization

59

required for treating IPV. Without being able to consider experiences that fall outside the dominant discourse (Frieze & McHugh, 1998), women's voices become silenced, and their experience of violence continues to be misunderstood (McHugh, 2005).

Swan and Snow (2002) provide a useful typology of women's use of violence, highlighting the motivational component the women studied had for perpetrating violence. Findings revealed specific differences in reasons why women acted violently, illustrated within four separate categories:

1 *Victim* (34%)—Partners committed more severe violence and coercion against the women than vice versa: (a) *Type A:* Partner committed more of all types of violence than woman did; (b) *Type B:* Partner committed greater levels of severe violence or emotional abuse.

2 *Abused aggressor* (12%)—(a) *Type A:* Woman commits more of every type of violence than partner commits against her; (b) *Type B:* Woman commits more severe violence and coercion. Partner commits equal or greater moderate violence or emotional abuse.

3 *Mixed-male coercive* (32%)—Woman is equally violent to or more violent than partner. Partner is more coercive than woman.

4 *Mixed-female coercive* (18%)—Partner is equally violent to or more violent than woman. Woman is equally coercive to or more coercive than her partner.

Although this typology expands the discourse surrounding women's intentions and motivations for using violence, highlighting the various possibilities that could drive such aggression, this research has also come under some methodological scrutiny. For example, a particular concern is how the findings were interpreted—little distinction was made regarding the types of abuse reported and their severity and impact (such as controlling tactics vs. actual physical violence)—along with concern for the instrument used (the Psychological Maltreatment of Women Inventory; Tolman, 1999), which was specifically designed to measure men's behaviors (Hamel, in press). Consequently, the categories within this typology for women's violence may be somewhat misleading.

But even with such critiques, this research continues to emphasize the relational component of IPV, given that intimate violence never occurs within a vacuum. IPV often transpires within relationships that replicate familiar patterns of childhood violence and abuse (Feerick, Haugaard, & Hien, 2002; Kernsmith, 2005, 2006; Lewis, Travea, & Fremouw, 2002). In order to understand women's use of violence, however, it is necessary to first recognize that there is no simple cause-and-effect explanation to represent all cases of women who perpetrate violence.

THEORETICAL AND PRACTICAL ORIENTATION

I am a trained couple and family therapist who teaches in the graduate programs of couple and family therapy at Drexel University. I am also in clinical practice with the Council for Relationships in Philadelphia, where I primarily treat couples. Over the past 10 years, I have spent many sessions hearing women describe *initiating* acts of violence toward their male partners. Some men would report retaliating violently, whereas others would not.

I use an integrative model in treating clients. When I am seeing women who experience rage, I theoretically draw from various modalities. For example, I use Bowen theory for exploring intergenerational patterns of family violence, while using genograms for tracking such patterns. I use feminist theory for identifying areas of oppression and marginalization that can often fuel rage. Contextual therapy (Boszormenyi-Nagy & Krasner, 1986; Boszormenyi-Nagy & Sparks, 1973) is helpful when I try to understand areas of destructive entitlement that would lead to acts of violence, along with exploring invisible loyalties to parents who may have been similarly violent. Object relations theory is also necessary for understanding how past abuse is internalized and how pain gets projected onto partners, as well as for exploring attachment patterns to early caretakers for understanding selection of current partners. Experiential therapy is often used for working in the moment with clients, helping them identify the painful emotions that may be coming up, as well as using their bodies in the moment as tools to prevent future violence and aggression.

I have also treated both male and female offenders of domestic violence, serving as a treatment provider for the Bucks County (Philadelphia Suburb) Adult Probation and Parole Department. Men and women who had been arrested for acts of IPV were mandated to 26 weeks of treatment. Because there were many more men than women arrested for these acts, men were treated in groups, whereas women were treated individually. As the dynamics with intimate partners were addressed and explored among the women I saw, past experiences of trauma and abuse were often disclosed over the course of treatment. This experience began to inform the way I conceptualized treatment for women's rage.

In addition to treating violent offenders on probation or parole, I have also worked with incarcerated women in a Philadelphia prison as a forensic family therapist. I was able to conduct many couple and family therapy sessions with inmates and their loved ones, when loved ones would be willing to enter the prison for therapy sessions. It was quite a common experience during these sessions to hear stories discussed between the inmates and their partners of past IPV.

CONFRONTING WOMEN'S VIOLENCE

A few years ago, after working in the prison, I was invited to attend a statewide meeting to determine the appropriate philosophy for treating female offenders of domestic violence. The meeting left a lasting impression because it embodied a heated controversy debated between clinicians and prominent women's advocates and attorneys. Strong words were exchanged as conflicting positions collided. The advocates had great difficulty accepting clinicians' reports of women being violent toward their partners without the violence being an act of self-defense or in response to a perceived threat. Clinicians offered multiple examples of women seeking therapeutic help for fear of losing control of their anger and taking it out on either their partner or their children. The room became increasingly uncomfortable as the assumed role of "female victim" was challenged.

I was intrigued that rage was being described with greater intensity and fury than anger. The group consensus seemed to suggest that rage was associated with being out of control. Even more interesting was that many of the attendees of the meeting revealed having their own rage, but somehow they perceived themselves—unlike female offenders of domestic violence—as having a mechanism to manage it. This undefined mechanism seemed to be the boundary that separated the people at the meeting from the women offenders they were discussing and considering for treatment services.

I left the meeting wondering, "How does a woman's anger transform into rage? How are some women able to manage feelings of rage while other women are less able to do so?" I wondered how much of a woman's act of aggression, whether it be out of self-defense and retaliation or some sort of premeditated form of violence, is housed within feelings of rage. Little research has been published about women's expressions of rage and violence, leaving clinicians and researchers with limited knowledge or understanding.

I reflected on the many stories that I had heard while working in the prison when women would describe their experiences of rage and acts of violence toward their partners. I specifically recalled one woman telling me that she knew she needed something *more* than anger management. What she was feeling was far more than anger, which is why she stopped attending those groups; she did not find them useful. I realized that anger management was the only form of treatment (at that time) that was currently available to treat women who were violent, and I questioned its effectiveness. As a result, I wanted to better understand women's experience of rage and violence.

Present Rage Links to Past Trauma

Based on in-depth interviews with 37 incarcerated women who reported experiencing rage during IPV, rage was discovered to be a *distinct* experience from anger, where something "snaps" and leaves women feeling out of control (Flemke & Allen, 2008). The emotional precursors of rage that were discovered include initial feelings of fear and being threatened; tears (not connected to sadness) were often released from feeling overwhelmed, which then would culminate into a detonation of rage and violence. Specific inward and outward physiological changes were reported during rage, such as having increased heart rate, shaking hands or clenched fists, or blurry vision; feeling bigger and stronger; and sometimes "blanking out." This specific research has been very useful to me in my current treatment of women who experience rage. I no longer work in the prison system but have a clinical practice where I am able to see both couples and women individually who are reporting this problem.

The women in my study described their various experiences of rage toward their intimate partners, including traumatic memories from many years ago until present. Almost 90% of those interviewed described at least one vivid memory from childhood that *still* triggers them to feel rage as adults. From the 33 women who were able to identify such experiences, all but two descriptions fell into four significant categories: (a) physical abuse, (b) sexual abuse, (c) feeling unprotected by caretakers, and (d) observing domestic violence.

More than half the participants discussed painful memories from their past that arise when feelings of rage are triggered in the present.

Among the 21 women who identified such memories, 15 women specifically thought of distressing memories involving their parents or caretakers, 6 women recalled memories dealing with their mothers, and 9 women recalled memories dealing with their father figures. Nearly half of the women, 18 participants, specifically discussed types of emotional pain or abuse occurring within their adult intimate relationships that elicit rage. The most common illustrations included scenarios of emotional pain that involved forms of both verbal and emotional abuse.

We still know very little about how past trauma impacts women's current acts of rage and violence toward their intimate partners. My research explored past and present links to rage by asking women to describe any childhood memory that still has the ability to trigger rage inside of them as adult women (Flemke, 2006). Examples of questions asked include the following: Do you remember the first time you ever felt rage? How old were you? What caused you to feel that way? How did your body respond? What has caused you to recall that childhood memory as an adult? How does your early rage connect to rage you have as an adult?

When exploring the intersection of past trauma with present behavior, it becomes necessary to understand the nature of trauma. Despite the personal and subjective experience of enduring traumatic events, clinically evaluating a person's degree of traumatization requires that the client cite exposure to an event that continues to cause significant distress for at least 1 month following the incident (American Psychiatric Association, 1994). Recommendations for clinical intervention regarding past trauma, as in the treatment for posttraumatic stress disorder (PTSD), are based on the prevalence of key, persistent symptoms from the American Psychiatric Association's *DSM–IV*, which include (a) repeated reexperiencing of the trauma, (b) emotional numbing and avoidance of things associated with the trauma, and (c) heightened arousal to the trauma. As a result of finding past trauma intersecting with current triggers for violence, I incorporate into my work with violent women the use of eye movement desensitization reprocessing (EMDR) (Shapiro, 1989, 1991), in which key traumas that still fuel rage are targeted and reprocessed.

CASE STUDY: ELLYSE

I specifically selected the case of Ellyse, an attractive woman in her early 30s who was a medical student attending an Ivy League school, to counter the widespread prevailing myths and stereotypes that surround "violent women." Within my current practice I have treated many professional women who are highly educated, affluent, and independent; some of these women also come in specifically seeking help with the rage that they experience toward their partner. Because these women are high-functioning and do not present as being out of control, many therapists would likely fail to assess for any current or past perpetration of IPV if it were not specifically reported by the client. This is a disservice to those women who desperately need help and clinical intervention. Unfortunately, I believe that many women who do not appear full of rage in session or who do not match expectations for what a violent woman should look like are consequently being overlooked for potentially needed assessment and evaluation. It is important that clinicians challenge their own prejudgments and biases of what violent women supposedly look like in order to help those women who may not initially feel comfortable disclosing their perpetration of violence.

Assessment

Ellyse came to me after reading something that I had written on women's experience of rage and IPV. She explained that she and her boyfriend, Adam, who was a law student in the same Ivy League school, had been together for the past 3 years and were having increasing amounts of "conflict." She said she was afraid that if she did not get control of the rage she has inside, her boyfriend would ultimately leave her. She described both Adam and herself as being very jealous and possessive of each other. She also admitted that her biggest fear was him deciding to move out, leaving her for another woman.

When I met Ellyse for the initial assessment, she explained how she came to realize her need for help after their most recent argument, when she exploded in rage and physically attacked Adam. She said her violence resulted from having checked his phone and there discovered numerous text messages from various women she did not know. She explained that leading up to her attack, she was trying to tell him something, and he seemed disinterested in what she was saying, preoccupied with a text message he had received. She then reported being so angry that she ran over to him and grabbed the phone out of his hands so that she could read the message. She remembered that she just "lost it" and felt completely out of control when she realized it was a text message from another woman. When he tried to yank back his phone from her, she suddenly punched him in the head.

When I asked her to think about her emotions leading up to her violence, she cited the feeling of betrayal as the trigger for her rage. When

I asked her how she felt after the incident, knowing that she had caused him physical pain, she stated, "Honestly, it felt good that I successfully hurt him. . . . [I] finally felt like I was in control. . . . I definitely didn't feel sorry for what I had done. If anything, it felt physically satisfying." She demonstrated little remorse in the telling of the story but described now feeling embarrassed by her actions. She admitted that this was not the first time she had used violence against him, but rather she had been violent with him on numerous occasions in the past. She also admitted that her behaviors were worsening and that she was worried about what she might be capable of doing eventually.

I asked Ellyse if this was her first dating relationship where there had been violence. She explained that she had also initiated violence with her last long-term boyfriend. She explained that the violence between her and her ex-boyfriend eventually had escalated into bidirectional violence, whereas with her current boyfriend, there was no violence reciprocated back from him. When I asked how Adam reacts to her acts of aggression, she reported that he had never retaliated using physical violence, although he would say very mean things to get back at her and hurt her.

Family History

In this first session, I spent time with Ellyse constructing her genogram and trying to get a sense of the contributing factors to her feelings of rage. Ellyse came from a very prominent family in New York, with parents who had been together over 30 years; both parents held positions of power and influence and were each highly regarded within their respective disciplines. Her mother was a well-known attorney, and her father was a provost at a very prestigious university. Ellyse had a twin brother who was completing his MBA at the same Ivy League school Ellyse was attending and a younger sister in her late 20s who was working and living abroad.

After Ellyse gave some background information on her family of origin, I began exploring family patterns that may have been absorbed and were possibly being replicated. Specifically, I began looking for intergenerational patterns of rage and violence. As I began asking questions regarding any possible "modeling" of rage by either parent, it seemed there was a legacy of rage and violence created primarily by her mother. Ellyse said that she had never witnessed either of her parents hurting the other physically; however, she described her mother often demonstrating "out of control" behaviors toward Ellyse's father, with lots of screaming, yelling, and throwing of objects. Ellyse reported currently having a good relationship with both of her parents, but she also seemed to have an invisible loyalty toward her mother in how she would emulate her rage and frustration.

I explored whether there was ever violence between Ellyse and her siblings while growing up together. She reported that one time when she was a teenager, she became very physically aggressive with her sister, with whom she described always feeling in competition for her parents' love and attention. She admitted that she had gotten into a major argument the previous summer with her sister, which had led to Ellyse losing control and punching her sister in the stomach. She openly expressed shame and regret over this incident, far more in comparison to how she felt about her recent attack on her boyfriend. I also asked about any past childhood abuse, which Ellyse denied experiencing.

Screening and Danger Assessment Tools

After completing her genogram, I assessed Ellyse's level of dangerousness to her partner. I pulled out the Power and Control Wheel (Pence & Paymer, 1993) and spent time going through each slice of the pie. I was trying to ascertain what other types of abusive behaviors were being played out in their relationship that had yet to be identified. It seemed that Ellyse's primary area of abusiveness, in addition to her physical aggression, was demonstrated in her attempts to isolate Adam; she would repeatedly use jealousy to justify her violent actions, hoping to control whom he would meet and spend time with when she was not with him. I then spent time going through the wheel with Ellyse about Adam's efforts of using power and control against her. It seemed that he too was responsible for a number of various forms of abuse in the relationship, although they were never previously identified as abuse. Despite Adam's lack of physical violence, he was abusive in using intimidation, emotional abuse, efforts of isolation, and tactics of minimizing, denying, and blaming, along with constant threats of leaving if Ellyse would not do something he wanted.

I then used the Danger Assessment scale (Campbell, 1995) to determine the level of risk and danger in the relationship between Ellyse and Adam. The primary area that was noted for dangerousness centered on Ellyse's violent jealousy. There were no guns in their apartment, she was not using any type of drugs or getting drunk, and she did not believe that she could kill him. Nonetheless, the initial goal of treatment was to immediately end all acts of aggression and violence toward her boyfriend. Although Ellyse denied that Adam exhibited any of the Danger Assessment items except having moments of intense jealousy (which she admitted as having potential for violence), we discussed a safety plan in case she suddenly felt that she was in danger if Adam ever became unexpectedly violent. I also provided her with crisis hotline numbers for abuse shelters.

I told Ellyse that I would like to meet with Adam alone, and she told me that he was 100% unwilling to come to therapy. She explained that was not an option, and he was willing to stay with her only if she went to therapy to take care of her problem. I explained that I generally meet with the partner to get a fuller picture of how the partner experiences the woman's rage, as well as to help me become aware of aggression that may go unreported. She told me that I could call him myself and see what he said about coming in for treatment, which I did at the end of our session, with Ellyse still present. When I invited him to meet with me, he adamantly refused, stating that he firmly believed that this was Ellyse's problem and that she needed to take responsibility for it and deal with it on her own. He did, however, agree to speak with me by phone on a weekly basis if I felt that would be helpful.

Finally, I gave Ellyse homework to be completed for our next session. I assigned an EMDR exercise, borrowed from a colleague, in which she was asked to list the 10 worst experiences she had ever had in her life, half from before age 18 and the other half after age 18 (D'Antonio, 2005). I then asked her to rank them against each other, with the least upsetting event labeled as number 1 and the most upsetting labeled as number 10, and to write her age alongside each event in the margin. I also told her to asterisk any of the events that caused rage to be triggered.

TREATMENT AND INTERVENTIONS

Ellyse came back in the following week reporting no violence between her and her boyfriend. She described it as being a "good week." We then went over her homework, listing the significant traumas from her past. Themes of jealousy and fearing abandonment were present in the majority of the traumas listed, giving me a sense of some underlying attachment issues. There were vivid memories of jealousy from childhood, usually involving competitiveness with female peers; she explained that often she would recall these events even now when she was feeling jealousy in her adult relationships. A common belief she held about herself that seemed to fuel such feelings of jealousy was that she was not good enough.

I asked that Ellyse describe her earliest memory of feeling rage, and she described her brother holding her down so that her sister could hit her. I asked Ellyse to give a feeling that captured that early experience of rage. She said she felt totally helpless. I asked her to think about any other significant memories from her childhood that left her feeling intensely helpless. She described watching her mom seriously hit (abuse) her sister when they were little and feeling like she could not do anything to rescue her sister. Ellyse recalled crying as she watched it happen, causing her brother to come over and cover her ears.

Additional memories of rage connected to feeling helpless included scenes from early adolescence—Ellyse stated that she often felt left out and not good enough to be included with the most popular girls at school, and she felt rage remembering herself eating alone at lunch. She also described being intensely jealous of two girls in particular because everyone seemed to like them, including the boys. The majority of her adult scenes involved feeling jealous about other women and the attention her dating partner gave them. The majority of the described scenes seemed to underscore her feeling inadequate and helpless.

It was apparent that the emotional memories still held tremendous power over Ellyse; this was particularly true after exploring the cognitions that correlated with the traumatic events. As we reviewed each of the 10 memories, two negative cognitions that Ellyse had about herself continued to rise to the surface: (a) I am not good enough, and (b) I am not worthy of being loved. I asked Ellyse to reflect on her most recent episode of jealousy with Adam and to tell me about the thoughts running through her mind. She reported a series of uncensored beliefs: "She's better than me; I'm not special; he's not special to me; what we've shared is not special; I'm lonely; I'm an outsider; he'll find someone better than me."

EMDR Therapy

Before I was able to target these painful thoughts and feelings using EMDR, I needed to first have Ellyse create an image in her mind, a safe place, which would represent her feeling relaxed, in control, safe, and calm. This scene would be used to conclude our session each time that we did any EMDR on past, upsetting scenes. Ellyse described a scene that was linked to her spirituality, a part of her life where she feels strong and in control; she saw herself kneeling on a beach at sunset and connecting to God. I also had Ellyse imagine a scenario that would normally trigger her to feel rage, such as one in which she is feeling jealous about Adam, but to instead watch herself in the scene handling the situation with total control and composure. I used EMDR to install this scene so that she could quickly draw from it to help guide her when she was feeling inclined to repeat past abusive behaviors when jealous. She reported finding great hope in being able to imagine that scene and thought of it often.

Over the course of many weeks, both the emotions and the negative beliefs from Ellyse's list of worst events were targeted using EMDR. As a result, the past traumas that were currently impacting Ellyse's inability to stay in control of her rage were resolved; the intense emotional responses were eliminated. The key traumas that were fueling much of Ellyse's rage, including the distorted cognitions underlying much of her feelings of jealousy, no longer had the triggering effect they had previously had on her.

Experiential Therapy

Another key component of Ellyse's treatment was experiential therapy. It was critical for Ellyse to begin to notice, log, and keep track of her bodily sensations and changes prior to and during an episode of rage. We spent weeks closely focused on how her body gives physical signals to help her recognize when her rage is beginning to simmer. The specific cues she started to recognize and track leading up to experiencing rage included an increase in her breathing and heart rate, a marked increase in body temperature that she specifically noticed feeling in her head, a burning sensation in her stomach, her fists balling up, and a surge of adrenaline that she described making her feel much stronger in those moments. She described feeling emotionally overwhelmed, which would trigger her to cry as a way to release the build-up inside once she was done releasing her rage. Over time Ellyse used these physical cues as warning signals to both herself and her boyfriend, enabling her to choose more constructive outlets for her growing feelings of rage.

Learning to master the physiological changes leading to rage became a turning point for Ellyse. She described feeling more empowered and in control of herself the more she was able to successfully tune in to her body. Being able to identify the triggers in her body enabled her to then be able to implement an alternate plan, which included choosing to remove herself from Adam for a minimum of 20 minutes. This physical separation from Adam helped Ellyse regain focus on how she wanted to manage her preliminary feelings that had the potential to escalate and explode into rage. We discussed various options that could be useful to her, including breathing exercises, calling a friend for support and accountability, and going downstairs to the gym (their apartment had a gym on the first floor). Ellyse decided that her first choice would be to use the treadmill downstairs or to run outside for a minimum of 20 minutes, which over time proved to be a very effective intervention to calm down.

Relational Dynamic of Violence

Over the course of therapy, however, an interesting dynamic between Ellyse and Adam was revealed; the more in control that Ellyse became over her rage outbursts, the less in control Adam was over his ability to manage his anger. It is important to note that in the beginning of the relationship, Ellyse reported, she was the only one who had acted violently in the relationship. However, as she sought to manage her rage and tried to calm herself down during their heated arguments, Adam would physically block the door so that she could not leave. This often caused arguments to escalate into mutual verbal abuse, and inevitably bidirectional violence would follow. Although Ellyse was very upset to see her progress sabotaged, she refused to move out or call the police, despite her risk of danger and injury increasing.

Adam refused to speak with me on the phone once he began using violence against Ellyse, at which point she demanded that he seek professional help. As Ellyse actively worked on stopping her violent behaviors toward Adam, Ellyse described noticing Adam trying harder to provoke her to become violent again. The more that she was able to maintain staying in control and was able to disengage during high stress and conflict, the more out of control Adam would appear. It was becoming clearer over time that Adam was not feeling in control in the relationship, particularly because he no longer knew how to "trigger" Ellyse back into their unhealthy dance of violent intimacy. I warned Ellyse that this change to their relationship dynamic might put her at greater risk of getting hurt, assuming that Adam would continue to escalate in aggression if he could not successfully bait her into her former behaviors where she would be the primary perpetrator of violence. We discussed a safety plan again, so that she would be able to leave if she needed to go somewhere else for safety.

According to Ellyse, my prediction of violence came true. Once she had completely stopped initiating violence between them, Adam's aggression eventually led to his initiating violence toward her. The situation became increasingly distressing to Ellyse because Adam would actively deny his attacks on her; he refused to admit that he was now in the role of being the violent aggressor and instead blamed her for his acts of aggression. Ellyse would fight back once Adam attacked her, and Adam used that to manipulate Ellyse's understanding of her self-defense by blaming her for his actions, saying that she *made* him act that way. He explained that he was simply trying to stop her from becoming violent toward him because he knew from the past what she was capable of doing.

The turning point for Ellyse came when she did not fight back during one of his recent attacks. It was later that night when Adam noticed the numerous bruises on Ellyse's throat and forearms, as he recognized that he had no marks on his own body, that Adam finally faced the reality of his own violence and aggression. It was Ellyse's choice to stop participating in the mutual violence that forced Adam to take responsibility for the bruises and injuries he had caused her; he was no longer able to rationalize his behaviors as a result from them *both* fighting.

Ellyse explained that this realization was traumatic to Adam because he had formerly taken great pride in being different from his abusive father. Although Adam recognized he would be mean to Ellyse and give her occasional verbal lashings (this was never considered to be verbal abuse, however), he always maintained that he was not an abusive man because he had never laid a finger on Ellyse in the past. Once he saw the effects of his physical abuse on Ellyse, he agreed that he needed his own treatment for violence. He took my referral and went to a men's battering group.

It was important to understand the dynamic pull of violence between Ellyse and Adam. I warned Ellyse in the beginning of treatment that it was possible that as she became more able to control her rage and violence, she herself would be at greater risk for abuse from Adam. Because Adam and Ellyse were so possessive of each other, they had developed their own methods of trying to control their partner. For example, Adam would threaten to leave Ellyse if she decided to hang out with any guy friends, causing Ellyse's circle of friends to dwindle. Gradually, she stopped having not only any male friends but also any female friends. Ellyse explained that she would often feel embarrassed when her girlfriends heard how abusively Adam would speak to her, although she admitted that she would always defend him to her friends. Ellyse would similarly try to sabotage and ruin any opportunities Adam had to study with female friends after classes either by showing up, where she would cause a scene and embarrass him, or by constantly calling him until he came home. Although Ellyse was responsible for trying to control Adam through her acts of violence, Adam was also highly controlling of Ellyse in the relationship, using both verbal abuse (e.g., calling her names such as "slut" and "whore") and emotional abuse (such as threatening to break up with her and move out of the apartment).

It was necessary for Ellyse to understand that the healthier she might become, without Adam getting his own treatment, the greater the likelihood that the patterns that had once held them together as a couple would no longer have the same effect and would thus change the way they connected to each other. For example, the pattern of Adam saying abusive things against Ellyse as a way to bait her to engage with him, which would historically trigger an aggressive response, might eventually lose its power over Ellyse. This long-lasting unhealthy interaction between them provided each with reassurance that they were still emotionally connected to the other, essentially quelling their individual fears of abandonment. It is quite likely that enmeshment and intensity were being mistaken for intimacy.

My concern for Ellyse was the possibility that her growth would be interpreted as her disengagement from Adam in the relationship. I predicted that once Adam's controlling techniques were rendered ineffective, he likely would begin to feel scared and helpless, no longer feeling able to control *her* loss of control. It seemed likely that at this point he would feel the need to "up the ante" and take more drastic measures to draw Ellyse back into their dysfunctional dance of intimacy. He would be seeking a sense of security that their bond of enmeshment continued to exist. This was unfortunately proven correct toward the end of Ellyse's treatment with me.

Although Adam initially agreed to attend the batterer intervention group, he wound up refusing to attend at the last minute. Ellyse was very upset by this, understanding the potential risks to her safety if he did not receive some treatment. She also began to see his refusal of help as a direct reflection of a lack of care for her and the relationship, which led her to consider that she may not want to remain in this relationship. She agreed that she would be open to calling the police in the future, given that he chose to ignore getting help. I saw Ellyse for approximately 10 months, at which time she had to move to begin her residency.

OUTCOMES AND CONCLUSION

Overall, this case was a success. There were clear limitations in having a partner who was unwilling to be involved in treatment, as a source of either support or accountability. Ellyse was highly motivated and remained that way throughout her time with me. She clearly felt better about herself once she felt more in control of her rage and acts of violence. This also helped her feelings of jealousy and insecurity about other women. The past attachment issues linked to her intense fear of abandonment were only minimally addressed; a more thorough exploration might have helped in her decision to leave her abusive relationship. Over the course of therapy, Ellyse made marked improvement in how she learned to control her violent attacks. She will hopefully continue using all that she learned and apply it to the years ahead with whomever she chooses for a partner.

REFERENCES

American Psychiatric Association. (1994). *Diagnostic and statistical manual of mental disorders* (4th ed.). Washington, DC: Author.

Archer, J. (2000). Sex differences in aggression between heterosexual partners: A meta-analytic review. *Psychological Bulletin, 126,* 651–680.

Boszormenyi-Nagy, I., & Krasner, B. R. (1986). *Between give and take.* New York: Brunner-Routledge.

Boszormenyi-Nagy, I., & Sparks, G. (1973). *Invisible loyalties.* New York: Harper & Row.

Busch, A., & Rosenberg, M. (2003). Comparing women and men arrested for domestic violence: A preliminary report. *Journal of Family Violence, 19,* 49–57.

Campbell, J. C. (1995). *Assessing dangerousness.* Newbury Park, CA: Sage.

Chen, P., & White, J. R. (2004). Gender differences in adolescent and young adult predictors of later intimate partner violence. *Violence Against Women, 10,* 1283–1301.

D'Antonio, M. (2005, October). *EMDR exercise: 10 worst experiences: Working with EMDR targets.* Presented at the Council for Relationships 2005 Annual Relationship Conference, Philadelphia.

Dutton, D. G., & Nicholls, T. L. (2005). The gender paradigm in domestic violence research and theory: The conflict of theory and data. *Aggression and Violent Behavior, 10,* 680–714.

Emery, B. C., & Lloyd, S. A. (1994). A feminist perspective on the study of women who use aggression in close relationships. In D. L. Sollie & L. A. Leslie (Eds.), *Gender, families and close relationships: Feminist research journeys* (pp. 237–262). Thousand Oaks, CA: Sage.

Feerick, M. M., Haugaard, J. J., & Hien, D. A. (2002). Child maltreatment and adulthood violence: The contribution of attachment and drug abuse. *Child Maltreatment, 7,* 226–240.

Flemke, K. (2006, November). *Women's experience of rage towards their intimate partner.* Paper presented at the 68th National Conference on Family Relations, Minneapolis, MN.

Flemke, K., & Allen, K. R. (2008). Women's experience of rage: A critical feminist analysis. *Journal of Marital and Family Therapy, 34,* 58–74.

Frieze, I. H., & McHugh, M. C. (1998). Measuring feminism and gender role attitudes. *Psychology of Women Quarterly, 22,* 349–353.

Hamel, J. (in press). Toward a gender-inclusive conception of intimate partner violence research and theory: Part II—New directions. *International Journal of Men's Health.*

Holtzworth-Munroe, A. (2005). Female perpetration of physical aggression against an intimate partner: A controversial new topic of study. *Violence and Victims, 20,* 253–261.

Kernsmith, P. (2005). Exerting power or striking back: A gendered comparison of motivations for domestic violence perpetration. *Violence and Victims, 20, 173–185.*

Kernsmith, P. (2006). Gender differences in the impact of family of origin violence on perpetrators of domestic violence. *Journal of Family Violence, 21,* 163–171.

Lewis, S. F., Travea, L., & Fremouw, W. J. (2002). Characteristics of female perpetrators and victims of dating violence. *Violence and Victims, 17,* 593–606.

McHugh, M. C. (2005). Understanding gender and intimate partner abuse. *Sex Roles, 52,* 717–724.

McHugh, M. C., Livingston, N. A., & Ford, A. (2005). A postmodern approach to women's use of violence: Developing multiple and complex conceptualizations. *Psychology of Women Quarterly, 29,* 323–336.

Pence, E., & Paymer, M. (1993). *Education groups for men who batter: The Duluth model.* New York: Springer Publishing.

Shapiro, F. (1989). Efficacy of the eye movement desensitization procedure for the treatment of traumatic memories. *Journal of Traumatic Stress, 2,* 199–223.

Shapiro, F. (1991). Eye movement and reprocessing procedure: From EMD to EMDR—A new model for anxiety and related traumata. *Behavior Therapist, 14,* 133–135.

Steinmetz, S. (1977–1978). The battered husband syndrome. *Victimology: An International Journal, 2,* 499–509.

Straus, M. A., & Gelles, R. J. (1988). How violent are American families? Estimates from the National Family Violence Resurvey and other studies. In G. T. Hotaling, D. Finkelhor, J. T. Kirkpatrick, & M. A. Straus (Eds.), *Family abuse and its consequences: New directions in research* (pp. 14–36). Thousand Oaks, CA: Sage.

Swan, S. C., & Snow, D. L. (2002). A typology of women's use of violence in intimate relationships. *Violence Against Women, 8,* 286–319.

Tolman, R. M. (1999). The validation of the Psychological Maltreatment of Women Inventory. *Violence and Victims, 14,* 25–35.

Walker, L. (1983). *The battered woman syndrome.* New York: Springer Publishing.

QUESTIONS FOR REFLECTION AND DISCUSSION

1 The author began exploring Ellyse's past trauma in the first session, using a genogram. Why do you suppose she decided to do this so early in treatment? What else could she have done first? If you were the therapist, how would you have begun Ellyse's treatment?

2 According to the author, eliminating Ellyse's violence was her number one treatment consideration. When it became evident that Adam was beginning to engage in violence himself, the author discussed with Ellyse a plan to help keep her safe. She does not, however, mention having discussed a similar plan for Adam to address his own safety needs. Why not? Do you think Adam's safety was at risk? In general, do you think that a therapist working with a perpetrator is obligated to provide a safety plan to the victim or simply to refer him or her to appropriate victim services?

3 The author draws an important distinction between rage and anger. What, in your view, are the differences, and what are the implications for treatment of domestic violence? How well are traditional psychoeducational models equipped to help clients with rage?

4 The research cited by the author on women's typologies of IPV concluded that "women's violent behavior can only be understood when placed in the context of their male partners' violence against them" (Swan & Snow, 2002, p. 310). Do you agree? How well did the case of Ellyse and Adam illustrate this point? Do you think this is also true of men's violence toward their female partners?

5

The Souzas: Using Problem-Centered Systems Therapy With IPV

ALISON HERU

The McMaster model of family functioning and the problem-centered systems therapy of the family originated at McGill University in Montreal 50 years ago, under the direction of Nathan Epstein. Development of the McMaster model continued at McMaster University in Hamilton, Ontario, and progressed further at Brown University in Providence, Rhode Island, where Epstein developed the Family Research and Training program. The McMaster model originally emanated from psychodynamic models but is essentially a systemic, behavioral approach, recognizing that insight is not a necessary or sufficient ingredient for change. Treatment is aimed at the processes occurring within the family that produce or maintain dysfunctional behaviors. Family therapy is directed at changing the system and thereby changing the behavior of the individual. I was trained by Nathan Epstein and Duane Bishop, the originators of the model, and ran the Brown Psychiatry Residency Family Training program for 17 years. I have adapted the model for use with intimate partner violence (IPV).

Results of a recent study indicate that the prevalence of intimate partner violence among patients hospitalized with suicidality is surprisingly high (Heru, Stuart, Eyres, Rainey, & Recupero, 2006). Over 90% of these patients reported severe physical violence on the revised Conflict Tactic Scale (Straus, Hamby, Boney-McCoy, & Sugarman, 1996). Male and female patients in this study did not differ significantly on violence perpetration or victimization (all p values $> .05$). Poor family functioning predicted physical violence victimization in both male and female suicidal inpatients, even after controlling for alcohol use and demographic characteristics. Currently, we are conducting a pilot study for patients with major depression and marital violence, comparing couples treatment with treatment as usual. This chapter describes the successful treatment of a couple in the study.

The treatment model used is the problem-centered systems therapy of the family (PCSTF; Epstein, Baldwin, & Bishop, 1983; Ryan, Epstein, Keitner, Miller, & Bishop, 2005). A core belief of this treatment model is that the steps of problem solving can be taught. These steps are identification of the problem, communication of the problem, discussion of alternatives for solving the problem, deciding together on a solution, and checking back with each other on whether the solution worked and, if not, choosing another solution. An IPV-psychoeducational module is added to the PCSTF when treating couples with marital violence. This module uses a cognitive-behavioral approach and is based on the work of Stith and colleagues (Stith, 2005). A negotiated time-out tool is also taught (Rosen, Matheson, Stith, McCollum, & Locke, 2003). This treatment model has been used to treat couples where one partner has major depression, with significant reductions in depression and suicidal ideation when compared to treatment without family therapy (Miller et al., 2005). Treatment is completed when the problems on the list have been satisfactorily resolved. Couples with violent behavior can also have strengths (Heru, 2007). Emphasizing positive attributes is therapeutic because couples can be easily shamed when discussing their violence. At a minimum, couples can be commended for coming to treatment and acknowledging such a difficult problem as family violence.

CASE STUDY: PETER AND MARIA SOUZA

Maria Souza, a White 25-year-old mother of two, was admitted to the general psychiatric unit with depressive symptoms and suicidal ideation. She was treated with an antidepressant, Prozac (20 mgs), and received milieu therapy. A meeting was held with her husband, Peter. He described her deteriorating functioning at home and her recent loss of supervisor status at a fast-food restaurant where he also works. They both expressed conflict over managing bills and the care of their two children, who were 2 and 5 years old. He emphasized his need to work extra hours and "do what they say" because he was afraid of losing his job. They easily quarreled about his work situation and her dissatisfaction with staying home and caring for the children. They engaged in bidirectional violence, with each person initiating the violence and experiencing victimization.

Maria and Peter Souza were asked to participate in a study of depression and partner relationships. After giving informed consent, the couple completed a screening assessment designed to exclude high-risk couples. Exhibit 5.1 gives a description of the questions asked during the assessment. These questions ask about acts of extreme violence, uncontrolled use of alcohol or substances, violation of restraining orders, sadistic behavior, stalking, and injury requiring medical intervention (Bograd & Mederos, 1999). Based on their responses, Mrs. and Mr. Souza passed the screening and were assigned to couples treatment.

Exhibit 5.1

PROBLEM-CENTERED SYSTEMS THERAPY OF THE FAMILY

Assessment

Presenting Problem: What are the major problems facing your family? For each problem, when did you first notice the problem, how have you tried to resolve the problem, and what prevented it from being resolved?

Dimensions

Roles: How family members fulfill practical and emotional family functioning.

Practical: How do you divide up the chores? Who does the cooking, grocery shopping, laundry, yard work, car maintenance? Are things divided fairly? Does anyone feel overwhelmed or feel that he or she has too much to do? Are some people doing jobs that they should not be doing? How do you check that jobs get done? Who does that? What do you do if jobs are not getting done? How are finances organized? Who brings in the money? Are there separate bank accounts? Do the bills get paid? If not, do you have a plan for paying off debts? Do you discuss spending money? Do the children get an allowance? Do they have to do chores? *Nurturance and support:* Whom do you go to when you need support? Are they helpful? What do they do that's helpful or unhelpful? *Sexual relationship:* Do you have an intimate relationship? What difficulties are there? When did they start? Do you both agree, or do you see the relationship and difficulties differently? *Life skill development:* Who oversees the children's education? As

(Continued)

Exhibit 5.1 *(Continued)*

adults, do you discuss your careers, changes in jobs, and so on? *Management of family system:* Who has the final say? Where does "the buck stop"?

What is the relationship between violence and your dissatisfaction with responsibilities in the couple? Are there expectations that make you angry?

Problem solving: Ability to resolve problems to maintain effective family functioning.

Practical problem solving: Problems of everyday life (household repairs, etc.) and emotional problem solving (e.g., when a family member is angry or sad). *Identification:* Who first notices the problem? *Communication:* When you notice a problem, whom do you tell? Does anyone notice the problem but not tell anyone? *Development of alternatives:* After you notice a problem and communicate the solution, do you think about alternatives? Who thinks of the plan? Does anyone else have ideas? Do you share them? *Decisions and actions:* How do you decide what to do? Who decides? How do you decide on that alternative? *Monitoring the action:* When you decide on an action, do you follow through? Do you check to see that things get done?

Do you ever use violence to exert control over your partner? Do you ever use violence to get what you want? Do you ever use violence so that you win the argument and things get decided in your favor?

Communication: Recurrent patterns of exchanging practical and emotional information.

Extent: Do people in this family talk with each other? Who does most of the talking? Can you talk freely or are you guarded about what you say? What stops you from talking freely? *Clarity:* How did X let you know that? Did you get the message? What is X getting at? *Directness:* Do you feel others understand you? What happens when they don't? Can you get straight to the point? Do others let you know they have understood you? What happens when they don't?

How often do you threaten violence? When do you do this? Do you always know when you are going to get angry or violent? Does your partner? Do you ever use violence instead of saying you are angry?

Affective Responsiveness: The range of emotions experienced by each family member. Is it appropriate and in proportion to situations? Do you experience feelings of happiness, joy, sadness, anger, fear? Do you feel that you over-respond with any one emotion? Do you underrespond? Do you think you get angry, depressed, and so on in situations where others would react differently? Are you concerned about how you respond in some situations? *Do you think you have excessive anger? Do you think you have the same amount of anger as other people but you choose to "let it rip" rather than hold it in? Do you think your anger is more extreme than other people experience?*

Affective Involvement: The extent to which family members show a genuine interest in each other. Who cares about what is important to you? What activities and interests are important to you? Is your spouse supportive of your interests? How does your partner show his or her interest? Does your partner

Exhibit 5.1   *(Continued)*

show too much interest? *Does violence ever occur when you feel rejected or insecure with how your partner feels about you?*

Behavior Control: Patterns for handling behavior of children and adults in dangerous situations. Do you have rules? What are they? Are they the same for everyone? Are they clear? Do you agree on the rules? Which rules do you differ on and how? Do you work together in disciplining your children? How do you enforce the rules? What happens if you break a rule? Who is toughest in terms of consequences? Do you stick to being tough, or do you give in later? Does anyone have a problem with drinking, drugs, or violence? *What are the rules about violence? What stops you from being able to keep to those rules?*

TREATMENT GOALS AND TREATMENT PLAN

In the first session, Peter described his wife's violence as being problematic and said that on a scale of 1 to 10, her physical violence was a 4 to 5 and psychological violence was around a 6. Maria described "being like my dad towards Peter. That's how I feel."

Peter described his physical violence as a 2 to 3 and his psychological violence as a 6 to 7. They both agreed on the other's assessment and stated, "We do it to provoke each other." They described hitting each other with their fists, yelling and pushing, pulling hair, and throwing any object at hand at the other person. They admitted to fighting when arguing about everyday things. Neither had ever hurt the other person badly, but both were afraid that might happen. The Souzas were very open, and we easily developed a good rapport.

I explained the process of assessment and treatment. "The first session will focus exclusively on education about the role of violence in your relationship and the signing of the no violence contract. The second session will focus on the learning of the negotiated time-out tool. The third session will focus on an assessment of your whole relationship and the generation of a problem list. Subsequent sessions will focus on problem resolution. Most likely you will come for 6–12 sessions. Is this acceptable?" They agreed.

TREATMENT

In the first session, the couple and I reviewed a psychoeducational handout, which discusses how to develop better ways to manage anger.

I read each topic and asked them to note their responses on the handout. I kept their responses on my copy in the chart as a record of the session. Following are extracts from the handout and descriptions of the couple's responses.

> Violent behavior is a behavior that may be passed down through the generations and a behavior that is culturally enforced. Can you give examples from your own lives of how violent behavior is passed down through the generations of your family?

Maria identified with her father, who was the disciplinarian during her childhood. "He used to line us up, all four of us girls, and say, 'This is the Board of Education.' He then took a board and hit us all." She could not remember why he hit them. Both Mr. and Mrs. Souza agreed that her father had had a significant impact on their disciplinary style with the children. They did not use physical discipline on their 5-year-old son, Joey, and instead only yelled at him when he hit his 2-year-old sister.

Peter's parents died when he was young, and he lived in various group homes "where there was no discipline, just consequences for bad behavior." He described a childhood injury secondary to violence from a relative, which had precipitated his entry into child protective services. He was not taught how to manage himself; the only consequence to bad behavior was a short time in room restriction, which he described as pleasant and a way to get some quiet time away from the others. He identified his lack of discipline of his son as a result of his own lack of any parental role model.

When discussing the bidirectionality of their violence, Peter said, "I have never told anyone about this because the men would all laugh at me!" Maria reiterated that she learned her violence from her dad. The couple appeared unsure of how to proceed. I encouraged them to write down how previous generations have influenced their current behavior.

> New behaviors can be learned. Can you give examples from your own lives of how you have learned new behaviors? This can include work skills, parenting skills, caring for elderly, etc.

Peter said that he was controlling his drinking and was proud of this. He knew that his drinking bothered Maria, and he wanted to do his part to improve their relationship. Instead of drinking a few beers when he came home from work and watching TV by himself, he instead sat and talked with her. Maria Souza agreed that she was less worried about his alcohol use, although she noted it had been only 1 week since he stopped drinking.

Maria was pleased with her ability to learn negotiating skills at work. I kept her focused on the new skills even when she veered off to talk about how useless she felt "being stuck at home without a job."

> Each person is responsible for his or her own behavior. Can you give an example from your own life that illustrates this point?

Peter again spoke about his alcohol use and his responsibility to stay sober. Maria said she was responsible for her own behavior because she sought treatment for her depression.

Next, the handout described various points the therapist should discuss, depicted in the following paragraphs in italics. *The family therapist describes different types of violent behavior.* I reviewed the current understanding of violence in relationships. I discussed the role of alcohol, spending some extra time describing studies on alcohol and violence because this topic was of particular importance to the Souzas. I also described the relative frequency of violence by both partners: "In a study done here on the inpatient unit, over 90% of patients with depression reported violence both *towards* their partners and *by* their partners. There was no difference between the men and women. So, your experience is the most common we find here in this hospital."

The family therapist discusses resources in the community. I discussed with the Souzas the availability of women's shelters and gave them cards for the domestic violence hotline. (There are no shelters available for men in Rhode Island.) I explained the role of the police and the courts. I also described resources for men, such as support groups and anger management classes.

The family therapist outlines the concept of safety planning and helps each individual develop his or her own safety plan should violence escalate. I explained that Maria and Peter should have their own individual safety plans that they do not share with their partner.

Each participant will be given a copy of the material covered in this meeting and given the opportunity to ask questions. At this point in the session, the couple signed a no-violence contract, and Maria signed a release allowing me to communicate with her treatment team.

Second Session

In the second session, both Maria and Peter stated that there had been no violence in the previous week. When I asked what had enabled them to stay safe, they said that they had reminded each other about the no-violence contract and that they both really wanted to get over the violence. Both agreed that they were looking forward to the session so that they could figure out what to do next. Peter said that he "wants to find a different way to deal with it." When I asked for clarification of "it," he said he meant "being angry."

In this session I gave both of them a copy of the negotiated time-out tool. I explained that this tool must be learned properly and that they have to adapt it to specifically suit them. In my experience, couples often rush through this session, moving quickly through the exercise. My main task during this session is to slow them down and provide multiple opportunities for reflection and the creation of alternate action. The tool's steps are outlined in the following pages.

> Step 1. Awareness: Learning to recognize internal cues that anger is escalating. Partners may have different levels of comfort with intense emotion. One may be ready for a time-out before the other has reached his or her warning level. Both partners take ownership for their responses and agree to act in a way that maintains safety.

It is hard for individuals to recognize and describe their anger; for this reason I have found it helpful to have clients draw how their anger builds. Maria drew a curve that sharply escalated, peaked, and then quickly diminished. Peter, on the other hand, drew a line with a slower build and a more sustained peak (see Figure 5.1).

Mrs. Souza   Mr. Souza

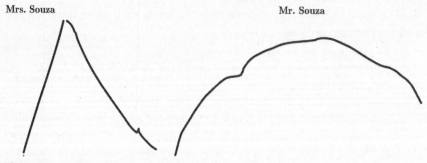

Figure 5.1 Anger curves.

We spent time reviewing Maria and Peter's awareness of this pattern and how they recognize it in themselves and each other. I asked clarifying questions such as the following: Do you feel your face muscles tighten? Do the muscles in your arms or your fists clench? Do you notice your voice rise and get shrill, or do you get loud? Do you move around a lot? Do you stamp your feet? Do you move your arms around? The couple gave multiple examples of how they can see the patterns in themselves and each other. Some couples find this part difficult; however, with coaching and demonstration, they can eventually become aware of their anger. I may describe how I experience anger and my own physiological response. Referring back to the visual description given earlier is helpful.

Step 2. Staying within the Safety Zone: Deciding that anger may escalate past the safety zone and a time-out is needed. Either partner may initiate a time-out.

Maria and Peter agreed that raising their voices is the sign that they are moving out of the safety zone.

Step 3. Signaling: The initiator signals a time-out using a hand gesture such as the "T" symbol and saying in a calm manner, "I am going to take a time-out."

The couple selected a clear and nonthreatening time-out signal. I asked them to role-play so that they could feel comfortable with the time-out tool. They made several attempts at this and then changed the signal to one with which they felt more comfortable (choosing to make the universally accepted sign for a time-out: one vertical hand with the other hand placed horizontally on the fingertips of the first hand). Steps 4 and 5 were included in the role-playing.

Step 4. Acknowledging: The other partner acknowledges the time-out. Partners plan ways to resist the urge to continue arguing.

Step 5. Disengaging: Partners go to separate locations. Partners negotiate a specified location, plans for caring for the children, and amount of time needed for the time-out.

The Souzas decided that 10–15 minutes is the optimal time for their time-out. (For nearly all clients, anything less than 1 hour is optimal.)

We discussed all contingencies: for example, Peter will go outside for his time-out, but if it is raining or cold, he will go to the shed. Maria will go to the bedroom. Both stated that their fights usually escalate when the children are not present, but they agreed that when the children were present, Maria would supervise the children during the time-out and would either stay with them or go to the bedroom.

> Step 6. Cooling Off: Partner who initiates time-out spends time doing calming activities. Both partners may need to cool off and may need help in finding ways to calm themselves.

Maria and Peter each picked an activity that is soothing and allows them to get back in control. Maria chose music or exercises; Peter chose a cigarette, deep breathing, or a short walk. Many couples spontaneously identify activities that keep them angry, so the therapist needs to educate them about relaxing activities. Examples of activities that keep couples angry are continuing to ruminate about the disagreement, continuing to try to argue with their spouse, raising their voices, and so on. It is important to remind couples that the goal is to work together on remaining in control and not "nursing anger."

> Step 7. Returning: Partners reconnect and continue discussion if calm. Partners know they have the option of taking another time-out, tabling the discussion until their next session, or dropping the discussion altogether.

Both agreed to return to a neutral place (not either one's time-out zone) such as the living room or kitchen and continue the discussion if calm. They could discuss the topic twice, and if this was unsuccessful, they would agree to table the discussion until the next appointment. If they decided to table it, they would then engage in a pleasant activity together such as a board game or listening to music.

Third Session

We began this session by reviewing the no-violence contract and their use of the negotiated time-out tool. Instead of going outside for 15 minutes, Peter had decided to take a ride in the car and had not come back for an hour. Maria said she was shocked to see the car drive off and did not know what it meant.

I reiterated that there was no right or wrong here and that they have to agree together on what they want and work together to make it happen. They both looked at me for a while, and then Maria stated, "I don't mind if he drives off for an hour. What I mind is that he didn't tell me and that he broke the agreement." Peter replied, "Yes, you are right. I shouldn't have agreed to one thing and then done another." After a pause, I encouraged them to keep talking it through and come to an agreement about what to do. Maria asked her husband what he wanted to do for his time-out. He said that he would go outside as he originally agreed and would not take off in the car again. He added that it was pointless and just wasted gas. Maria said nothing. I asked them if they had agreed on something or not. They replied that they had and repeated their original agreement. I asked them to be sure about it because I was writing it down and planned to ask them next week. Peter laughed and said he was sure. Maria nodded. We moved on to the family assessment.

The assessment revealed that the couple had poor problem-solving skills. They identified problems and communicated them to each other but did not discuss solutions, each trying out different options without discussing it with their partner. This led to disorganization and frustration. One example is how the decision about the evening meal was made. A few hours before Peter was expected home, Maria would start calling him at work. They would have several heated exchanges about what they might eat and what Peter might buy on the way home. When he came home, they were frustrated and angry.

The exchange about the evening meal, Maria Souza agreed, was more about her need to have her husband care for her. Peter expressed frustration because he is busy at work when this happens and does not know what she really wants from him. They both agreed that they were doing a bad job of communicating their emotional needs to each other. Each person spontaneously talked about why they were indirect about their emotional needs, citing negative experiences in childhood. Peter stated that he did not learn to ask for what he needed—that he had been abused and tried to hide any feelings of vulnerability when he was a child. Maria described her father "turning everything into an argument" whenever she or her siblings asked for anything, and so she learned to consider his feelings first before asking for anything. She said that she would try to be nice to him, in the hopes that her father would be nice to her in return.

The family history also revealed that the couple had poor division of roles and responsibilities, and Maria and Peter expressed strong motivation to organize their lives better. The couple wanted to be more involved with each other and develop mutual interests, perhaps continuing to do the things they had enjoyed before the children were born.

In affective responsiveness, anger is highlighted. The couple agreed that they want to be more open about their warm feelings for each other and less angry at each other. Regarding behavior control, they agreed that they have lost control over their anger, lashed out, and thrown things and that this is a poor example to set their children. They agreed that they have no rules for their children regarding the children's behavior. Maria stated that her husband drinks too much but he disagreed.

Together we identified important dysfunctional transactional patterns. In this couple, the most dysfunctional pattern begins with Maria's bullying of her husband. He gets angry and then withdraws and drinks or lashes out and becomes violent. Her bullying can escalate into violence but quickly subsides, whereas he remains angry for longer. Peter does not confront her and shuts down while she continues to "rant and rave." They agreed that this is the most destructive cycle that they get into.

We generated a problem list from the information gathered during the assessment. IPV is always identified as the first problem on the problem list even if couples state that IPV occurs as a consequence of other problems.

1   Violence
2   Difficulty deciding what roles each will have in the family
3   Communication is unclear around emotional needs
4   Emotional needs not identified
5   Shared hobbies and interests
6   Disagreement about Peter's alcohol use
7   Rules for children and adults

After the problem list was agreed upon, I asked them to think of a homework task to tackle before the next week. I emphasized that it should be easy and focused on one of the problems. Maria suggested they draw up a daily schedule for such things as cooking, shopping, and cleaning and caring for the children. Peter agreed. The homework task at this stage should be easy and something that the couple can achieve successfully. This homework seemed hard to me, but the couple insisted that they wanted to try it.

Fourth Session

At this session, Maria reported that there had been one violent incident, one small slap on the hand in the context of a disagreement in the kitchen while they were making lunch. They both smiled and said they had done well because in the past this would have escalated to physical abuse. Instead they had apologized to each other and successfully used the time-out signal as a reminder to calm down. Immediately Peter had regained control, and no time-out was needed. No other episodes had occurred.

We reviewed the problem list and identified which problem to tackle. Maria stated that she had been able to express her emotional needs and had made fewer phone calls to Peter at work. Peter said he was reluctant to say how he feels to her because "it won't matter." She agreed to listen to him more but said that she did not know when he was going to say something important. "Maybe we need a signal so the other person can listen." They discussed how to get the other's attention when they need to talk about their emotional needs. They decided to state their intention clearly and directly, saying, "I would like to express how I am feeling right now." I asked them if this was the right phrase because it seemed too long to me. They confidently stated that they were sure.

The couple went on to discuss their daily schedule and who would cook and shop. Maria was expressing her emotional needs more clearly at this point. Peter was finding this more difficult because his wife tended to dismiss his needs. He was beginning to use a signal to communicate more clearly, and she was trying to pay attention to this.

Fifth Session

No violence had occurred. The couple had used the time-out tool once in a modified fashion that they had negotiated on their own. They did their weekly goal setting on the morning of the appointment. (Nothing like a deadline to get homework done!) They had put the corkboards on the kitchen wall, one for each of them, including their son, Joey, and had written their goals on the boards. This included expressing feelings. They described an improvement in their ability to express affection. They could identify feelings in the other person and were developing a language to talk about feelings.

Peter identified a problem that he wished to discuss in the session. His wife continued to call him frequently at work about a variety of things, ranging from shopping to Joey's behavior. He described an incident of her calling while he was meeting with his boss and the difficulty he had terminating the phone call. He stated that his preference is for him to initiate a call to his wife. She agreed. He looked surprised that it was that easy. She laughed and replied that she had been wondering when he would get around to telling her not to call so much! We reviewed the problem list. The house rules were well established, and his alcohol use remained low. She said she did not mind his having the occasional beer. Next on the problem list was a lack of mutual hobbies. The couple agreed on playing a board game weekly, on Monday evenings, and to look in stores and online for a mutual hobby.

Sixth Session

No violence had occurred. Maria and Peter had used the time-out tool once, but Peter had gone into the bedroom instead of outside. They had renegotiated so that he had the option of going into the bedroom if she agreed. They had not played the board game on Monday as discussed. Peter's alcohol use was still low, but Maria said she remained cautious. I asked them what they were going to do about not following through with the board game. They agreed to add the board game to the wallboard in the kitchen. I remarked that their improved communication had reduced other problems, and I gave them positive feedback on their progress and ability to solve this problem. I emphasized that problems will always arise and that it is how they deal with problems that matters. They should anticipate that solutions may not always work out and that they will need to renegotiate.

Seventh Session

This session was scheduled for 4 weeks later. The couple had had no violence and had used the time-out tool on two occasions. She stated that she had never trusted him before because she knew he always just gave in to her. Now he was able to assert himself appropriately and did not go drinking, and she could trust him to be an equal partner in the marriage. They noticed that their children were more settled and happy. We agreed that they had successfully resolved the problems on the list. We decided on a 6-month follow-up appointment.

Eighth Session

No violence had occurred, and they had used the negotiated time-out tool frequently. They had adapted it to include arguments that occur while driving. When they recognized the escalation, one would call a time-out, and they would drive to either their own home or her sister's home, where she would stay while Peter would drive off for 15–30 minutes to cool down. Then he would come home or pick her up at her sister's, and they would continue the exercise at home as described previously.

OUTCOMES AND CONCLUSION

This couple is an example of a successful treatment of IPV using a no-violence contract, psychoeducation, and a modified PCSTF. This treatment is suitable for couples where there is bidirectional violence. This treatment was successful for several reasons. The screening process excluded high-risk couples. The couple was motivated, and they worked hard between sessions and displayed openness in working with the therapist. It is important to assess the couple's motivation as soon as possible. This can be observed during the psychoeducational portion of the first session and in each person's willingness to follow through on the homework assignments.

The treatment model educated the couple about how violence had become such an important part of their lives and taught the couple new skills in managing dangerous situations. The comprehensive assessment and PCSTF allowed them to discuss all aspects of their relationship and work collaboratively with the therapist on solving each problem they identified.

REFERENCES

Bograd, M., & Mederos, F. (1999). Battering and couples therapy: Universal screening and selection of treatment modality. *Journal of Marital and Family Therapy, 25*(30), 291–312.

Epstein, N. B., Baldwin, L. M., & Bishop, D.S. (1983). The McMaster family assessment device. *Journal of Marital and Family Therapy, 9*(2), 171–180.

Heru, A. M. (2007). *Family factors in intimate partner violence.* Manuscript submitted for publication.

Heru, A. M., Stuart, G. L., Eyres, J., Rainey, S., & Recupero, P. R. (2006). Prevalence and severity of intimate partner violence and associations with family functioning and alcohol abuse in psychiatric inpatients with suicidal intent. *Journal of Clinical Psychiatry, 67*, 23–29.

Miller, I. W., Keitner, G., Ryan, C. E., Solomon, D., Cardemil, E., & Beevers, C. (2005). Treatment matching in the post-hospital care of depressed inpatients. *American Journal of Psychiatry, 161*(11), 2131–2138.

Rosen, K., Matheson, J., Stith, S., McCollum, E., & Locke, L. (2003). Negotiated time-out: A de-escalation tool for couples. *Journal of Marital & Family Therapy, 29*(3), 291–298.

Ryan, C. E., Epstein, N. B., Keitner, G. I., Miller, I. W., & Bishop, D. S. (2005). *Evaluating and treating families: The McMaster approach.* New York: Brunner/Routledge.

Stith, S. M. (2005). *Couples treatment for domestic violence.* Family Therapy Association Workshop, Washington, DC. (Available from stith@vt.edu)

Straus, M. A., Hamby, S. L., Boney-McCoy, S., & Sugarman, D. B. (1996). The revised Conflict Tactics Scales (CTS2). Development and preliminary psychometric data. *Journal of Family Issues, 17*(3), 283–316.

QUESTIONS FOR REFLECTION AND DISCUSSION

1   The couples program described by the author and illustrated in this case example is between 6 and 12 weeks in duration. Do you think this is a sufficient amount of time in which to help a couple stop engaging in abusive behaviors and alter a dysfunctional system for the better? Why or why not?

2   During the course of treatment, the author explains to the couple that bidirectional violence is the most common type, by far more prevalent than unilateral violence by a male partner. What is the significance of Mr. Sousa's remark, "I have never told anyone about this because the men would all laugh at me"? Do you think this is a common feeling among men in situations of bidirectional violence? How might this impact assessment and treatment of bidirectional violence?

3   The PCSTF model used to treat this couple focuses primarily on skills acquisition to effect behavior change, in contrast to some of the other approaches outlined in this book that focus on emotions and cognitions. Do you think it is more effective to first teach violence reduction and relationship skills and then proceed to address a couple's relationship issues, or can the two be done concurrently?

6

Mary and Mark: Couples Therapy With a Female Batterer and Her Husband

MICHAEL MESMER

This case study concerns Mary and Mark, a recently married couple who sought help in stopping violence and abuse and reducing anger in their relationship. Mary had been arrested and convicted in the spring of 2006 for attacking her husband during an argument and was newly enrolled in a batterers' treatment program in Marin County, California, when I first met her and Mark in June of that year. They attended 11 one-hour sessions of couples' therapy over 6 months, ending in January 2007.

I am a marriage and family therapist (MFT) and have been licensed in California since June of 2000. I have a private psychotherapy practice in San Rafael, California, where I work with adults, teens, and children in individual, couples, and family therapy. Among a diverse population of clients seen in short- as well as long-term therapy, I have provided treatment for several women who were concerned about their own anger and violence in their relationships as well as about, in some cases, the abusiveness of their partners or family members. I have also worked with several individual male adults and teens as well as many heterosexual couples in which the focus was on the man's anger, as well as with a transsexual (male transitioning to female) who participated in sadomasochistic and violent sexual activities with several male partners. Mary and Mark were the first couple I had worked with in which the female partner had been identified by law enforcement as the batterer and the male as the victim in a domestic violence case.

I am also cofounder and codirector of Building Better Families, Inc. (BBF), a provider of batterers' treatment groups certified by the Marin County Probation Department since 2003. BBF clients include both court-ordered and voluntary clients working on ending family and other forms of violence in their lives as well as on managing their anger better. To date, BBF groups have served over 160 male clients; female and teen groups are forming as this is written. Since BBF's founding, I have led at least one group and sometimes two or three each week for 2-hour sessions, with as many as 10 group members or as few as 2. (Mary attended another provider's program during the months I provided couples' therapy to her and Mark.)

BBF promotes respect and responsibility as essential elements of healthy relationships, and through lectures, meditation, group exercises, and individual check-ins and storytelling, it provides its clients with tools and techniques to behave more respectfully and responsibly toward themselves and others. Responsibility is presented as empowering rather than burdensome and as a point of view that can be considered ("How am I responsible, if at all?") in any situation but particularly those in which we feel victimized by external events or others.

THEORETICAL AND PRACTICAL ORIENTATION

I understand psychotherapy to be a process by which one person helps another to help him or herself. My approach is eclectic, varies by client, and reflects my training and interest in a wide range of sometimes disparate psychotherapeutic approaches, including the expressive arts (including music, art, and movement therapy); crisis intervention; holistic health and the unity of mind, body, and spirit (see "Holistic Health," 2007); grief therapy; 12-step and other self-help methods of healing addictive and self-destructive behaviors; meditation, guided visualization, and auto-suggestion (such as affirmations); narrative therapy (see especially White & Epston, 1990); and Hakomi therapy, a body-oriented approach to working with trauma and other concerns (described in detail in Kurtz, 1990).

In particular, my work with both male and female perpetrators of abuse or violence has been strongly influenced by Alan Jenkins's fascinating book *Invitations to Responsibility* (1990). Jenkins describes an approach to working with men who have been violent or sexually abusive that begins by modeling respect and by adopting a constraint model instead of a causal model in attempting to understand how these clients came to behave as they did and, more importantly, how to engage clients in discovering more respectful and personally rewarding ways of relating to others. In a manner reminiscent of the stance taken by therapists when conducting motivational interviewing (Miller & Rollnick, 2002), Jenkins addresses his clients in a disarming fashion, inviting them to wonder with him *what keeps them* from behaving respectfully and non-violently toward others rather than *what causes them* to do so. In his view, promoting responsibility is more difficult within a causal model of behavior—both the client and others in his (or her) life can use causes as excuses instead of recognizing one's responsibility for one's own behavior. Constraints, however, are more easily resisted by both client and therapist in promoting nonviolent relationships and in encouraging clients to act more responsibly.

As someone who understands because of personal and professional experience that people of any gender (whether male, female, hermaphroditic, or transgender) can behave violently or abusively toward others, I have been less interested in patriarchal theories of the origins of domestic violence and more in theories and therapies that lend themselves to a pan-gender model of violence in relationships. Attachment theory is one that offers a different view of the possible genesis of violence resulting from childhood trauma in men and women. Sonkin provides a good introduction to its potential in psychotherapy in general (2005) and in responding to domestic violence in particular (Sonkin & Dutton, 2003), the latter albeit with a male-perpetrator focus.

Although often founded in real experiences, the historical and cultural significance of male-perpetrated violence and abuse that has informed much of the work to date in the field of family violence has proved unhelpful to me in the face of actual situations brought to my attention in the course of my work with various clients. The practical problem of treating both male and female perpetrators has led many practitioners, including me, to recognize the universal challenges that face people of all genders in mastering the self-soothing and self-assessment practices so helpful in living respectfully and nonviolently with others.

These are aspects of the theoretical background behind the interventions I employed during my work with Mary and Mark. It should be noted here that I use the terms "batterer" and "victim" to mean a person so identified by law enforcement and others, but with the understanding that neither label is of much help to clients and clinicians seeking not only to understand the clients' anger and violence but also to manage the former and end the latter. I also view the distinction between court-ordered and voluntary clients to be a false one: all clients freely choose to participate to the extent and in the manner that they do, whether in a group or in life. Probation and its requirements are chosen by each probationer instead of other available options, such as a trial of unpredictable length and expense with an unpredictable outcome or an unpredictable sentence including time in jail. In this way, all clients are voluntary, though some are more aware of it than others.

CASE STUDY: MARY AND MARK

Mary called me initially to ask if BBF had any women's groups available (we did not) because she was "required by probation to attend a 52-week program" after being convicted of assaulting her husband during an argument. I referred her to another provider in the county (where she subsequently enrolled). She also told me on the phone that she and her husband were seeking "couples counseling" to help them "learn how to communicate better." I cautioned her that therapy was not appropriate for all couples, especially when violence was a concern, but agreed to meet with her and her husband to find out if I could or should work with them.

At our first session, Mary and Mark identified themselves as "White," "Catholic" (her), and "one-fourth Jewish" (him). They had married only 6 months earlier after a long-distance courtship of several years; her parents lived back in Wyoming and were Christian Scientists, whereas his lived somewhere in the Bay Area. Both gave their age as 29, with Mark the younger by just 6 weeks. Mary seemed to be about 5'3" tall, with broad hips and thighs (which she described as evidence she was overweight) but a small head and delicate shoulders, giving an overall impression of being "bottom heavy." From her physicality and firm voice, I immediately got a sense of Mary's strength and ability to assert her needs and views.

Mark, on the other hand, may have been about the same height as or a few inches taller than Mary but presented as a person of smaller stature because of the way he hunched over, whether moving or sitting. Although he had a full head and beard of dark hair, he was slight of build and spoke in a quiet voice that was sometimes hard to hear. Mark held Mary's hand or reached out to touch her hand frequently during this first session (as well as in future ones), and they kissed frequently (albeit chastely), especially after one of them had spoken of something distressing or disturbing to one of them. Mark was invariably polite and soft-spoken even when, during later sessions, discussing anger or fear (either his own toward Mary or his work or hers toward her jobs or him). Mary, on the other hand, would become loud, even strident, sometimes verbally attacking Mark or others when agitated or upset in our meetings.

Mary self-identified as a "part-time baby-sitter and home-care provider" with a BA. Mark spoke a little about his work as a manager for a San Francisco Bay Area company; he held a Master of Science degree and was concerned about a recent takeover of his employer. Their financial situation was "tenuous," and Mary was looking to increase her income. Neither was in individual or other counseling, besides the 52-week program Mary had begun 2 days before our first meeting. Both reported moderate diets but little structured exercise, although Mary got "out and about" on her part-time jobs more than Mark did. Neither felt they were very spiritual.

Both Mary and Mark spoke at length about Mary's anger and violence in their marriage. Taking turns, each described their arguments as primarily about Mary wanting something that Mark either could not or would not give her. An example they gave me that we focused on during later sessions was that Mary wanted Mark to stay awake at night or, as an alternative, to fall asleep on the living room couch rather than "all the way" in the bedroom while she worked at the dining room table, until she was ready to fall asleep, even though he felt he needed more sleep and had to get up earlier than she did in the morning.

Mary described her arrest somewhat briefly although she acknowledged straightforwardly that she had scratched Mark's face during their argument. (A neighbor's call to 911 on the day of Mary's arrest reported "loud yelling.") But she became agitated when I pressed for more details. Mary again emphasized, "We're here to work on both of us," and she worried that I might be prejudiced against her because she had been identified as a batterer and because I was a man like Mark and therefore more likely to bond with him. Mark described himself as "more passive" than Mary and wondered if he was somehow "enabling" Mary's anger and violence by failing to be, perhaps, more patient or cooperative with her agendas or needs.

TREATMENT

Before learning this information from Mary and Mark, I began our first session, as with all clients, by discussing confidentiality, including my responsibilities regarding child and elder abuse reporting and the limits these imposed on the privacy of our meetings. Knowing that Mary had been violent toward Mark, I emphasized the importance of safety limits to confidentiality, especially regarding "danger to self or others," and briefly discussed Mark's safety plan with him (he had money, a car, a cell phone, and friends and neighbors close by), while Mary listened and became somewhat agitated. (At one point she commented, "I hope this isn't going to be just about my anger.") I also described my policy of not holding secrets from either party in couples therapy should information arise during conversations or meetings with one of them. Notwithstanding, I encouraged both of them to feel free to call me on my cell phone, reminded them of 911, and gave them the Marin County Psychiatric Crisis Center phone number as well as the 24-hour volunteer-staffed hotline number in San Rafael.

Also knowing that Mary was enrolled in a batterers' treatment program operated by someone with whom I attended meetings at the Marin County Probation Department every other month, I took time to explore whether Mary thought it might be helpful for me to acknowledge her status as a client of mine in any contact with the program provider and to perhaps consult with him regarding Mary's progress in their program. Mary declined. Mark agreed with her decision, saying, "We're here to work on our relationship, not Mary." I thus had no contact with her program provider regarding her participation in batterers' treatment groups.

In our first session I discussed with Mary and Mark the problem that can arise in couples therapy when a therapist, being neutral and seeking to help all parties make changes that contribute to reaching their collective goals, inadvertently endangers one or both parties by inattention to the dynamics of a violent or abusive relationship. We agreed that, in this regard, I should remain mindful of ways in which I might be inadvertently blaming the recipient of abuse or violence rather than the perpetrator, however these roles were acted out by Mary and Mark, and that either of them could bring up this topic at any time, either in sessions or by calling me.

I proposed a hierarchy for us to adopt in our work, beginning with "safety first" for Mark *and* Mary (as well as neighbors, police, and others affected by the anger and violence in their relationship). This meant that anyone—Mary, Mark, or I—could call 911 or anyone else we thought would be helpful in ensuring everyone's safety. This was followed closely by establishing "personal-truth telling" as the standard for statements made in therapy as well as at home—that is, using "I" statements whenever possible and relative language rather than absolutes, particularly when describing the other (as in "it felt cruel to me" rather than "it was cruel" or "sometimes you . . ." rather than "you always . . .").

Because Mary already took some responsibility for her violence and had enrolled in a weekly batterers' treatment program, was being supervised by Marin County Probation (which I knew would include, from previous work with BBF clients on probation, phone calls and personal meetings with the victim and other family members and neighbors, random house calls, and regular meetings with the probationer), and showed remorse and some empathy for her husband, I was willing to work with Mary and Mark. Their positive, forward-looking statements indicated that an ongoing conversation leading to positive change could be established, although only time would tell.

I should note that my interest in Mary and Mark's stated intentions was not whether they were believable or not (they were) but whether they could be used as benchmarks against which their future behaviors could be compared. I have found this to be a highly motivating practice for many clients who want to improve themselves and their relationships but find themselves feeling constrained by personal histories, cultural patterning, and the (usually negatively told) story of their family at the beginning of therapy.

We ended the first session by agreeing on a goal for treatment: help Mary and Mark communicate with each other about their differences in nonviolent and more respectful ways. In practical terms, this would look like Mark being more assertive and Mary using less abusive and less violent ways of expressing her anger. I asked if anyone thought that Mark needed help with expressing anger nonviolently or Mary with speaking out more loudly—none of us did.

Privately, I also held an additional goal for Mary and Mark—I hoped that both could learn to take better care of themselves on their own, given that Mary had already shown an unhealthy dependence on Mark for meeting her needs and that Mark felt that this was appropriate in some ways.

From the standpoint of attachment theory, Mary could be viewed as having a disorganized attachment style with extreme ambivalent features. She became highly agitated or angry, even violent, on occasions of unstructured or spontaneous separation from Mark—in fact, her arrest followed an argument about whether Mark ought to go to the store for milk even though Mary wanted him to stay with her. She had trouble caring for herself while alone for long periods of time. Yet, instead of welcoming Mark when he *was* available to be with her, Mary often attacked him verbally regarding their times apart. "Why did you take so long to come home?" was a common question, according to Mark, that Mary asked him when he arrived home at night. Mark could be viewed as having an avoidant attachment style in that he was happier apart from Mary in some ways than he could be when he was with her. Of course, Mark's tendencies to isolate from Mary were in some respects a response to her excessive need for his company, which in turn was exacerbated by his isolating behaviors (such as going to sleep early).

I sent them home each with a copy of a handout I have adapted and successfully used with couples as well as with anger-management and domestic violence group clients, included here as Table 6.1 (Scotberg, 2002). This set of standards for healthy relationships was intended to

Table 6.1

THE GOALS OF A GOOD RELATIONSHIP		
WHAT HELPS: SELF-SOOTHE. SELF-EXAMINE. SELF-DISCLOSE. SELF-SOOTHE.		
Behavior That Supports a Good Relationship	The Responsibilities of a Good Relationship	Behavior That Interferes With a Good Relationship
Share your thoughts and hear your partner's.	**Show goodwill** toward your partner and yourself.	PHYSICAL OR EMOTIONAL VIOLENCE
Express your enthusiasm and delight in your partner's.	**Encourage** your partner and yourself.	THREATENING WORDS OR ACTIONS
Reveal yourself and reflect your partner.	**Establish healthy boundaries** for yourself and respect those of your partner.	ABUSIVE ANGER
Value yourself and esteem your partner.	**Appreciate** and acknowledge positive and nourishing behavior from your partner as well as from you.	ORDERING OR CONTROLLING
Enjoy your creations and treasure your partner's.		ACCUSING OR BLAMING
Pursue your growth and nurture your partner's.	**Hear** your partner's views, especially if you have a different one, and **express** your views appropriately.	JUDGING OR CRITICIZING UNFAIRLY
Cherish your solitude and honor your partner's.		NAME-CALLING
		DENYING
		COUNTERING

(Continued)

Table 6.1 *(Continued)*

WHAT HELPS: SELF-SOOTHE. SELF-EXAMINE. SELF-DISCLOSE. SELF-SOOTHE.		
Behavior That Supports a Good Relationship	The Responsibilities of a Good Relationship	Behavior That Interferes With a Good Relationship
Follow your interests and encourage your partner's. **Act** at your own pace and accept your partner's. **Indulge** yourself and give to your partner. **Involve** yourself and assist your partner. **Protect** yourself and comfort your partner. **See** yourself and behold your partner. **Be** yourself and let your partner be. **Love** yourself and love your partner.	**Acknowledge** your partner's feelings and experiences as real, and **share** yours appropriately. Treat yourself and your partner with **respect**. **Speak** of your own and your partner's family, friends, and interests **courteously**. **Give clear, informative answers** to your partner's questions that legitimately concern your affairs. **Admit to** and work to change any of your behavior that interferes with a good relationship (list at right). **Sincerely apologize** for statements your partner finds offensive, even if you did not intend that result. **Ask for helpful feedback** from your partner and provide it when requested of you, and seriously consider your partner's feedback when it is given. **Seek assistance** from people you trust if problems in your relationship become unmanageable.	DISCOUNTING OR TRIVIALIZING BLOCKING OR DIVERTING UNDERMINING VERBAL ABUSE DISGUISED AS JOKING WITHHOLDING IGNORING FORGETTING

From a handout for couples created by Kass Scotberg, MFT.

further several treatment goals: the opening formula offers a clear alternative to the codependency apparent in Mary's need for Mark to be there for her and to comply with even unreasonable requests as well as Mark's fears of upsetting Mary versus taking more responsibility for getting what he needed from Mary, especially nonviolent and respectful behavior toward him. The list of "behavior that interferes with a good relationship" on the handout provided a way to further assess the level of violence or abuse in the relationship, as well as naming it for the couple, in particular for Mark. And the "responsibilities of a good relationship" made clear at the beginning of our work together that I, as a therapist, was promoting relationships with balance and respect for all participants—this would give Mark and Mary more information on which to base their decision to return to work with me, as well as give them an opening to raise a different set of standards in response if they wished.

Second Session

Mary and Mark returned 6 days later. (Because of all of our respective work schedules, our appointments all began between 7:00 and 7:45 p.m. This became a factor as we began to focus on sleep concerns in later sessions.) Mary began by asking if confidentiality in our sessions would be threatened if she spoke of behavior that violated the terms of her probation. Although I said that I could not break confidentiality for past behavior, I asked her to consider whether she would rather be honest here in our sessions and with her husband, her probation officer, and others in her life or be someone who lied or hid parts of her life from us. She admitted to a preference for honesty, and Mark agreed honesty was what he preferred as well. But I also made it safe for Mary to withhold information in treatment if she felt it was not in her own best interest, by asking both her and Mark if that was important for either of them; they said it was. In the process, Mark acknowledged, "Sometimes I might be too willing to give in when Mary gets upset." Mary enthusiastically agreed and said she wanted Mark to be more honest with her.

This conversation was part of my ongoing efforts to help Mary and Mark establish clear goals and standards, even ones they might not be ready to actualize. In cases such as this, rather than focus exclusively on the batterer's violence or other problems in the marriage, I think it can be very helpful to engage clients in positive, forward-looking conversations, using questions such as, "Five years from now, when your life is working again, what about yourself now will you look back on as having contributed to your healing?" I continued in the same vein by revisiting the previous week's handout and asking them if they had questions or comments or perhaps disagreed with anything on the table or found something important to be missing.

It was also important to continue practicing with the couple the naming of abusive or violent behavior. So we discussed which behaviors were common among them from the list of "behavior that interferes." Mary acknowledged engaging in most of the top half—including physical and emotional violence, threatening words and actions, and abusive anger—whereas they both agreed that Mark tended to block and withhold.

I finished this second session by giving them a handout on "structured time-outs" that we use in the BBF program (see Exhibit 6.1) and saying that it was an important tool to learn if they wanted to realize some of the relationship goals we had been discussing. We reviewed the main points, and Mary and Mark agreed that, in the coming week, they would each practice using time-outs as a way to soothe themselves and not to control the other.

Exhibit 6.1

TAKING STRUCTURED TIME-OUTS

Purpose

<u>The purpose of a structured time-out is to stop violence.</u> Time-outs build trust and improve your communication, safety, and responsibility in your relationship. They also de-escalate anger, stress, and hostility. Time-outs can be used in any relationship in which anger or violence is a concern, at work or at home. They are helpful any time we feel annoyed or irritated.

How to Take a Time-Out

In order for time-outs to be effective, both partners must agree to the following guidelines. Specifically:

1 Never use a time-out to punish or avoid your partner.
2 Agree ahead of time with your partner that it's okay for anyone to take a time-out and how long a time-out usually is. One hour is recommended—allow enough time to lower the effects of anger in your body.

(Continued)

Exhibit 6.1   *(Continued)*

3   Announce your time-out; don't just leave. Include an "I" statement that describes your feelings. Example: "I am beginning to feel angry/frustrated/etc. I need to take a time-out."

4   Leave the room (or the house if there is no place to be alone inside) for the agreed-upon length of time or until you are ready to listen and to talk without anger or violence, whichever is longer. If you're going to be out longer than the agreed-upon time, you must make sure your partner knows when you will return. If you don't know, check in periodically.

5   Upon returning from a time-out, check in with your partner to learn if he or she is ready to listen and to talk. Respect your partner if he or she doesn't want to talk yet. Spend time apart until both feel safe and are ready to resume contact.

6   When all partners are ready, talk about what made you angry first before taking up other concerns.

Do

1   **Do** engage in physical activity while on your time-out, such as walking, running, riding a bicycle, or hiking, or **do** something relaxing, such as breathing or meditation.

2   **Do** come back when you said you would.

3   When you resume speaking with your partner, **do** talk about what made you angry in a calm, nonjudgmental, and non-blaming way. If you can't, take another time-out.

Do Not

1   **Do not** get into an argument about taking the time-out. Announce it appropriately and leave. Remember, you and your partner already agreed that this is okay.

2   **Do not** drink alcohol or use drugs on your time-out. Avoid bars or places where others are using drugs or alcohol.

3   **Do not** drive unless necessary, and if you do, **do not** drive far.

4   **Do not** obsess about or play over in your mind the current situation with your partner while you're away. It's supposed to be a time-out mentally as well as physically.

5   **Do not** plan arguments to prove your point or new things to say when you return.

6   **Do not** go to a person's house if this will affect your partner in any way, such as someone your partner is jealous of or does not respect.

Remember . . .

Time-outs are hard to do initially but get easier with time and practice. In the beginning, it can be helpful for you and your partner to both practice taking time-outs even when things are good. You build trust whenever you are able to walk away and not stay with the impulse to finish the fight or have the last word. Sometimes, your partner may express fear that you won't return from the time-out. When you do, this also builds trust. Trust, safety, communication, and responsibility will grow in your relationship if you use time-outs properly.

Third Session

Our third session was a full one (we went over by 15 minutes) in which we continued to introduce many of the primary concepts I think are essential to reducing anger and ending violence in relationships. First, Mark and Mary each spoke with a lot of energy about their experimenting with time-outs. Mary found it particularly distressing when Mark took a time-out for more than 15 minutes; she had worries he might not return, wondered how upset or hurt he was, and berated herself for "being bad" again. Mary also found it somewhat distressing to take a time-out herself because she became focused on being alone and did not feel calmed or relaxed; she did acknowledge, though, that she too was only staying away for 15 minutes or so. I reemphasized the biological factors, including dropping adrenaline levels in our bloodstream and returning blood flow to the cerebrum, that suggested longer durations for one's (successful) time-outs. To reduce their anxiety, I suggested they try doing time-outs literally as a practice—that is, time-outs taken during a time of harmony between them rather than stress or upset. And, not wanting to struggle with Mary's defenses (evidenced in the limited tolerance she had for separation from Mark at times of disagreement), I suggested they do the time-outs for only 5 minutes; this, I explained, would be permissible in a practice time-out because they would be doing them when they were feeling calm and okay about their situation at the moment.

Next, I initiated a discussion with an accompanying handout (see Figure 6.1) about the differences between passive, passive-aggressive, aggressive, and assertive communication styles and asked Mark and Mary to identify their own predominant styles, or combination thereof. Mary spoke out immediately. "Oh, I'm the aggressive one, no doubt." Mark said quietly, "I guess I'm more passive, but I don't want to admit that, somehow . . ." Mary leaned over and said, "Awww," and she and Mark kissed quickly.

Mark had reported and exhibited with me fear of Mary's reactions to his feelings, especially anger or disappointment; Mary could become "hurt" (her word) if Mark thought badly of her, and he acknowledged his tendency to "let things go," meaning he would overlook Mary's minor transgressions because he did not want to face her disappointment. Could it be that some of Mary's aggressiveness was related to efforts on her part to get more information from Mark about his feelings? This was still controlling behavior, of course, and no excuse, but it could indicate that, while working to reduce codependency by helping Mark to be

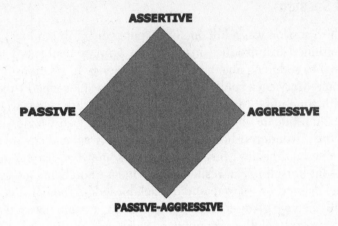

Figure 6.1 Communication styles.

more assertive, we might also help support empathic behavior between Mary and Mark that could become the new norm for them and help eliminate Mary's violent behavior.

We finished by setting up their next "homework assignment," as they had begun to call it despite my repeated assurances that these were suggestions. (The label may have signified something reassuring for them, or they may have been making clearer that they still felt apart from me.) I had in mind for Mary and Mark an exercise I first learned as a participant in the Insight "Awakening Heart" seminar I attended over 20 years ago (see www.insightseminars.org). In this exercise, each person takes turns telling the other something he or she dislikes or wants to change about the other; the recipient responds with a spoken, formulaic answer: "Thank you for caring enough to share that." Then they take turns sharing something positive about the other; the structured response is "I know." This exercise potentially gives the participants practice in unapologetically accepting praise (which can deflect or undermine it) and in more calmly accepting criticism. I was curious if Mary and Mark would be willing or able to practice it at home.

I then presented a short description of the "cycle of violence," which I described as a pattern occurring in many relationships wherein a "honeymoon" period of bliss is followed by a period of increasing stress, with disagreements and confrontations escalating in seriousness, ending with an abusive or violent explosion of anger and consequent separation, cooling down, and resumption of the honeymoon phase. How can one intervene, given this pattern? We usually do not want to "rock the boat" during the honeymoon cruise, nor do the initial or even medium-level upsets of the tension-building phase seem to warrant any comment— they are "minor," after all. And the explosion, once it occurs, is usually unstoppable, and few people can listen or think during these confrontations. The answer, I suggested, was to intervene all along the way. The honeymoon phase presented an ideal time to raise difficult concerns; it is a time when we are most connected, probably calmest and most secure, and most likely to be able to listen and respond appropriately. During the tension-building phase, we should indeed mention, albeit respectfully and productively, many of the "minor" upsets of the day, the better and sooner to resolve them before they get out of hand. Finally, there is a way to intervene in the explosion—take a structured time-out as soon as we realize we are involved, either as perpetrator or as victim or both, in an abusive or violent interaction.

Both Mary and Mark expressed interest in trying all of this at home. We agreed to meet in 2 weeks because of scheduling issues.

Fourth Session

Mary and Mark began by speaking at length about the progress they had seen at home between them. They had wholeheartedly taken to the practice timeouts and found that, by doing that every evening, they had reduced their conflicts and increased their sense of connection. (They held hands on the couch and sat closely together during most of the session.) They also felt that this had contributed to an improvement in their ability to discuss problems, their initial treatment goal. I cautioned, as I often do when clients report early successes in therapy, "Progress can sometimes look like 'two steps forward, one or two steps back.'" (I learned a while ago that, besides helping to avoid unrealistic expectations in clients, this statement invites a restatement by the client of the progress. It is always better for the client to be dragging us along the path to health than the other way around.)

They also said they had practiced the "praise and criticism" exercise and that they had seen how they could use this as well to improve their ability to communicate about disagreements. I wondered silently if a physicalization of their patterns of struggle or control could be helpful, perhaps to me as an assessment tool but preferably for them as an externalization and demonstration as well. So I suggested that we try an exercise together right there in the room instead of sending them home to try it. As always, I described the exercise first and emphasized that they could take it or leave it after hearing what was involved. I also emphasized that I thought it might be helpful for at least one of us.

This exercise was introduced to me as part of the comprehensive training in Hakomi therapy I completed in 1998. (See www.hakomiinstitute.com for more information.) A power and control exercise, it works like this: two people each take the part of "leader" and "follower" during three separate but related experiments. In all three experiments, the leader and follower begin by standing a little more than arm's length apart, facing each other. The leader extends his or her arm toward the follower and holds his or her hand palm up, 6 inches or so from the follower's face. The leader can but is not required to move his or her hand anywhere in the room, as long as he or she complies with two firm rules: the hand can be moved only at a pace slow enough to allow the follower time to move with the hand, and the leader must safeguard the follower at all times (i.e., not lead him or her into any dangerous situations). The follower must try to keep his or her face at the same 6-inch distance from the leader's hand throughout the experiment until told that time is up (about a minute).

In the second experiment, the parties switch roles so that the follower is now the leader and vice versa. In the third experiment, both parties hold their hands out in front of the other's face; both parties are the leader and the follower together. They must learn how to move, if they choose, while they compete or cooperate, depending on whether they struggle with their apparently conflicting roles or whether they discover ways to minimize conflict. I have seen this exercise used successfully (and have participated myself several times, as a therapist/student and in my own marriage counseling). It usually brings out either sadistic or otherwise controlling behaviors, sometimes from both participants, for all to see. It can also be a fun exercise during which people often giggle or laugh.

We took some time to outline and agree on the rules and then took about five minutes to run through each portion of the exercise. To me it appeared that they barely moved at all, standing almost motionless regardless of who was leader or follower. Each spoke afterward about not wanting to challenge or upset the other. There was very little energy, and neither demonstrated much in the way of controlling or sadistic behavior. The results were different from what I had expected, and Mary and Mark later said they felt they did not get much from it.

Fifth Session

After the previous week's experiment, I thought it might be more helpful for me to shift to a more receptive and listening stance instead of the more directive and active stance I had employed to date. As I often do, I engaged them at first in a review of the last session for a few minutes (in which they reiterated their "ho-hum" experience in the exercise we had tried). But for much of the session, I listened to them speak about their experiences since our last meeting (again, 2 weeks earlier).

Both Mary and Mark talked together and separately about several incidents in which Mary got upset but handled it by taking a "real" time-out (albeit for only 20 minutes). She found she could sit in her car outside their home with the radio playing soothing music and calm herself down. They both also spoke at length about ways in which Mark was "speaking up a little more" about feeling hurt or attacked by Mary's words and anger.

They also spoke again of an ongoing problem that they had mentioned early on—Mary did not want Mark to go to sleep in the bedroom while she was still awake in the living room, even though the rooms are only about 10 feet apart and even when the bedroom door is left open. Mary spoke at length about how angry she got that Mark would not give her this "little bit" of support when she "needed it." Mark said it really was not a problem for him to sleep on the couch while Mary worked at the dining room table, their current compromise on the issue. When Mary was ready to go to bed, she would wake Mark (gently, both reported), and they would go to bed for the night. This practice had meant that Mark often felt he was not getting enough quality sleep because he was awakened after a few hours and because he worried all evening as this arrangement's time approached whether Mary would get upset again. We ended the session agreeing that this recurring situation would be our focus the following week.

Toward the end of the session, Mary said they would be away for several weeks in August; the next appointment we could arrange was a month later. I noted that this meant a longer time between sessions than previously taken and wondered whether it might mean that they were concerned about our sessions in some way. Mark admitted that money had become a problem for them and that he felt the sessions were helpful but became "a little stressed" about paying for them, given his uncertainties about his job and their finances. I saw immediately a way in which I could be punishing the victim if I pressed for more sessions. Considering their overall progress and this particular scheduling issue, it seemed best to make the appointment when we could and not make too big of an issue about it at the moment.

Sixth Session

We reviewed their previous month of travel (to see her parents in Wyoming) and then shifted to a more detailed discussion of the sleeping issue. I engaged them in a conversation about the exact ways in which this problem manifested, including questions such as the following: What time and in what room? Who speaks first, and what is said? How do you feel, Mark, and you, Mary, when that happens? Then I asked them whether this happened every night and if not, why not? Not so surprisingly, there were occasions when (a) Mary went to bed at the time Mark wanted to, (b) Mark did not want or need to go to bed any earlier than Mary, or (c) Mary did not mind if Mark slept in the bedroom (usually because she would read in bed beside him). We then spent a fair amount of time wondering about what might contribute to these exceptions to the rule and how they might be able to encourage more of them. I imagined that, by pointing out exceptions to their problem-focused story of their evenings together, I might enable them to develop some hopefulness about solving their problem. And at first, this seemed to have occurred. Both Mark and Mary spoke in the session about how "it's not all bad" and "we don't always argue about this." But another scheduling issue because of the approaching Labor Day holiday (and their finances) led to scheduling our next appointment 4 weeks away.

Seventh Session

Mary and Mark arrived visibly uncomfortable about being there and soon revealed their reason: they had had a "relapse," in other words, a big fight, just the week before, when Mark had tried to take a practice time-out (a now-regular practice in their home) by sitting at the computer to play video games. The difference for Mary seemed to be that when he sat outside or took a walk, she knew he was working on their relationship, but she felt the opposite when he sat at the computer. She argued that, because he had other options, he should not use one that upset her. We spent the next 30 minutes discussing options for how Mary could soothe herself when she got upset at Mark, as well as acknowledging that Mark seemed to be more willing to risk upsetting Mary if he felt he was taking care of himself. ("Thanks a lot!" Mary complained.)

I was concerned that our month-long break had contributed to their problems rather than relieving them. But then they gave me reason to adopt a more positive attitude about their prognosis. Mary surprised me by saying that their sleep problem had improved. Mark had slept in the bedroom, with the door open, while she watched television in the living room. Also, Mark was able to sleep with "much less anxiety" about how Mary was feeling. For her part, Mary said she thought about how she could calm down in a time-out and tried to "feel the same way." We agreed to meet in 3 weeks.

Eighth Session

This session began with an extended description by Mary and Mark of the several ways they had been working on the sleep problem and seeing some progress in their goal of communicating about their differences more respectfully. But then Mary again surprised me by saying that she had noticed how upset she got if, when she was taking a time-out, Mark was sitting at the computer. Somehow, she felt this was "abandoning her" and that he should be "sharing my experience if he loved me."

This led to a discussion of independence, interdependence, and codependence. I likened the latter to a model of relationship in which each of two people is leaning on the other, making in effect an A-frame; neither party can move away without the other falling, and lifting the fallen one up from flat on the ground could be difficult. Independence is when neither person leans on the other but stands on his or her own two feet; in this scenario, either can move as far from or as close to the other without causing anyone to fall. Interdependence is when two independent people choose to associate for mutual support while standing and moving on their own. Moreover, as a self-supporting person, one can better stop the other's fall, catch him or her partway to the ground, and help him or her stand again; this is much easier than lifting the other person completely up. We ended there.

Ninth Session

Meeting again 3 weeks later, Mary spoke in this session about her batterers' treatment groups for the first time since we began working. She felt some resentment toward the group leader, and we spent some time discussing among us how Mary could (a) soothe herself and (b) communicate (see Table 6.1).

For the first time we discussed explicitly the self-assessment skills needed to take a time-out before getting too upset. But Mark changed our focus by speaking about their respective families and their effects on his relationship with Mary. He felt that his own family members, though they lived close by in the Bay Area, were not nurturing of Mary and that she was mostly alone here in California, where he had wanted them to move the year before. Mary started crying, saying that she did feel lonely but that she wanted her marriage with Mark to be the relationship that replaced all others. This admission was followed by much hand-holding and quick kissing between them as Mark seemed to comfort her. Mark led the discussion to his family again, speaking about their religious beliefs and how they grated on Mary. We ended inconclusively.

Tenth Session

This session occurred a month later, after Thanksgiving had come and gone, and much of the session was taken up by a discussion of Mark and Mary's experiences visiting Mark's parents for the holiday. Mary felt that Mark's parents were cold toward her, but Mark differed, seeing them as "still getting to know" Mary. In the process, it was mentioned that Mark's household had been calm and quiet in his memory of growing up, whereas Mary's family was large (four siblings), loud and boisterous (a farming family), and somewhat overwhelming for her. I noted the differences and wondered aloud if either one saw how their families could have contributed to their expectations and standards about marriage. Mark said he thought that he had problems dealing with Mary's anger because it was so foreign to him. Mary said she felt that Mark was too easily disappointed in her because of that.

Before we could explore family-of-origin issues further, though, they spoke about recent challenges that Mark felt had arisen regarding Mary's anger; he wanted to be able to go to the computer without Mary getting upset, and she still felt that this was disrespectful. I noticed, though, that the tenor of their story had changed. Although Mary still got upset, she self-soothed in almost all the incidents they discussed by taking a time-out or using some other technique that we had discussed or that she had learned in her group meetings. They discussed as well several ways in which they felt they had worked on their sleep problem. I ended the session feeling that they were making progress.

Eleventh Session

This proved to be our last session, although it began like many others. We had last met a month before; during the intervening weeks, Christmas, Hanukkah, and New Year's Day had passed, as well as, perhaps more significantly, Mary and Mark's first wedding anniversary (December 31). They spoke for several minutes about the fact that, much more often than before, Mark slept in the bedroom when he felt tired, and Mary either joined him or stayed up doing whatever she was doing (watching television, reading, and so on). They had also reached a provisional compromise regarding Mark's use of the computer, a ritual in which Mark notified Mary several hours ahead of time when he planned to be using the computer, and Mary could thereby "get ready" through self-talk and other self-soothing tools we had discussed.

I then introduced to them a meditation exercise for us to do together in this session or the next in which one "scans" one's body by directing attention to each part of the body, beginning with the soles of the feet and ending at the top of the head after observing briefly everything in between. I offered it as a self-soothing as well as a self-study tool, but Mark cut me short in my description by saying, somewhat haltingly, that he and Mary wanted to "take a break from couples counseling for a while."

I was completely surprised. I asked if this meant we would not meet again ever or if they wanted to suspend meeting for a fixed period of time and then resume. Mary and Mark held hands throughout this part of our session and kept looking at each other, as if for reassurance.

Mark said, "Money is part of it . . . but . . . I think we should . . . we should be able to work on this on our own."

I asked if he could explain further what his concern was.

"I'm worried . . . that we're not going to know how to do this . . . on our own if we . . . don't take a break."

"So you're worried, if I understand you correctly," I said, "that you won't learn how to practice the things you've learned or treat each other respectfully if you don't have the 'crutch' of therapy, is that it?"

Mary nodded vigorously and agreed. Mark interrupted her, though, to say, "I want to know that we have learned something we will know in ourselves without you reminding us."

We had only a few minutes left in our session. I suggested we meet for one last session in which we could use the full amount of time to review and in several other ways maximize their benefit from the work they had done. Mark replied, "We'll think about it and call you." I then spent a minute or two, suspecting this might be my last chance, to remind them of the number of sessions and calendar time they had spent working with me and what I remembered they had worked on. I asked if they felt they had benefited—they immediately agreed, and for a moment, it felt again that we were in the middle of our work rather than at the end. Mary spoke for several minutes (we ran over again) about how her weekly groups and our now-monthly couples therapy had made a significant improvement in her feelings of hopefulness for their relationship. Mark spoke about the growth he had seen in Mary's ability to calm herself when angry, and Mary responded by speaking of Mark's increased assertiveness at home. We ended with mention of a possible phone call the following week to discuss a final session, but the message I left for them was not returned.

OUTCOMES AND CONCLUSION

Given that, during our work in couples therapy, Mary attended a weekly batterers' treatment program, it is hard to know, perhaps more than with other couples I have treated, how much our sessions contributed to Mark and Mary's progress. The abbreviated termination process we engaged in did not provide as much time for acknowledging their successes and pointing toward future issues as I would have liked; I prefer at least two sessions for summing up and cleaning up any loose ends, if necessary.

Despite this and other problems that arose in the course of treatment, I see several ways in which Mary and Mark grew more respectful and responsible with each other during the time I knew them. Mary no longer exploded into anger after badgering Mark about some concern or other of hers. Instead, she was now more likely to take a time-out or retreat from angry communications into more cooperative and empathetic conversation. Mark was more likely to assert his needs even if Mary might get angry, and he had shown himself more able to stand his ground in disagreements in the face of Mary's distress, as when he went to sleep sooner in the evening without worrying as much about Mary's reaction.

But we had only begun to scratch the surface of their respective family-of-origin issues, nor had I had much success in trying to direct our discussions toward a consideration of individual therapy for Mary and Mark. Mary exhibited attachment disturbances in her clinging and dependent behaviors, and Mark's story of "no anger in my family growing up" left me wondering whether that could be entirely accurate, given the passive-aggressiveness shown when Mark played computer games to avoid resolving issues with Mary.

Perhaps the changing schedule of our sessions made it difficult to realize more results. We met initially once a week for three sessions. Significant progress was reported by the 3rd session. We then changed to a biweekly schedule for a month. After more progress was shown by the 5th session (at the end of July), we met thereafter once a month until terminating therapy after the 11th session. It seemed at each juncture that the increasing gaps in our schedule were preceded by signs that Mark and Mary were benefiting.

It may also be that our shift to a more talk-oriented approach was not as helpful as I imagined it would be. Although they reported progress even in the last session, Mary was still prone to strong feelings of abandonment, and Mark was, by his own admission, still learning how to assert himself with her. It may be that more skills instruction and additional psychoeducation would have engaged the couple in their treatment for a longer period of time.

In conclusion, it seems that Mary and Mark benefited somewhat from the combination of couples therapy and batterers' treatment groups. One can imagine that the contributions commonly found in the latter—requiring accountability and promoting responsibility and empathy—were impacting Mary positively and perhaps Mark as well. Their apparent ability to use didactic interventions to improve their relationship suggests that further work in that modality could have provided additional benefit.

REFERENCES

Holistic health. (2007). In *Wikipedia: The free encyclopedia.* Retrieved October 7, 2007, from http://en.wikipedia.org/wiki/Holistic_health

Jenkins, A. (1990). *Invitations to responsibility: The therapeutic engagement of men who are violent & abusive.* Adelaide: Dulwich Press.

Kurtz, R. (1990). *Body-centered psychotherapy: The Hakomi method.* Mendocino: Life-Rhythm.

Miller, W. R., & Rollnick, S. (2002). *Motivational interviewing* (2nd ed.). New York: Guilford Press.

Scotberg, Susan "Kass." (2002). *The goals of a good relationship.* Unpublished manuscript.

Sonkin, D. (2005). Attachment theory and psychotherapy. *The Therapist* (January/February).

Sonkin, D., & Dutton, D. (2003). Treating assaultive men from an attachment perspective. In D. Dutton & D. Sonkin (Eds.), *Intimate violence: Contemporary treatment innovations.* New York: Haworth.

White, M., & Epston, D. (1990). *Narrative means to therapeutic ends.* New York: Norton.

QUESTIONS FOR REFLECTION AND DISCUSSION

1   Although Mary is clearly the perpetrator in her relationship with Mark, and Mark has no prior history of intimate partner violence, the author established as a primary treatment goal the safety of *both* parties. Why do you think the author did this?

2   Discuss the "cycle of violence" as a teaching tool. How does the author use it as a means of helping this couple reduce their relationship conflict?

3   The author does not address family-of-origin issues until the 10th session and does so only after the clients bring this up following a visit with Mark's family. Compare this case with some of the others in the book, in which family-of-origin issues are brought up almost from the beginning of treatment. What may be some of this author's reasons for choosing his particular strategy?

4   Over the past few years, an emerging body of research has appeared examining the role of adult attachment styles in the dynamics of intimate partner abuse. Are certain combinations of attachment styles more likely to result in physical assaults? What about those of Mary and Mark?

7

Vivian "Rae" Bailey: Reciprocal Family Violence With a Female Batterer

LAURA DREUTH ZEMAN

The client whose case study is presented in this chapter, Vivian Rae Bailey, is a composite of a case that I saw at my independent social work practice during the 1990s outside of Nashville. Clients at the practice were typically referred by the courts, local doctors, their friends or family, and the several domestic violence programs. Most clients' fees were paid by public insurance, Medicaid or Medicare, though some clients paid through employer-supported insurance or out of pocket. The majority of my practice involved work with individuals and families with histories of family sexual assault. Many experienced co-occurring conditions of mental illness and substance abuse.

I was trained as a therapist during a 2-year post-master's position in a private central Tennessee psychiatric hospital. As a practitioner of individual therapy, I consider my role to be helping people examine their inner world so that they might better understand their attachments and perceptions and grow emotionally. As a family therapist, I draw heavily on the work of Virginia Satir in helping troubled families use crises to create a new status quo so that the well-being of all family members may be enhanced. I embrace the strengths concept of resilience and draw on feminist interpretations of power, particularly in confronting imbalances among individuals, independent of gender, and within families where sexual assault has contributed to pervasively distorted boundaries, identities, and interactions. The case of Vivian Rae Bailey reflects these theoretical influences and illustrates the client's ability to affect therapeutic process and outcome by identifying treatment problems and personalizing solutions.

CASE STUDY: RAE AND HARLEY

Vivian Rae Bailey, Rae to her friends, was referred for counseling by her partner after she "started acting crazy" and "went off" on him during a fight in which she hit, kicked, and threw things at him. At age 19, Rae was a tall, thin, beautiful woman. Her long curly brown hair bounced around her ivory face and down her back. She appeared polished in faded jeans, a white baby doll top, a belt with a large silver buckle, and a pair of white shoes sporting a pink corporate logo. She was joined by 34-year-old Harley Kipp, a man that Rae referred to as her "common-law husband." Harley was a musician who was often on the road traveling with his band. His short red hair showed his receding hairline. He was dressed in a black button-up shirt pulled over his blue jeans, which hugged his dusty Western boots at the ankle.

Rae and Harley presented as a middle-income couple typical of the country music–influenced culture that was prevalent in the communities surrounding Nashville, Tennessee, in the 1990s. The couple agreed that they had communication problems and relationship tensions heightened by Harley's absences and his hectic touring schedule. Both believed these troubles could be reduced if Rae learned to control her anger. Rae admitted that her anger seemed to have been getting worse in the 2 years since she gave birth to their son, Dale Kipp. She reported specific problems maintaining friendships and finishing tasks and said that she was often upset. To demonstrate their concerns, Harley described several conflicts between Rae and his mother in which he characterized Rae's behavior as cruel and threatening. Harley's mother was Enid Kipp, the matriarch who operated the family restaurant on their rural Tennessee compound. Rae, a waitress at the restaurant, reported that she refused to share her tip money with the staff, and Enid accused her of stealing. Harley reported that Enid did not pay Rae; instead, Enid let Rae live in a cottage on the family compound in exchange for working in the restaurant.

Assessment

The initial phase of treatment consisted of history taking, assessment, and treatment planning, which spanned the course of three sessions.

The psychosocial report combined direct verbal questioning in a face-to-face interview, problem checklists, and observation. The couple did not have a prior social service or legal history to review for this evaluation. This model of assessment describes the aspects of each client's environmental functioning as prescribed for social workers (Sheafor & Horejsi, 2006). The face-to-face interview gathered information on current strengths and stressors; family-of-origin patterns, culture, and beliefs; current social and occupational functioning; and a legal, medical, and psychiatric history.

Rae and Harley also completed personal substance-use inventories and personal abusive-behavior checklists prior to the interview. The substance-use information was gathered using a generic inventory that contained two pages of alcohol, prescription drugs, and common street drugs that the clients identified as substances they had used historically and in the last 6 months. This self-report questionnaire enabled the clients to provide a detailed account of their substance use as part of the assessment process. The couple also completed an abusive-behavior checklist, derived from the batterer assessment model developed by Dutton (1992), a two-page self-report inventory that asked about personal incidents of abuse categorized as physical (including extent of injuries), sexual, coercive, psychological, economic, intimidating, isolating, minimizing, and involving the use of children.

Insisting that Rae was the problem, Harley completed the assessment focusing primarily on her, though he did agree to provide some background information. Harley had no formal education. He was homeschooled and claimed that he had played music all his life and that his earliest childhood memories included playing with his father, uncles, and brother, either traveling or at the restaurant. He reported daily use of marijuana, alcohol, and prescription drugs for anxiety. While on the road, which was most of the year, he reported using cocaine. Harley dismissed the substance use as typical for musicians who "lived on buses." Harley claimed that he had "too many" sexual partners and that most of his sexual behavior involved concert attendees or girls who traveled with the band. While at home he reported being "mostly faithful" to Rae, who had been his domestic partner for 3 years. Harley admitted to wrestling and physically restraining Rae and to using threats, insults, and humiliation to control her. Harley attributed his actions to his need to manage Rae's out-of-hand behavior. He reported that he had met Rae when she was 15 and that he had initiated a sexual relationship with her when she was 16. He also admitted to occasionally filming them during sex against Rae's wishes and to enjoying anal sex more than she did to the extent that he admitted coercion, though he dismissed the idea that this was abusive and considered their relationship to be normal.

Rae reported drinking alcohol occasionally, mostly beer, Kahlúa, and Irish cream, and to smoking marijuana almost daily since her early teens. Rae said that her mother had begun giving her "speed" to keep her from gaining weight when she was 8 years old and that she had also used diet pills to lose weight after the baby. She reported occasionally using cocaine with Harley. Rae described her abusive behaviors as reasonable responses to coercion or manipulation. She admitted to her outbursts but shifted responsibility for her actions to either Harley or Enid. She claimed that Enid encouraged Dale to be disobedient and that Enid also threatened to take custody of the child. Rae also claimed that Enid isolated her and made it difficult for her to contact her mother and sister.

Family History

Rae was the eldest of her mother's two daughters. Rae's mother told her that she married after she found out she was pregnant, and she maintained that her first husband was not Rae's real father. Rae described her father as an alcoholic and musician whom she did not really know. When Rae was 6, her parents divorced, and her mother married her stepfather, who adopted her younger sister. Her stepfather owned a successful construction company, and her mother managed the office. She described her mother as a cruel and abusive alcoholic who took prescription drugs to calm her nerves. Rae said her mother frequently lost control and used humiliation, threats, hitting, pushing, and throwing things. Rae reported that she was frequently emotionally and physically wounded during her mother's rages and that she lived in fear. Her sister was 4 years younger, and Rae reports spending most of her childhood babysitting.

Rae admitted to having multiple boyfriends in her early teens and said that her conflicts with her mother increased when she was 15 and started staying out all night. Rae said that when she was 16, her mother arranged with Enid Kipp, a business contact, for Rae to live and work on the compound. Her mother also encouraged her to respond to Harley's sexual advances with the expectation that if Rae provided sex, Harley would support her financially. Rae followed through and became pregnant with their son, Dale, within a year of moving to the compound.

Rae and Harley described their relationship as a hierarchical one in which Harley was the authority, a role that was assumed by Enid when

Harley was traveling, and in which Rae was expected to submit to both figures. Within this relationship, Rae was defined in terms of her compliance, and her value was defined in terms of her contribution to the compound. She was also regarded as a bad mother and often referred to by Harley as "young and foolish." He dismissed her goal of attending school, moving to town, and living independently as "childish fantasy." Harley was defined as responsible and mature. Though she was frustrated by his lack of financial support, Rae did not expect Harley to be monogamous or to participate in parenting.

The multi-method assessment produced insight into this family system's long-standing patterns of reciprocal violence, sexual abuse, and addiction. The assessment identified Rae's three primary batterers, Harley, Enid, and Rae's mother, who perpetrated a range of emotional, physical, and sexual abuse. Harley exerted his control over Rae through minimizing, humiliating, and blaming Rae and treating her as if she were inferior to him. He also committed acts that not only were abusive but that also could be considered rape or coercion. The mothers, Enid and Rae's mother, engaged in ongoing bullying and cruelty, and they acted together to initiate and maintain the sexual relationship between the minor Rae and Harley. Rae, on the other hand, vacillated between victim and batterer. As a victim of her mother's rage in childhood and then of Enid's domineering cruelty and the sexual abuse by Harley in her teens, she learned placating acts that provided her safety and that served to suffocate her identity and diminish her self-worth. As she emerged into adulthood, she targeted Harley and Enid as victims. She engaged in rage attacks that included verbal and physical assaults. At the time of intake, there was no evidence to suggest that any of the adults battered Dale, but it was necessary to evaluate his risk and to build a safety plan for him.

INITIAL TREATMENT GOALS AND TREATMENT PLAN

The primary treatment goal for this family was to identify and alter abusive behavioral patterns. The treatment process to which the couple agreed relied on dialogue and role play to reconstruct Rae's family of origin, to help Rae identify the feelings, patterns of behavior, and expectations that she associated with her mother. Virginia Satir developed the reconstruction process in family therapy to help people recreate their family stories in order to form understandings that facilitate growth (Satir, Banmen, Gerber, & Gomori, 1990). The reconstruction process was intended to help Rae identify similarities and differences with her mother that may underlie her actions and safety risks. They also agreed to use family reconstruction to examine their courtship and early relationship, to understand each other's experiences, and to understand the impact of those experiences on their current expectations, feelings, and behaviors.

A second treatment goal was to reduce the use of alcohol and other substances and to understand its role in family dynamics. The couple agreed that Rae would participate in interpersonal psychotherapy while Harley was on the road to address her family-of-origin issues with addiction and that he would join in the family therapy sessions when he was in town to examine the impact of substance use on their relationship. Interpersonal therapy examines the client's use of defenses and perceptions of self and others that impact choices and disputes (Walsh, 2006). The use of psychotherapy with persons who abuse substances has been effective in reducing substance use when combined with 12-step programs (Woody, 2003). The couple agreed that Rae would attend Al-Anon meetings regularly. Al-Anon is a 12-step support group for families that serves a twofold benefit: It provides support to family members and engages them in treatment. Studies have found that Al-Anon benefits include empowering family members to reevaluate their dysfunctional system in order to make positive changes (Friedemann, 1996). Harley agreed that he would work with Rae to identify ways he could reduce his use of substances while at home and that he would participate in discussions to identify whether substance use impacted their relationship.

The final treatment goal was for Rae to establish autonomy. Harley agreed to deposit a small monthly allowance in an account for Rae to use to support Dale and to request that his mother pay Rae for her work in the restaurant. The couple agreed that Rae may benefit from putting a lock on the door of the cottage to establish boundaries from Harley's family and in the future that Rae may consider moving into town. Rae also identified a local college that she wanted to attend, and Harley agreed that she could pursue financial aid for school if it did not interfere with her work in the restaurant and raising Dale.

The treatment plan included an agreement on a safety plan for each of the family members. Harley required Rae to abstain from physically striking him or throwing objects during anger outbursts. Rae also agreed to seek help prior to engaging in physical assault. Rae required Harley to refrain from physically restraining her and to engage only in sexual acts to which she consented. If either partner threatened the safety of the other, the plan required the victim to separate immediately and call the police. Both agreed to make a police report in the event the other became aggressive. Rae also required Harley to intervene on Rae's behalf to end disputes between Rae and Enid. Both agreed that Dale required protection. Specifically, they agreed that if either party was concerned about Dale's safety, he or she could remove him from the situation or ask someone to care for him until safety was restored.

As a result of this treatment plan, relationships were established with social service agencies prior to the treatment phase. Rae was referred to and visited the domestic violence center for a service intake. She agreed to contact their hotline if she required emergency shelter for her and Dale, but she declined group support. Rae and Harley were given a list of local Al-Anon meeting times, and they agreed to attend while Harley was in town. Rae and Harley visited the school to investigate financial aid and scheduling options that were appropriate for Rae to balance her obligations to Dale and the compound.

THE MIDDLE PHASE OF TREATMENT

The middle phase of treatment involved two courses of therapy that spanned two years as Vivian Rae Bailey emerged from her life with Harley and passed through a brief marriage that produced a second child. The first phase of treatment included Harley and Rae. The second phase of treatment followed a crisis pregnancy that returned Rae to counseling to complete her treatment plan and included Rae and Dale as the family system. What follows is an account of these two phases of treatment as Rae progressed toward completing her treatment goals to reduce abusive patterns and patterns of harm related to substance abuse, to create safe relationships for herself and her child, and to establish an autonomous identity. This account is a composite of therapeutic themes that demonstrate the technique and that highlight transitions in Rae's perceptions and expectations during the course of treatment.

During her first treatment phase, Rae's growth focused on her relationship with alcohol and drugs and the other people in her life who used them. She used her exposure to the 12-step program Al-Anon to test out areas of her relationships that she wanted to change and to bring those insights into family therapy for examination. Her primary experience of Al-Anon was empowerment through mutual aid rather than growth through working a personal program fashioned after the 12 steps.

In fact, it was never clear that Rae understood the concept of moving through the steps to achieve growth, as is consistent with the literature on these programs (Friedemann, 1996). Her choice not to buy in to the 12 steps was a barrier to forging relationships with sponsors, persons with advanced Al-Anon growth who could guide her recovery.

Rather, Rae used the groups to identify personally with the participants' stories, which she used as therapeutic metaphors, stories that paralleled her situation and offered insight. For example, her conflicts with Enid would provoke a discussion in which group members shared their experiences with mothers who controlled them. These stories helped Rae understand alternative interpretations of events and to see the impact of similar events on other people's circumstances. Satir (1990) believed that metaphors serve two functions in family therapy: They create possibilities of what may happen if the family changes, and they serve to switch the context, often to someone who is safe or less threatening. Rae's pattern included going to a meeting, sharing the portion of her story that she considered examining, listening to related life stories, piecing these stories together into possibilities for change, and bringing the insight to therapy. During therapy, she shared the insights, validated portions, identified options for change, and made choices about her personal possibilities. Between therapy sessions she practiced these options, returned with insight into the outcome of these choices, and made intentional selections toward the next step. She returned to Al-Anon when she sought feedback or was seeking alternative possibilities. Rae benefited from sharing portions of her story that she wanted to change within the mutual-aid setting. She perceived the members' stories as safe because their context was different from hers, and she was therefore less emotionally connected.

Issues that Rae examined within the context of family therapy supported by Al-Anon included her perceptions of her economic and social dependence on Harley. She also examined Enid's dominance and her own obedience. In both cases, Rae's placating masked her feelings of anger and fear directed toward Harley and his mother. Although it appeared functional on a superficial level, Rae's placating served only to postpone her expression until she engaged in abusive outbursts. During the first phase of therapy, Rae exposed her conflicts between her desire to stand up to Harley and her fear that she would be kicked off the compound if she rebelled against Enid. Discussion of these fears and conflicts contributed to her understanding that she trapped herself in her situation.

Rae considered examination of her inner world as a means of understanding her family-of-origin issues and their impact on her abusive choices to be less important than establishing independence and exploring the role of alcohol on her relationships. On one occasion, Rae disclosed an aspect of herself that was molded by Harley and her desires to please him that showed her use of placating to the extent that she subordinated her identity as a means of pleasing. She came to a session sporting a new haircut. Her once long, bouncy brown waves were replaced with a blond spiked cut that stood on top of her head and boxed her face and hugged her neck. This drastic change of hair was accompanied by Rae's need for reassurance that she looked good. When I asked why she cut and dyed her hair if she was uncertain it looked good, she explained that she cut it because another woman who was a favorite girlfriend of Harley had cut her hair. In fact, it was at this point that Rae disclosed that she had a notebook of pictures of the other woman, and she used them as a guide for her choices to style her dress and hair.

Through this disclosure, Rae gained a greater understanding of how placating affected her lack of self-worth and how this related to her rage. However, she was resistant to further examining her inner world for two reasons. First, the progress she had made on substance use and independence had resulted in major life changes that she hoped would get her away from the people to whom she had problems relating. Rae believed that it was in her best interest to follow through on her efforts to become independent and then determine if her abusive behavior persisted. Second, she preferred to understand her abusive actions as reactions, and thus, through blaming, she was able to redirect focus from her inner world to others. As a result, her understanding of her role in the abuse was limited to superficial verbalization that she harmed others and a rudimentary agreement to follow behavioral plans to move away from conflict by leaving the compound or by finding someone to babysit Dale so that she could go for a drive and "cool down."

For his part, Harley expressed frustration as the first phase of therapy progressed to the point where Rae enrolled in school, he paid child support, and Rae earned salary and tips for her work at the restaurant. His resentment included feelings that he was targeted and blamed for Rae's behavior. Further, he expressed disappointment over his perceptions that the therapy did not support their hierarchy and that he would have to change if their relationship was to continue. Therefore, he agreed that it was best for Rae and for their relationship with Dale to end their domestic partnership. It appeared that Harley believed he would be relieved of responsibility for his role in Rae's life events if he removed himself from the relationship. Ending the domestic partnership also allowed him to freely engage in substance use and sexual activity without the accountability to Rae that had emerged as she progressed in therapy. He agreed to maintain his child support and agreed that his mother needed to allow Rae to find a balance between work, parenting, and going to school. Harley stayed on the road and away from Rae as he removed himself from the therapy and the relationship.

It appeared that as Harley stepped out of the relationship, his role in the domestic partnership was assumed by Enid. Conflicts with Enid and Rae escalated, and Enid made ongoing threats that she would take custody of Dale in the event that Rae tried to leave. During these conflicts, Rae engaged in verbal abuse and in throwing things or breaking Enid's property. Rae continued to blame her actions on others but did get child care for Dale as part of the safety plan. She also maintained that her choice to destroy property represented harm reduction in that her actions were less directed toward others and more directed at property and that overall her number of abusive incidents were reduced.

Rae ended the first phase of treatment approximately 1 year after it began. She moved into her own apartment and began to balance school and caring for Dale. She worked in a local restaurant and was paid in salary and tips. She began to make friends at school and occasionally went to Al-Anon meetings as a means of testing new approaches to establish her independence. Dale had infrequent contact with Harley, who was touring and using substances heavily when he was in town, per Rae's report. Both parents agreed to a legal custody, support, and visitation agreement in which Enid did not have visitation when Harley was on the road. Rae decided to end treatment yet leave the door open to return in the event that her problems with abuse persisted.

NEW TREATMENT PHASE

A little over a year later, a woman with wavy shoulder-length red hair who was dressed in jeans and a sweatshirt appeared at the therapy office with her well-groomed and quiet, yet active, 4-year-old son, requesting an appointment that day. She identified herself as Vivian Scott, a long-term client, and said that she was 8 months pregnant and wanted to come in that day because she was concerned that she would be homebound after her next doctor's appointment.

This was Rae, now Vivian Scott, the wife of a contractor whom she had dated briefly and married during her first trimester. Vivian, as she preferred to be called, returned to therapy over concerns that she might hurt someone and that her pregnancy may be compromised because of her anger. According to Vivian, the night before her return to therapy, she had gone to a local steakhouse with Dale and her husband, Buddy Scott, where Buddy had expressed his desire to end the marriage. As Vivian recalled, Buddy informed her that he was no longer interested in having sex with her, that he planned on hiring strippers for sex, and that the only thing he wanted from her was the baby. After dinner their dispute escalated in the parking lot. Their yelling led to Vivian repeatedly striking her husband in the chest and shoulder, pushing him against his truck, slapping him across the head, and trying to pull out his hair. Buddy tried to restrain his wife at the arms or shoulder. Instead of grabbing Vivian, who was moving as she lunged into him, Buddy grazed her face with his fingers, causing her to back away. At that moment, Dale said, "Buddy, why did you hit my mom?"

Vivian explored the events of that evening and pieced together feelings of rejection and betrayal. She examined her expectation of monogamy in the marriage and her expectations that pregnancy would provoke Buddy to financially provide for her. She examined the blame that she placed on Harley for failing to support her and her resistance to assuming personal financial responsibility. She followed these conclusions to understand that she expected to be economically supported if she became pregnant. She understood that she may have been acting out her mother's irrational expectations and that she may also be responding to events with rage and blame, similar to her mother. As Vivian sat in therapeutic reflection, she became aware that her behavior was impacting Dale. Specifically powerful for Vivian was how Dale had blamed Buddy for hitting his mother but had chosen not to acknowledge her assault of his stepfather.

Vivian's new safety plan was coordinated with the domestic violence shelter. This plan included emergency shelter for Vivian and Dale, if Buddy tried to return to their apartment. The shelter's case manager also agreed to coordinate care with the crisis pregnancy center where Vivian would receive maternity and baby supplies, transportation to her doctor's appointments, and childbirth support. Vivian also negotiated with Enid and Harley to provide care for Dale from her labor and delivery through her first days at home with the baby. Vivian declined treatment that incorporated substance-use goals because she believed that she was no longer affected by drinking or drugs. She reported being drug- and alcohol-free during her pregnancy and said that Buddy's use of drugs was limited to smoking marijuana while golfing with friends and drinking beers after work. She committed to completing her therapy plan by addressing her abusive behavior, which included an examination of her own childhood abuse and its impact on her self-worth and its relationship to her abusive actions. Vivian requested that therapy include Dale to improve her parenting and to address the impact that witnessing her domestic partner battering had on him.

Vivian visited a support group meeting at the domestic violence center in the weeks that followed her return to therapy. She shared her perceptions of the other women as dependent and as victims. She explained that she did not belong in a meeting with them because she did not identify with their circumstances. At this phase of therapy, Vivian had come to understand herself as a domestic partner batterer, and as such she was no longer able to identify with the concerns of victims. This perception represented a shift in self-identification for Vivian from the first phase of therapy, when she understood herself as a victim responding to others' behaviors. This shift helped her recommit to therapy with the goal of reducing her abusive behavior through reflective self-examination and reconstruction of her family-of-origin dynamics to alter her current family interactions.

Vivian and Dale's family sessions began with a review of her ongoing parenting concerns and then shifted into examining their parallel to her family of origin. These concerns were typically associated with Dale's lack of response to Vivian's most frequent form of redirection. Vivian expected Dale to remain quiet and calm, and when he did not, she expected him to correct his behavior either independently or following one redirection. She preferred him to put his toys away and to keep himself occupied with his toys or to play while watching television. Vivian used the interactions with Dale as a way of reconsidering her own childhood as she saw parallels between her expectations and those of her mother. She also saw an inconsistency between her acceptance of Dale's behavior as normal and the blame she internalized for her mother's unprovoked rages. By examining her relationship with Dale, she was able to deconstruct her mother's abuse and began to recognize that her mother's actions were unprovoked and unwarranted. This process allowed Vivian to release the blame she assumed for her mother and helped her understand that she could have reasonable expectations of Dale and did not have to recycle those of her family of origin. In family sessions with

Dale, she discussed behavioral options with him and began to allow him to participate in forming their relationship.

The birth of the baby, Buddy Scott Jr., or JR as Vivian preferred to call him, temporarily reunited Vivian and Harley. Dale wanted to stay with Harley, which she allowed. Vivian tried to develop a routine that balanced self-care with infant care. Part of Vivian's self-care was to move to her own apartment and go back to work and school. Harley helped Vivian find an apartment and paid several months' rent in advance. Conflicts arose when Harley decided he wanted to keep Dale with him because of concerns that Vivian was unstable and that she posed a safety risk. Vivian agreed in principle but objected to Dale staying with Enid when Harley began traveling again. Harley addressed these concerns by taking Dale on tour. Although Harley viewed his actions as supportive of Vivian and consistent with Dale's safety plan, Vivian was outraged. She felt betrayed by Harley. She responded by making numerous phone calls to Enid and making threats. She escalated her behavior to include following Enid. Enid responded by filing a harassment complaint with the local police.

This was the first formal police contact for Vivian Rae Bailey. Able to maintain a private profile prior to this incident, Vivian was now publicly exposed as a domestic batterer. Along with that identification was the threat of child protection oversight of JR, who Enid claimed was in the car several times when Vivian stalked her. Vivian was devastated. She was cut off from Enid. She had left her husband and was alone with JR. She did not have Dale, nor could she get him returned without hiring an attorney, which was out of the question because the only person to whom she could turn for money was Harley. Harley refused to help her unless she demonstrated that she was emotionally stable. At 21, after two failed relationships, two children, and 2 years of therapy, Vivian Rae Bailey was trapped in a confrontation with her abusive self.

With no way out of her circumstances but to change, Vivian committed to aggressive individual therapy twice weekly. She attended Alcoholics Anonymous meetings several times a week because she felt a fellowship with the group members who were examining their use of blame and the impact of their behavior on others. Vivian used role-playing to recreate her conflicts with her mother, Harley, and Dale. Through role-playing she gained insight into her motivation and drew on that insight to create change. Applying Virginia Satir's model of molding into the shape of oneself or others during significant conflicts or events, Vivian sculpted her mother stances and examined their parallels to her own mother. These poses allowed her to gain insight into unspoken or ignored experiences that shaped her reactions and self-worth. She created and practiced perceptions of her relationship with JR and Dale that reflected her new insights.

The birth of JR had thus provoked the chain of events that led to the rebirth of Vivian Rae Bailey. In one of her later therapy sessions, Vivian expressed frustration that her issues with her mother seemed to appear randomly and influence her thoughts of self-worth and choices. She described her inner world as one in which new images and interpretations of meaning consistent with her new self-worth were consistently presenting themselves, but then, quite unexpectedly, a negative thought or self-talk that she traced to her mother's abuse would pop in her head and distract or depress her. She practiced examining these old thoughts and tried to understand their impact. Fearful that these random thoughts would reappear, she sought to put them aside so that she could focus on her reconstructed family relationships.

Vivian agreed to participate in a visualization exercise to organize these "mother thoughts." She imagined a scene from her favorite movie, *The Wizard of Oz*. The setting involved the beautiful witch floating in a bubble. The witch represented her negative self-manifestation attributed to her mother, and she imagined each of her mother's character flaws as they affected her. She then visualized a physical flaw to correspond to the character flaws. For instance, she added a crooked nose, a wart on the face, or a hunched back. She then integrated each one into her witch visualization, thus transforming the once beautiful witch into a hideously deformed and disfigured being. She then recalled the negative thoughts and self-talk that had been so distressing to her. Vivian focused on each thought, moved them one by one into a bubble, and then moved each bubble off into the landscape. With this visualization, Vivian organized her random abuse memories into a protective bubble.

Vivian completed her intensive inner journey 6 months after returning to therapy. She ended the second phase of her treatment after Dale had returned home, JR had turned 4 months old, and she had returned to work and school. She left therapy with the agreement that she was welcome to come back if she felt it was necessary.

OUTCOMES AND CONCLUSION

At 19, Rae was a tall, thin, beautiful woman involved in a domestic partnership with Harley that involved reciprocal battery. Both partners believed these troubles could be reduced if Rae learned to control her anger. Harley attributed his actions to his need to manage Rae's out-of-hand behavior. Rae described her abusive behaviors as reasonable responses to coercion or manipulation. The assessment identified Rae's three primary batterers, Harley, Enid, and Rae's mother, who perpetrated a range of emotional, physical, and sexual abuse. Rae, on the other hand, vacillated between victim and batterer. Rae's placating masked her feelings of anger and fear directed toward Harley and his mother. The placating was often followed by explosive abusive acts targeted at these two individuals.

The treatment involved two courses of therapy that spanned 2 years as Vivian Rae Bailey emerged from her life with Harley and passed through a brief marriage that produced a second child. Vivian Rae Bailey used therapy to supplement her growth from substance use, childhood abuse, and domestic battery into life as an independent mother of two and college student. In the process she learned to define herself and to identify patterns that were disruptive in order to create her own life. The first phase of treatment included Harley and Rae and examined the impact of substances on their relationship and supported her independence. Rae believed that her family-of-origin issues and her abusive behaviors were secondary to her need for independence and understanding the role of alcohol in her relationships.

The treatment progressed as the family selected opportunities for change that appeared to produce the most immediate results with the least amount of inner turmoil. Rae's choice to become independent and use Al-Anon as a sounding board represented a least-resistance approach to change. Although these approaches ultimately resulted in major upheaval of the family system, they also allowed each member to engage in the least amount of reflection. For instance, though he let Rae leave and supported her independence, Harley was able to continue to use substances and sex without examining their impact on his relationships. Rae, by leaving, was able to continue to blame Harley and Enid for her abusive patterns.

Rae continued to avoid reflection on her own contributions to the domestic violence until she was confronted with the impact of the abuse on her son in a later relationship. The assault she perpetrated on her husband, coupled with the police report following Enid and Harley's decision to take Dale, created circumstances that forced Rae to confront her inner-world experiences of abuse and battery. It was only after she made the commitment to tunnel into her inner world in order to alter her patterns that Rae made progress toward creating long-lasting change. She progressed beyond the survival tactics of placating and blame as she examined her contributions to the chaotic events in her life. She also identified and released dysfunctional expectations from her family of origin, such as the belief that providing sex or children leads to financial security. In the end, she identified as a parent and sought ways of interacting with her children that supported her relationship with her sons and sought to end her cycle of abuse.

This case illustrates the complexities of treating reciprocal family violence. It demonstrated the application of a multi-method psychosocial assessment process that included checklists for substance use and family violence combined with an in-depth interview. The assessment produced insight into a complex victim and batterer profile for each of the adults in the primary family system. It also revealed the predominant coping and blame strategies that enabled family members to remain engaged in both the relationship and the abuse. Though many problems emerged that could have been addressed with therapeutic interventions, the treatment goals that resonated with these clients were those that matched their expectations and desires at the time.

REFERENCES

Dutton, M. (1992). *Empowering and healing the battered woman: A model for assessment and intervention.* New York: Springer Publishing.

Friedemann, M. (1996). Effects of Al-Anon attendance on family perception of inner-city indigents. *American Journal of Drug and Alcohol Abuse, 22*(1), 123–134.

Satir, V., Banmen, J., Gerber, J., & Gomori, M. (1990). *The Satir model: Family therapy and beyond.* Palo Alto, CA: Science and Behavioral Books.

Sheafor, B., & Horejsi, C. (2006). *Techniques and guidelines for social work practice.* Boston: Allyn and Bacon.

Walsh, J. (2006). *Theories for direct social work practice.* Belmont, CA: Brooks/Cole.

Woody, G. (2003). Research findings on psychotherapy of addictive disorders. *The American Journal on Addictions, 12*(Suppl.), 19–26.

QUESTIONS FOR REFLECTION AND DISCUSSION

1   Considering the impact of her mother's abuse, as well as Enid and Harley's controlling behavior (e.g., dismissing her goal of attending school or living independently), would you consider Rae primarily a victim or primarily a perpetrator?

2 Do you agree with the author's decision to refer Rae to a battered women's shelter? How might Rae's treatment and ultimate outcome have been different if she had been referred to an anger management or batterer intervention program instead?

3 The author initially referred Rae to Al-Anon, rather than Alcoholics Anonymous. Do you agree with this choice? Why or why not?

4 The author appears to make the argument that independence is not always best for individuals involved in abusive relationships because it denies them an opportunity to work out their relationship issues and inhibits the process of self-transformation required to take responsibility over one's life. Do you agree? Why or why not?

Work With Families

8

Treating a Family in Crisis: The Christiansons

ELLEN L. BOWEN

I have been a clinical social worker for 34 years, and my understanding of domestic violence has evolved and changed significantly from when I first started in this field. One year before I started my career in social work (1972), Erin Pizzey established the first shelter for battered women in England. The same year that I completed graduate school and earned my MSW, Lenore Walker published her landmark book, *The Battered Woman* (1979). About then, California began requiring licensed therapists to have continuing education in the topic of child abuse. I had never even heard of the term *domestic violence,* let alone understood the complexities of what it meant.

I worked in private nonprofit settings, served on the staff of a local church as a counselor for 5 years, and then opened a private practice in 1985. I worked with children, adolescents, families, couples, and individual adults. Many who saw me came with presenting problems of eating disorders, child abuse, childhood molestation, and addictions. Not surprisingly, I often found myself working with victims of some sort of trauma—often domestic violence.

In the early days of my work, I believed that domestic violence was a phenomenon characterized by a man (always the perpetrator) who used power and control tactics to batter his female partner (always the victim). I assumed, as Walker maintained, that domestic violence follows a fairly predictable three-phase cycle that tends to increase in severity and frequency over time. I believed that men were the problem and that women were the victims and were powerless in their lives over their abusers. I accepted the commonly held belief of the time that if a woman was violent in her intimate partnership, it must be because she was first a victim of domestic violence.

From the experience of working with children and women who had been hurt by domestic violence, I became increasingly interested in understanding the men in their lives. The eventual outcome of this curiosity came in 1997, when two colleagues and I established Non-Violent Alternatives (NOVA), a 52-week program for domestic violence offenders. Our certification was contingent on the program being based on the Duluth model, which was considered at the time to be the best approach for treating batterers. I obtained training at the National Training Project in Duluth, Minnesota.

Not long after we started NOVA, my traditional social work roots (establish a trusting therapeutic alliance with the client, begin where the client is, support and encourage strengths, empower clients to be self-determining in their lives, etc.) bristled at the Duluth contention that men must be reeducated in their use of power, male privilege, and male entitlement in their relationships with women (Pence & Paymar, 1993). I found this approach to be shaming and countertherapeutic. Research studies have found this model to be ineffective in decreasing male violence against women (Babcock, Green, & Robie, 2004).

I found that although sometimes men truly are the dominant aggressors in their relationships, sometimes women are actually the more dominant aggressors, and most often, the relationship dynamic is a complex dance in which both partners are abusive to each other. Men have told me of experiencing serious violence from their wives and girlfriends. In telephone contacts with the female partners, women candidly told me of their own violence and how they had, at times, lied to probation or to the court in order to retaliate when they were angry. I came to recognize that the motivations, reasons, and expressions of domestic violence are myriad and complex and that good treatment must reflect this.

In my search for better information, I came across writings of several researchers (Dutton & Golant, 1995; Holtzworth-Munroe & Stuart, 1994; Jacobson & Gottman, 1998). Based on their findings, they proposed that there are actually different types of people who batter and who also present with different underlying psychological problems, suggesting that treatment should be tailored to the unique qualities of the individual batterer. Not only did this make intuitive sense to me, but it also mirrored my experience in my private practice as well as in my NOVA groups. Domestic violence is not a one-size-fits-all problem.

As I have come to know more about the family-of-origin experiences of my clients, I have recognized that most are truly doing the best they can to cope with life experiences and relationships that are overwhelming and terrifying for them and for which they have been ill-prepared. I believe that the best treatment outcome happens when there is a positive, collaborative therapeutic alliance between client and therapist. This requires the therapist to balance two oft-opposing roles: having empathy and respect for the client yet also holding the client fully accountable for his or her violent behavior. I now consider my treatment approach to be gender-inclusive (Hamel, 2005) and based on attachment theory (Dutton, 2006; Sonkin & Dutton, 2003) and trauma theory (Schore, 1994; Siegel, 1999), incorporating cognitive behavioral therapy techniques.

I continue to maintain a private practice where I see children, adolescents, and adults with a broad range of presenting problems, including domestic violence. Through NOVA, I facilitate separate treatment groups for male and female domestic violence offenders. I also co-teach a continuing education course for relicensing therapists titled "Understanding and Treating Intimate Partner Abuse."

The following case study illustrates the long-term damaging effects on family members and the many challenges of working effectively to end domestic violence. This family represents, to some degree, a composite of cases. All identifying information has been disguised or changed. The fundamental narrative of the family's journey through treatment, however, remains faithful.

CASE STUDY: THE CHRISTIANSONS

As often can be the case, the Christianson family did not initially seek treatment because of domestic violence. Rachel and Joe Christianson had been married for 20 years and were parents to two children: Alicia, age 16, and David, age 14. As fundamentalist Christians, they were very active in their church and prided themselves in supervising their children closely and "raising them right."

Alicia, a 16-year-old White girl, modestly dressed, was brought by her mother to see me at the insistence of her favorite teacher. Alicia had confided one day to her teacher that she had been anorexic for 2 years and also that she had been raped by several neighborhood boys when she was about age 4. Her teacher was horrified and pressed Alicia's parents to take seriously their daughter's revelations.

Assessment Interview

In her initial individual interview, Alicia sat upright and poised on the sofa, moved slowly, and spoke in a soft voice with an ethereal smile on her face, no matter what she was saying—an unsettling experience to witness. She answered my direct questions, corroborating her mother's information but exhibiting little emotional self-awareness. She was convinced that her anorexia was simply a result of the sexual molestations she had experienced years before, she was already feeling much better, and she did not really think she needed therapy after all, but was willing to attend because her teacher wanted her to.

She then told me she often thought of stabbing herself to death with a knife but added that she did not want to talk about that. I told her I was very worried about her because if things were going so well for her, it did not make sense to me that she would often think of wanting to kill herself. She shrugged. She agreed to have her mother, Rachel, join the session and to tell her mother what she had told me.

Rachel was neatly and conservatively dressed and wore no makeup. As Alicia told her mother details about her frightening history with anorexia and her suicidal thoughts, Rachel seemed bewildered. She perched on the edge of the sofa next to her daughter, but without touching or looking at her, and told me that she herself had been molested by her brother when she was growing up. She seemed to be so distracted by her thoughts about her own history that she was unable to respond meaningfully to her daughter's distress.

Alicia's gaze wandered around my office as her mother then told me about the many stressors their family was experiencing. Rachel had recently been fired from her job as a bookkeeper for a small store following an argument with the owner about Rachel's interaction with a vendor. Both Rachel's mother and her brother were mentally ill. The brother was homeless and often showed up at their doorstep at all hours of the night. Her father, an alcoholic, was slowly dying of heart disease, and her mother would call her several times a day to ask whether she should call 911. Rachel was overwhelmed by these problems. I was especially troubled by her inability to be present for her daughter.

Based on this initial assessment interview, I recommended that Alicia see her primary care physician for a complete physical exam and a child psychiatrist for a medication evaluation, that Alicia see me individually for further assessment, and that Rachel and Joe next meet together with me. I was alarmed at Rachel's difficulty in being emotionally available to her daughter and hoped that Joe, the father, might be more accessible to Alicia.

When given specific concrete direction, Rachel pulled herself together and became more focused, ready to take action. She committed to making appointments with the pediatrician and psychiatrist that day and insisted to Alicia that she must continue in therapy. Both she and Alicia signed releases for me to speak to the pediatrician and psychiatrist.

Rachel balked at meeting together with Joe. She complained that he had his own serious problems that she should not have to deal with, namely that he "drinks too much and looks at pornography," thinking she did not know. She firmly stated that she would meet separately with me and that I could contact Joe myself for his own appointment. She added that she handles most of the important issues regarding the children and that she did not think he would want to be involved. Clearly, their marriage was not as solid as they portrayed it to be to the outside world.

Individual Session: Rachel

In her individual session, Rachel told me that 2 months before, Joe had been enraged at their 14-year-old son, David, because he was on the verge of being expelled from school for fighting. Having been diagnosed with ADHD, David was taking medication and seeing a counselor but still had trouble getting along with his teachers and with some of his peers. That night, Joe blew up at David, screaming at him for being in trouble again at school. Rachel was afraid Joe might hit him, so she touched Joe's shoulder to pull him away. Joe then turned, grabbed her, and pushed her out of his way, leaving bruises on her arms. The incident ended hours later with each family member isolated in separate rooms. The next morning, they did not talk about it and continued as if it had not happened.

Rachel did not like Joe screaming at David, but she also understood his frustration. She said that both kids pushed the parents to the limits and only settled down when one of the parents exploded. She said that Alicia was often mouthy and disobedient and that she had slapped Alicia on occasion, for instance, for flirting with construction workers. She felt somewhat guilty for hitting Alicia but thought it was justified. Joe had slapped David for swearing at his mother and calling her a whore.

Joe had been violent in the past with Rachel. When they had just returned from their honeymoon 20 years before, Joe and Rachel had argued intensely. Rachel locked herself in the bathroom; Joe unlocked the door with a nail and threw her over his knee, spanking her 30–40 times until she was black and blue. Rachel's parents were present but did not intervene in any way. Soon after, Joe apologized and did not directly assault Rachel again, instead venting his anger and frustration by punching holes in walls and throwing things.

Individual Session: Joe

Soon after meeting with Alicia and Rachel, Joe came in for his first session. He had just come from his job as a letter carrier and was wearing his uniform. Joe's initial presentation was affable. He joked about seeing a "shrink" and then admitted he felt nervous because he was not sure what I might say to him. He readily told me that he was frightened about Alicia's anorexia, the molestations, and her suicidal thoughts. And then he began to open up more.

Joe had experienced a chaotic childhood. His parents drank heavily and engaged in terrifying physical fights before their divorce when he was 5. A year later, his mother, without warning, left him at the babysitter's house, never to return. He bounced from foster family to foster family, eventually reuniting with his father during adolescence and reconnecting with his mother in his 20s.

He felt like a failure as a father and husband—the roles that were most important to him as a Christian man. He said that Rachel typically handled everything involving the children—their activities, homework, and problems—and that often he felt left out of their lives, not finding out about important issues until it was too late for him to do anything. That is when he would blow up. He then told how he had been enraged at David a couple of weeks before and had grabbed and pushed Rachel for interfering when he was trying to discipline David, who since then had been running away from home for a day or two at a time.

Joe believed that it was his responsibility as spiritual head of the household to create a stable and loving home and enforce rules with the children and with his wife. He recognized that what he had been trying so far had not been successful. His family was a mess, and he was overwhelmed. In fact, he often experienced debilitating migraine head-aches and had contemplated suicide.

Joe said that his marriage had been an unhappy mistake from the start and that he only stayed because of the promise he had made to God. He loved his children and tried to love Rachel but often felt that no matter what he tried, nothing was enough to make her happy. During arguments, she told him he was a pathetic loser and a disappointment to God, and she threatened to leave him.

To say that this family was in crisis does not do justice to the depth of overwhelming pain, panic, and despair that each family member was experiencing. Both Joe and Rachel had fearful attachment styles, a result of childhoods marked by extreme trauma, abuse, and abandonment. As adults, they consequently expected that their deepest emotional needs would never be met, and each vacillated between fearing intimacy and fearing abandonment. They were each abusive to the other and also to each of the children. Both children were exhibiting dangerous acting-out behaviors, and the parents were at a loss to know how to begin to respond. For Joe and Rachel, Christianity provided not only spiritual comfort but also some sense of internal psychological organization. Still, neither had any organized strategy for responding effectively to the immediate family crises, let alone for managing their individual underlying attachment anxieties.

TREATMENT GOALS AND TREATMENT PLAN

The development of effective treatment goals and a corresponding treatment plan must always be done in collaboration with the clients. Without their active participation in this process, clients are less likely to be motivated to do the work necessary for constructive, genuine change.

Treatment Goals

Both parents expressed the greatest motivation to help Alicia recover from her eating disorder and her suicidal thoughts. For herself, Rachel wanted to focus on helping her children, but she also believed that the real underlying problems in the family were a result of Joe's temper, his drinking, and his use of pornography. She thought that if he were a more godly man, they would have a happier marriage, she would be happier, and the children would be better behaved. She did not feel unsafe living with Joe and pointed out that for most of their marriage, she had been able to recognize when the tension was building and had been able to respond without getting physically hurt. Joe described himself as "insecure, wound-up a lot of the time, and short-tempered, especially at home." He admitted that he had a hard time controlling his anger, even over small incidents, like David using his comb without asking. From the start, Joe was introspective, able to reflect about himself and his inner thoughts and feelings. He admitted being afraid of failing and yet feeling doomed to do so.

Both Joe and Rachel agreed to the following initial treatment goals:

- Stop family violence. This includes physical as well as verbal and emotional abuse.
- Learn communication and problem-solving skills so that the parents can respond more effectively and nonviolently when crises arise. Learn to work through and resolve conflicts.
- Build healthy relationships with each other and with the children, where each family member can feel loved, supported, understood, respected, and safe.
- Help Alicia recover from anorexia and suicidal thoughts. Help improve her self-esteem.
- Help David to be able to get along with teachers and peers, to not be in trouble at school, and to want to stay home (rather than running away). Help improve his self-esteem.

I told Rachel and Joe that these were worthy and appropriate goals that, to be accomplished, would necessitate other steps along the way. From the beginning I took a very strong position that violence was *not* an appropriate solution to their problems and was enormously destructive to the family, their marriage, and the individual members. I also maintained that each family member had the ability to learn new and different ways of behaving and relating. I proposed the following additional necessary goals:

- Each family member will take responsibility for his or her own behavior, without denying, minimizing, or blaming someone else: "No one else *makes* you decide to be violent, abusive, or hurtful to someone else. Two wrongs don't make a right. Even if someone is hurtful to you, it doesn't justify retaliating with hurtfulness."

- Each family member defines his or her own boundaries and will respect others' boundaries.
- Joe and Rachel will learn to parent constructively and nonviolently as a team and to share responsibility for decision making so that each feels respected, supported, included, and not alone.
- Joe and Rachel will increase their coping skills and ability to manage anxiety. This will mean learning to tolerate pain in order to grow, learning to self-soothe one's own hurts and pains, and maintaining a clear sense of self while being nonreactive to a partner's anxiety.
- Each parent will learn to have empathy and compassion for the other and for each of their children.
- Each parent will begin to examine their crisis-bound family life and consider the impact on family members. Each will take responsibility for his or her own role in maintaining the state of crisis.

Treatment Plan

Because of the pressing medical risks of Alicia's eating disorder and suicidal thoughts, the parents' first concern was for her well-being. The identified treatment goals were used as context to define a treatment plan that was specific first to Alicia's urgent health problems and then to the other family crises. Alicia was seen individually and with her mother. I worked collaboratively with her physician and her psychiatrist, who prescribed antidepressant medication.

An immediate concern was that the family access as much support as possible because they were so overwhelmed by serious problems and needed more than what one therapist could provide. As fundamentalist Christians, they were suspicious of programs, treatment, support groups, and so on that were not clearly Bible-based. This had to be considered in recommending ancillary treatment options.

With respect to family violence, Rachel viewed herself primarily as the victim. She felt victimized by Joe, Alicia, and David. She believed that any time she had been abusive to any of them, she had done so because they had first been abusive to her. She was so entrenched in this position and defensive of her behavior that to try to explore this with her in the presence of other family members would have totally alienated her from the therapeutic process. When seen individually, she was somewhat more willing to acknowledge her own pain and fears, to consider exploring her role in the marital and family problems, and to consider how she could change her behavior to make things better. Joe, on the other hand, readily acknowledged that he had problems with his anger, and he wanted help. Although he had been violent over many years, he was the higher-functioning parent and the one more motivated to change.

The initial treatment plan that they requested and agreed to was as follows:

- Individual therapy for Alicia, with mother joining for part of the sessions. Collaboration with physician and psychiatrist, who prescribed antidepressant medication.
- Individual therapy for Rachel plus participation in a faith-based support group for women who were sexually abused in childhood.
- Individual therapy for Joe plus participation in a faith-based men's support group and a 12-week peer-led domestic violence recovery class. He refused to go to AA but agreed to stop drinking and to be forthright about any times he broke that commitment, so that this could be addressed. He also agreed to attend a support group for parents of acting-out teenagers. Rachel refused to go because it was not Bible-based.
- Collaboration with Joe's physician and a psychiatrist regarding his depression, suicidal thoughts, headaches, and alcohol abuse. His psychiatrist prescribed antidepressant medication.
- Conjoint therapy for Rachel and Joe.
- Continued therapy for David with his own therapist at a teen crisis agency and a psychiatrist, with his parents participating in his treatment as requested.

THE COURSE OF TREATMENT

Establishing a therapeutic alliance with this family was no easy feat. By the time the Christiansons came to therapy, they were overwhelmed with many serious crises and on the brink of collapse as a family. Each family member was experiencing enormous fear and pain and acting out in different ways: Joe in physical violence within the family; Rachel in passive-aggressive, verbal, and physical violence within the family; Alicia in violence against her body; and David in physical violence within the family and in the community.

Besides seeing me in various combinations several times during the week, they also followed through with the recommended educational, medical, psychiatric, and support group interventions and therapy with other providers as detailed in the treatment plan. In the early stages, therapy focused on the here and now, the current issues that required attention. Between sessions, I was available for the many emergency phone calls for support and advice. I believe that an essential role of the therapist is to provide clients with a "secure base, a safe harbor"—the very experiences they likely missed during childhood that contributed to their insecure attachment styles.

A major complication in working with this family was their belief that much of the violence in their family was acceptable. They all believed that children should always obey their parents and that parents were justified in hitting, slapping, spanking, or paddling their children as punishment for any misdeed. Arguing against this perspective with Bible verses (although I tried) was futile.

A more successful approach was to have them process each situation in very concrete problem-solving steps: exploring the facts of what the problem was and how each person was involved and affected, what their goals were, the options for responding to the problem, and the likely outcome of each option and how it would affect each person in the short and long term and then choosing the best option. We role-played how they wanted to speak to each child involved and discussed how they thought each family member might feel and think in response to their interactions. This process helped Joe and Rachel to calm down and manage their anxiety, facilitated their working together as an egalitarian team in setting appropriate boundaries with the children and Rachel's brother and mother, gave them a sense of mastery over everyday family dilemmas, and helped them to be more sensitive and observant of each other and the children. It may sound self-evident to others, but Joe and Rachel had never considered that their children had feelings, thoughts, opinions, and experiences separate from their own.

Both Joe and Rachel held to a view that the husband was the head and final authority in the family. This presented problems when Joe was not sure how to handle an issue but felt pressured to solve a problem. He was the "enforcer" but also the "fall guy" when his efforts did not succeed. Rachel often reminded him of his responsibilities.

To the outside world, it appeared that Joe was the adult who had the most power and control in the family. In reality, Rachel did. When she did not agree with Joe, she went behind his back to try to effect a different outcome. Sometimes, she would not tell him about major problems involving the children's welfare because she thought she knew better how to deal with them. When confronted in therapy about this, she appeared surprised and said she thought she was doing what was most helpful to all. In both individual and conjoint therapy sessions, she had great difficulty putting herself in the other person's position and considering how that person felt. This sabotaged Joe's efforts to participate in a positive way in family life and undermined his relationships with the children. He was trying to establish his own more caring, open communication with each child so that they would not be afraid of him. At the same time, he wanted to be supportive of Rachel and convey a united front to the children.

Alicia's medical condition deteriorated as she lost more weight. Her physician and psychiatrist recommended hospitalization. Rachel resisted this recommendation, and rather than telling Joe about it, let alone discussing it with him, she polled other people. She had no close friends, so she approached acquaintances at church, former coworkers, and Alicia's favorite teacher, who had remained very involved with Alicia. Unbeknownst to Joe, one day the teacher and Rachel took Alicia to a 3-hour "spiritual warfare" session with a local pastor. Afterward, Rachel declared that Alicia was "cured" and no longer needed treatment for anorexia.

A sidebar is appropriate here: my position in working with people with histories of domestic violence is that anger is a normal, human emotion. The goal of treatment is, not to eliminate the experience of anger, but rather to learn to recognize the physical, emotional, and cognitive cues of anger and then to learn skills for respectfully expressing what is often a very valid emotion: acknowledge feelings; choose behavior. Sometimes anger is a defense against feeling or showing other more painful and vulnerable emotions. Other times, righteous anger is the most appropriate response and can provide the energy and courage necessary to stand against wrongs in our world.

When Joe found out what Rachel had done, he was furious. He called Alicia's psychiatrist and physician and discovered for himself what they had recommended and why. By this time in therapy, he was able to clearly express himself to Rachel and do so without intimidation, threats, or violence. He told her that this experience left him feeling excluded, unimportant, and alone. In addressing this in conjoint therapy, they were able to eventually agree to send Alicia to a Christian residential eating disorders treatment program that was out of state. She stayed at this facility for 9 months. Joe and Rachel visited for a weeklong intensive family therapy program and were able to begin to understand their daughter. When Alicia was discharged, she moved into a private foster home.

About the same time as Alicia's medical condition was deteriorating, David's behavior problems escalated. He was expelled from school, and so Rachel homeschooled him. He resisted her efforts to teach him, and they ended up in screaming and hitting matches. Rachel would call Joe at work and demand he come home immediately to deal with David's disrespectful behavior. Joe was worried that time away from work could cost him his job and told her he could not do that anymore. Rachel felt abandoned and helpless. One day, she screamed at David and threatened to send him away like Alicia. David took off and was gone by the time Joe got home from work.

By now, Joe had come to terms with his own limitations in controlling the behavior of his children and had developed some empathy and compassion for Rachel. He pointed out to her that David usually runs away to a friend's house, stays a few days to cool off, and ultimately returns. He promised to try to contact David and talk with him to be sure he was safe. Rachel told Joe she had already contacted a wilderness program and wanted to have David kidnapped and taken there. Joe disagreed but eventually conceded. Over the next year, David completed the wilderness program, came home briefly, went in and out of juvenile hall (shoplifting, assault, breaking and entering), ran away a few times from an out-of-state residential treatment program, and then found a family on his own that was willing to take him in. This devastated Joe and Rachel because they saw this as bold evidence of their failure as parents.

Also during this time, I was encouraging Rachel to examine her role in these many family crises. She was reluctant to do this, preferring to focus on how wrongly everyone else had behaved. My efforts to back up, join in with her, acknowledge her distress, and so on did not comfort her.

Rachel went to a weekend women's conference through her church. The speaker urged the attendees to "take a chance and try something new." She gave examples such as learning a new hobby or starting an exercise program, but Rachel decided the message to her was that she should separate from Joe and divorce him. She also told me she was discontinuing therapy with me and going to see someone who would pray with her during each session. She saw a series of five other therapists after me.

Joe was undone. Even though he had continued to tell me privately that he still expected all along to eventually divorce Rachel, he was devastated at her declaration. Losing his daughter, his son, and now his wife resurrected all of his early feelings of rejection and abandonment from childhood. He had suicidal thoughts and considered drinking again but decided it would not ultimately help him or his children. He continued in individual therapy and decided to redouble his efforts to be a better father. He understood the impact of his own chaotic and sad childhood and decided that he did not want his children to suffer as he had. He had never believed Alicia's claims that she had been molested by neighborhood boys when she was 4, but he recognized that this subject offered him an opportunity to build a more empathic relationship with her. He told her that he loved her, had always wanted to protect her, and felt devastated that something so horrible could happen to her. The ensuing conversations over many months helped them to turn a corner in their relationship. Alicia began opening up to her father about herself, confessing her fears and insecurities and asking for advice. This in turn helped Joe to feel needed, loved, and *competent.*

Joe rented an apartment after moving out of the family home. As with Alicia, Joe made great efforts to establish his own direct relationship with David. He visited him frequently at juvenile hall and at each successive place where David stayed. Joe encouraged David to get involved in sports as an outlet for his energy. Every weekend Joe drove him to soccer meets all over the state. This gave them lots of time together for establishing a relationship different from any they had ever had before. Joe agonized about many of the life decisions his son was making, but he was ultimately successful in conveying to David that in spite of everything, he loved him.

Joe continued in individual therapy for another 5 years. In spite of his physical violence, he had always been the higher-functioning parent and the one more motivated to change. He learned to be assertive with Rachel, including after their divorce. He stopped drinking and stopped using pornography. He became the safe, supportive adult in his children's lives. After a few years, he began dating and eventually married a kind and loving woman. Both Alicia and David have positive relationships with their father and stepmother. They have minimal and guarded contact with their mother, who has remained single.

OUTCOMES AND CONCLUSION

Therapy with a family such as the Christiansons can seem like being first on the scene to a train wreck—utter chaos, with everyone screaming out in pain, begging for attention and care. The therapist must triage, deciding which ones get emergency response first, which can hold on a little while longer, and which might be able to assist in caring for the others who are injured. I was very aware of needing to stay calm myself and to maintain my own clear boundaries.

I was also keenly aware of my own countertransference throughout this experience. I recognized that as inadequate as Joe and Rachel were as parents, they truly were trying the best they could. I felt sad for them and sometimes frustrated at their intransigence. I felt sympathy for the kids and secretly knew that if I were in their spots, I would probably also want to get out of this family as fast as I could. I admired their resourcefulness in finding safe places and people and ultimately their ability to survive. Although I wanted to be a safe person for them, I knew that what would be the most helpful in the long run was for them to have a parent, or parents, who provided that "secure base, safe harbor" for them.

Although many helping professionals were involved with this family, I regret a few decisions I made early in treatment. Even though David was already seeing his own counselor, it would have been worthwhile to meet with the whole family together at the beginning. This would have allowed a more efficient assessment of the family dynamics and perhaps engaged the whole family more powerfully and effectively in working together to change.

I do not think I ever succeeded in developing a therapeutic alliance with Rachel. Working with both partners in such a dysfunctional marriage can be tricky. The risk is that one partner can feel like the therapist is siding only with the other and then discount whatever the therapist says, no matter how applicable, insightful, or wise. Rachel was receptive to my every intervention except when I evenly, gently tried to suggest it could be helpful to explore her own role in the family drama. Sadly, none of her subsequent therapists were any more successful.

The irony of this family's journey in treatment is that the person who was initially identified as the most violent in the family was actually the one who made the most changes, grew the most psychologically, and became the healthiest parent. The parent initially identified as the victim was the more disturbed one; by clinging to her identity as a victim, she never realized the real empowerment she could have attained.

REFERENCES

Babcock, J., Green, C. E., & Robie, C. (2004). Does batterers' treatment work? A meta-analytic review of domestic violence treatment outcome research, *Clinical Psychology Review, 23,* 1023–1053.

Dutton, D. (2006). *Rethinking domestic violence.* Vancouver, BC: UBC Press.

Dutton, D., & Golant, S. (1995). *The batterer: A psychological profile.* New York: Basic Books.

Hamel, J. (2005). *Gender inclusive treatment of intimate partner abuse: A comprehensive approach.* New York: Springer Publishing.

Holtzworth-Munroe, A., & Stuart, G. (1994). Typologies of male batterers: Three subtypes and the differences among them. *Psychology Bulletin, 116,* 476–497.

Jacobson, N., & Gottman, J. (1998). *When men batter women.* New York: Simon & Schuster.

Pence, E., & Paymar, M. (1993). *Education groups for men who batter: The Duluth model.* New York: Springer Publishing.

Schore, A. (1994). *Affect regulation and the origin of the self: The neurobiology of emotional development.* Hillsdale, NJ: Erlbaum.

Siegel, D. (1999). *The developing mind: How relationships and the brain interact to shape who we are.* New York: Guilford.

Sonkin, D., & Dutton, D. (2003). Treating assaultive men from an attachment perspective. In D. Sonkin & D. Dutton (Eds.), *Intimate violence: Contemporary treatment innovations* (pp. 105–133). New York: Haworth Press.

Walker, L. (1979). *The battered woman.* New York: Harper & Row.

QUESTIONS FOR REFLECTION AND DISCUSSION

1   Although Rachel does not engage in physical aggression toward her husband, Joe, the author describes both parents as being abusive toward each other and the children. Do you agree, and if so, why? Is Joe automatically the dominant aggressor because of his history of physical violence?

2   What was the most significant problem in this very troubled family—physical violence, emotional abuse and control, or one or more of the mental health issues? To what extent were they interrelated?

3 What does this case tell us about gender roles with respect to women's use of abusive and controlling behaviors?

4 In her conclusions section, the author expresses regret at not having seen the entire family from the beginning, including the son, David. Do you agree? How would seeing the entire family have changed the therapy?

5 Do you agree or disagree with the author's observation that Rachel, "by clinging to her identity as a victim . . . never realized the real empowerment she could have attained"? What does this case tell us about victims and their role in family violence?

Who's Holding the Baby? Infant-Led Systems Work in IPV

9

WENDY BUNSTON

Work within the arena of domestic violence has been dominated by the same political landscape, cultural shifts, and ideologies that influence the rest of society. The theoretical paradigms that dominate the war against family violence are as flawed as the humans that have created them. And human beings are complex, as are the multiple systems in which we operate. We obfuscate the complexity of self and thereby of our relationships if we overidentify with polarities that reduce rather than enlarge our understanding of the dynamics that play out in landscapes dominated by violence. This in turn limits our ability to effectively respond.

In late 1996, staff at the Royal Children's Hospital Mental Health Service in Victoria, Australia, began working in what was then unknown territory for our Child and Adolescent Mental Health Service (CAMHS)—the area of family violence prevention. In collaboration with a community-based health center running groups for women who were identified as victims of family violence and groups for men who were identified as perpetrators, a children's and parents' group-work intervention was developed. The involvement of a CAMHS worker, co-located at their center to improve accessibility to mental health, brought about an unexpected development in the way those involved thought about their work with women and men. This development became what could now best be described as "child-led" and "infant-led" systems group work in the area of addressing family violence (Bunston, 2006b), provided by a small team of CAMHS workers within the Royal Children's Hospital whose sole role was to run specialist mental health group-work programs (Bunston, Pavlidis, & Leyden, 2003).

This chapter primarily discusses a systems group-work approach to working therapeutically to address family violence that is child- and infant-led. This approach is illustrated through the journey of an infant/ mother dyad within our group work program for infants and mothers affected by family violence and the additional family work with the mother/father/infant triad. The mother of this infant was identified as the primary aggressor in the couple relationship, and the infant had been placed in the care of the father through an interim court order. The chapter concludes with a discussion of the outcomes for the family and the implications of this approach to practice.

CHILD-LED SYSTEMS WORK

The feature of this particular intervention, distinguishing it from other children's group work being run at that time within Victoria, was its commitment to a child-led philosophy that challenged the adult-centric mentality that continues to pervade work undertaken within the field of domestic violence where children are involved. This approach, attuned to the systemic nature of familial dynamics, subverts the "adult-down" lens most professionals look through in trying to understand families and instead promotes a "child-up" perspective:

> Remaining true to a child sensitive focus meant remaining true to a process that was child led and not set by the compass of adult expectations. We believed that children felt safe when they felt heard, irrespective of whether their communication with us occurred verbally or non-verbally. They also felt safe when their environment could meaningfully tolerate who they were and what they had to offer, and reflect back an affirming and respectful image of self. The focus of our intervention was to repair, rebuild and/or develop new families relationships through honoring the experience and attachments of the child. (Bunston, 2001, p. 9)

Our group work model consisted of separate adult and children groups, both run by the same therapeutic team. This model aimed to provide a bridge between the two groups, mediating and realigning the often-fractured attachments between the parent and child (Bunston, 2001, 2006b; Bunston, Crean, & Thomson-Salo, 1999). The children's group always preceded the parents' group. The circular and recipro-cal nature of this model used the material emerging from the children's group to build the foundation for work undertaken and reflected on in the parent group, with the work from the parents' group being fed back into the children's group. This systemic approach was further enhanced by an appreciation of "the primary motivational system" of attachments (Bowlby, 1973) and psychodynamic early childhood development theo-ries. Rather than viewing certain theoretical paradigms as holding the "exclusive truth" with regard to the complexity of humans and their in-teractions, our systemic base called for an openness to different systems of thinking that ultimately might better lead to improving family rela-tionships. Inherent in this approach is the importance of discovering the reality of an infant's or child's world as they live it and as they see it.

What children told us was not gender- or relationship-exclusive, but rather gender- and relationship-inclusive. Their experience of fathers only as perpetrators was rare, as was their experience of their mothers as victims. Sometimes they experienced their mother, father, and other family members, such as siblings or grandparents, as perpetrators or vic-tims or rescuers, or maybe all three. Sometimes they told of their own emotional distress and behaviors that violently played out in these com-plex roles and their confusion about how they made sense of themselves as either good or bad, just as they heard people describe their mother or father. This rigidity in thinking made it difficult to see themselves as multidimensional beings, open to choice or change. As noted by Pynoos and Nader (1993),

> The treatment must address the pre-existing relationship with the perpe-trator . . . complicated issues of identification, intense conflicts of loyalty, issues related to loss and often pre-existing vulnerability arising from a chronic impulse ridden environment. (p. 545)

Additionally, whether the father or the mother was the perpetrator, the child seldom experienced the parent as such. Instead the parent was someone these children had complex attachments to. Their stories about their families revealed complex patterning of sequential and reciprocal violence. Recognition of the complex configurations of violence that can ripple through family systems led to an inclusive approach to our work where we accepted referrals that led to "child and mother/father" parent groups and a recognition of same-sex parental violence, as well as sibling violence.

As our experience in this approach grew, so too did the evidence that the majority of children we worked with in these groups had been exposed to violence from birth, if not in utero (Bunston, 2006a). The decision to undertake infant-led family group work (Bunston, 2006a) was hastened by the knowledge that the infant brain experiences its most rapid growth spurt within the first 2 to 3 years of life and that the quality of the care and attachments infants experience has an immediate impact on their neurological development (Cozolino, 2005, 2006; Perry, Pollard, Blakley, Baker, & Vigilante, 1995; Perry & Szalavitz, 2007; Schore, 2001, 2003a, 2003b; Siegel, 2006; Streeck-Fischer & van der Kolk, 2000; Teicher, 2002). Our experience was that the majority of children remained in the care of their mothers, so we ran our first infant/mother group in early 2005, utilizing the knowledge we had accumulated through our work in running child-led systems groups in addressing family violence, and grateful for the interest and support of the expert infant mental health team operating within our hospital and their provision of weekly supervision to our groups (Thomson-Salo & Paul, 2007).

INFANT-LED SYSTEMS GROUP WORK

Our infant/mother group consisted of an individual assessment session with each dyad, six weekly group-work sessions, a post-group individual dyad feedback session, and a post-group reunion. A maximum of six infants and their mothers were accepted, and three therapists ran the group using an experiential, activity-based, and interactive format. The need for such a group was based on our belief that many mothers living with domestic violence were operating in survival mode. They were often so overwhelmed by their own trauma that they were emotionally unavailable to their infants and failed to understand their need for a relationship with them. By offering both infant and mother a different experience of relating, we opened up the infant/mother system to a new awareness of one another.

The power of infant-led systems work lies in allowing the infants to let us know what it is they need through observing and attuning ourselves to what they are telling us they need (Thomson-Salo et al., 1999). An example of this can be found in one group where singing and dancing to a nursery rhyme unexpectedly frightened one of the infants. Rather than not return to singing this song, each week we attuned its delivery and played with the words until this infant comfortably engaged with, and even looked forward to, this song during our singing time in the group.

The essence of the group was to encourage the mothers to see and relate to their babies as "a subject" in and of their own right (Thomson-Salo & Paul, 2007). The effectiveness of the intervention has been measured through the administration of a pre-and post-intervention standardized questionnaire called the Parent–Infant Attachment scale (Condon & Corkindale, 1998), which measures quality of attachment, absence of hostility, and pleasure in interaction. Additional measures have recently been included, and preliminary outcomes to date have been positive (Bunston & Dileo, 2006).

CASE STUDY: MOLLY, BREE, AND TONY MAKE THREE

Molly was 6 months old when she and her mother, Bree, were referred to our group for newborns (up to 12 months of age) and mothers affected by family violence (Bunston, 2006a). The high-risk infant team within our local Statutory Social Services had made a number of referrals into this particular group, two of which involved women who were identified as the primary aggressors, with their infants placed in the care of their fathers. Given our recognition of the complex patterning of violence within families, we accepted both referrals, despite the group primarily targeting women who were not identified as the primary aggressors. As our experience in this work had borne out over time, a number of mothers in both our infant and children's groups have been unable to reveal, acknowledge, and attend to their own feelings of aggression and acts of violence (Bunston, 2006a).

One of these two referrals did not eventuate. However, Statutory Social Services assured us that Bree was most keen to attend with Molly, and Tony, Molly's father, was supportive of their involvement. Molly was the only infant in the group to have an established and ongoing relationship with her father. The referral information indicated that Molly had been placed in Tony's care not long after her birth because Bree had made threats to harm her. Tony had decided to end the relationship with Bree soon after, and he was reported to have a very close and appropriate relationship with Molly. Bree was boarding with a family from her church, having increased contact with Molly and wanting to participate in the group in order to improve her relationship and feelings of connectedness with her daughter. The referral information indicated that Bree had been violent in her relationship with Tony, but there had been no evidence of physical violence in her relationship with Molly.

My first contact with Bree was by phone, and I experienced her as brisk and perhaps understandably suspicious. As is not unusual, what the group involved and its purpose were less clear to Bree than to those referring her, and I found myself having to work hard to engage her. We set up a time for Molly and Bree to come in for an assessment session, and she asked if Tony should come along. I said he was welcome and asked her to allow for a full hour and a half for the session. Bree was not ordered by the courts to attend the group, nor were any reports required. Thus it was her decision to participate.

Assessment

Bree presented as a petite, feisty, and earnest young woman who felt ashamed at not being involved in the full-time care of her daughter. As the session progressed, it appeared that she worked hard to conceal a slight speech impediment, and her brisk demeanor was intended to minimize the amount she had to speak to others. Molly was asleep in her baby stroller when Tony wheeled her in through our waiting area. Tony was a large, physically imposing man who was well educated and articulate, and he relished his command of the English language. Both clearly adored their daughter, almost amazed that they could have created such a perfect human, untainted by the adversities that had plagued their own lives.

Our assessments are guided by systems theory, ideas about violence and power, and our understanding of infant mental health. We state clearly that we will not hesitate to notify Statutory Social Services if we believe an infant is at risk. We demonstrate early our infant focus, greeting them and establishing a comfortable gaze and exchange with the infant. We are thoughtfully observant and curious about their experience, aware they are in a strange place and meeting new people. We try to create a picture of the quality of the attachment between mother and child and their perception of their infant as separate from and in relation to themselves, their father, their grandparents, and significant others. We also explore how the women perceive themselves as mothers. This process is guided by a structured interview called the "working model of the child interview" (Zeanah & Benoit, 1995). Further questions relate to the nature, extent, and length of violence occurring within the family and its perceived impact on the infant and on the mothers. This is set against a backdrop of inquiry that seeks to collect information that illuminates the interactional dynamics that play out in the family system and their reconstruction of their family history.

Family History

Bree described a family history of neglect, with a mother who was promised into a loveless marriage with a philandering husband who left the family on Bree's 10th birthday. She described herself as running wild as a teenager. Tony was from a successful professional family where he felt very supported by his mother but forever judged by his father as "never good enough." A recurring back injury had prevented Tony from pursuing an accountancy career, and he had been largely unemployed for the past 7 years. Bree and Tony had met at a religious revival service and saw religion as an important part of their lives. Bree was well known for her fiery temper and occasional violent outburst toward Tony, most of which was dismissed as harmless enough by outsiders, given their disparity in size, with Tony towering over her.

The violence appeared to escalate when Bree felt dismissed by Tony and had occurred with some regularity in their 3-year relationship. Bree felt that in these instances, Tony had used excessive force in response to her punching at and pushing him. An exploration of what played out in these sequences suggested that Bree's attachment style was ambivalent, whereas Tony's interactional pattern suggested avoidance. The further Bree intruded into his space, the more he withdrew. Her aggression would then escalate until he would use considerable force to end the altercation, and order would be restored. Tony felt that he could on occasion be "overly rough," but he felt he had no choice because Bree's actions backed him into a corner. He indicated that he felt more concerned about her verbal abuse and worried about Molly being exposed to any form of violence.

Bree was unaware of being pregnant until having tests for another medical condition, but both parents were delighted with the discovery. Bree became quite ill toward the end of the pregnancy, and after a very difficult labor, both baby and mother remained in the hospital for a number of weeks, but with little contact. The impact of this early initial separation on Molly's attachment experience and emerging sense of self and her world would have been considerable. Infants are from birth hardwired to engage with their environment, organize information, and demonstrate extraordinary cross-modal fluency (Stern, 2003). It is likely that in Molly's first weeks of life, she would have been bombarded with multiple medical, social, and environmental intrusions, despite the best intentions of medical staff. This is in contrast to coming home from the hospital and participating in a reciprocal social exchange with her parents while they endeavor to establish some mutual communication and physiological regulation. "The hospitalized, and usually traumatized, infant may not be able to accommodate so many impingements and may protest, acquiesce or dissociate, to manage the stressful experience" (Jones, 2007, p. 148).

It was also during this time that Bree told hospital staff she was fearful of hurting her baby, and a report was made to child protection. Bree's disclosure, coupled with their discovery of a history of her being violent toward Tony, led to the decision to remove Molly from her care and grant an interim accommodation order to Tony. This immediate and significant separation was followed by Bree being available to Molly only intermittently, as workers from Statutory Social Services assessed her capacity to parent. The disruption to their relationship at such a sensitive time in Molly's development undoubtedly contributed to compromising the quality of their attachment.

Molly

Molly was so snuggly wrapped up in her pram that it was almost difficult to see her. She remained asleep for most of the assessment session and only seemed to awaken toward the end. She did not cry out or make any demands once she woke, and if I had not looked over to where she was lying, I may have missed the chance to introduce myself and meet her gaze. This introduction and noting her presence became an important part of our work together, that of seeing Molly and inviting her out to play.

Bree's perception of Molly was that she was "like a gift from God," and it was almost unbelievable that they had been blessed with such a child. Tony was excessively proud of his daughter and, as the main caregiver, much more confident in his attachment with his daughter and what he believed she needed. Both parents presented with an over-idealization of their infant, foreclosing an ability to see Molly as an ordinary baby and a subject in and of her own right. This also made it difficult for them to see themselves as ordinary parents and be comfortable in their own exploration of this new role as parents, learning through trial and error.

Bree had been working with a local maternal and child health nurse service, was gaining in confidence, and had Molly in her care 2 days a week but would see her almost daily. The two parents had different opinions about what was the best routine for Molly, but in the current circumstances, Bree felt she should defer to Tony's judgment. The courts had awarded Tony the provisional caregiving role of his daughter, and it seemed evident from their interactions that Tony used this leverage to his advantage in their decision-making capacity as parents. On the basis of our assessment, I considered it important to offer them some additional family sessions alongside the group-work intervention. It seemed that Tony's inclusion was critical and that he would also benefit from and was entitled to feedback about Molly and her experience within the group.

TREATMENT

In the early sessions it was not unusual for Molly to either arrive at the group already asleep or fall asleep soon after arriving. We ascertained that the group did not clash with her normal sleeping routine, and it soon became evident that she was behind in some of her milestones. Bree had informed us that Molly's early medical difficulties had resulted in some delays, but she felt these difficulties had largely been attended to. We began to wonder, however, if Molly's withdrawal through sleep or inactivity was indicative of an avoidant response, her way of managing her emotional experience through shutting down. She seemed to carry a tiring burden, the hope, dreams, and future of this couple.

When Molly was awake, she was watchful but flat in affect. She seemed hesitant in her interactions with the other infants, and we noted that Bree would sometimes instigate removing Molly from the group, suggesting she was tired or needed a bottle when this was not obviously apparent to others. The mothers in the group were very curious about what the others did as mothers. As Bree observed other mothers engaging with their infants in various activities, she began to follow their lead. Bree also began to notice and hear what the group therapists heard and noticed. It was as though she followed her eyes along the line of our vision and in reaching their destination saw what we saw: her daughter Molly trying to make vocalizations when the group was singing and trying to engage with this new experience; her daughter Molly beginning to protest when she felt uncomfortable on her cushion and wanting to better see what everyone else was doing; her daughter Molly beginning to explore her environment and find her own place in this new system. As we became curious about what Molly might feel in this new experience, Bree became curious too.

We spoke to Molly directly, as we did all the infants, about what we were doing, and through discussion, activities, and music we invited Molly and her mother to play. Bree initially seemed unable to attune herself to the idea of Molly having her own agency or a self-directed need to explore her environment. The medical, physical, and psychological separation during their early mother/daughter relationship appeared to have disrupted their courtship of one another. Yet it appeared to encompass more than this. Bree seemed frightened of Molly. Bree did not know how to be close to her without being hurt by what she anticipated to be a likely rejection. Her own unaddressed early familial trauma and subsequent relational experiences threatened to repeat themselves, as did her pattern of becoming violent in relationships. How was she to see Molly with all her imperfections and still be capable of loving her fully? She seemed terrified of being hurt by her and terrified of hurting her. Our work with Molly and Bree involved playing with different ways of seeing and being with one another:

> Where parents seem unable to think about their infant, there has often been a very early fixed identification with the infant, rather than an empathic one, with the result that the parents' relationship is not with a subject and, in consequence, no transitional space is possible. . . . In our work we create a space in which thinking can start again. (Thomson-Salo et al., 1999, p. 49)

In one of our early sessions, we brought in a mirror for each infant, large enough for them to easily look into and explore themselves as well as to explore others. Initially the mothers held the mirror so that the infant could see him- or herself and play with his or her own image. Some of the mothers then maneuvered the mirror so that their infant could look up at them (the mother) in the mirror, and much to the delight of the infants, their mothers began to play peek-a-boo with them. Bree found that Molly could not meet her gaze in the mirror and became quite distressed. The group therapists encouraged Bree to just wait and see if Molly might bring her gaze back to her, which she did, but very briefly. This activity led to a discussion with the mothers about how they felt they managed their feelings, in particular, stress. Managing anger also featured strongly in this discussion, with different participants talking about how they tended to bottle up their feelings, taking themselves away from their children to cry or scream into their pillows.

It was at this point that Bree bravely disclosed that she was different from the other mothers in the group and talked about her history of violence toward others and her reason for being in the group. She also gave more details about her past, telling of an uncle who had beaten her severely as an adolescent for what she thought were her many misdemeanors. She concluded with her fear that others in the group would now distance themselves from her. Another member of the group disclosed that she too had done some things she was not proud of, and another stated that she did not think any less of Bree and was glad she was in the group.

> As one's image of self is more often than not derived from the reflection we see in the eyes of others, group work therapy can offer a very creative, intensive and personally exciting way of enhancing and strengthening one's sense of self. . . . The intensity of the group work experience can offer an opportunity to tolerate and sometimes transcend the political intimacy that group dynamics can bring to bear, as well as potentially offer a chance for some level of relational reparation. (Bunston et al., 2003, p. 39)

In that moment, Bree was able to see herself in the eyes of these other mothers as someone they wanted in their group, not as someone they rejected, judged, or were frightened of. Her disclosure also opened up the capacity for other mothers in the group to make known parts of themselves previously hidden, including their own feelings of rage. What infants see when they look into the eyes of their mothers and what infants see when their mothers look into theirs is inextricably intertwined. Winnicott (1971) noted that ordinarily, when infants look into the eyes of their mothers, what they see is themselves. What did Molly see of herself when she looked into the eyes of Bree? Was what she saw so frightening that Molly could not bear to look at her mother? Did Bree find it difficult to look "into" rather than "at" her daughter, anticipating what she needed rather than seeing what Molly communicated to her? What was Bree's experience of being seen, or possibly not seen, by her mother, her father, her uncle, Tony, and even Molly?

There was a seismic shift within this session that reverberated throughout the remainder of Molly and Bree's work together as a daughter/mother system within this larger social system called a group. Bree became curious about how Molly might perceive her and played with ideas about how she would give Molly different messages about who she was, in contrast to those given to Bree by her mother. In a later session Bree concluded that because of the extremity of her behavior as an adolescent, she probably deserved the beatings she had received at the hands of her uncle. When another group member asked if Molly would deserve to be beaten if she played up as Bree had, Bree immediately rallied, stating she would never allow anyone to hurt Molly in that way, no matter what she did. Bree was shocked when another group member indignantly asked what, then, made it OK for Bree to have experienced it.

The group took great interest in Molly and held her in their minds as they welcomed her out to play. Mothers would bring their infants over to greet her, and on the occasion when Tony drove them to the session and helped Bree bring in Molly with the pram and all her luggage, they welcomed him as well. Bree began to give expression to her fear that Molly was a little slower in her development than the other babies in the group and sat with another mother while they compared notes about their pediatricians. She was also able to hear from others how much progress they had noticed Molly had made from earlier group sessions in which she had largely slept and had been less mobile. The return to play with the mirrors in a later group saw Molly initiate eye contact with her mother and show her sheer delight when the mothers gathered all the infants together to look at one another.

The experience of joining with this therapeutic group was very powerful for Bree and Molly, individually and as a dyad. They benefited from the sense of hope and healing created by the group, the validation they were offered by others, and the capacity to safely bring up and process aspects of their lives that had remained hidden. All those participating in this group had found their first experience of belonging to a group—their family of origin—incredibly damaging. This experience allowed Bree in particular an opportunity to transcend, rather than replicate, her earliest interactional patterns of relating and to practice imitative behaviors, which can "unfreeze the individual enough to experiment with new behaviour" (Yalom, 1995, p. 16). Bree was able to watch how others engaged and played with Molly and how other dyads in the group interacted with one another and with her, allowing an opportunity to imprint a different way of how she and Molly could be together.

Family Sessions

We met for our first family session a month after Molly and Bree commenced the group. Tony wheeled in Molly's pram and parked her to one side of the circle we had made with our chairs. Molly was awake and seemed keen to check out her new surroundings. Bree sat her up next to her on her chair. Her eyes seemed to travel around the room and then moved to each parent as he or she they spoke. As Tony adroitly outlined his concerns and complaints about the differing routines they were using with Molly, Bree's speech impediment seemed to become accentuated. There was an awkward air to their conversation, with both still testing out how to relate to one another as parents, given that they no longer lived together. Bree was clear that she wanted to try reunification but felt Tony was holding the past over her head, making her too afraid to say or do anything for fear of repercussions. Tony was adamant. He believed the relationship was over, and were it not for Molly, he doubted they would have any reason to be in contact at all. Tony began to take on a disparaging tone with Bree and became unwilling to discuss it further. Bree became increasingly distressed, and the tempo of the room changed considerably, as an old familiar pattern in relating returned.

I noticed that Molly, who had been curiously engaging in her surroundings, suddenly became stock-still. Bree was sobbing, and Molly just watched her and waited. Tony was looking away from Bree, his eyes rolled upward as if to say, "Here we go again." Both seemed oblivious to Molly. I asked if either of them had just noticed what had happened to Molly, and both seemed surprised, taking a while to consider just what I was asking. They looked at me and then at Molly, unsure of whether I was asking a trick question. I relayed back what I had just observed during their interaction and asked what they thought might be happening right then and there for Molly. Tony ventured that perhaps they were upsetting her, and Bree seemed surprised that Molly would be attentive to her reactions. The shift in the room was palpable. We began to explore what impact their pattern of relating might have on Molly and where and how she fits into this family unit they had created.

The remainder of this session focused on just how they planned to conduct themselves as parents, irrespective of whether they reunited or permanently separated, and how this might serve as the foundation for how they would grow into their new role as parents of their daughter, Molly. This shift in focus was as startling for them as it was for me as their therapist. After years of working as a family therapist, this new infant-led focus had opened my eyes to seeing what was before me, an infant who was a subject in and of her own right and as extraordinary a part of the system as any other. Not having acquired language skills yet did not mean she could not speak. As all three adults in that session that day began to think about the mind of this infant, I believe we all experienced a change of mind in ourselves.

Changing Systems

Bree's internal working model of attachment appeared to be one of anxious ambivalence. The harder she worked at being seen, the more she was ignored. Molly adapted to the intrusiveness of Bree's interactions by becoming increasingly compliant and avoiding her gaze or dissociating. The facilitation team was able to hold Bree's anxiety well enough to allow her a transitional space within which she could think about Molly as a subject, in and of her own right (Thomson-Salo & Paul, 2007; Thomson-Salo et al., 1999). Rather than being someone she could impinge on, Molly was someone Bree could interact with.

Molly and Bree attended every group, and their capacity to read each other's cues grew, as did their enjoyment of one another. Molly became more animated in her engagement with the group, and while more secure in the space of the group, she was also more conscious of her mother, following her with her eyes and comfortable in meeting and returning her gaze. Bree's post-group questionnaire indicated a significant increase in how she rated her quality of attachment with Molly, their pleasure in interacting, and the absence of hostility. Tony, Bree, and Molly participated in one further infant-led family session. Although both remained unchanged in their thoughts about the future of their relationship as a couple, Bree was able to tolerate the idea that they may never reunite, and both were able to entertain the thought that they needed to alter the way they related to one another for the benefit of Molly. Their ability to engage respectfully as parents with a shared responsibility was markedly different. Tony was complimentary about the changes he saw in Bree's relationship with Molly, and Bree was able to respectfully hold her emotional world in check while still acknowledging her desire for them to be together as a family.

Molly and Bree returned for our group reunion and then for a further end-of-year farewell for all the infant groups we had held that year. The positive shifts in their relationship continued, with Molly making noticeable strides in her development. Tony and Bree had not reunited but sought some relationship counseling to sort through how they could better communicate, and Bree appeared to have begun building a supportive social network separate from that which involved Tony and had taken on shared care of Molly. She even made a joke about someone from her church setting her up on a date. The Statutory Social Services unit had also recently ceased involvement, and that was the last contact we had with the family and the last we know of their progress.

OUTCOMES AND CONCLUSION

Children, and infants in particular, do not and cannot exist in isolation of their caregiving system, however that system functions. Most often we think of the new infant as entering our world, rather than considering that we may have as much to learn by entering the infant's. Appreciating all that infant mental health theory has to offer and acknowledging the complex internal representations and communications that an infant possesses may jump start the primary system into change, just as occurred with this family. Their therapeutic journey could be considered successful from all accounts. Bree and Molly were able to make great use of the therapeutic space and interactional opportunities of the group, and both Bree and Tony demonstrated a motivation to embrace new ways of operating as a family system through thinking about and seeing Bree as possessing her own personhood.

Purely infant-led and child-led systems work, like all other therapeutic approaches, does not guarantee obvious or even successful outcomes. It is through an ability to embrace an openness to different systems of thinking, however, that the richness and texture of the therapeutic landscape we inhabit with our clients is enhanced. This requires a receptivity on the part of the professional and the familial systems to entertain different and new ways of seeing and thinking while ensuring that the safety of its most vulnerable members is never compromised. Seeing infants and children not as an extension of, but in addition to, the parental system, particularly when that system's interactional patterns are violent, takes a considerable shift in thinking. As noted by Sved-Williams (2003), a perinatal and infant psychiatrist,

Family Therapists understand systems, and systemic intervention. The exciting challenge for Infant Mental Health and Family Therapists is to increase their knowledge of each other's strengths and capabilities to ensure best use with this clinical population. As prevention and early intervention become increasingly seen as effective, time-efficient and appropriate, Family Therapists with an understanding of attachment theory, systems theory, brain development and intergenerational family problems will make successful and worthwhile clinical interventions. (p. 31)

To apply this knowledge to the area of addressing family violence and adopt an infant- or child-up lens to our work with systems may unveil patterns not yet seen. Motivation for change in a closed and unyielding system can sometimes emerge from its newest members. As we retrain ourselves to see the world from their eyes and take clear action to affirm and support their views, we invite parents to think back to their experience of being parented and how in years to come they want their children to remember them as parents. Promoting an infant- and child-led approach can enlarge our understanding of the complex dynamics that play out in families dominated by violence. This is turn expands our ability to effectively respond.

REFERENCES

Bowlby, J. (1973). *Attachment and loss: Vol. 2. Separation: Anxiety and anger.* London: Hogarth Press.

Bunston, W. (2001). *PARKAS (Parents Accepting Responsibility—Kids Are Safe) manual.* Victoria, Australia: Royal Children's Hospital Mental Health Service & Djerriwarrh Health Services.

Bunston, W. (2006a). The Peek a Boo Club: Groupwork for infants and mothers affected by family violence. *DVIRC Quarterly, 1,* 3–8.

Bunston, W. (2006b). One way of responding to family violence: "Putting on a PARKAS." In W. Bunston & A. Heynatz (Eds.), *Addressing family violence programs—Group work interventions for infants, children and their families.* Melbourne, Australia: Royal Children's Hospital Mental Health Service.

Bunston, W., Crean, H., & Thomson-Salo, F. (1999). *PARKAS (Parents Accepting Responsibility—Kids Are Safe).* Melbourne: Federal/State Government—Partnerships Against Domestic Violence.

Bunston, W., & Dileo, J. (2006). Last but never least: Evaluation. In W. Bunston & A. Heynatz (Eds.), *Addressing family violence programs—Group work interventions for infants, children and their families.* Melbourne, Australia: Royal Children's Hospital Mental Health Service.

Bunston, W., Pavlidis, T., & Leyden, P. (2003). Putting the GRO into groupwork. *Australian Social Work, 56*(1), 40–49.

Condon, J. T., & Corkindale, C. J. (1998). The assessment of parent-to-infant attachment: Development of a self-report questionnaire instrument. *Journal of Reproductive & Infant Psychology, 16*(1), 57–76.

Cozolino, L. J. (2005). The impact of trauma on the brain. *Psychotherapy in Australia, 11*(3), 22–35.

Cozolino, L. J. (2006). The social brain. *Psychotherapy in Australia, 12*(2), 12–17.

Jones, S. (2007). The baby as subject: The hospitalized infant and the family therapist. *Australian and New Zealand Journal of Family Therapy, 28*(3), 146–154.

Perry, B., & Szalavitz, M. (2007). Stairway to heaven: Treating children in the crosshairs of trauma. *Psychotherapy Networker, 31*(2), 56–64.

Perry, B. D., Pollard, R. A., Blakley, T. L., Baker, W. L., & Vigilante, D. (1995). Childhood trauma, the neurobiology of adaptation, and "use-dependent" development of the brain: How "states" become "traits." *Infant Mental Health Journal, 16*(4), 271–291.

Pynoos, R. S., & Nader, K. (1993). Psychological first aid and treatment approach to children exposed to community violence: Research implications. *Journal of Traumatic Stress, 1*(4), 445–473.

Schore, A. (2003a). *Affect regulation and the repair of the self.* New York: Norton.

Schore, A. (2003b). *Affect dysregulation and disorders of the self.* New York: Norton.

Schore, A. N. (2001). The effects of early relational trauma on the right brain development, affect regulation, and infant mental health. *Infant Mental Health Journal, 22*(1–2), 201–269.

Siegel, D. J. (2006). Attachment and self-understanding: Parenting with the brain in mind. *Psychotherapy in Australia, 12*(2), 26–32.

Stern, D. N. (2003). *The interpersonal world of the infant.* London: Karnac Books.

Streeck-Fischer, A., & van der Kolk, B. (2000). Down will come baby, cradle and all: Diagnostic and therapeutic implications of chronic trauma on child development. *Australian and New Zealand Journal of Psychiatry, 34*, 903–918.

Sved-Williams, A. (2003). Family therapy and infant mental health: Natural partners. *Australian and New Zealand Journal of Family Therapy, 24*(1), 26–32.

Teicher, M. H. (2002). Scars that won't heal: The neurobiology of child abuse. *Scientific American, 286*(3), 68–75.

Thomson-Salo, F., & Paul, C. (Eds.). (2007). *The baby as subject* (2nd ed.). Melbourne: Stonnington Press.

Thomson-Salo, F., Paul, C., Morgan, A., Jones, S., Meehan, M., Morse et al. (1999). "Free to be playful": Therapeutic work with infants. *Infant Observation Journal: The International Journal of Infant Observation and Its Applications, 3*, 47–62.

Winnicott, D. W. (1971). *Playing and reality.* London: Tavistock.

Yalom, I. D. (1995). *The theory and practice of group psychotherapy* (4th ed.). New York: Basic Books.

Zeanah, C. H., & Benoit, D. (1995). Clinical applications of a parent perception interview in infant mental health. *Child and Adolescent Psychiatric Clinics of North America, 4*(3), 539–554.

QUESTIONS FOR REFLECTION AND DISCUSSION

1 In her introduction, the author writes, "The theoretical paradigms that dominate the war against family violence are as flawed as the humans that have created them." How does her

child-led systems group work advance our efforts to effectively treat intimate partner violence and child abuse? How empirically grounded is this model, in comparison with others in the field of family violence? Are there limitations to this model, and if so, what might they be?

2 This case study illustrates the importance of attachment bonds in understanding family violence, both in infancy between child and caregivers and in adulthood between intimate partners. What is the link between the quality of Bree's early attachment to her mother and her attachments to her own child, Molly, as well as to Tony?

3 The author does not say whether Bree had previously attended an anger management or batterer intervention group, but the implication is that she stopped being violent to Tony only because he left her, and Bree's unresolved anger continued to affect her child. What unique features of the parent group accounted for the dramatic improvement in her relationship with Molly? Do you think attendance in a batterer intervention program would have had the same results?

10

The Movable Genogram: Family Intervention Techniques Toward Breaking Cycles of Intergenerational Conflict

KAREN COHEN

The terms *cycle of violence* and *intergenerational transmission* are often used interchangeably by therapists and in the family violence literature, referring to at-risk children who have experienced or witnessed abuse and who later become victims or offenders themselves. Certain factors that increase the probability of families becoming at higher risk for violence include social isolation, substance abuse, poor interpersonal skills and high-conflict relationships, financial and employment problems, and lack of family and emotional support. Multifamily group therapy is a combination of group treatment and family therapy, first introduced by Peter Laqueur (1972), which research indicates can be used effectively to help families overcome their intergenerational transmission of violence. Deschner (1984), for example, reported that in an 8-month follow-up study of 15 couples who completed a 10-week session for multi-couples group intervention programs using cognitive-behavioral approaches, 8 out of 15 were violence-free.

My contribution to this work comes from 20 years of clinical experience with troubled families. These families were all assessed as exhibiting the most common form of violence, with low to moderate levels of physical aggression (Johnson & Ferraro, 2000), and therefore were considered suitable for this type of counseling. Ideally, the multifamily group contains a minimum of three couples, and the facilitator focuses on one couple at a time while the others observe the conflict and then elicits feedback from everyone in the group. The families discussed in this chapter were required to complete 12 weeks of mandatory multifamily group counseling in order to qualify for family reunification by Child and Family Services. They were also encouraged to maintain outside contact with other multifamily group members once they completed the program.

THE MOVABLE FAMILY GENOGRAM

In 1988 I was the outpatient drug and alcohol program director of a Los Angeles County family services agency. I directed and facilitated a multifamily group treatment program for parents who had been arrested and convicted of child abuse and who had as a consequence temporarily lost custody of their children. Families were referred by case workers from the Department of Children and Family Services to receive mandated multifamily group counseling sessions. During that time I developed a systemic visual family therapeutic intervention technique known as the movable family-of-origin genogram.

Family-of-origin work typically looks at the family an individual was born into and his or her parents' background (Bowen, 1978). Therapy involves analyzing family messages, values, communication styles, traditions, and ways of dealing with feelings. Family-of-origin therapy helps individuals who are experiencing current family and marital difficulties comprehend that their problems largely stem from unresolved conflicts in their childhood.

A family-of-origin genogram is an efficient and effective pictorial diagram for explaining repetitive, intergenerationally learned behaviors and patterns. It includes basic information about the individual family members, the number of children in each family, birth order, divorce, stepfamilies, and death. Additional data can include major life events, chronic illness, social behaviors, and the living situations and disorders that become intergenerationally transmitted learned behaviors. The movable family-of-origin genogram is constructed with chairs. The way the clients position the chairs and the family members (either current or past family members, or both) they assign to sit in each can effectively provide a mobile and graphic representation of their family structure and history.

A movable family genogram can reflect and project an individual's point of view and uncover the causes of a conflicted interpersonal relationship. Although most family members generally agree on the basics of their self-reported family trees (a genealogical diagram of a family's ancestry), family members can experience major differences when describing complex interpersonal dynamics among themselves. The interpretation of a movable family-of-origin genogram is influenced by the creator of the genogram; different family members may have differing perspectives on family relationships and will therefore construct the movable genogram of the same family differently.

For example, two adult siblings acknowledge that as children they both saw their parents become violent with one another, but they do not agree on which parent was to blame for causing the violence. The older sister blames her father because she thought he was always the first to physically strike out. This is why she sided with her mother. The younger sister blames her mother because she witnessed her slapping her father and therefore aligns with him. There is no absolute "right" genogram for any one family. The goal of the movable family genogram is to reconstruct the family structure to communicate information openly and to flow freely within the family system.

Structural family therapy (Minuchin, 1974) can be used to help in the creation of a movable genogram, assisting family members to join in the process and to structure and restructure both old and new relationships. Group members are able to observe and assess how the various families are influenced by their families of origin. The invisible set of functional demands that organizes the ways in which family members interact is demonstrated effectively in the way each person positions the chairs to show his or her interpersonal relationships. In a family system, conflict is structured by assigning the members unconscious roles and rules in order for the family to function. With the movable chairs a client creates a visual family structure and helps to identify and understand how the unconscious and conscious family roles and rules function—for example, when an adult child with an abusive alcoholic parent moves the alcoholic's chair out of the circle to show he or she is disconnected from the family unit both emotionally and physically.

Family Systems Theory and the Movable Family Genogram

Family systems theory approaches the family as a whole, as the unit of treatment, and emphasizes such factors as relationships and communication patterns rather than traits or symptoms in individual members. The family is a system in which each member has a role to play and rules to enforce. Members in a family system are expected to respond to each other according to their roles, which are determined by the interpersonal relationship dynamics that include a transmission process of learned behavior. Within the boundaries of the family system, patterns develop in certain family members' behavior, which is then transmitted into ways that are predictable. A family operates as a closed, rigid system when its members maintain the same patterns of behavior, also known as homeostasis. When there is homeostasis, the family system seeks to maintain its customary organization and functioning over time. It tends to resist change. An example of a closed rigid homeostasis system is when families continue to enable intergenerational family violence, incest, and addiction by keeping them a family secret.

The movable family-of-origin genogram employs family systems techniques in order to open up the family system. Once the rigid closed system has been opened up, such as through breaking a family secret, this causes chaos and creates an imbalance in the old system. The imbalance comes from changing the closed system and restructuring it so that it can become open and flexible. The system can remain open and flexible, or it can go back to the old system through denial and resistance to change. When the system chooses to stay open and flexible, the family is implementing new problem-solving approaches to resolve conflict, instead of using the familial dysfunctional behaviors in dealing with its problems.

Treatment Goals

The primary therapeutic goal in applying the movable family genogram in a multifamily group session is to empower family members to restructure their own system in order to break the cycle of intergenerational family violence. In achieving this goal, family members acquire alternative problem-solving skills and improve their interpersonal relationships. Through group feedback and support, participants experience the increase in ego strength necessary to construct their movable family-of-origin genogram. Once family conflicts are being addressed in the multifamily group, the treatment objective is to have group members practice modeling communication and behavioral techniques in ongoing sessions. The facilitator's treatment objectives for constructing a movable family-of-origin genogram are as follows:

- Assist in restructuring their family system so as to promote the changes and growth that come from learning to problem-solve conflict.

- Help family members visually observe and understand the inter-generational transmission process in order to gain new insight into old and new behaviors.
- Encourage participants to utilize their strengths and overcome the resistance they have to problem-solving conflict.
- Help participants experience and practice new communication skills and behaviors with other family group members through imitation learning. This multifamily group therapy technique is known as learning through identification (Lacquer, 1972).

The Multifamily Family Group Therapist

Most of the studies on multifamily group therapies have found that the role of the therapist should be a proactive one. Donner and Gameson (1968) discuss the therapist as a participant-observer. The facilitator works with all the family group members and encourages them to join in and work with other families outside of their own. To ensure group containment so that the families can work in a here-and-now process, the facilitator must structure the group and maintain safe therapeutic boundaries, based on the premise that families in group can bring to consciousness what is happening on an unconscious level. When boundaries and limits are consistent in group process, family members are less resistant to reenact family-of-origin roles and rules with other couples and families. This type of learning through identification (Laqueur, 1972) becomes invaluable for encouraging members in taking risks to separate from their family of origin's dysfunctional communication and behaviors.

A key task for a family group facilitator is to restructure family communication patterns in order to create positive expression through assertive means. As part of the group process, family group members are encouraged to learn new interpersonal communication techniques such as engaging and accepting positive and constructive criticisms from each other. The facilitator helps to safely empower members to resolve conflict by problem-solving their own solutions by using the movable genogram.

Before using the movable family-of-origin genogram, a therapist should have experience in working with families as well as in working with cases of domestic violence, treating both victims and perpetrators. When treating family violence, clinicians not trained in domestic violence and family therapy are at greater risk of becoming triangulated in the family system. Family systems theory maintains that emotional relationships in families are usually triangular. Whenever two persons in the family have problems with each other, they will "triangle in" a third member as a way of stabilizing their own relationship. The triangles in a family system usually interlock in a way that maintains family homeostasis. Common family triangles include a child and the child's parents; two children and one parent; a parent, a child, and a grandparent; and a husband, a wife, and an in-law. The therapist's role is to intervene when necessary to expose these triangles and directly effect change.

The Intake Interview

I conduct a clinical interview separately with each family member, to gather information and assess whether a family member is appropriate for participation in multifamily group sessions. As both the interviewer and the group facilitator, I have the opportunity to assess and follow up on responses they may have made during the course of the clinical interview and psychosocial history. Through many years of experience in interviewing clients, I have found ways to provide a safe transition for those who are resistant to participate in multifamily group sessions.

I employ a direct, empathetic approach to encourage clients to open up, usually beginning the interview by asking the person directly, "Can you tell me what brought you here today?" Before the interview is over, each person has signed an agreement, agreeing to comply with the multifamily group rules. The rules for treatment compliance in the multifamily group sessions are the following:

- Violence is not permitted.
- Group participants must agree that all children shall not be punished by their parents, siblings, or legal guardian for what a child has said during and after family group sessions.
- Spouses, partners, and family members are not to discuss what occurs in session with other family group members outside of the group.
- Termination of the group must be announced by family members 1 week in advance of their final session.

Individuals who were mandated for family group counseling but have now been reassessed as inappropriate referrals are sent back to either the court or social services agencies to become reevaluated for other services for the following reasons:

- A low level of psychosocial functioning
- Pathological personality disorders

- Diagnosis of psychotic symptoms
- Lack of medication compliance
- Use of nonprescribed drugs or alcohol or reasonable cause for suspicion of being under the influence

The remainder of this chapter focuses on the first of 12 scheduled family group meetings I held with Sam and Maria, a 90-minute session that demonstrates the construction of a movable family genogram. It shows how this intervention tool can help in the development of new communication techniques with which to undo learned behaviors and to problem solve conflict.

CASE STUDY: SAM AND MARIA

Sam and Maria were referred by their son's caseworker to attend family counseling as a condition for regaining custody of their son, after Antonio had been removed from his parents' home by the Department of Children and Family Services for child endangerment. He was placed in the custody of his grandmother because of a violent incident that occurred between his mother and father in their home.

Sam is a Latino, age 26. Maria, his wife, is a Latina, age 25. Sam had lost his job several months before and had started to go out drinking frequently. Maria worked while Sam stayed at home to take care of their son. As soon as Maria would get home after work, Sam would leave to go out drinking and would often come home late. On the night of the incident, Sam arrived home late and very intoxicated. Maria confronted him, complaining that she was tired of him coming home late and drunk. Knowing that they would get into an argument, he tried to avoid her, but the argument continued to escalate to the point that he lost control and slapped her so hard that she fell down. She became frightened and got up to reach for the telephone. When Sam grabbed the phone away from her, Maria kicked him in the groin.

Awoken by the commotion, Antonio came out from his room to investigate. He found his parents in the living room engaged in intimate partner violence and began to scream and cry, causing the downstairs neighbor to call 911. When the police arrived they noticed the red mark on Maria's face and the presence of her frightened child. The police arrested Sam for domestic violence.

Sam's Intake Interview

Sam showed up a few minutes late for his appointment. He had just gotten off work from his new job as an auto mechanic. Sam appeared anxious in the interview. He admitted that on the night of the incident, he had been drunk, in an effort to escape feeling angry and frustrated with himself about being unemployed. After he was arrested, he became very depressed about his son being taken away. He stated he was attending Alcoholics Anonymous (AA) meetings and had completed classes in anger management and parenting. He also mentioned that this was the first time he and his wife had gotten into a violent argument. In the past when she had confronted him about his drinking, he had just avoided her by leaving the house. Sam reported in his intake interview that Maria blamed his drinking for the problems in their marriage. He said he would like to be able to improve his relationship with his wife and son but was fearful of confronting Maria about their financial problems.

Sam's Family-of-Origin History

Sam reported that his mother divorced his father when he was 2 years old. He is the older of two children, with a younger half-brother. His mother remarried when he was 5, to a man who would beat her when he was drunk. Growing up, Sam often would go and stay in his room by himself to avoid his stepfather when he was angry or when he got drunk. His stepfather constantly blamed his mother and Sam for problems that occurred in the home. Sam left his mother's home at age 18. He sought his biological father but found out through family members that the man had died of cirrhosis of the liver. After living with relatives for a while, Sam enlisted in the army. Four years later, after an honorable discharge, he moved back in with his mother, who by now had separated from her husband. Sam and his mother would constantly argue. At times she would throw things at him and threaten to kick him out of her house. He moved out of her home when he met Maria.

Maria's Intake Interview

Maria showed up to her appointment on time. She soon began to cry, stating that she felt depressed and sad about losing custody of her son and that she wanted to have a better relationship with Sam because he is the father of her child. Although she previously confirmed to her son's social worker that Sam had never struck her physically in the past, she reported in her intake interview with me that he would come home drunk and angry and would throw things. Maria reported that on the night of the incident, she kept calling him to come home so that they could be together. She felt very angry with him for not returning several calls and intended to confront him about his drinking. That night, when he came home late smelling of alcohol, she decided she had had enough of his behavior. Maria decided she would take Antonio to her mother's home.

She reported to the police and to the social worker that she had kicked Sam in the groin in self-defense. The police arrested Sam for domestic violence and placed their son, Antonio, in the hands of the Department of Social Services for child endangerment, because of Maria and Sam's failure to protect their son and their exposing him to their intimate partner violence. Social services put Antonio into the temporary custody of his maternal grandmother until Maria had successfully completed her requirements for family reunification. By the time of her intake interview with me, Maria had completed a course of parenting classes with Sam.

Maria's Family-of-Origin History

Maria is an only child. She opened up in the intake when asked if there had been any history of child abuse in her family of origin. Maria reported that her father had begun to molest her when she was 3 years old and had told her to keep this secret from her mom. It remained that way until her mom came home from work when Maria was 11 years old and found him in bed with her. But her mother told her to keep the molestation a secret. When Maria was 12, her father left her and her mother for another woman. Maria felt that her mother blamed her for his leaving. After graduating high school, she left her mother's home and went into vocational school to become a medical assistant. Eventually, she married Sam after she became pregnant with Antonio.

MULTIFAMILY GROUP: CONSTRUCTION OF THE MOVABLE CHAIR FAMILY GENOGRAM

For their first of 12 weekly group sessions, Sam and Maria were joined by one other couple, John and Laura, who were referred by the Department of Children and Family for child abuse. I instructed the four parents to sit in a circle and introduce themselves to each other. Afterward, I asked them to state why they were sent here. They all said that they were sent here because they had lost custody of their children. Sam and Maria added that they wanted to learn how to improve communication in order to avoid another violent episode in Antonio's presence.

In the initial session with families that are joining the group, I educate and structure the movable family genogram as a visual tool for them to identify how their old communication patterns learned in childhood are still being used today in their troubled relationship. After the intervention has taken place, the group is taught and asked to practice over the next 11 weeks new communication skills, both in the ongoing group sessions and at home as weekly homework assignments. The remainder of this chapter focuses on the work done during the first of the 12 scheduled sessions.

Sam disclosed that he had difficulty speaking to his wife directly about their problems. Maria nodded in acknowledgement. They agreed to participate in the construction of the movable genogram to demonstrate their conflicted relationship. I instructed Sam to take three empty chairs from outside of the circle and place them inside the circle, with each empty chair representing his immediate family members. When he had done so, I asked him to place the chairs as if he and his wife and son were having Thanksgiving dinner. Sam complied and placed the three chairs side by side right next to each other. Sam's chair was placed to the left. He put Antonio's chair into the middle and Maria's on the right.

Sam's Movable Chair Genogram

I instructed Sam to describe his relationship conflicts with Maria. He proceeded to take another three empty chairs, placing the two chairs representing him and Maria on top of one another and then placing the chair representing Antonio several feet away from the inner circle. I asked Sam to describe why he had placed the chairs in this type of arrangement.

Sam: The chair on top is Maria. I feel that she tries to control me. At nights when she comes home from work and Antonio goes to sleep, she starts arguing about financial problems. I'm on the bottom chair because I always get frustrated, and I tell her I need to get away to cool off, but she doesn't listen and continues to go after me. I feel like I'm her kid instead of her husband.

Facilitator: Where is Antonio's chair?

Sam: I moved his chair out there because I don't want him to see his mother and I argue.

Facilitator: Maria, the way Sam put the chairs on top of one another—is that how you experience conflict with Sam?

Maria: I understand that's how he sees our relationship, but it's not how I see it.

Facilitator: What is your version of the conflict?

Maria was now invited to participate in the intervention process by offering her perception of conflict with Sam. I directed her to retrieve three more chairs. Like Sam, Maria placed them inside the inner circle, two of them on top of each other and the third outside of the circle several feet away.

Facilitator: Maria, whose chairs are the ones in the circle?

Maria: The chair on top is Sam, and the chair on the bottom is me. I see Sam's behavior as controlling. I feel frustrated because he will pull away from me whenever I try to talk to him; he just walks away or leaves the house. It used to be the bars; now it's the AA meetings.

Reconstructing the Movable Family-of-Origin Genogram

Next, I asked Sam and Maria to use the chairs to demonstrate how they communicate indirectly with one another over unresolved conflict, such as when Maria starts arguing about finances the moment that Antonio goes to sleep. Sam went to the first set of chairs, which he had placed side by side with Antonio in the middle, and indicated that this arrangement represented his need to be shielded and to avoid confrontation with Maria, confident that she will not verbally attack him in front of their son.

Maria said that Sam controls her by avoiding direct interactions with her. I asked the group for feedback from observing the family structure designed by Sam with the first set of chairs and then moved outside of the group. I encouraged everyone to respond to Sam's version of his family system and to join in at any time to reconstruct their own relationship, knowing that the marital conflict between Sam and Maria would elicit emotions from the other group members. I asked Maria to bring in another set of chairs to demonstrate how she envisions her conflicted relationship with Sam. Maria placed two of the chairs side by side, but placed the third one outside of the circle several feet away.

Facilitator: Maria, can you please tell the group who is who in the three chairs?

Maria: Antonio and I are sitting together at the table. I put Sam's chair outside to show that he leaves whenever I try to talk to him.

Facilitator: Sam, the way that Maria placed you outside of the family—is that how you want to resolve conflict?

Sam: Maria constantly complains about my drinking. That makes me angry, so I walk away.

Having Sam and Maria participate in constructing separate demonstrations with the chairs allowed both of them and the other group members to observe each other's interpretation of their own marital relationship problems. The demonstration also allowed observing group members to identify and perceive their own role in their marital dyad.

Facilitator: John and Laura, do either of you connect with Maria or Sam in how they perceive their conflict?

John: I relate to the way Maria put the chairs. That's the way I grew up in my family with my mom and dad. My dad was also an alcoholic.

Facilitator: John, how did you want your family to deal with conflict as a child?

John: I would have liked to have my dad be in the circle with my mom and me.

Facilitator: Sam, now that you are not drinking, how would you like to deal with Maria when you are arguing?

Sam: Different from my parents. When I was growing up, my parents would argue and beat each other up. My real father left when I was 2 years old.

Facilitator: John, can you show the group how as a child you would have wanted your family to sit at the dinner table on Thanksgiving?

John: [as he arranges the chairs] I would have had my dad sit across from my mom, and my younger sister who died last year sit across from me.

Facilitator: What you're showing by rearranging the chairs is your perception of being with the family on Thanksgiving and having everyone being connected in a circle facing each other.

Facilitator: Sam, what do you think of John's version of his childhood wish?

Sam: I have the same wish.

Facilitator: Can you show Maria and the rest of the group how you would have wanted your parents to spend Thanksgiving with you as a child?

Sam rearranged the three chairs in a circle similar to how John had modeled his version of his family being openly connected to one another.

Facilitator: Does anyone else identify with the way Sam has put his family together?

Laura nodded her head in agreement.

Facilitator: So, John, how would you want your relationship to be with Laura?
John: I want to be able to talk directly to her without having Angela [their daughter] around.
Facilitator: Can you show Laura and everyone how you would like to communicate with her directly?

John joined the circle with Sam and Maria, bringing in three chairs to demonstrate how he would like to restructure his own family system and change the way he interacts with Laura. He placed one chair directly facing a second and placed the third to face both of them. John sat in one chair and invited Laura to sit across from him. He indicated that the other empty chair facing both of them represented their daughter, Angela, who was taken by social services and placed in foster care after doctors found traces of cocaine in her placenta at birth.

With the chairs, John had restructured his family system to create an imbalance in the marital dyad.

Facilitator: John and Laura, what does it feel like to have both of you sitting and facing each other?
Laura: It feels uncomfortable to have him look at me directly.
Facilitator: John, how is it for you to sit across from Laura?
John: I like it, but it feels different.
Facilitator: What do you want to say directly to Laura?
John: Why is it every time you make arrangements with Angela's foster home, you never check with me to see if I can go see her?
Laura: Because when I try to let you know, you don't give me an answer right away. You always do this when I need to let the social worker know what day we can go see Angela.
Facilitator: Sam and Maria, what are you hearing from John and Laura?

Maria: I hear that John is upset with Laura for not checking with him first before she calls the social worker, and Laura is upset because he won't listen and give her an answer.

Sam: I heard the same as Maria.

Facilitator: How does it feel to see Laura and John facing one another?

Sam: I feel uncomfortable to hear them argue.

Facilitator: What feels uncomfortable for you?

Sam: How John arranged the chairs to face each other.

Learning by identification from family group observation in the multifamily group session (Laqueur, 1972) empowers old and new group members such as John and Laura to intervene, making it possible for Sam and Maria to connect with their own similar family structure. By observing the reenactment, Sam and Maria were encouraged to create an imbalance in the homeostasis of their own family system. Witnessing Laura's reaction helped Sam identify his resistance to join Maria in confronting conflict under the new system. According to family systems theory, if one person changes, it changes the whole family system. The change in the family structure caused an imbalance and was met with opposition by both Laura and Sam.

Once their reaction to changes in the system had been openly identified, I moved into the circle to validate their feelings of resistance, interpreting their resistance as fear of the unknown amid their family structure moving into a new direction. My next intervention would be to revisit Sam's family structure to include Maria and Antonio.

Sam had initially constructed a rigid family system, placing Antonio between him and Maria to avoid conflict, the three chairs close together, depicting a closed and inflexible system. Sam had structured his family to communicate indirectly with Maria and Antonio. I have often found that positioning a child's chair in the middle often represents a parent's avoidance of problem-solving marital conflict. When there has been violent conflict between the parents, this arrangement also visually represents the child being "caught in the middle," a victim of child endangerment and abuse. Adult children who were abused will demonstrate their version of a childhood fantasy of an idealized harmonious relationship without conflict. I asked Sam and Maria if I could rearrange the chairs by removing the ones that Sam placed side by side to face each other. They both agreed. I took Antonio's chair and placed him across from them. By moving the position of the chairs, I sought to alter the dynamics of their interaction. In the case of Sam and Maria, who were both abused and exposed to violent conflicts as children, using the movable family of origin empowers them to create changes as adult children.

Sam and Maria's Family-of-Origin Movable Genogram

The movable genogram helps group members learn how to identify unresolved family-of-origin conflicts and to problem-solve conflict by incorporating family therapy and cognitive behavioral techniques to safely address "here and now" problems. Any group member can assist in the chair work, to identify the old behaviors and model the new ones, so necessary to reduce the possibility of reexperiencing trauma and in deescalating anger. The therapist continually observes and assesses, ready to intervene at any time to get everyone to join in and express their feelings openly about what just happened and to maintain the safe therapeutic boundaries in which participants can act out their unconscious and conscious feelings and thoughts.

At my request, Sam and Maria shifted their chairs to face each other directly. This was the initial intervention in restructuring their marital dyad.

Facilitator: Sam, what is it like for you to move your chair to face Maria?
Sam: It feels strange, somewhat uncomfortable.
Maria: This feels uncomfortable.
Facilitator: It's understandable that you both feel uncomfortable. This is different than what you both are used to.

The discomfort that Maria and Sam were experiencing was an indication that their family system was becoming balanced and nonlinear. I directed Sam to take extra chairs to reenact his own perception of how his family dealt with conflict when he was growing up, hoping that this intervention would assist all of the group members in visually connecting with their own intergenerational familial patterns. Sam brought the chairs into the circle.

Facilitator: Sam, please arrange the chairs in a way that represents how you would like to have your family function at the dinner table.
Sam: You mean now, or when I was a kid?
Facilitator: Let's begin with now [here-and-now process]. How would you like your family to act now?

Maria and the other members watched as Sam placed the chairs in a circle.

Facilitator: Who is in each chair?
Sam: Maria sits across from me.

Sam had now positioned the chairs in a circle, in contrast to how he perceived his own family as being disconnected from one another.

Facilitator: Sam, is this how you would like it to be?
Sam: Yes.

I then checked in with Maria and the others to elicit their reactions to how Sam had positioned the chairs.

Facilitator: Maria, what do you think about Sam's wishes?
Maria: I like how he has put the chairs together.

Sam's positioning of the chairs, and Maria's appreciation of how he would like his present family to become, indicated a motivation by both to improve their relationship through direct communication. I asked John and Laura for feedback on the circular flow of the chairs, and they both had positive responses. This kind of encouragement from group members outside of the inner circle provides positive criticism, support, and the encouragement needed to take risks.

Facilitator: Sam, if this is the way you want to have your relationship with Maria, then it is important to see how, in your own family of origin, the chairs were positioned when you were growing up.

Sam started to move the chairs in the circle. I stopped him, pointing out that it is important to keep those chairs, representing his current family, separate from those that represent his family of origin. I instructed him to get another set of chairs in order to reenact his own family-of-origin genogram. Following my instructions, he placed three chairs in a circle as if they had sat at the dining room table when he was a child. I asked him to describe his family of origin as he began to position each chair and assigned the family roles. He took the chair representing himself and placed it several feet away from the circle and positioned the remaining two chairs back to back, to represent his parents' relationship.

Sam: The chair I moved far away is my chair. The two other chairs across from each other are my stepdad and my mom.

Facilitator: Is this how you wanted your family as a child?

Sam: No.

Facilitator: As a child, how would you have liked to have your family at the dinner table?

Sam brought his chair into the circle and then turned the other two chairs around so that they faced one another, creating a circle exactly as had restructured the second set of chairs for himself and Maria. I asked Maria and the rest of the group members if they could relate to Sam's family of origin.

Maria: My family is similar to Sam's, except that all chairs are distanced away from everyone.

Facilitator: Can you show what you mean by that?

Maria: Yes.

Maria was about to move Sam's chairs to depict her own family-of-origin genogram, but I intervened, instructing her to get a new set of chairs. Maria retrieved three additional chairs and proceeded to put two far outside of the circle and the one remaining chair inside the circle.

Facilitator: How many of you in the group relate to or connect with Maria's family system?

Laura: I connect because I feel so far away from my family when I use drugs.

Facilitator: Maria, can you tell the group who's in what chair?

Maria: [pointing to the two chairs that are so far apart] The chair on the right is my mother, and the other chair that is also far away is my dad.

Facilitator: Who's sitting in the third chair?

Maria: That's me.

Maria began to cry as she contemplated the chairs, arranged in a long-distance triangle. I approached her, noticing how the other group members were being affected, a reaction to their own emotions being projected from Maria's pain.

Facilitator: Sam, do you connect with how Maria is feeling?

Sam: Yes, I do. I sometimes wish I could cry. But I can't.

Facilitator: How many of you in the group can connect with Maria and Sam as children?

John: I can relate to Sam as far as not remembering the last time I cried.

Laura: I, too, can connect with both John and Sam as a kid. My mom would hit me if I cried.

Facilitator: Let's come back now to your present relationship. Maria, can you describe your relationship with Sam?

Maria: The chair that I moved away is Sam. The other chair is me.

Facilitator: How many others connect with Maria's relationship with Sam?

John: The way Maria put the chairs reminds me of my relationship with my wife.

Laura: I connect with Sam's perception of his relationship with Maria.

The encouragement, support, and validation from the group members helped Sam and Maria to feel supported enough to address their conflict openly. As they arranged the chairs to demonstrate this conflict, an imbalance was created in the group's family system. The group members observed how all the chairs in the circle were in disarray and disconnected from one another, evidence of the chaos in the group's family system when conflict was addressed. The chair work would become an experiential process in which Sam and Maria, as well as the other couple, could begin to function on their own, becoming interdependent between the old and new behaviors to constructively communicate with themselves and their families.

When a system is able to reorganize itself, it becomes empowered to create its own structure in which to function (Rubenfeld, 2001). After having constructed his childhood family of origin, Sam was able to recognize how he had used avoidance to withdraw from his parents' violent relationship. Maria and the others observed Sam's rearrangement of his chair to communicate with her. Now Maria went back and revisited her chair work as a child. She was able to make the connection between how her mother had placed the blame on her for her father leaving them and how she blamed Sam's drinking for their problems. Having now made the connection that blame was a family pattern, Maria felt empowered to take her childhood chair out of her family of origin and place it across from Sam so that they could be face to face.

Facilitator: Sam and Maria, now that you have placed your chairs to face each other, I want the two of you to practice here in the session and as a homework assignment communicating with each other using "I" statements. The "I" statement is used to directly tell each other what you want or don't want. Sam, how do you want to address Maria about her being upset that you are still gone from the house even though you are attending AA meetings instead of going to bars?

Sam: Maria, I need to go to my meetings so I can stay sober.

Maria: I understand, but I feel you attend more meetings than you should.

Sam: You're starting to tell me what to do again.

Maria: I'm not. Instead of being with me, you go to more meetings.

Facilitator: John and Laura, what do you hear from them?

John: They're starting to get defensive with each other.

Laura: They're going back to using "you" statements.

Facilitator: I hear the two of you going back to blaming each other. Try again, using only "I" statements.

Maria: I understand you have to go to your AA meetings, but I need you to spend time with me and help at home.

Sam: You're right—I've been going to more meetings than I need. Because I fear a confrontation from you when we're alone. I feel you have not dealt with being angry towards me even though I've stopped drinking.

Facilitator: Before we stop for today, I want the four of you to begin to practice the "I" statements at home. Each of you take a chair and sit down facing each other to address the problems that may come up during the week. If either one resorts to going back to the "you" messages, or if things get heated, take a time-out to calm down. Then go back to the same chairs and practice again.

OUTCOMES AND CONCLUSION

Both couples went on to complete the necessary requirements for family reunification by attending all 12 weekly sessions. Each week they reported being sober and violence-free. In the weeks following the interventions just described, Sam and Maria opened up more to each other and to Laura and John, addressing issues that had come up during the week. When a member of a couple had a problem with his or her partner, he or she would go into the inner circle and invite his or her spouse to join in, and vice versa. Whoever had a problem would move his or her chair around in the circle to face his or her partner. Both Sam and Maria learned to practice new communication tools such as listening, fair fighting, and applying negotiation skills to the problem-solving process. In their last session, Sam and Maria shared with the group that they had learned to compromise. Sam agreed to move his recovery meetings from the evenings to the mornings so that he could spend time with Maria after work. Maria also agreed to go to Al-Anon meetings, to learn how to live with a recovering alcoholic.

REFERENCES

Bowen, M. (1978). *Family therapy in clinical practice.* Northvale, NJ: Aronson.

Deschner, J. (1984). *The hitting habit: Anger control for battering couples.* New York: Free Press.

Donner, J., & Gameson, A. (1968). Experience with multifamily, time limited, outpatient groups at a community psychiatric clinic. *Psychiatry, 31*(2), 126–137.

Johnson, M. P., & Ferraro, K. (2000). Research on domestic violence in the 1990s: Making distinctions. *Journal of Marriage and the Family, 57*, 283–294.

Laqueur, H. P. (1972). Mechanisms of change in multiple family therapy. In C. J. Sager & H. S. Kaplan (Eds.), *Progress in group & family therapy.* New York: Brunner/Mazel, 400–415.

Minuchin, S. (1974). *Families and family therapy.* Cambridge, MA: Harvard University Press.

Rubenfeld, S. (2001). Group therapy and complexity theory. *International Journal of Group Psychotherapy, 51*, 449–469.

QUESTIONS FOR REFLECTION AND DISCUSSION

1   When describing the incident for which Sam and Maria lost custody of Antonio, the author says that Sam "lost control" and slapped Maria, hard enough that she fell down and suffered a bruise. The author infers that the violence was "expressive" rather than "coercive," something that happened in the heat of an escalated argument rather than in an instrumental manner. Many would argue that in incidents of intimate partner abuse, no one "loses control." Do you agree or disagree? Give your reasons why or why not.

2   Compare the movable family-of-origin genogram to the more common genogram typically used by clinicians. What are the advantages of the movable genogram? Can you think of any disadvantages or ways in which it might be improperly used?

3 Because of the mutual violence between Sam and Maria, social services took Antonio out of their home and placed him temporarily in the custody of his grandmother. Considering the well-known adverse effects both of witnessing violence by one's parents and of being separated from one's parents, how appropriate was the decision to remove in this case? What other information, if any, would you need in order to decide?

4 How would you characterize Sam and Maria's respective adult attachment styles—secure, preoccupied, dismissing, or fearful? Describe how they may have contributed to the cycle of abuse in their families.

5 Do you think that Sam or Maria would have benefited from continued in-depth counseling after completing the 12 sessions of multigroup therapy? Would you have recommended individual work or more couples sessions? What would the focus of this work be with Sam? With Maria?

11

Co-Parenting Counseling With High-Conflict Parents in the Presence of Domestic Violence

K. KERSTIN GUTIERREZ

As a licensed clinical psychologist working in the forensic arena, I find that families and children utilize my services for a variety of needs, ranging from individual and couples therapy to court-ordered family and co-parenting counseling. In addition, I also conduct parent/child dyadic relationship coaching to assist young and inexperienced parents in improving their parenting skills of young children, and I perform court-ordered custody evaluations and parent/child reunification counseling.

My clinical approach to cases necessarily varies depending on the reasons for and the source of the referrals, as well as consideration of the particular issues involved. For example, a couple or a single parent seeking therapy to address family, individual, and parenting issues will usually require a different case formulation from parents who have been ordered to participate in a therapeutic process in light of allegations of domestic violence or substance abuse. Often the variability has to do with the degree of insight the patients are able to muster, but in some cases this is confounded by the actual historical events driving the court orders (such as court documentation or allegations or incidents of domestic violence, child abuse, or substance abuse, etc.).

My therapeutic orientation is derived from attachment and psychoanalytic theory, but I also use cognitive behavioral and other more directive techniques, especially in those cases where the patients demonstrate low insight or the need for more concrete and practical tools. It is not unusual for many of my patients to have histories involving abuse and other traumatic experiences necessitating interventions that address anxiety or other borderline related symptoms, such as the tendency to split and to be reactive, especially when there is a perceived threat of loss or the failure of an emotional connection driven by court-related outcomes. As a result, careful assessment and attention to building a good early rapport require forethought and a road map for treatment progress.

The difficult histories of many court-driven therapeutic processes require the practitioner to utilize sometimes extraordinary care during the assessment and formulation stages of treatment in order to avoid breaches of physical or mental health safety. Additionally, it is imperative that practitioners doing this work attend carefully to ethical constraints and protocols unique to the legal context, in which mental health practitioners often find themselves inadvertently providing services in multiple roles (Greenberg & Gould, 2003).

It is important, also, to begin careful assessment of the safety issues even prior to seeing or hearing from the clients themselves, often during the first contact with the attorneys. For example, knowing whether there are current or past restraining orders, past or current cases with child protective services, or involvement by either party in the legal system will allow the practitioner to utilize a therapeutic "frame" appropriate for the presenting issues, beginning with the first phone contact with the prospective client(s).

Additionally, especially in cases where intimate violence has been a factor, assessment sensitive to the subtleties of this area is critical. McCloskey and Grigsby (2005) note that even among mental health practitioners trained in the use of violence-assessment tools, the majority fail to accurately identify or assess levels of dangerousness in approximately half the cases. These authors caution that clinicians should be aware that psychological sequelae resulting from partner violence may "masquerade as many of the standard gendered diagnoses" (such as depressive, histrionic, or borderline symptoms in women), possibly causing the issue of intimate violence to remain invisible. Furthermore, it is important to keep in mind that the gender of the assessor may also skew the assessment of the domestic violence context, severity, and sequelae.

CASE STUDY: ALBERT FIGUEROA AND SHERRY ROSE

Albert and Sherry, the patients in the following case, were ordered by the court to participate in co-parenting counseling to address the needs of their children following a contentious divorce. The conflict between the parents was ongoing and seemed unlikely to resolve even after a recent expensive custody evaluation that presented information concerning both parents' psychological issues that promoted the conflict.

The court's referral was made, in part, because of its awareness that the children in this family (ages 5, 8, and 11) were experiencing symptoms of anxiety (poor school performance and increasingly poor social relationships) and that there had been a past report to Child and Family Services regarding the father's harsh discipline. There had been numerous restraining orders against the father during the marriage and none against the mother, and a recent restraining order against the father concerned his abusive parenting. The father was currently attending a batterer's treatment program and was engaged in supervised visitation with the children. It was the court's order that co-parenting counseling address those individual and conjoint issues that continued to undermine these parents' ability to effectively co-parent the three children.

Assessment

In a court-referred co-parenting counseling case such as this, a thorough assessment is obtained from a variety of sources, including phone contacts with the attorneys (to maintain neutrality, these phone contacts are conducted as conference calls) and a review of the court documents, in addition to meeting with the parents. In this case, a court order was requested and obtained through the attorneys, to provide documented clarification regarding the concerns of the court and the goals of the clients and their counsel.

An early conference call to both attorneys revealed that there had been prior restraining orders against the father, although none existed at the present time, and that there had been a report to child protective services regarding the father's parenting. The father was alleged to have pushed and hit the mother in an escalating pattern of violence during the relationship and to have repeatedly called her and the children derogatory names; additionally, he was reported to have engaged in corporal punishment of the children, using his belt and a wooden spoon to spank them; the children also complained that he had punished them by withholding food.

My usual protocol with separated couples is to meet with the two parents together for an initial meeting and then to meet with each one individually before resuming conjoint sessions. However, because of the history of parental and parenting violence and ongoing conflict in this family, I decided to interview each parent on the phone and then meet with each one alone prior to meeting them jointly, in order to obtain more information regarding the relative safety issues for each parent, as well as the personality organization of each parent and the relationship between the individual issues and those of the co-parenting relationship.

It is important to keep in mind that in many cases of reported domestic violence, the context within which the reported incident takes place is sometimes overlooked by professionals involved in developing treatment plans. In this case, although there were past restraining orders involving this father, it was crucial to maintain an awareness of the role of the contextual issues (namely, loss of his children, mutually destructive behaviors in the marriage, etc.) prior to drawing conclusions about the individuals involved.

Clinically, the goal of co-parenting counseling with these parents was to provide a neutral forum within which they could find common ground (namely, the goal of raising healthy children). To assume that the past restraining orders against the father captured and continued to capture the entire picture regarding domestic violence in this family would have precluded the potential of later revelations concerning Sherry and her parenting.

Nonetheless, based on the information indicating the existence of domestic violence allegations, each parent was asked specific questions over the phone prior to scheduling the first joint session, in order to assess for potential threats to both psychological and physical safety. Each parent was interviewed with regard to current safety (context and precaution) and presence of current violence and then in a more in-depth, individualized assessment. Also assessed were levels of fear and frustration in each of the parents in relation to one another, as well as their mutual perceptions of the other's parenting and their respective views of the children's reactions to and perception of their own and the other's parenting. Among the specific parenting questions asked were the following: "What kinds of situations seem to make it difficult to be the kind of parent you want to be?" "Describe an example of parenting during which you lost your temper? Used physical discipline?"

Albert's responses to these initial questions, prior to the establishment of a therapeutic rapport, were somewhat different from those he offered later during the therapy. During the initial screening process, he was defensive, suspicious, and dismissive, even over the phone. After the first individual assessment session, his demeanor was noticeably less defensive, and his willingness to acknowledge his own role in the family's dynamics increased markedly.

Obviously important to effective co-parenting is the ability of the two parents to be able to tolerate one another's presence in order to find ways to talk about and focus on the children. Prior to joint sessions, each parent must demonstrate the ability to self-regulate and to communicate and manage his or her own discomfort, and therefore it is necessary to assess each parent's internal resources related to self-control. Albert, as is not uncommon, initially felt he had moved past feeling triggered by Sherry; but this was clearly not the case, as was observed during the initial interview with him in which he clenched his jaw, flexed his fist, and jiggled his foot up and down as he recalled slights and disappointments during the marriage. Sherry, interestingly, had at first indicated she might find it difficult emotionally to be in the same room with Albert but said she did not feel unsafe. However, when we later met for our first joint session, she appeared at ease and more confrontational and provocative than she had initially seemed. She interrupted Albert, insisted on the correctness of her position in spite of a neutral reframe, and laughed derisively several times.

SESSIONS WITH ALBERT

Albert, a tall, good-looking, muscular man in his early 40s, with dark hair and eyes and white teeth, entered my office from the waiting room with a broad smile and a flourish of his arm as he commented, "This is a really nice place." He called me by my first name (without asking) and looked directly into my eyes as he shook my hand and held it a little too long. He was dressed well (silk shirt and Rolex watch) and sat on the sofa with his arms outstretched on the back of the sofa to either side, resting one foot on the other knee and smiling. My impression, at this point, was that he was feeling uneasy but was reluctant to acknowledge it, struggling for a sense of control by employing a calm and charming demeanor. After brief introductions, I invited him to tell me why he felt he had come to see me and what he hoped to get out of the co-parenting counseling process.

Albert initially used vague terms to describe himself and declared, with what appeared to be feigned enthusiasm, that for the past year he had been in therapy on a regular basis and that he felt he had been fortunate to find a therapist who had helped him begin to truly understand "what's going on in my head." He described himself as a "reader" and noted that he continued to explore books on raising children; he said he could now see how his own childhood had impacted his ability to be the kind of parent he wanted to be, and he acknowledged that his past behavior in the marriage had been physical and violent. He also offered several alternative interpretations of his physical and emotional behavior in the marriage. For example, he suggested that he had always felt he was more emotionally invested in the marriage than his wife, and he recalled that his wife seemed to discount his efforts to be romantic. He complained that when he made the effort to celebrate their anniversary with roses and a nice dinner out, she "just didn't seem to realize how important our relationship was to me." As he described the effort he had made in arranging the dinner and providing his wife with "an extraordinary" evening, he became teary. Albert viewed his own role in the relationship as altruistic and self-explanatory, justifying his own frustration and disappointment that inevitably led to his angry outbursts and feelings of being treated unfairly.

As he described his parenting, Albert found it difficult to take responsibility for the inappropriateness of his actions and justified kicking his then-6-year-old son in the crotch from behind as teaching "him to respect his father." When he described examples of parenting he considered "good," he frequently linked the basis for his reasoning to his need to "teach the child about his father's feelings; he needs to know I'm human too." Albert tended to minimize the impact on the children of his poor emotional control, but when I asked him how his children viewed him, he blew out a sigh and dropped his head. "I don't know . . . but they respect me."

I asked him if he had observed anything in their behavior that might indicate they are afraid of him. His head snapped up, and he fixed me with a challenging stare and paused. I held my breath, determined to wait for a response. He sighed again, dropped his eyes, and said, "Yeah, I think so."

Albert related his personal history in fits and starts, but after several therapeutic confrontations, he became more forthcoming. One confrontation occurred at the beginning of the second individual session, which followed the first joint session with the two parents. Albert glided into the clinical office, took off his shoes, and then asked me if I minded. I responded, "I don't object if that helps you feel more comfortable." I was aware that he needed to feel in control of the environment and of the relationship with me, but I felt I would need to brace myself for a boundary contest to come.

An opportunity came within a few minutes, as we were discussing Albert's childhood and his more recent drug use. His answers and comments pertaining to his childhood were laden with emotional content, causing him to tear up and clench his fists as he fought for self-control. But as we moved closer to his more recent and potentially current drug use, he became tense and evasive: His breathing rate increased, he began to fidget, and his eyes took on a piercing glare as he looked at me. His comments became shorter, and he had the look of a cornered animal. I took a deep breath and reflected back to him that I had noticed these outward physical changes and wondered if he could identify internal changes also. He appeared stunned for a moment and shook his head slowly, appearing ready to leap off the sofa. In as soft a voice as I could muster, given my own visceral feelings of defensiveness, I recalled that he had made an effort to make himself feel comfortable in the session by taking off his shoes; I asked if he felt comfortable now. He acknowledged that he did not and said with a forced smile, "I think you're trying to trick me into saying something I don't want to."

At this point, I reminded him that he had already acknowledged that he was engaging in this process in order to benefit his children; that he himself had noted with pride that in addition to his own reading, his therapy was equipping him with tools to manage the discomfort of such conversations; and that my interest in the topic of his drug use was not to punish but rather to help him find ways to understand himself. My rational approach held no sway with him. I breathed deeply to calm myself and wondered aloud if the drug use was embarrassing and shameful to him. At this point Albert again teared up, put his face in his hands, and choked out, "I'm not stupid—I know it's not healthy. I've tried to quit. I've even told my kids that whenever they see drugs, or any of the paraphernalia they've noticed around the house where I'm staying, to leave it alone and to tell me."

Over the course of the two individual interviews, Albert Figueroa cried when he recalled being beaten by his father and then his mother as a young child and when he described how frustrated he felt when trying to protect his younger siblings from his father's drunken temper by stepping in the middle. Albert left home at the age of 15. "I figured it was their problem. I couldn't fix what was wrong. But I've always felt guilty about leaving my brothers there with my parents." Albert turned to alcohol and drugs not only as a means of self-medication but also as a way to create a social support system for himself, through his meetings with dealers and other users. Although he described the abuse by his father as damaging, he sobbed deeply when he acknowledged that his mother, with a quick and unpredictable temper, always seemed more frightening to him and his siblings.

Mr. Figueroa recalled periods of deep depression during his adolescence and adulthood; the episodes were linked to sudden ruptures in his primary intimate relationships. With each successive lost relationship, the depressive episode was deeper and longer-lasting. Albert was able to acknowledge a sense of desperation and shame related to his emotional neediness during these times.

Significant rapport was established with Albert during the individual sessions. However, during the joint sessions with his ex-wife, Albert continued to demonstrate a reactive anger, toward either his ex-wife or me. His reactions included noticeable physical cues: clenched teeth and fists, twitching foot, abrupt standing and pacing, pulling on his cheek, and loud sighs. During these moments his ex-wife would freeze mid-sentence and watch him nervously.

Throughout the therapy, but to a diminishing degree, Albert presented with narcissistic symptoms such as poor empathy, hypervigilance to emotional threats, and poor emotional regulation. However, he also was at times able, after self-soothing or because of feeling contained by the therapeutic setting, to take in the importance of focusing on the children's needs rather than his own. One incidence of this occurred when Albert heard Sherry describe, in a self-righteous tone, how she had felt humiliated during the marriage when he called her "worthless fat bitch," "cow," and "rag" and when, after she returned from working up to 14 hours a day as a housecleaner, he derided her inability to get a "real" job. Albert commented with a sneer, "I could never do anything right, could I? And what about you!? Remember the time I tried to . . ." To circumvent a historical rundown of past wounds, I reminded both parents that at this point in time, both of them were making heroic efforts to do "the right thing" by focusing on their children. Albert took a deep breath and calmed down. "I now am beginning to see how to do that. Even though *she* may not see it."

As our conversation, both individually and in the conjoint sessions, began to address Albert's fears of losing contact with his children, Albert shared that he was worried that Sherry's primary motivation was to keep his children away from him and that he would never be able to prove that he could be a good parent. Sherry acknowledged that she had in the past found it difficult to encourage a relationship between the children and their father but that if he could continue to take responsibility for his own issues, she, at heart, wanted the children to be with their father more. Albert's stance softened noticeably, and he was able to tell Sherry that he still had warm feelings for her and felt confident that she was a good parent; he said he wanted her to feel confident in him as a parent too. Sherry turned directly toward Albert and said, "Then keep working at this, and don't assume I'm trying to do something bad to you. Stop reacting to me and look at the kids and what they need."

SESSIONS WITH SHERRY

Sherry Ross, although heavy, was an attractive, engaging woman in her mid-30s with a quick step and a sparkle in her eye. She was 9 months pregnant with the child of her current husband of one year. She seemed unpretentious, and her intelligence and quick sense of humor were self-deprecating. She laughed easily and seemed candid and emotionally open in her full descriptions of her difficult childhood as an adoptee. Although she was affable, toward the end of the interview, it became apparent that beneath her affability was a rigidity that seemed to interfere with her ability to see alternative points of view. At one point during the process of setting up appointments, she seemed to find it difficult to modulate her frustration when her own scheduling needs could not be met.

The question of her ability to sustain her personable demeanor in the face of thwarted self-needs arose early. She spoke quickly and in an integrated fashion, pointing out for me the pride she took in her capacity to be helpful and giving, as well as in her strong work ethic, noting that she did not mind helping Albert out financially in the early years of their relationship but that she became more and more disillusioned and resentful as the physical abuse increased, and his ability to contribute financially decreased.

During the individual interviews, Sherry described her childhood as "over as soon as I could get it behind me." She noted that she was able to withstand the pain of repeated physical and sexual abuse at the hands of her adopted father because "I was smart and knew it wouldn't last forever." Sherry Ross ran away from her adoptive home at the age of 16 to live with an aunt, who encouraged her to finish high school and apply to college. Sherry acknowledged that during her adolescent years, she was sexually promiscuous, but through her own therapy, she had been able to understand that much of her behavior was linked to the sexual abuse and lack of boundaries during her childhood. She noted, also, that therapy as a young adult helped her immeasurably, and then she chuckled that in spite of this she fell into the "wrong relationship with Albert." She acknowledged that the three children loved their father and that she was aware that he loved them, but because he still was unable to control his anger, the children were afraid of him. "If there's only one thing I hope to come out of this, it's that the children have a better relationship with him than I had." Sherry patted her large belly and said, "I want them to have what this little guy is going to have with his dad."

Sherry felt the early years of her relationship with Mr. Figueroa were "superficial" and "out of balance." "I was doing all the work, literally and emotionally. He wasn't holding onto his jobs; he was charming and possessive, but there wasn't a real bond there." Sherry, "always a hard worker," supported the two of them as a secretary and part-time waitress. "When I became pregnant, he became physical." Sherry recalled that she left Albert after he tried to kick her in the stomach when she was 6 months pregnant. "He managed to clock me in the head first, though—knocked me out. I went back, couldn't see raising the baby by myself. After the baby came, he seemed calmer—for a while. Then I got pregnant again, and this time things just got ugly . . . he started drinking again, and I had to save myself and the babies. So I left. Went back to my aunt's until after the second baby was born." Albert and Sherry reunited twice and tried couples counseling, and Albert found a job "he actually stuck with. He's still there. I didn't think he could do it."

After the third child was born, the family looked for a home to purchase, and Sherry returned to work. Within a couple of years, Albert's "drinking made him a mean drunk several times a week. I just couldn't see putting my kids—and me—through this anymore." After Sherry left the home with the children, Albert begged her to return and then threatened her if she chose not to. Sherry sought refuge in a women's shelter for 6 months, during which time the children did not see their father. After finding a job and establishing a home for herself and the children, Sherry filed for divorce, and the court ordered supervised visitation of the father's parenting time with the children. During the prior 18 months, Sherry had met and married a man a few years older than she, who was "close to the children and very gentle with them—and me."

Sherry worried that once the supervision was dropped, Albert's temper would pose a problem once again for the children. She did not feel that she herself was at risk now from his temper, but she felt the children might be at risk while with their father. "I'd like to be anywhere but here, frankly, but I'm here for my kids. I want things to get better for them."

CONJOINT SESSIONS

As most couples therapists know, what you see in the room when the two partners are together can be very different from what you see when each is alone. And in co-parenting counseling, the process is complicated by the fact that the patients do not wish to work together but are forced to be there in the name of their children. Their identities as parents and adults are clouded by the referral and by the pain of their mutual history. As a result, the therapist must maintain an awareness of psychological issues on several levels at once: issues related to the individuals' history and development; their attachment history as children and with their spouses; their abilities to parent and to function as adults in their own lives; and their internal resources available during times of stress.

When Sherry and Albert were together, the static in the air was palpable. Albert was tense and alert, speaking in clipped phrases. Sherry spoke in long-winded, self-justifying language with a note of whininess, or she would not speak at all. During the sessions, Sherry tended to use a self-righteous tone of voice, seeking alignment with me. At other times she would say nothing, seemingly withholding information in a judgmental, manipulative way. Albert complained that this current pattern of communication was "just like it always was and probably will be." He offered his opinions and then would look away when Sherry began to speak, appearing to visibly cringe and cover up. A sense of hopelessness was palpable as this ex-couple engaged with one another, reflecting their past patterns of failed communication.

The attachment deficits and abuse in the history of each parent alerted me to the importance of establishing firm but warm boundaries for the therapy. The primary goal of treatment was to help each of them to experience a sense of emotional and physical safety while in the therapeutic environment and to understand how their respective coping mechanisms continued to contribute to the derailing of their common goal of healthy co-parenting. The secondary goal was to help each of them develop empathy for the other, to understand how it was that the other parent might react to the parenting challenges and to the co-parenting relationship. This would involve helping each of them understand the internal and external sources of their frustration and anger when dealing with one another.

The practitioner needs to remain aware that the parenting relationship often manifests the unfulfilled primitive needs and intolerable feelings of painful exclusion and loss experienced by the individual in the past (MacDonald & Leary, 2005), feelings that are then projected onto the children and often onto the other parent. Co-parenting counseling is not couples counseling, but in order to be effective, it must lay the groundwork necessary to address, to some extent, past experiences of loss and anxiety (see Chemtob & Carlson, 2004) resulting from the abusive histories, as well as the deficits in attachment (Lyons-Ruth, 1996). Therapeutic goals for these parents included finding ways to provide a more nurturing sense of self in light of the conflict each experienced historically in the couple relationship and to help them find ways to consider the co-parenting relationship as a source of parenting security and predictability. This is usually a difficult task, in light of the past experiences with each other. But with a neutral third party, this is not impossible.

One critical moment in the therapy occurred when I commented on the underlying sadness and sense of loss and hurt both parents seemed to feel as they verbally shared their initial hopes and positive emotions regarding the birth of their first child. Albert sobbed as he acknowledged feeling "so proud of the fact that our son had such a warm and loving mother; so different from my own mother." Sherry looked at him directly, with tears in her eyes. "Why didn't you ever tell me that?" I reflected to the couple that relating to one another as healthy co-parents required that the two of them communicate their respective perceptions and needs about their own and each other's parenting—in order to provide appropriate parenting to their children. Joining with the couple in acknowledging the need for recognition of self in the parenting role allows the couple to understand that the parent-role of each can exist separately from the other roles they fulfill in their lives but that it will always exist, and in order to benefit their children, they will continue to need to be able to rely on their unique relationship as co-parents.

Important to formulating treatment goals in this case was research drawn from diverse sources, such as that involving the relationship between development of emotion regulation and harsh parenting (Chang, Schwartz, Dodge, & McBride-Chang, 2003), as well as anticipating the ability of each of the parents to be able to develop an observing ego (Beitman & Soth, 2006). Chang et al. (2003) explore the impact of harsh parenting, to which both of these parents were exposed as children, and these authors suggest that even if not "maltreatment," harsh parenting is significantly related to a child's ability to regulate his or her emotions. The impact of harsh parenting is mediated through the communication of affect, in that in addition to the behavioral *modeling* of emotional dysregulation by the parent, the parent's chaotic emotional state also essentially fails to modulate or contain the child's own emotion, a necessary neuropsychological function of healthy parenting. Without a mirroring function of emotional containment, the child seems to develop neurologically without the ability to regulate. Albert, more so than Sherry, was less able to regulate his own emotional state, which seems to point to his own experiences as a child exposed to ongoing abuse by both parents, who seemed to remain detached from their children and dysregulated when interacting with them. The couple work in this case also revealed that Sherry, in spite of her affable demeanor, had a tenuous hold on effective emotion regulation as well.

Susan Johnson (2004) notes that as a "process consultant," the therapist helps the patients reprocess their relationship experience and in so doing helps them gain new insight regarding how each "self" becomes involved in the dynamic. Furthermore, slowing down the process assists the therapist, in my experience, in helping the patients begin to understand the subtle aspects of their own identities as parents in addition to individuals. It is often necessary for the individuals in co-parenting counseling to be referred to individual counseling to address the existential and identity issues that emerge as a result of uncovering the residual developmental and childhood issues currently impacting their lives as co-parents.

INTERVIEWS WITH THE CHILDREN

Most important to helping this particular couple move toward a healthier and more effective co-parenting relationship was information having to do with the phenomenological experience of their children. Interviews with children are invaluable as a means to ascertain the felt sense of being in the family. Initially, most parents are uncomfortable with the prospect of exposing the children to this type of professional inquiry, but it never ceases to provide useful emotional and psychological information for the adults trying to figure out what their children need and how these parents might provide it.

The oldest child, Alicia, although only in fifth grade, was experiencing some difficulty with her peers. She was described by her teacher as having a "superior attitude" that was off-putting to other children her age. Based on my interview with her, it was my opinion that she had developed a means of controlling her emotions by denying their existence and by remaining emotionally aloof. Additionally, Alicia had adopted a parental role toward each of her parents as well as her siblings. Although both parents described her as "older than her years," there was a brittle aspect to her, most notable when she declared, "I just want to hurry up and get through school." She acknowledged that she felt different from other kids and that she did not really feel she could talk easily to anyone. This pseudo-maturity merits concern regarding the ability of the child to effectively navigate appropriate developmental challenges; in such circumstances the child often is forced to forgo her own needs in order to meet the overwhelming needs of the parent or parents.

The youngest child, Jeremy, was doing well enough in kindergarten and seemed to rely emotionally on his oldest sister, deferring to her opinions and statements. Both parents described Jeremy as "no trouble." It seemed possible that he might have come through his early childhood relatively unexposed to the level of tension and violence the other two had experienced. An alternative hypothesis was that he had managed to learn how to fly under the radar and that his needs had not yet emerged.

Bart, the middle child, was described as oppositional by his teachers, and although he seemed able to manage the academic demands of school, he had difficulty making friends because he often would yell and throw things when he did not get his way; he would then cry and withdraw and be inconsolable. A particularly revealing statement regarding his view of his parents was his comment describing his family drawing: "my dad only sleeps or yells; my mom only cooks, works, and yells." And in a whisper, looking down at a black drawing of five small figures without features, he said, "and then they hit someone."

The interviews with the children in this case revealed that Sherry's perceptions were accurate. The children were hesitant to anger their father, and they viewed him as unpredictable and unable to "know" them as children; the middle child, a boy, acknowledged that his stomach often churned and hurt when he was with his father because he did not know exactly how to appease him. (When Albert learned of this, he cried.) All three children recalled feeling fearful as they watched their mother throw things and their father yell and threaten and push their mother to the ground; the oldest child, in particular, was articulate in noting that the "all tingly and scared" feeling she experienced "when they fought" sometimes happened currently when her parents were simply exchanging the children on a weekly basis and found themselves in the same time and place. The ongoing impact on children of witnessing past domestic violence has been well documented and researched by Chemtob and Carlson (2004), who note that children often exhibit symptoms of dissociation, depression, irritability, and poor concentration long after their exposure to the violence has ended.

Interestingly, and unexpectedly, the children also revealed that they were more than a little afraid of their mother as well. This information was at first difficult for Sherry to take in, but it was critical in helping this couple find some common ground toward becoming the kind of parents they wanted to be. Albert was also surprised to hear this about the children but gradually was able to provide instances from his own experience of Sherry's reactivity and irritability that contributed not insignificantly to the level of violence between these two adults, as well as harsh or reactive parenting toward the children.

O'Leary and Slep (2006) note that in their examination of partner incidents involving physical aggression, their research suggests that in many cases where women are the first to escalate a conflict through the use of physical aggression, "this escalation may disinhibit men's physical aggression and contribute to the risk of fear or injury from their partners' violence that women face." It was a clinical turning point in the therapy when Albert realized that he was not perceived as just the embodiment of the label "aggressor" (and Sherry the "victim"), but instead could begin to see that the dynamic between them, to which they both contributed, was rife with points of mutual escalation. Based on information provided by the children to me regarding their own anxiety related to their parents' discipline, Sherry divulged that she imagined she "might have a problem with emotional control too." The children had shared with me that although they had often been afraid that their father might hurt their mother, they could "tell when Mommy was upset and was going to make Daddy mad too, usually by laughing at him or yelling at him." I also related to the parents something Bart had told me: "One time my mommy even threw a glass at my daddy, and then she started hitting him; he was just sitting at the table. I don't know why she did that; I hope she doesn't throw anything at me sometime."

Alicia attempted to minimize her mother's emotional reactivity by adopting Ms. Ross's perspective regarding Albert: "My dad can be so childish; that's why my mom gets so upset." Part of the treatment involved identifying the impact on the children of this mother's too-open evaluative comments regarding the father, as well as how her reactivity toward him may undermine her own relationship with the children in the long run. As Albert observed the therapeutic work unfolding with Sherry concerning her own parenting, he began to take on more psychological responsibility for his own parenting. In this way, although both parents' histories contained abuse and attachment issues, the more integrated and sturdy ego of Sherry allowed for some good therapeutic interventions to begin as a foundation to later, deeper work with Albert.

The tension between these two parents began to diminish as the therapeutic focus shifted from blame to forgiveness of each other and then to a felt collaboration between them as they acknowledged their mutual hope of helping one another become better parents for their children. The identity work, as well as the attachment issues underlying their own ability to relate to one another and their children, became the foundation on which the more nuts-and-bolts problem solving could be accomplished: how to communicate with one another about the children's schedules, who would make the decisions about the extracurricular activities, who would help with which homework, how the two parents would discuss ear piercing and summer sleepovers.

OUTCOMES AND CONCLUSION

The co-parenting work, although utilizing information from the children's perspective, did not address the children's needs to find ways to recover from the abusive parenting they had experienced or their recovery from the issues raised by the separation and the divorce and the high-conflict relationship between their parents. Additional referrals were made for each of the children to participate for at least a year in individual therapy with a licensed practitioner whose expertise is in treating children impacted by high-conflict parenting and divorce. (I generally refer each child to a separate therapist to ensure that the children are able to experience the solidity of boundaries over which they have control. However, in this case, scheduling and financial considerations dictated that two of the children would need to see the same therapist. The children were therefore referred to one practitioner.)

Chang et al. (2003) note that the impact of harsh parenting has more deleterious effects than previously thought on the child's neurological ability to emotionally self-regulate and contributes to the child's difficulties in managing peer relationships through pathways other than behavioral modeling. Levendosky, Leahy, Bogat, Davidson, and von Eye (2006) suggest that maternal parenting (when the mother's poor parenting is a result of depression and emotional disorganization and mental health) may pose more significant risk in terms of the child's potential for externalizing behavior and the ability to emotionally regulate, especially when there is domestic violence in the home. In this case, Sherry's parenting seemed to be warm and supportive, following separation from Albert. But while she was in the relationship with Albert, her parenting could be characterized as distracted and emotionally unpredictable from the children's points of view.

It seemed clear from the co-parenting counseling sessions, as well as the children's reports, that Sherry's parenting role was not the role she felt to be primary. Instead, according to her own description, "I was consumed with trying to find a way to make him happy, to keep him calm, to bring in enough money. I couldn't even think about who I was or about how I was doing." Levendosky et al. (2006) suggest that interventions targeting the mother's mental health are critical to the mental health of the children, with the "goals of this therapy . . . for the mother to learn to understand her responses and feelings toward the infant in the context of the Domestic Violence, as well as to understand how her own behaviors may be aversive to the child. Treatment helps the mother understand and empathize with her child's behavior problems (in particular aggression) in the context of the DV" (Levendosky et al., 2006).

Katz and Windecker-Nelson (2006), as well as Lindquist, Barrett, Bliss-Moreau, and Russell (2006), point to the ways that the child's emotional regulation and adjustment are mediated by language, domestic violence, and emotion coaching. The child's ability to regulate emotion also appears to be linked to the ways both parents, but especially mothers, assist the child's developing language skills and how the parents' emotional expressivity affects the children's ability to demonstrate or respond with empathy (Valiente et al., 2004). According to these authors, both language skill level and empathy appear to be linked to whether the parents' expressivity is positive (laughing, praising, etc.) or negative (angry, contemptuous, threatening). The child's ability to display and respond to sympathy seems to be linked to positive expressivity, whereas the child's expression of distress and low empathy seems linked to negative expressivity of the parents (Valiente et al., 2004). Lindquist et al. suggest that emotion language influences emotion perception—namely, that the way parents use language is related to the shaping and accessibility of emotion and words depicting emotion in the children and that this in turn has an effect on the children's ability to perceive emotion in another's face.

This family, similar to others for whom co-parenting counseling is appropriate, needed help in restoring a vision of itself as "still a family." The parents, in spite of their long history of mutual deficits in emotional control and empathy, were able to marshal their respective good intentions, to share and support one another's varying ego strengths, and to find ways to restore a sense of dignity to their respective roles as parents. The history of violence and abuse in this family was seen as a manifestation of long-standing attachment and ego deficits, but not as necessarily static. In fact, probably the most important therapeutic intervention in cases such as this occurs when the parents can begin to visualize a sense of hopefulness regarding their own and their children's futures. The children's needs, much as the parents' own ongoing and unresolved developmental issues, were recognized as warranting additional interventions as well (it should be noted, however, that in most cases of high-conflict parenting, the approach most effective in helping children is that which addresses the co-parenting issues).

REFERENCES

Beitman, B. D., & Soth, A. M. (2006). Activation of self-observation: A core process among the psychotherapies. *Journal of Psychotherapy Integration, 16*(4), 383–397.

Chang, L., Schwartz, D., Dodge, K. A., & McBride-Chang, C. (2003). Harsh parenting in relation to child emotion regulation and aggression. *Journal of Family Psychology, 17*(4), 598–606.

Chemtob, C. M., & Carlson, J. G. (2004). Psychological effects of domestic violence on children and their mothers. *International Journal of Stress Management, 11*(3), 209–226.

Greenberg, L. R., & Gould, J. W. (2003). The treating expert: A hybrid role with firm boundaries. *Professional Psychology: Research and Practice, 32*(5), 469–478.

Johnson, S. M. (2004). *The practice of emotionally focused couple therapy.* New York: Brunner-Routledge.

Katz, L. F., & Windecker-Nelson, B. (2006). Domestic violence, emotion coaching, and child adjustment. *Journal of Family Psychology, 20*(1), 56–67.

Levendosky, A. A., Leahy, K., Bogat, A., Davidson, W. S., & von Eye, A. (2006). Domestic violence, maternal parenting, maternal mental health, and infant externalizing behavior. *Journal of Family Psychology, 20*(4), 544–552.

Lindquist, K. A., Barrett, L. F., Bliss-Moreau, E., & Russell, J. A. (2006). Language and the perception of emotion. *Emotion, 6*(1), 125–138.

Lyons-Ruth, K. (1996). Attachment relationships among children with aggressive behavior problems: The role of disorganized early attachment patterns. *Journal of Consulting and Clinical Psychology, 64*(1), 64–73.

MacDonald, G., & Leary, M. R. (2005). Why does social exclusion hurt? The relationship between social and physical pain. *Psychological Bulletin, 131*(2), 202–223.

McCloskey, K., & Grigsby, N. (2005). The ubiquitous clinical problem of adult intimate partner violence: The need for routine assessment. *Professional Psychology: Research and Practice, 36*(3), 264–275.

O'Leary, S. G., & Slep, A. M. S. (2006). Precipitants of partner aggression. *Journal of Family Psychology, 20*(2), 344–347.

Valiente, C., Eisenberg, N., Fabes, R. A., Shepard, S. A., Cumberland, A., & Losoya, S. H. (2004). Prediction of children's empathy-related responding from their effortful control and parents' expressivity. *Developmental Psychology, 40*(6), 911–926.

QUESTIONS FOR REFLECTION AND DISCUSSION

1   In conducting co-parenting counseling, the therapist's goals are mostly of a practical nature, primarily to help the parents set aside their past differences and negotiate an agreement on how to make the right decisions for their children. To do this, it is essential that the therapist help foster a working alliance between the parents. How successful would the author have been in building such an alliance with Mr. Figueroa and Ms. Ross had she not helped "each of them understand the internal and external sources of their frustration and anger when dealing with one another"? How important was the therapist's understanding of their respective abuse histories and their impact on their current relationship?

How did the therapist go about helping the parents build a working alliance? What role did the therapist's understanding of the parents' respective abuse histories play in the counseling process?

2   When Mr. Figueroa began the co-parenting sessions, he appeared guarded, tended to blame his ex for his own shortcomings, and exhibited little insight into the nature of his abusive behavior. What aspects of the counseling process as described contributed to Albert's progress toward taking responsibility for

his actions? By the end of the sessions, he had made considerable progress toward taking full responsibility for his actions. Do you think that the therapist's evenhanded and systemic approach, and willingness to also address Ms. Ross's contributions to the abuse dynamics, helped or hindered his progress?

3 What procedures were followed to maximize victim safety? How well did they work in this case?

4 As this case clearly illustrates, children who witness high conflict and abuse between their parents are affected in many ways. According to the author, "the child often is forced to forgo her own needs in order to meet the overwhelming needs of the parent or parents." Who, in this family, might have been thus affected?

12

Multimodal Treatment: The Wyman Family

CATHERINE LIEB

"What do you want from me?" David Wyman asked his wife, Cynthia, in a tone both pleading and exasperated.

"I'm not going to tell you," she responded firmly. They stared at each other and then turned to look at me.

I knew refereeing this stalemate would not help. This was not the first time I had scrambled to stay balanced while I witnessed David asking, "What do you want?" and Cynthia refusing to answer. When I first met this couple, David was the one most easily identified as having an anger problem. He was often rigid and irritable and yelled at his wife and children. As the therapy unfolded, however, Cynthia's cool rage became the biggest obstacle to progress.

This session occurred during the third attempt at couples therapy in the course of the Wymans' family treatment. Cynthia initially called our family counseling agency almost 4 years before to request therapy for her children. They had recently completed a sexual abuse counseling program at another agency where perpetrators were treated separately from the victims and the rest of the family. Robert, her oldest son, who was now age 17, had molested his two younger siblings. According to his mother, he was a "star participant" in the offenders' program, but she doubted that he had gotten much out of it. The other two children, Zack, age 14, and Emily, age 12, had participated in some sessions with a "victims' counselor" where Emily denied any abuse and Zack "didn't say much." The mother stated that she was concerned that her children would have long-term problems if they did not receive additional treatment.

As the clinical supervisor of our family counseling agency, I explained to Cynthia that we provided an integrated family therapy program that did not segregate victims from offenders. Our protocol started with individual assessments for each family member, after which we would discuss the risks, appropriateness, and timing of family therapy sessions. We would request releases to communicate with the children's teachers and other professionals who were helping the family. She told me that finances were very tight, and she needed to use their state victim-of-crime compensation benefits. There was no funding for Robert beyond the offender program he had already completed. After the sessions from victim compensation ran out, she thought we could use funding for counseling through Zack's school district. He had met the criteria for severely emotionally disturbed (SED) children and had been in special education classes for years. He seemed to have above-average intelligence, but his academic performance was very poor largely because of not completing assignments. His behavior was not disruptive at school, but he was socially and emotionally withdrawn from peers and was often perceived as intrusive or weird. I was used to dealing with insurance programs that structured payment around individual victims or pathology, so I offered a strategy for doing the family therapy as an adjunctive service as long as we had an "identified patient." It is hardly ideal for family therapists to form coalitions with insurance providers to single out individual family members as the problem, but this is often what we have to do to use insurance benefits. Cynthia proceeded to set up appointments for Zack, Emily, her husband, and herself.

ASSESSMENT

After everyone was established with an individual therapist, I scheduled a consultation for the four clinicians to pool their assessment information, discuss risk factors, and develop a treatment plan. Neither of the victims had spoken to anyone about the molestation until 3 years after it had occurred, when Zack, the middle child, told a friend at school, who told a school counselor. A sexual abuse report was made to Child Protective Services, and the police showed up at the Wymans' house unannounced to interview everyone in the family. Robert admitted that he had fondled his siblings, and he was taken away to juvenile hall. Two weeks later, he was mandated to live away from home for a year and to participate in a mandatory offenders program. A family friend agreed to have him live with his family. At the time of our assessment, Robert had recently returned home.

Emily's therapist expressed concern that she and Zack might still be at risk for sexual exploitation. Emily, a shy, dark-haired 12-year-old, eventually acknowledged that her brother had molested her, but she did not want to talk about it further. Robert was her favorite brother, and she felt partly responsible for what had happened. Emily's therapist feared that her guilt and avoidance increased her risk for being victimized again, and she wanted to know if the parents were taking responsibility for keeping her safe. Zack's therapist had similar concerns but a lot less information. Zack, gangly and withdrawn, wanted his mother with him in sessions and was saying as little as possible.

Cynthia's therapist went next. Although it was not mentioned as a presenting problem, Cynthia revealed that since they first married, her husband had been very critical of her and yelled at her "every day." In one incident several years ago, his anger had escalated to hitting her. She stated that neither of them hit their children, but her husband would yell at Zack for up to an hour over issues such as not doing his homework. Zack also had anger problems, and Cynthia was his primary target. He would verbally attack her, shouting things such as, "Stop controlling my life!" His weird, uncooperative behavior alienated him from his siblings and peers. Emily was embarrassed to be around him at school. Robert teased him mercilessly, often getting Emily to join in. How the family dealt with anger and power was not addressed in the previous therapy in part because of the limitations of treatment organized around the offender/victim dichotomy but also because the family did not want to volunteer this information for fear of more intrusion from the criminal justice system. How power was used to dominate others would be incorporated into the family's treatment plan.

The therapist assigned to David reported that he knew he had an anger problem and was working on it, but Cynthia still felt intimidated by him. His anger management problems were compounded 4 years before when he developed a potentially fatal neurological disease. During the first year of his illness, he was in and out of the hospital several times and was taking a medication that made him very irritable, exacerbating his angry outbursts when others did not do what he told them to do. For 3 years after that, he was not able to return to work as a computer program analyst, so his wife went back to work full-time as a hospital pediatric social worker. He stayed home as the children's primary caretaker, a job he was willing to do but at which he did not feel very skilled. He eventually was able to stop the medication that made him so irritable and had recently returned to work. Cynthia had resumed her role as the stay-at-home parent, working as a part-time consultant from her desk in a hallway.

In the family dynamic, Zack easily stood out as the "identified patient," but everyone else had psychiatric diagnoses and were on psychotropic medications as well. The mom took medication for depression, the dad for depression and attention deficit disorder (ADD). Emily was on medication for separation anxiety. She did not want to participate in social activities with peers and often stayed home from school because of stomachaches or other somatic complaints. Zack, who had cleverly defeated a psychologist's effort to measure his IQ, was presumed to be very bright but had chronic academic and social problems. He had taken medications for many years for various diagnoses, including ADD, pervasive developmental disorder, bipolar disorder, and Tourette's. The mother's description of her firstborn, Robert, was echoed by the other family members: He was charismatic and was a "good kid" and good athlete with lots of friends. He did well in school, especially since starting medication for ADD in middle school.

Genogram

We sketched out a genogram. This White, middle-class family had no history of substance abuse or other physical or sexual abuse. Cynthia and David's families of origin were pretty traditional two-parent households with three children each. The only thing that stood out was that Cynthia's biological father was unknown. She was conceived when her mother was in her late teens. Her mother briefly married the father, divorced him, and moved back home with her parents. After her parents refused to take care of her baby so that she could take a job that involved traveling, she settled into marriage at age 21 with another man, who adopted Cynthia. They had two more children, a daughter and a son. Cynthia stated that the family never talked about her mother's first marriage; in fact she was not even sure whether it was a legal marriage. She was remarkably incurious, shrugging off further questions by stating that her stepfather was the only father she knew or cared about.

From a family systems point of view, some interesting hypotheses began to take shape. The molestation was clearly a self-centered, exploitive act by the prepubescent oldest child. But was it also a cry for help for a family in distress? Could Emily's anxious attachment to her mom and Zack's "pathologic" behavior function to distract the family from the parents' marital problems and protect the family from divorce? Would the couple's issues devolve into a crisis if the children were more successful, individuating, and moving along developmentally? Although there appeared to be a low risk of physical violence reoccurring, there certainly were problematic patterns of dominance in a rigid system of hierarchies: dad over mom, Robert manipulating his younger siblings, Robert and Emily ganging up on Zack, and Zack teeter-tottering between the passive victim and an angry tyrant who made it nearly impossible for the family to enjoy activities together.

Some elements of traditional, patriarchal family organization appeared to be valued in this family, especially by Cynthia, who had recently joined a fundamentalist religious community and was trying to get everyone more involved with her. Her projection of an ideal, all-knowing, all-powerful but caring father-god was confusing for David. She wanted him to be a strong father figure but also wanted him to respect her opinions. She was profoundly disappointed by his limitations, and she was very critical of him. David was comfortable with being in charge but felt undermined when Cynthia did not go along with what he thought was best. On a less conscious level, he seemed overburdened by family responsibilities, especially since his illness. Ironically, they both started their marriage thinking that they wanted a more collaborative, modern marriage that was not tied to traditional gender roles. Over the years, however, they said they had shifted to wanting more traditional marital roles and family structure.

There were other problematic polarities. Robert appeared to be operating in a narcissistic pattern of being both the charismatic first-born son whom everyone loved and the bad boy who used others, including sexually exploiting his younger siblings, to get what he wanted. Cynthia's history included an element of children being both a landmark in a woman's development and an impediment for a happy and successful adulthood. Her mother's pregnancy "out of wedlock" had created a crisis that had prevented her from exploring the world in her early adulthood as she had wanted. Her mother resolved this by marrying again and having a successful career later in real estate, but she remained hostile toward Cynthia. Cynthia entered motherhood in her early 30s after traveling, partying, and working at what she called "not very adult jobs." She and David were both very clear about wanting a family, and she got pregnant within the first year of their marriage. But her firstborn was difficult to soothe, and she had difficulty breastfeeding. When she turned to her mother for help, her mother scolded and criticized her. David tried to help with the baby and be emotionally supportive, but he was focused on getting his career going. Although they agreed that he did better than his father's generation, he never felt like he was good enough for Cynthia, and Cynthia became increasingly resentful. After the birth of their second child, Zack, Cynthia sank into postpartum depression, which did not lift until 2 years later, after Emily was born.

TREATMENT GOALS AND TREATMENT PLAN

We could not fully assess the family system until we saw everyone together, but the treatment team agreed that it was too early to start family sessions. We needed more information to assess the risk factors and more time for the family, especially for Zack and Emily, to feel safe with the therapeutic process. I shifted from being the clinical consultant to the lead family therapist as we proceeded to mix and match individual sessions with sessions for different family subsystems (Freeman, 1992). We scheduled sibling sessions for Zack and Emily, hoping that they would move a little out of their developmentally immature dependence on their mother and into a more collaborative sibling relationship. Zack was the one who had triggered the sexual abuse report. He could benefit from experiencing himself as a "big brother," as a resource instead of as the primary consumer of the family's attention. Perhaps Emily could learn from Zack to be more assertive about the molestation.

Couple Sessions: David and Cynthia

I began to work with David and Cynthia in couple sessions. Increasing empathy and communication seemed essential to ensure a healing environment for the work in the family sessions. Two years after intake, David was controlling his anger better, but he was frustrated because his wife remained distant and rejecting. He attributed his success to self-control, taking antidepressant medication, and backing off to let Cynthia be in charge. Cynthia insisted that keeping her distance was necessary because his temper continued to flare up even if it was not as often. She stated how helpful it was for her to have her individual therapist, who had previous experience in a domestic violence program, tell her that her husband's behavior was emotionally and physically abusive. It was such a relief for her to know that she was a victim, which meant that the problems in her family were not all her fault.

Cynthia was getting increasingly more assertive in talking about the things David had done to hurt her, including watching pornographic videos. David stated that he had not done this in a long time, and he rationalized that pornography is something that men are naturally drawn to, especially when their wives cut them off sexually. It was less damaging than having an affair. This was a spot where I could easily have been drawn into a triangle, taking sides on the issue of pornography. It might have been useful at some point in the couples therapy to explore how pornography portrays exploitative relational patterns and functions to regulate emotional distance, but at this point I chose not to comment. David asked Cynthia directly if she blamed him for the molestation. She answered, "Yes."

The distance and aggression in Cynthia and David's relationship was complementary. She withheld, blamed, and was covertly hostile; he was overtly angry, critical, and sarcastic. In spite of our lack of progress, Cynthia and David clearly stated that they were not considering divorce. The only glue that seemed to be keeping them together was their strong commitment to family, but even this was a bone of contention. Cynthia complained in a tone that conveyed hopelessness about their nuclear family that David's family was not as "close" as hers. Even though David was very involved with caring for his elderly parents, she perceived him and his two sisters as very individualistic. In contrast, Cynthia spoke fondly of her family's togetherness, especially with regard to the extended family gatherings at her parents' beach house. That her family's solidarity was enforced by her mother's harsh criticism and control did not diminish its value in Cynthia's eyes.

In spite of the lack of progress in the couple sessions, the clinical team agreed to move forward with the family sessions on the strength of the parents' commitment to help their children. There was some behavioral progress—for example, David's anger was breaking through into behavior less often, and they were talking to each other more about their concerns for the family—but lack of progress on the deeper, unresolved issues that we had identified suggested that the family would regress without ongoing therapeutic support. Perhaps the family sessions would spark more sustainable, second-order change in a way that the individual and couple sessions had failed to do.

We decided to structure the family sessions around Robert making an apology for the molestation, a strategy derived from the concept of healing through confession, repentance, and restitution (Herman, 1997, p. 190). This structure was consistent with the presenting problem and was designed to help everyone feel a little safer around what to expect in the family sessions. We knew that the real work would occur in a more spontaneous process, but structure provides a safe container in which deeper emotional experiences can occur. The molestation narrative would serve as the jumping-off place from which we could address roles, attachment patterns, and how coercive power was exercised in the family. We would not assume that this was the most traumatic thing that had happened, but this was clearly the trauma that the family recognized and wanted to address. I would take the lead in the family sessions, with Zack and Emily's therapists alternating as co-therapist. It was important to have two therapists to keep track of what was going on, to stay balanced and avoid emotional triangles as much as possible, to model collaborative interactions, and to nurture more secure attachments among family members. It was also essential to have ongoing consultation to help the clinicians with their own feelings as they joined the tumultuous world of a troubled family.

Individual Sessions: Robert

It was time for Robert to come in for the couple of individual sessions that I thought we could justify with the insurance provider to prepare for the family sessions. Athletic and handsome, he was just as engaging as the family had described him to be. We quickly moved from getting acquainted and from me introducing him to our method of working with families to speaking about the molestation and his role as a healing agent. I asked him to tell me what had happened and what had stopped it, first in an individual session and then in a session with his parents. He stated that the molestation was primarily sexual exploration, and he stopped on his own because he realized it was wrong and harmful. It occurred four or five times while he was in middle school, when he was having lots of difficulty adjusting to a new school, the family had just moved to a new house where the three children shared a bedroom, and their dad was very sick. According to him, he did not coerce his siblings. I talked to him about how sexual exploitation is often about power over more vulnerable people. Perhaps he felt powerless over what was happening to him at school and at home, and the molestation was a way to compensate? He said his other therapist had brought this up in his offenders group, and at the time he went along with it, but he really did not think this applied to him. Given his history of telling therapists what they wanted to hear, I decided to validate and thank him for his candor rather than pursue my hypothesis about power.

Robert readily agreed to the family therapy plan, welcoming the opportunity to express his remorse to everyone. He said that he had already apologized to his brother and sister, but he doubted that they remembered it. I consulted with Emily and Zack's therapists. In order for Robert to make repentance, it would be helpful for them to speak about how he had hurt them, but they still were not willing to open up about the molestation. At least they did not object to hearing what Robert had to say. This was very important assessment information in preparation for the family sessions. It was the family therapists' job to first do no harm. When it comes to trauma, memories should not be explored in any detail until the client has demonstrated the ability to manage the emotional and body sensations that go with the telling (Rothschild, 2000). We would keep any remembering that came up in the family sessions limited and matter-of-fact to keep it safe.

Family Sessions

We started the family sessions focusing our interventions more on process than content: coaching communication skills, reinforcing David's involvement and encouraging Cynthia to be less intensely involved, and working with anything that came up to strengthen the parental and sibling subsystems. Usually in domestic violence cases, it is helpful to open up the family's boundaries to outside support. In this case, however, it was helpful for the family to turn inward in certain ways. They were underdeveloped in their ability to turn toward each other for help and seemed hampered by too much outside influence, especially Cynthia, who used selective comments or opinions of mental health professionals to avoid talking about her own experience and to blame her husband. Psychiatric labels were used frequently to explain behavior and fuel hopelessness. We repeatedly reframed problems from a family systems point of view while emphasizing that the more everyone took responsibility for his or her part, the more optimal the outcome. In the process we tired to reinforce the parents' roles as leaders and authority without promoting an authoritarian power structure.

The biggest surprise of the first few family sessions was that Zack, the "identified patient," articulately took the lead. He initiated conversation about fighting with his parents over chores and schoolwork and complained about his siblings picking on him. He even made a comment about how his role as the scapegoat in the family matched his mother's role in her family of origin given that grandpa was not her "real dad." Robert and Emily and their dad agreed. Cynthia chose not to join in with this family observation. The second surprise was that the children had much more to say about their mother's anger than their father's. They complained about her yelling at them about chores and demanding that they tell her about what was going on at school.

After several family sessions, there was less interrupting, more empathic listening, and some small problem-solving successes. The family appeared ready to deal with the molestation. We started with a process of developing a collective narrative of what had happened. As each family member told what he or she remembered, starting with the Child Protective Services report, our goal was to develop a shared family memory by having each member tell his or her version of the story while the others were supportive witnesses. In clinical terms this was creating a more functional family myth (Minuchin & Fishman, 1981) while balancing the family functions of nurturing individual autonomy and family solidarity (Freeman, 1992). We carefully avoided going too deep around the details of the trauma itself, knowing that this was beyond the scope of what we could reasonably accomplish.

Robert's amends were sincere and well received. Emily took a big step forward by telling Robert, as her family supportively witnessed, that what he had done was wrong, and she was glad that he had been taken to juvenile hall. Zack said that he was glad that the truth had come out, even though he did not like that his friend had betrayed his confidence to the school counselor. His tone was matter-of-fact without the victimization he usually expressed. Throughout the four sessions that focused on this content, David tended to be much more emotionally available than Cynthia, tearing up several times and making supportive comments to his children.

Changing Family Dynamics

As the therapy shifted to other content, the therapists addressed the scapegoat issue by trying to nurture Zack's shift toward a more active, developmentally mature role and focusing on anything but him as the problem. The family dynamic began to shift as Zack made positive contributions in the form of ideas to solve problems and provided support to others by making humorous statements. In turn, his family changed toward him. Robert made a special effort to stop picking on him and to include him in his activities (a form of restitution). This fit well with Robert's developmental task of developing more empathy and more genuine expressions of self in lieu of the hero/bad boy role he had learned to play. We encouraged Emily to speak up more to nudge her along in her individuation process and to shift her from her anxious attachment to her mother to more secure attachments among all her family members. Everyone appeared to be making progress except Cynthia. A session focusing on their aging dog, Cookie, one of several pets in the family and a favorite of hers, provides a good example.

At the beginning of the session, Zack autocratically announced that it was time to put Cookie down. She was too old, was suffering, and required too much work. Robert quickly aligned himself with Zack's solution but with an empathic comment about how this was not what Emily or their mom wanted. David chimed in that putting Cookie down would be hardest on Cynthia and Emily, but he sadly added that getting up in the middle of the night to let Cookie out was taking a toll on his ability to work the next day. The therapist used the softer tone of David's comment to coax more emotional material into the conversation. Emily expressed ambivalence. She hated the thought of losing the dog but feared she was suffering too much. A discussion ensued about the quality of Cookie's life. They wondered, how did the dog feel about her declining health? Up to this point, Cynthia had not joined in the conversation. Robert brought her in by indirectly speaking for her.

"I know that Mom thinks Cookie still enjoys life, but she's way too much work."

Cynthia responded with a tease about how he and his brother just wanted to get out of their chore of bathing her. Then she chided Zack about his reluctance to shower.

Zack's anger quickly escalated. Raising his voice, he said, "I'm tired of everyone getting on me about showers. I've taken a shower every day for the last 12 years!"

Cynthia calmly and logically began to probe the probability of anyone showering every day for 12 years.

It was evident that Zack's reactivity served to divert attention away from his mother's feelings of loss. Robert had sensed the emotional undercurrent and spoken for the silent member in an unconscious effort to get unspoken feelings out into the open so that they could be resolved. Cynthia had deflected this exposure by moving the conversation into territory that conformed to her role as mother, albeit chore enforcer, which felt more safe to her. To get even more distance from her feelings, she had thrown in a zinger aimed at Zack, the child with whom she had the most conflicted feelings. Zack had taken the bait and set himself up for more negative attacks with a grandiose statement about how "good" he is. He and Cynthia moved into the familiar but painfully alienating territory of arguing about who had the facts right while the others look on.

After letting this play out for a couple of exchanges, the therapist redirected by repeating the question that had stirred up all the anxiety and defensiveness: "So how is everyone feeling about Cookie's situation?" The conversation softened again, and this time around, there was evidence that the speakers not only had their own opinions but also had taken in what others had said. Collaboration was happening.

After a pause, Robert stated the obvious: "So Mom, everyone's said how they feel except you."

Cynthia said, "I know that Cookie has a lot of problems, but you kids haven't followed through with what you said you would do to help out . . ."

Robert interrupted with a dismissive laugh: "Mom, I asked how do you feeeel," dragging out the word "feel" in a sarcastic version of this standard therapeutic question. Everyone including the therapists got the joke, and his humor effectively dissipated the tension.

Cynthia, looking a little stunned, shrugged and responded, "I don't know."

This was a breakthrough in the family sessions, or at least the therapists thought so. Cynthia's inability to emotionally engage was out in the open. It had become increasingly clear that although Cynthia was very involved with her children, she was not emotionally there. It was as if she was good at going through the motions of doing what mothers do, but she could not express the warm, loving feelings of a mother. Zack helped bring the family session back to a less emotionally charged place by suggesting a compromise for the Cookie problem. They would continue as they were for the time being as long as they could agree to put her down if she got worse. The therapists moved to facilitate this agreement to end the session with a concrete solution on a positive note, a good place from which the deeper emotional content could settle in.

In subsequent sessions we tried to get the family back to exploring the revelation about Cynthia, but this was not working. Instead, Zack reverted back to refusing to help take care of Cookie and other annoy-ing "identified patient" behaviors. He would sit in session, silent and sullen, hiding under the hood of his sweatshirt. As the therapists did their best to focus on other issues, he would periodically interject some angry comment or instigate some terrible blowup in between sessions that kept short-circuiting the process back to a negative focus on him. Robert started missing sessions because of soccer practice. Emily was getting bored.

Deterioration of Family Sessions

As the family sessions deteriorated, we continued to monitor the risk for violence and refine our assessment hypotheses. In one session Cynthia brought up an incident mentioned earlier but not fully explored in which Zack had waved a knife at her during a period that he was not taking his medication. It came out that Zack had a collection of knives and swords with which he decorated his room, a collection that had started with a pocketknife that he inherited from his grandfather when he was 10 (a year or so before the molestation occurred). Alarmed by this informa-tion, the therapists asked more questions to assess risk. Both parents assured us that they did not think Zack's collection posed a risk to him or others. Zack had never verbally or otherwise threatened anyone. In the incident with his mother, he had waved around a kitchen knife, but Cynthia said she did not feel threatened; the worst thing he had said to a teacher was that he was going to sue her. But the revelation about the sword collection created a lot of anxiety for the therapists. Ironically, a diagnosis came to mind that Zack had not succeeded in acquiring yet: conduct disorder.

We struggled with the possibility of using our power as the mental health "experts" and our duty to protect to intervene to have the knives locked away. But this kind of intrusive intervention would run the risk of undermining the parents' authority and the family's sense of compe-tence to keep themselves safe. There was also the possibility that the blade collection represented a revenge fantasy (Herman, 1997, p. 189) for all the humiliation Zack had suffered throughout his childhood. Para-doxically, his collection could have the function of keeping his aggression under control. He may symbolically have needed his knives and swords to keep himself and his family safe from the rage he felt inside. If we did not directly intervene, he would have the opportunity to mature out of his use of symbolic power to become more self-confident and powerful in his real life. The parents' lack of anxiety and acceptance of Zack's collection did not seem reckless, so we decided to maintain our positions as consultants and go along with their evaluation of the risk.

The regression in the family sessions illustrated the inevitable push in families to expose the roots of anxiety, thereby opening up possibilities for healing and deeper change, and then pull back to homeostasis and the safety of what is familiar. There were some signs of progress, however. David continued to decrease his angry outbursts and was having more positive interactions with his children. Cynthia was trying to give her daughter more space to venture out into the world, and Emily was clinging less. Her school attendance had greatly improved, and she was enjoying extracurricular activities for the first time. Cynthia had backed off her intense involvement with Zack, which resulted in them having fewer arguments. Zack was making a little developmental progress, was participating in their church's youth group, and was on track for high school graduation, something his parents doubted when we started therapy.

Shifting Back to Couple Sessions: David and Cynthia

We set up a couple session to advise the parents that continuing the family sessions was becoming counterproductive and to gently confront Cynthia about her difficulty being emotionally engaged. We suggested that Zack's passive-aggressive behavior—for example, verbally lashing out at her and then retreating into the hood of his sweatshirt and refusing to speak—might be his way of trying to get some emotional connection with her. Cynthia repeated that she knew that she was emotionally shut down but this was because she had been beaten down for so many years in her marriage. She was digging in her heels around being a victim. So we suggested a shift back to couple sessions to focus on their relationship. David thought this was a good idea, but Cynthia remained noncommittal. Instead, she advocated for us to continue individual therapy with Zack because it was obvious that "he needed it." She told us that a previous therapist had used an anger management workbook with Zack, and it had helped (unlike us, who were not very helpful). Blaming David was one defense; blaming mental health professionals who were not effective was another. On her way out the door, she put her hand on the middle of her chest and quietly told me, "You know, I'm afraid if I talk about my feelings, there'll be too much pain in there." Her eyes were sad and moist with tears.

We stopped the family sessions and for 2 more months continued weekly individual sessions with Zack and couple sessions with Cynthia and David. In our frustration and hubris as helping professionals, we considered the anger management option for Zack, but it was clear that a psychoeducational approach was not likely to work. Zack was in the powerful position of being an expert at withholding participation. The concept of the self-defeating character style (Johnson, 1994) was very useful for understanding this dynamic. Zack was a master at trying to win by losing, gaining power by acting as if he was always the victim. He was compliant about coming to appointments, but he sat in session stonewalling, sitting slumped over, frustrating his therapist's efforts to help him. Unconsciously (or maybe more consciously than we knew), triggering an angry reaction in others facilitated him playing out the family drama of victim-perpetrator. His therapist, not wanting to repeat this cycle, did not react to his long bouts of silence by trying to cajole or pull Zack into conversation. Instead he invited Zack to talk and then patiently waited, sometimes using his time to do paperwork. Cynthia continued to use her status as a victim to play out her version of the victim-perpetrator duality. The victim label functioned to entrench her blame and resentment toward her husband as she repeated her accusation that he was "a bad role model."

When Zack reached his 18th birthday and legal adulthood, he refused to sign his updated treatment plan, so we advised his parents to support him in making his own decision to quit therapy and strongly urged them to continue with their couples work on a fee-for-service basis. They stated that they could not afford it and dropped out. Three months later, David, concerned that he was getting increasingly frustrated and losing his grip on controlling his anger, called to resume couples therapy. Cynthia had asked him to move out. When they came to their appointment, Cynthia explained that she did not want a divorce; she wanted a separation so that David could think about what he had done. David refused to accept full blame by complying with her request. For months I tried to help them work through this standoff, and in the process my empathy for Cynthia was waning. David seemed much more flexible, emotionally available, and willing to look at his side of their difficulties.

My self-doubt mounting, I thought maybe I should refer them to a different therapist. A cynical voice inside my head said, why don't they just go ahead and get a divorce and get it over with? Reaching for some analytical distance from my feelings of failure, I thought maybe this was a couple who had gone as far as they could go for now in therapy. Then something remarkable happened. In the middle of one session where I was laboriously trying to get Cynthia to explore some family-of-origin issue, David quietly got up, sat at my desk, and began writing the check for the session. He said maybe it would be better if he left. It finally occurred to me that there was something we had not tried yet: individual sessions with Cynthia. They agreed, and as we began to meet in individual sessions, I immediately felt a shift in my experience with Cynthia. Over the next 2 months, the closeness in our sessions grew as she gave me more and more details about her life, the hurts, the disappointments, and the losses. In one session she complained that David had bought Zack a motorbike without consulting her. I commented that at least it sounded like David was making progress in sharing a fun activity with their son.

"I hate David," she replied.

The most stunning thing about this moment was how close I felt to her. Tears welled up in both of our eyes as I reflectively listened, and she began to work the paradox. As soon as she spoke of her hatred, she saw the illogic of it and spontaneously started to list David's good qualities. Distancing herself while blaming David for everything was not over, but she had made an important shift that day.

OUTCOMES AND CONCLUSION

At the point of this writing, Cynthia and I both look forward to our sessions together. Periodically I check in with her about the possibility of shifting back to couple sessions, but she is not ready. I do not get the feeling that the relationship-focused work (Hycner & Jacobs, 1995) we do is transferring to her marriage, but maybe it is. Robert is moving to another part of the state to continue his college education in a few months, and Cynthia is able to talk about the loss and fear she feels. Zack is tentatively talking about taking some classes at the local community college and successfully worked with his psychiatrist a few months ago to decrease his medications. To play it safe, his parents locked up all the weapons in the house, and there have not been any aggressive incidents. Emily is driving, continues to enjoy her friends and school, and is demonstrating some mild adolescent rebellion.

Hierarchies came into play throughout this case, from the family's preference for diagnostic explanations for human behavior to the authoritarian stance of hatred and the antagonistic dualities of victim versus perpetrator, blame versus innocence, right versus wrong. The feminist advocacy assumption that a witness of abuse has only two moral choices—take the side of the victim or take the side of the perpetrator—is intrinsically hierarchal. As healing professionals working with domestic violence, taking the side of the victim is clearly appropriate in the most egregious cases. But an advocacy approach, when universally applied, can be rigid and too simplistic and get in the way of change and healing, as illustrated by this case. A family systems framework provided a much more flexible basis for understanding how power, hierarchies, and aggression functioned in this family and how to help the family develop healthier ways to keep everyone safe and get enough of their needs met. The use of power to dominate was distributed throughout the Wyman family, between spouses, among the siblings, and in Cynthia's family of origin. As David once put it, "I yell with a hammer; she uses a thumbscrew." The parents' handling of Zack's sword and knife collection provided an important insight for the therapists regarding their beliefs about aggression and their acceptance of the reality of coercive power as long as it is restrained and without malign intent.

While working toward more gender-inclusive treatments for domestic violence, it will be important not to deconstruct the important contributions feminist theory has made to the understanding of human behavior, family organization, and the practice of psychotherapy. Cynthia's story is one of alienation and the myths she created to understand her experience (Roy & Steiner, 1994). Although Cynthia is a woman with a master's degree, she felt within herself that she could not think, for example, relying too heavily on mental health professionals. She felt powerless, so she became superficially self-sufficient and disconnected from others; she became passive-aggressive to counter the coercive power exercised over her; and she became a disciplinarian in her family, turning to rules and mandates of a conservative religion, to fill the void. Her alienation was a result not only of the conditions of her childhood but also of the oppression of a patriarchal society where "out of wedlock" means you are not wanted here. Cynthia's motherhood appeared on the surface to be the strongest thread holding her together, but this was dependent on blaming her husband for all of the family's difficulties. Underneath was the crushing pain of a mother's guilt: a good mother would have protected her children. A good mother would not have abandoned her children in postpartum depression. Most tragically, Cynthia was dead inside, alienated within from feelings of joy and love.

Feminist theory explains that the road to healing is the path of connection (Roy & Steiner, 1994). Cynthia's liberation, it is hoped, will come through compassionate, consistent contact (the primary goal of her individual therapy); through a fuller awareness of her ability to be a "good enough" mother along with acceptance of her and society's role in creating the problems in her family; and through incrementally and repetitively claiming her power as a woman and doing things differently in her marriage, if she chooses to stay in that relationship, and in the relationships she cares about most deeply.

REFERENCES

Freeman, D. (1992). *Multigenerational family therapy.* Binghamton, NY: Haworth Press.

Herman, J. (1997). *Trauma and recovery: The aftermath of violence—from domestic abuse to political terror.* New York: Basic Books.

Hycner, R., & Jacobs, L. (1995). *The healing relationship in gestalt therapy: A dialogic/ self psychology approach.* Highland, NY: Gestalt Journal Press.

Johnson, S. (1994). *Character styles.* New York: Norton.

Minuchin, S., & Fishman, H. (1981). *Family therapy techniques.* Cambridge, MA: Harvard University Press.

Rothschild, B. (2000). *The body remembers: The psychophysiology of trauma and trauma treatment.* New York: Norton.

Roy, B., & Steiner, C. (Eds.). (1994). *Radical psychiatry: The second decade* (2nd ed., reformatted). Available by contacting author at broy@igc.org

QUESTIONS FOR REFLECTION AND DISCUSSION

1 The author alternated between several modalities in working with this family, using individual and couples sessions and sometimes meeting with the entire family. What are the advantages to this multimodal approach? How did this flexibility help advance, or hinder, the family's therapeutic progress?

2 How does this case view victim-perpetrator dichotomies, and do you agree with the author's assertion that "an advocacy approach, when universally applied, can be rigid and too simplistic and get in the way of change and healing"?

3 The author suggests that feminist theories of domestic violence have both merits and shortcomings. What does she mean by this? How are power and control manifested in this family on multiple levels—cultural, interpersonal, and individual?

4   Explain the relevance, if any, of Cynthia's relationship with her mother and her role both as a wife and as a mother. What were the consequences on the family structure and family roles?

5   One advantage of family therapy is the participation of children in helping to confront abuse between the parents. How did the initial focus on Zack, the "identified patient," contribute to a better understanding of the parents' relationship?

Multicultural Aspects in Partner Violence

Subject to Change: Elder Abuse in an East Indian Family

13

MELISSA C. ANDERSON

I began working at the Institute on Aging (IOA) in San Francisco as the elder abuse counselor in 2002, as a marriage and family therapist intern for the San Francisco Consortium for Elder Abuse Prevention. The IOA houses a number of organizations committed to enhancing the lives of older persons and helping them remain safe and independent for as long as possible. The Consortium for Elder Abuse Prevention is a network of nearly 40 public and private agencies dedicated to addressing the needs of vulnerable and abused seniors and dependent adults.

My background in abuse and trauma is both clinical and biological: Prior to becoming a therapist, I worked as a research scientist studying the biochemical basis of anxiety and trauma. My clinical work in sexual assault began at that same time, when I helped found the Rape Crisis Intervention Program (now known as the Sexual Assault and Violence Intervention program) at Mount Sinai Hospital in New York City. This is also where I did graduate work in neurobiology.

As a clinician, I have since worked in domestic violence and with dual diagnosed patients, among other groups. My current clinical practice tends toward psychoanalytically informed psychodynamic therapy, usually long-term. In the work described in this chapter, an experience-near psychodynamic theoretical base was utilized (Lundberg, 1990), emphasizing the relationship as key to working through trauma and as a place to experience emotional support, and additional multigenerational

237

awareness was incorporated in both individual and family sessions. Although this particular therapy lasted 33 sessions, spanning 9 months, the therapy was not time-limited.

WHAT IS ELDER ABUSE?

Elder abuse, broadly defined, includes physical, sexual, and emotional abuse; financial exploitation; neglect and self-neglect; and abandonment. Elder abuse awareness first came on the national scene in the 1970s and is the most recently recognized (and often *unrecognized*) family abuse, following domestic violence and child abuse. In response to institutional elder abuse, the federal government established the Long-Term Care Ombudsman Program under the Older Americans Act in 1972 (*Elderly Abuse in Nursing Homes,* 1996). However, to the general public, domestic elder abuse remains unthinkable, even though as of this writing, it is either a misdemeanor or a felony in 45 states. It often goes unnoticed, ignored, underreported, and untreated.

Our theoretical understanding of elder abuse as the abusive use of power and control owes much to the domestic violence community. The abuser can be a spouse or partner, but just as easily an adult child, a relative of adult-child age, or an unrelated person who is in, or who assumes, the role of caretaker.

Research shows the primary predictor of abuse is a prior history of abuse in both the victim and the caregiver (Reis, 2000). A phenomenon noted in elder abuse is a kind of domestic violence by proxy in which, when an abusing partner dies or is otherwise incapacitated, an adult child "steps in" to continue the abusive relationship (Brandl, 2000). Although the notion of "payback" is often evoked when considering elder abuse— that is, a child who was once abused is now in a position of power over the former abuser—research does not support this idea. Rather it shows that a lack of coping skills, including the ability to form and maintain lasting relationships, is a more valid indicator of abusing (Reis, 2000).

One interpretation of longstanding abusive relationships is that they are somehow familiar and comfortable. Although this does not make obvious sense—abuse is painful—at the same time, attention and predictability in a relationship enable an individual to maintain a sense of interpersonal contact and identity (Gottman & Notarius, 2000). Abuse can be experienced as a form of connection, and as death approaches, the desire to remain connected often intensifies. The immediate and intimate nature of any relationship—even an abusive one—presents an alternative to the confusion and isolation of incipient dementia, mental illness, and the social marginalization of aging.

The special case of domestic abuse in later life generally falls into three categories: domestic violence where both abused and abuser have aged; domestic violence that is the result of or traceable to disinhibition (Starkstein & Manes, 2005), a neurological phenomenon secondary to stroke or dementia; and "new" domestic violence occurring when an older person remarries or gets involved in a domestic partnership later in life. In the second category, it should be noted that disinhibition does not *cause* elder abuse, but the impulsivity, emotional lability, and lack of judgment and insight that accompany disinhibition of the frontal lobe may exacerbate abusive tendencies or help escalate verbal abuse to physical abuse.

In California an elder is defined as someone over the age of 65; dependent adults are defined as persons between the ages of 18 and 64 with physical or mental limitations that restrict their ability to carry out normal activities, or a person between those ages admitted into a 24-hour health facility (California Elder Abuse Law, 1982). This means any adult admitted as an inpatient to a hospital *for any reason* falls under the rubric of dependent adult and can benefit from mandated elder and dependent-adult abuse reporting laws and the provisions under the law.

OUR CLIENTS

At the outset of my tenure with the Elder Abuse Consortium, psychotherapy for victims or survivors was a fledgling program and one of only a handful in the country. Since then, the program has grown and is currently part of a multilevel training program in geriatric psychology for both master's and doctoral students. Upward of 90 elder abuse patients were seen in the San Francisco Bay Area in the final quarter of 2006 by student and faculty therapists, quite an increase from the 12 to 14 patients I saw during the same time period in 2002.

The majority of our clients are referred by official agencies: the police department, Adult Protective Services, the district attorney's office, and other social service providers and hospitals. Occasionally, individuals or their families contact the agency directly. Our referrals are generally for the victim; however, whenever possible, we explore the safety around, and feasibility of, including family members in some aspects of treatment. Many of our clients are used to public intervention and expect concrete help. As a cohort this group often initially resists the idea of psychotherapy, finding it unfamiliar or distasteful; however, once the first meeting begins, most seem to intuitively grasp that this is a safe place where they can talk about something traumatic and taboo, and I often have a hard time getting clients to stop talking long enough to sign the consent forms.

In general, our intake begins by screening for history of family violence and abuse, other mental health issues, general health, and mobility. Information about history helps us determine continued risk and the degree of acculturation to the concept of abuse. As with other types of family violence, without intervention, elder abuse clients remain at risk for further abuse and retraumatization.

General health concerns are more prominent in the elderly: diabetes, chronic obstructive pulmonary disease, and arthritis are widespread. The painful physical symptoms that typically accompany these diseases compound a client's experience of abuse and subsequent therapy. For many elderly clients, mobility is limited; we support our clients by meeting them wherever they are, literally as well as psychologically. I have seen patients in homes, long-term assisted living residences, single-room occupancy hotels, board-and-care homes, and skilled nursing facilities, as well as the consulting room.

Home visits allow those too sick or frail to participate in consistent psychotherapy and to have an ongoing relationship with the therapist; these visits also drive home the concept of the therapeutic frame. Maintaining boundaries is crucial, and we have discovered that introducing the concept of boundaries is therapeutic for our clients. In the patient's home, I have been exposed immediately to parts of the person that, under different circumstances, would unfold more slowly over time. This is sometimes helpful, alerting me to issues that are dangerous (such as hoarding and cluttering or lack of food or heat), but at other times it hinders or alters the direction of the work. The combination of real danger and the client's wish for physical intervention and rescue can pull a therapist in the direction of doing more than is actually beneficial. Sometimes a therapist might end up trying to see too many family members or take on tasks better left to Adult Protective Service workers and other caregivers. In addition, many elderly clients are lonely and (not unlike their younger counterparts, or even sophisticated analysands) want their therapist to be their friend. Meeting in the client's home blurs this distinction, so I have had to learn to occupy a professional role in the space traditionally "owned" by the client. Some of the containment or neutrality of the consulting room must be present in the body of the therapist. When first starting this work, I fantasized about a portable therapist kit—my imaginary brief case held a mat, a clock, and a box of tissue and would make it clear to my patient what it was we were doing.

CASE STUDY: SUMI AND XENA

Sumi, an 88-year-old widow, and her daughter Xena, a woman in her early 60s, were referred for joint therapy by the Multipurpose Senior Services Program (MSSP) and Adult Protective Services (APS). MSSP is California's social and health care management service for low-income, frail elderly clients who qualify for placement in a nursing facility but wish to remain in the community.

Sumi was born in what is now the state of Kerala in southern India. She was fluent in English as well as her native dialect. She lived with Xena and Naved, her son-in-law. Robin, her case manager, contacted APS in response to Sumi's statement that Xena pushed her and Robin's own observation of heated verbal exchanges between the two. Referral was voluntary, with the hope that intervention would address the verbal abuse, de-escalate the violence, and help mother and daughter communicate. The referral also noted Xena's need for respite, which would entail temporary alternative care for Sumi. In addition to the respite, Xena, her sister Jaisudha (Jai), and Naved would be out of the country for an extended period of time in the not-too-distant future.

Sumi's second daughter, Jai, and her husband, Madhur, figured in the therapy as well. Minor players were Vickie, Sumi's granddaughter, and Margie, a family friend. Xena and Naved's son John attended a family meeting in support of his mother.

First Session

I spoke with both Sumi and Xena by phone, and we agreed to meet in their home, a pleasant-looking split-level in San Francisco, with a well-tended garden to the side. An elderly Indian gentleman answered the door, shook my hand, and introduced himself as Naved, Xena's husband and Sumi's son-in-law. He had a wide grin and an air of relief as he led me upstairs to the living room. He informed me that his mother-in-law was waiting for me, and I spied Sumi right away, as she rose with an unexpected exuberance from the plastic-covered sofa with the aid of her cane, extended her hand, and welcomed me.

A short woman whose age was present in her white hair yet conspicuously absent in her fairly unlined skin, childlike posture, gaze, and tone, she asked if I was Melissa and then told me she had practiced my name. Off to one side, the living room opened into a kitchen, and a short, dark-haired woman, dressed in brightly colored clothes that were Western but suggested the traditional Indian sari, stood with a pot of tea that she brought into the living room. This was Xena.

At this first meeting, which rapidly deteriorated from tea party to standoff, the tension between the two women was palpable. Through a series of almost imperceptible nonverbal exchanges, I sensed a barely containable rage and a demand for reparation. My guess (made later, and not entirely wrong) was that Sumi saw herself as the wronged party and would want her daughter's wrong recognized. I immediately learned that the impasse between Sumi and her daughter was ongoing and likely historic, although few details were revealed. Sumi appeared at first to have unilaterally decided that she should be the sole recipient of my time and attention; to this, her daughter responded with annoyance and an attempt at dismissal. The old woman stood her ground. Next I mentioned the incident that had brought me into the room—the push—and things became even more charged.

Both clients shied away from my direct naming of the act. They spoke in hushed tones as if my words admitted shame into the room. I had failed to grasp the significance of both the push and my unintentional cavalier treatment of it. I was struck by its power as a unifying force for the two women.

Xena now reinforced her mother's request for individual therapy. My attempts to learn more about the emotional tone in the room and Sumi's wish for individual therapy were met with silence from mother and daughter. I asked both women what they hoped for. Sumi said she wanted Xena to change and not send her away; Xena said, "my mother needs someone to talk to." Sumi again requested an individual session, and I agreed this time, with the stipulation that we meet jointly in one month to clarify goals. The immediate task now was to de-escalate tension to a level where verbal communication was possible. More ambitious goals—such as figuring out how to live together and to discuss their expectations for the future—were on hold. This first change, in the unit of treatment, executed in an indirect and coercive style, and at the threshold of our work together, was indicative of an important issue for this family: *how to mark change.*

Assessment

Assessment began by phone; I asked both Robin and the APS worker about their impressions of Sumi and Xena's therapeutic suitability and relevant medical issues. Some questions were posed to the clients by phone prior to meeting and were elaborated on in person. Through these interviews I determined that the degree of violence was minimal and not a safety factor for either clients or therapist. Both clients seemed to have a desire to participate in therapy, which is the main criterion for acceptance in the elder abuse prevention program.

Sumi's health played a large role in determining where to meet and the unit of treatment. Her multiple medical conditions included type I diabetes, with secondary retinopathy; mobility impairment from both arthritis and peripheral neuropathy secondary to the diabetes; and some concern that she showed signs of incipient dementia. Her daily insulin injections were administered by Naved because she could not see well enough to fill the syringe properly, nor did she possess significant eye-hand coordination to safely inject herself. She was, however, able to prick her finger and monitor her own blood sugar levels; the device she used had a large, highly contrasting LED readout. She required a special diet, which Xena cooked for her in addition to the traditional Indian food she prepared for the rest of the family. Inside, Sumi moved about using a cane, but she needed a walker for greater distances, and she needed assistance dressing and bathing, which her daughter and son-in-law provided.

Sumi attended a social day care program 1 day a week and a hospital-based program for physical therapy 3 days a week, which Xena had arranged and coordinated. Sumi had been going to these programs for a number of years, and throughout the course of therapy, she referred to her friends at the centers, both peers and professionals. Her score of 23 out of 30 on the mini-mental state exam (Folstein, Folstein, & McHugh, 1975) suggested confusion but was not high enough for a diagnosis of dementia. Her sleep patterns, mood, and affect indicated mild depression. Further knowledge of the client identified early trauma and multiple loss as an organizing psychological principle, leading to some characterological traits, notably use of primitive defenses, such as splitting, projective identification, omnipotence, and devaluation. Elements of personality disorder along the narcissistic borderline spectrum were present and affected her relationships.

Xena suffered from high blood pressure, for which she used medication; however, her blood pressure fluctuated, and her doctor and family feared stress from interacting with her mother exacerbated her symptoms. She also presented as exhausted and with symptoms of mild depression. I later learned that her eldest daughter suffered from "mental problems." The severity and extent of these problems were revealed in the family meeting, at the culmination of treatment, and in a dramatic way. Also curious was that Xena had had considerable experience with therapy yet presented as naive about the practice.

Naved had type I diabetes, which was better controlled than his mother-in-law's. He was relatively absent from the joint therapy between Sumi and Xena; however, he attended a family meeting. Sumi made frequent reference to him in individual sessions.

Family History

The family had lived in the Bay Area for the last 20 to 35 years. Xena and Naved came first in the 1970s, following a stay in South Africa where both were employed. Their three children were born in Johannesburg.

When her father died in the mid 1980s, Xena, as eldest, assumed responsibility for her mother. She arranged Sumi's transit to the United States from her home village, where Sumi was born and raised and where she had married and raised her own family. Xena's younger sister, Jai, and Jai's husband, Madhur, lived in London and the Middle East before coming to America in the 1990s. Xena and Naved sponsored her mother, sister, and brother-in-law. Jai, Madhur, and their children settled near Xena's family, and the sisters came to rely on one another for companionship and respite in taking care of first their children and later their mother. The brothers-in-law had a congenial relationship, and the cousins grew up together, although they later grew apart. A youngest sister, relatively distant from the rest of the family, remained abroad.

At times, Sumi took pride and ownership in her decision to relocate to another country late in life. When she first moved to California, she lived with Xena, and although they had a contentious history, both were eager to make the arrangement work and gained comfort from one another in their shared loss of husband and father, respectively. Sumi got to know her grandchildren, and Xena got child care. In addition, Sumi showed an adventurous side, learning the bus system and delighting in having some disposable cash; she qualified for General Assistance in San

Francisco and had relatively few expenses. She became active in her parish and after a few years moved to an apartment with a woman friend from church named Kay. She and Kay remained on good terms until Kay's death in 1995. By that time, Jai and Madhur lived nearby, and Sumi stayed with them for a few years.

Sumi next moved into a Catholic home for the elderly, St. Teresa's, where she reported being quite content. Although it is unclear why she left St. Teresa's, her worsening medical conditions, finances, and inappropriate behaviors probably contributed. Among these behaviors may have been a strong and inappropriate attachment to one or all of the priests; she often spoke of "helping the priests" and said that other residents were jealous of her.

Sumi eventually returned to her daughters, being cared for by Xena and Jai, in turn. In 2001 Madhur, Jai's husband, was afflicted with a debilitating and progressive neurological disease, forcing Jai to quit her job and to end her caretaking responsibility for Sumi.

While living with Xena, Sumi's preference for Jai was clear and her criticism of Xena loud and frequent. She eventually revealed that even prior to Madhur's illness, she had left Jai's house, stating in what would become a refrain, "I will never burden your doorstep again." (She has through the course of her stay in California decreed never to burden the doorstep again of both daughters, a grandson and his wife, a granddaughter, and some well-intentioned cousins from Canada.) At other times, Sumi blamed her children, specifically Xena, for forcing her out of her home in Kerala.

The situation proved more complex. As the therapy unfolded, it was learned that ownership of Sumi's home had reverted to her brother-in-law at her husband's death and that the brother-in-law had evicted Sumi. This home had recently returned to the family when that brother-in-law died, given that he had no heirs. The specter of this home and its return not to Sumi, but to Xena (who, as eldest daughter of the deceased, holds a more prominent role in Indian culture than his widow), may have precipitated the most recent round of conflict between mother and daughter. Jai, Xena, and Naved would be traveling to India to settle the property in the spring. The relevance of this to the therapy on a practical level was concern about how and where to care for Sumi during this time. On an unconscious level, long-buried issues of birthright and belonging, jealousy between mother and daughter, and loss were also coming to light. Someone was being *pushed* out of the house.

Sumi

Sumi was an only child whose mother died during childbirth (as did her only potential sibling, a sister). When she was age 6, her father either died or left the family, and she was raised by her maternal grandparents. Her grandfather died when she was age 12. His loss affected her profoundly, and during the therapy, she recalled many instances where she spoke with him and related to me things she had learned from him. He may have been the first of her many early losses she was able to openly acknowledge and grieve.

At that time, India was under British rule, and local customs were unfavorable to widows or unattached women. Sumi was barely a woman. She stated that as a teenager she learned to sew and worked as a seamstress to support her grandmother and herself, and then she married at age 17 to an older man; however, she may actually have been married much younger or found other ways of supporting herself (the details are unclear). Throughout her marriage, she worked periodically, sewing for all of her children. Her husband, a mid-level bureaucrat, made an honest, albeit small income. Sumi spoke highly of him in a childlike way, venerating him and likening him to a saint and a prophet. She was and remains a devout Catholic.

Bearing children was difficult for Sumi. She did not carry a child to term until age 25, and even then, the birth was complicated, and both mother and daughter were at risk. In session, she stated that Xena "was born dead" and that her husband chose her life over the child's when asked by medical staff whom they should try to save, a fact she seemed proud of; yet, miraculously, the "good doctors" allowed them both to live. What was the legacy and meaning of this so-called miracle? The meaning of not outliving her daughter, of living with a daughter she fantasized was reminiscent of her absent and perhaps oft-wished-for sibling? Her guilt at surviving what her own mother did not and thus giving her daughter what she was deprived of are key elements in Sumi and Xena's relationship dynamic. She may also have secretly viewed herself as "deadly"; given that the doctors thought at first only one would (should?) live, did she unconsciously fear that she posed a danger to Xena in some way and that Xena in turn was potentially harmful to her? Surely all of these conflicting and seemingly paradoxical primitive beliefs informed their relationship.

Jai's birth 5 years later was comparatively mild. In addition to Sumi's improved health, much of her anxiety about parenting was allayed with this second child. It was easy for Sumi to love and dote on Jai. Sumi's third daughter is considerably younger than the first two, and little was learned about her birth.

Xena

Xena and Sumi both characterized their relationship as stormy and always difficult. Given the life-and-death stresses surrounding her birth and the similarities to Sumi's own life story, one can assume that Xena's mother had abundant and mixed feelings about her. This was probably as bewildering to Xena, who was at once cherished and despised by her mother, as it was to Sumi. In addition, the disparities between her and her sister's relationships to their mother may have exacerbated developmentally appropriate jealousy and sibling rivalry. Xena reported having a good relationship with her father, a source of jealousy between mother and daughter.

Sumi spoke a great deal about her difficulties with Xena during adolescence, which she attributed to a willful streak. According to Sumi, "she was very smart and always thought she knew best." On one occasion, she explained that "we married her young" because of this "character flaw." This marriage came to symbolize the fusion Sumi experienced with Xena and her confusion of roles: mother, sister, and, perhaps, a wished-for self—that is, a daughter raised by a mother. Sumi's ability to differentiate and relate to her daughter as a whole object appears impaired. Xena's response to the marriage can be interpreted as acting out in much the same way that Sumi acted out in this therapy: *transition must be marked dramatically.*

As a parent, Xena appeared unremarkable; she seemed to have good relationships with her children, two daughters and a son. The extent of Xena's eldest daughter's "mental problems" was rather successfully omitted from the therapy and therefore unavailable to the therapist or other professionals affiliated with the case for most of the time we were actively working with Sumi and her family. It was only at the family meeting that I learned that the unmarried daughter had a diagnosis of schizophrenia and lived in a board-and-care home. The impact of a schizophrenic child in the family and the prejudices and beliefs held by Xena, her husband, and her mother surely contributed to the relationship dynamics uncovered through the abuse referral and subsequent therapy.

Naved

Naved was the first member of the family whom I met in person. His body language and demeanor conveyed much: the long-standing discomfort and tension in the household as well as his hopefulness that there would be relief. Naved's connection to Xena and her family dated back to the relationship between his father and Sumi's husband. Naved's father was a protégé of Sumi's husband and may have been (or felt) indebted to him and the family, according to Sumi. I knew little of his childhood or early adult life.

Naved himself was a quiet and contained man who seemed to genuinely care for his mother-in-law despite the hoops she forced her daughter to jump through and her many outrageous claims of maltreatment by Xena and him. My firsthand knowledge of him came from his presence: stolid, placid, resigned, the calming force between mother and daughter. When I saw him with Xena, they appeared easy and comfortable together. I learned that he missed his work, even though he was happy to spend more time with his grandchildren. Naved did not participate in therapy sessions with Sumi and Xena, but he would appear silently near the end of the session or be visible moving about in an adjacent room, nodding while Xena described what she did to accommodate Sumi or made aggrieved pleas for her mother to speak directly to her. (As mentioned earlier, one of the pitfalls of doing therapy in a client's home is the difficulty in establishing a private space.)

Sumi was openly jealous of her daughter's relationship with Naved, stating, "I have no one, while she has Naved," and often reminding me (and also her daughter, I imagine) that she had "picked him for her." At one time, she listed the tasks he did for her, such as putting her hearing aids in for her in the morning, giving her insulin injections, and driving her to and from her many medical appointments, as evidence that her daughter should not be receiving funds from the state because she (Xena) did very little for Sumi. She did not seem to think Naved should receive the money either because he was doing these things out of genuine concern and perhaps obligation. When I observed them together, Naved was attentive, and Sumi appeared comfortable in his care, while simultaneously childlike and flirtatious.

Xena and Naved's Marriage

The marriage was arranged when Xena was still a child and Naved a young man, 14 years her senior. Naved was closer in age to Sumi, a fact that later may have had profound meaning for Sumi and possibly contributed to her sense of position and entitlement in her current relationships with both Naved and Xena.

Xena did not want to marry an old man and certainly not someone of her mother's choosing. She defied her parents and fell in love (an expression Sumi used with disdain) with Madhur, a bright and ambitious young man from school. When she informed the family of her plans, her mother was outraged, and her father was shamed and adamant. They insisted she marry Naved. True to her headstrong ways, Xena put up a fight and ran away from home; yet after a short while, she returned to marry Naved.

Madhur, however, was not going to sacrifice his standing in the community, his education, or his future; perhaps he had not fallen in love. Sumi and her husband decided that Madhur would make a good husband for Jai. Sumi gave little information as to why he became the obvious choice; she related this story as explanation of her perceived maltreatment by Xena. Xena's comments on the story reflected a tone of nostalgia, amusement, and bewilderment. The provocative elements of the relationships seemed to be of most interest to Sumi.

Xena and Naved married and almost immediately left India for South Africa. Later Sumi commented that her relationship with Jai was better because Jai had stayed in Kerala and had her children, whereas Xena was a bad girl who had run away from home.

TREATMENT

Initially, the wished-for outcome of therapy, as articulated to and intuited by caregivers, MSSP, and APS workers, was to ease tension between mother and daughter and, in the ensuing calm, work out a collaborative agenda regarding Sumi's care. Their historic conflict was unknown at that time, and both parties joined with their helpers in supporting the notion that logistics were dictating the tension. Independently, each party appeared to hold the fantasy that the therapist, as an outside and neutral (read: on *my* side) agent, would mediate the current dispute (and therefore all disputes), clarify roles, and dictate actions and that the offending party would follow direction.

In accepting the rapid and poorly explained change in the unit of treatment (from joint treatment to treating Sumi alone), the therapist entered into an enactment with the clients. The initiation of a new phase is marked by an explosion, in this case, Sumi's desired change in treatment. Far from "never" burdening the doorstep again, Sumi marked each doorstep or transition with an explosion.

The intended benefit behind meeting alone with Sumi (in addition to the fact that it was the only intervention to which she would agree) was that through relationship with the therapist, she would tell her story and might establish boundaries, including some distance from her anxiety. This would, in turn, de-escalate the tension between her and Xena and have a calming effect on her daughter. Eventually we hoped she and her daughter might recall the ways they had comforted each other when Sumi's husband died. In this way, she could explore her feelings of loss, as well as her fears about the future.

The secondary goals of creating a safe space for logistical planning were more important to agency workers and family members seeking to contain the tension, anger, and anxiety present in both Sumi and Xena than to the clients. The role of treatment was ultimately about bearing witness to Sumi's process, which was the de facto family process. The therapy unfolded regardless of these goals and in a dramatic and traumatizing way. On one level, Sumi got what she professed to want: for her anger and disappointment to be heard. However, the therapy also ultimately led to her being placed, temporarily, in the state hospital. This was also familiar, being again *pushed* out of her home and paradoxically not at all what she wanted.

Individual therapy sessions with Sumi focused on her anxiety, which at the outset centered almost entirely on Xena: her feelings of exclusion from Xena, Xena's family, and the decision processes she felt affected her, such as when they went on vacation and how soon she was informed and her outrage at not being allowed to do things for herself, such as cook or light candles. (It is important to note the significance of *not being allowed* to light candles given their role in Sumi's practice of Catholicism. Prayer without candles minimized both the solace and the compassion she received through this act and also exacerbated fears of judgment and damnation.) As the therapy progressed, Sumi was eager to share her personal history with me, often in the context of larger world events. The act of bearing witness to her life eased anxiety and allowed her to open to the possibility of seemingly more dynamic therapy. We addressed her grief over the loss of independence and her frustration at not being able to do the things she wished for herself, which was different from not being allowed to do them. She was able to talk about feeling included when with Jai's family and speculate on the differences, including differences within herself; her still at-times-acute grief over the loss of her husband; and her identity as his wife.

As the client identified areas where she felt like part of the family in her current life, both client and therapist were encouraged to set up a joint meeting with Xena. It is important to note that both mother and daughter successfully avoided joint therapy for more than 3 months and did not honor my request for a joint session within 1 month of individual therapy. For the first few weeks, I was complicit with this nonverbal decision. Unconsciously, I carried the wishes of my clients: Sumi's desire to remain in the privileged role of patient and both Xena and Sumi's wish to avoid another explosion. Only by addressing the failure to meet the goal of a joint session in supervision did I recognize my reticence to move forward. Then I was able take the necessary steps: after discussing the joint session in individual therapy with Sumi and in collateral meetings with Xena, the joint session was finally scheduled.

The Joint Session

This second meeting with mother and daughter was entered with few expectations for concrete outcome but with optimism that Sumi felt supported enough to hear Xena's position and acknowledge her feelings. The rapid change in psychic climate that occurred during the first session was all but forgotten, and I was unprepared for the explosion that surfaced. I had barely mentioned the ground rules for discussion and confidentiality when Sumi accused her daughter of plotting to put her away in the state hospital forever. She expressed outrage at being told at the last minute about a trip the family was planning 3 weeks hence and declared that Robin (the social worker from MSSP) was aiding Xena in stealing her allotment. She said that she wished to leave Xena's house and demanded that I find alternative housing for her immediately!

I was both stunned by and curious about this side of Sumi that I had not fully encountered. Xena also appeared surprised, although I later surmised her astonishment was more directed toward me and the fact that I was unable to contain her mother. I attempted to address Sumi's process in session, while the daughter took a submissive role and answered the allegations. She further elaborated on the services offered through the state hospital for respite care and made an effort to persuade Sumi of the merits of the hospital by informing her that a trusted caregiver at her adult day health treatment center suggested the stay. Sumi then "remembered" this conversation and began to cry, imploring me to "go there, see for yourself, you would not want me there."

For Sumi the concrete outcomes of the joint session were that she obtained information from her daughter that she felt would influence me, her therapist. She believed that with this information I could produce the results she wanted. What she did not expect was my assurance that, should she enter the state hospital as a temporary resident, our therapy visits would continue; I was familiar with the hospital and met with other residents there. In the short term, her outburst resulted in arrangements for her to stay with her grandson and his wife during Xena and Naved's upcoming vacation. Her allegations about financial fraud were addressed by her social worker, and I became acquainted with her cunning use of anger and manipulation. Another explosion to mark another transition. In several months this process would be repeated on a grand scale.

As might be expected, after the vacation, Sumi complained about her stay with her grandson and was relieved to be back at home, stating her granddaughter-in-law was "worse than Xena." The therapy continued as supportive and with explorations of Sumi's early life, her good feelings about the therapist, and her disappointment that the therapist was unable to change her daughter's mind or prevent what appeared to be inevitable, a stay at the state hospital.

The State Hospital

As stated at the outset, Xena, Naved, and Jai were planning an extended trip to India and were unsure who would care for Sumi during that time. They agreed to persuade Sumi to stay at the state hospital, for the duration of a shorter trip, with the hope that she would adjust once there. Xena requested a joint session to discuss this plan, to which Sumi agreed. Prior to the meeting Sumi told me she would speak with Xena, but during the session, she refused to speak directly to her daughter and expressed outrage that I would not act as go-between. Xena stated repeatedly that she needed her mother to tell her how she was feeling. Sumi eventually did speak directly to Xena, saying she would go to the state hospital, dramatically adding that she would stay there until she died. Near the end of the hour, both clients cried and appeared to make up. Sumi said that she would try the hospital and that she did love her daughter. Elaborate plans were made, including naming friends who could visit during Xena's absence. Sumi received an 11th-hour offer to stay with her grandson again, which she stoically (and manipulatively) refused. She confided to me that she would be homesick for a day or two but would adjust. She left on a Monday.

On Thursday, in our scheduled session at the state hospital, Sumi presented as happy and engaged with other residents. She showed me her blood-sugar level numbers, commenting that they were better than at home and that she felt better. She showed me her drawings and commented on how much she liked the food. It may have been all manic defense, but I did not think so. She still complained about Xena and said she wanted to move away from there, but she was worried now that this might be her only choice. Her major complaints were that Xena had arranged for *too many* friends to stop by and of the smell of urine that permeated the building.

On the following Monday, I was rather shocked (although in hindsight I probably should not have been) to learn from APS that the hospital had filed a report of neglect against Xena. The allegations were based on Sumi's accounts, which her granddaughter Vickie had corroborated. I was rather shocked to learn of this granddaughter I had never heard of, Jai's daughter. I felt I had been taken in by Sumi, and she no doubt felt that way about me. I had failed to address her feelings of abandonment and betrayal. Chaos ensued.

Xena learned of the charges after picking her mother up (underlining the confusion in bureaucracy at the state hospital, which could file a report of neglect against the very individual to whom they were releasing an alleged victim). Robin, the MSSP worker, along with the APS investigator, called for a family meeting. The mysterious granddaughter Vickie demanded to be at the meeting as well as "Margie," a woman she seemed to assume we all knew. (Margie was unknown to Robin and me.) An experienced family therapist was called in to facilitate the meeting, and after a number of sessions with Sumi and my supervisors, we agreed it would be best if Sumi were not present. Thus, the meeting convened with Xena, Naved, Vickie, and Margie as well as Xena's son John, Robin from MSSP, the APS investigator, and me. Judy, an experienced family therapist and mediator, facilitated. Jai was notably absent. The room was tense, the acrimony palpable. Another explosion loomed as Sumi neared another transition.

The Family Meeting

The family meeting itself was dramatic and tense; accusations were hurled, family secrets revealed. Judy was responsible for the deft handling of grandchildren and wronged daughters, loyal sons, and Naved, the stoic son-in-law and supportive husband. In spite of our efforts to frame the meeting as a problem-solving venue, both Xena and her family and Vickie and Margie entered the conference room as if it were a judge's chambers: Xena to meet her accusers, Margie and Vickie to continue accusing. Vickie seemed to imagine herself Sumi's defender, and Margie was her cocounsel. Although Margie was unknown to us (professionals from IOA, MSSP, and APS), she was known to Xena and her family; we learned in bits and starts that she was the daughter of an elderly man whom Sumi had befriended some 10 years prior and considered herself an "almost daughter-in-law" to Sumi. She remained connected to the family but only through Jai's family.

Early in the session Vickie accused Xena of neglect and maltreatment, citing nonspecific reports and complaints from Sumi. John defended his mother, and Naved also added many examples of the care they both had given Sumi. Vickie further elaborated that she knew exactly how much money Sumi got each month and that Xena and Naved must clearly be pocketing it because Sumi did not see it. The amount she received from General Assistance was small, less than $900 a month, and her expenses many: health care, including medication; transportation to and from adult health day programs, as well as the fees for the programs; and food, housing, and clothing. Vickie presented this information as if it would clearly indict Xena, while all the professionals agreed that Xena and Naved were probably supplementing Sumi's allotment to provide her with the extra necessities she equated with having her own money.

Vickie further speculated that Xena could not care for Sumi (or anyone!) because her own daughter was schizophrenic. This is how I learned the extent of Xena's eldest daughter's so-called mental problems. There was a hush in the meeting, and although John and Naved had been defending Xena, she now chose to speak on her own behalf. She turned to me, stating, "Yes, this is true. This has been difficult for the family, but we are responsible for her; she lives in a board-and-care residence."

At the start of the meeting and several times throughout, Judy reminded us that the purpose of the meeting was to find a best solution for Sumi. Xena remained firm that Sumi must find another place to live. In a manner reminiscent of her grandmother, Vickie, Xena's chief accuser, appeared genuinely surprised that Xena was "throwing Sumi out" of her house. When it began to dawn on her that her grandmother might have nowhere else to go except to return to the state hospital, she attempted to cajole Xena, calling her "auntie" and affecting an odd, out-of-place childlike voice. John and Naved rolled their eyes. Xena asked Vickie if she would like to care for Sumi; perhaps she could do a better job. Vickie backed off, countering that she could not possibly do that because of her other responsibilities, to a 15-month-old daughter. Xena commented that, as we all now knew, she also had other responsibilities.

Margie was relatively quiet through most of the meeting; she was reserved in agreeing with Vickie's charges or in clamoring in support of Xena. Near the end of the meeting, she suggested that Sumi might find a place at the convalescent hospital where she worked. This was where her father had been 10–15 years earlier and where Sumi had met him when volunteering. Time was just about up.

After 2 hours, tensions eased, and a plan was formulated. Margie agreed to find alternative care for Sumi and remarkably did so in less than 2 weeks. In what was described as a permanent relocation for her, Sumi became a resident of a private convalescent hospital in the suburbs of San Francisco, which was paid for by General Assistance. Concretely, her allegations of abuse brought results: she was no longer waiting to be pushed out of her home—she made certain it would happen.

Xena and Naved recognized how difficult it was for them to say no to Sumi, recalling the many times she had left, "never to burden their doorstep again," and then returned. They decided to meet with a therapist to help them negotiate this transition and to figure out how to forge a new type of relationship with Sumi. They stayed in therapy for 6 months with a therapist from the Elder Abuse Prevention program.

I met one last time with Sumi, to say good-bye. Because of her relocation outside of our catchment area, we were unable to continue our work together. I found her in the convalescent hospital where she seemed quite content. She gave me a tour. She knew many residents and informed me that when she was younger, she had volunteered at this very hospital. The staff knew her. She said that Xena came to see her sometimes. She said she was sad that she had had to leave her daughter's house, but that this was better.

OUTCOMES AND CONCLUSION

Several themes emerged from this therapy, some specific to this case and others that are relevant to many cases of elder abuse. These are marking transitions, the meaning of the push, burdening doorsteps, and repeating the past. A common occurrence in elder abuse is that although the precipitating issues have merit and basis in reality, they also serve as a screen for more primitive and terrifying anxieties that surface with the nearness of death. In Sumi's case, this is the ultimate transition, and she is afraid of it, as well as what might follow. Her Catholic faith, with both its compassion and its promise of harsh judgment, informed her fears as well as the way she lived her life. Using explosions to mark each change was a way to dissipate her anxiety (not very effective) as well as make her anger about change, which historically was dramatic and inflicted on her from outside (early death of mother, abandonment by father, etc.), known to others.

In this case (as is often true in elder abuse) both clients were elderly, and the distinction between abuser and the abused was vague. Although Sumi was pushed, and this generated the referral, Xena was subjected to verbal attacks, which became apparent as the treatment progressed. The subtle use of manipulation and emotional blackmail by Sumi and, at times, Xena was also seen during the course of treatment and later, not very adeptly, by Vickie. In the very first meeting, the push was discussed, although that word seems too big. I mentioned it, thus giving the clients a platform from which to respond, and although not denied by either party, it remained an unacceptable topic of discourse. The unstated consensus was that it would not be repeated, perhaps because of the fact that it had generated outside interest.

This was viewed as good and bad for both: good for Xena because she would get some help but bad for Xena because she was still the "not good enough" daughter; good for Sumi because someone was there to witness her abuse but bad for Sumi because the work/change she agreed to meant giving up the power she knew in her position of victim. Given her age and cultural background, manipulation may have been her only power options.

Although physical violence was not the general form of abuse in this family, the culture of blame and shame and victim and abuser influenced their relationships. Normal losses associated with aging, health problems, the loss of motor control, and diminishing sight and sound were made to fit into blaming categories—they were "someone's fault." It was Xena's fault because she was still young (in Sumi's eyes), still the daughter; Sumi's fault for not trying hard enough. Inevitable losses of friends and family because of illness, frailty, and death were also perceived as the result of bad intentions, or acts of bad faith by others. This culture of blaming effectively blocked grief.

The theme of burdening doorsteps is another important consideration for this family—from Sumi's historic sense of displacement from the early loss of her mother to her feeling out of place as Xena's mother because of the complications of Xena's birth, through to the loss of her home by eviction. She struggles with her right to be "home" and also with the strange feelings that accompany being "at home." Her disappointment at being pushed out is more comfortable because of its familiarity. Finally we see her repeating the past.

The outcomes in this case are bittersweet: an elderly, at-risk client was removed from what on one level was a threatening situation, yet at the same time she was choosing (albeit unconsciously) to repeat the familiar cycle of losing her home. She retained her childlike position, where anger could be expressed and simultaneously dismissed by others and herself, through placating her on a physical level, such as finding her new accommodations. For Xena and Naved the outcome may have proved better; I have little knowledge of their therapy.

In rethinking what I might have done differently in this case, I consider that I might have pushed harder for joint therapy at the start and insisted on at least one more meeting together before switching to individual sessions. And were it possible, as it might have been had I worked longer with this family or gained insight sooner, I would have brought Naved officially into the therapy. In addition, because I was inexperienced and found the shift from individual to family dynamic difficult to negotiate, I held back on interpretations that might have been helpful for the family in understanding the situation: the meaning of the "push," more directly exploring the meaning of Sumi's home in India returning to the family, and Sumi's repetition in being evicted from her many homes, all in light of her proximity to death.

REFERENCES

Brandl, B. (2000). Power and control: Understanding domestic abuse in later life. *Generations, 24*(2), 39–45.

California Elder Abuse Law, Elder Abuse and Dependent Adult Civil Protection Act, California Welfare and Institutions Code 15610 *et seq.* (1982).

Elderly abuse in nursing homes, Testimony before the House Older Americans Caucus, U.S. House of Representatives, 104th Cong., 1 (1996) (testimony of William F. Benson).

Folstein, M. F., Folstein, S. E., & McHugh, P. R. (1975). "Mini-mental state": A practical method for grading the cognitive state of patients for the clinician. *Journal of Psychiatric Research, 12*(3), 189–198.

Gottman, J. M., & Notarius, C. I. (2000). Decade review: Observing marital interaction. *Journal of Marriage and Family, 62*(4), 927–947.

Lundberg, S. G. (1990). Domestic violence: A psychodynamic approach and implications for treatment. *Psychotherapy: Theory, Research, Practice, Training, 27*(2), 243–248.

Reis, M. (2000). The IOA screen: An abuse-alert measure that dispels myths. *Generations, 24*(2), 14.

Starkstein, S. E., & Manes, F. (2005). Neural mechanisms of depression, anxiety and disinhibition. In G. Gainotti (Ed.), *Handbook of neuropsychology* (Vol. 5, pp. 263–286). Amsterdam: Elsevier.

QUESTIONS FOR REFLECTION AND DISCUSSION

1   The author says that long-standing abusive relationships continue because they are "familiar and comfortable." Do you think this applies only to elderly abuse?

2   Describe the alliances in this family, both within and across generations. How did they contribute to the conflicts between Sumi and her daughter Xena, sometimes leading to elder abuse? How well did the author succeed in keeping herself from getting caught up in the power struggle?

3   The author writes that Sumi's "guilt at surviving what her own mother did not and thus giving her daughter what she was deprived of are key elements in Sumi and Xena's relationship dynamic." How did this issue contribute to the conflict between them?

4   What does this case suggest about the complexities of family violence, or how "abuse" ought to be defined? What do you think was the overall impact of physical abuse in this case, in comparison with more subtle forms of abuse such as manipulation?

5   It is common practice in the field of domestic violence to respect a victim's wish not to participate in conjoint sessions with his or her abuser. How well does this case argue for exceptions to this rule?

14

Use of the Medicine Wheel and Other Experiential Approaches in Domestic Violence and Anger Management Therapy

LORI BLOOM

R. D. Lang (1985) said that the thing people fear above everything else is other people. My own experience has led me to believe that this is so. I also have found that both men and women who are in violent relationships feel that they are victims. I believe that we do our clients a great injustice if we support the idea that our clients are either victims or perpetrators when most often they are both.

My experience working with violent people began in 1978, when I began my practicum for my master's program at an inpatient drug rehabilitation center. Many of my clients were murderers and rapists who had been released after the Supreme Court ruled that indeterminate sentences were unconstitutional. I was the first counselor to conduct groups at the facility, and I can remember clearly walking into a room of 23 men, most of them with huge muscles from working out in prison. They were sitting in a circle, slouched back in their chairs and looking very intimidating. As I passed the biggest man (he was 6 feet, 6 inches, and about 280 pounds), he said in the loudest voice he could, "Hey, honey, why don't you come over here and sit on my face?"

The room became absolutely still. Everyone was looking at me. To say that I was not prepared for this is an understatement. Nothing in the books I had read or in the theories that had been discussed in class came even close to this. But something told me that this was an important moment. If I did the wrong thing, I would lose them. So I looked right at him, smiled, and said, "Now that's the best offer I have had all day, but that's not what we are here for." He looked right back at me and laughed and said, "Okay, let's see what you've got." For the next 2 years, I did psychodrama groups with mostly heroin addicts. My best student and protector was this huge man who had challenged me on my first day. He made sure that no one got out of line, and he himself turned his life around and was clean and sober 5 years later.

I relate this incident not to shock but to pass on what I learned on that first day with the worst of the worst. This work is a dance. The people who come to you are distrustful of authority. They will challenge you, and if you shame them or take them on, you will be justifying their beliefs about you. They may say what you want to hear to get through your classes, but they will never trust you. The question that comes up over and over again is whether it is better to be right or to be kind. This is true for both the therapist and the client. If you model for your clients a way of allowing people their dignity, even when they challenge your more powerful position, you give them a very important tool. Most of-fenders do not know that they have a choice when threatened. The most important role we play as therapists is providing a model for a relation-ship that is based on respect, honesty, and the willingness to see and accept all the many facets of the client. We are mirrors for our clients. If we reflect back the positive qualities that we see in them, we will also be able to confront them honestly when we see them making choices that will keep them in negative patterns.

It is important to be able to create a safe space where people can speak honestly and begin to see themselves clearly. Rather than using blaming words such as *good* or *bad* and *right* or *wrong*, I talk about patterns of behavior that are no longer useful or effective. It is helpful for clients to remember the first time that using violence and intimidation worked for them. Most of them can bring up the situation where they stood up to someone who was threatening them. Usually they were around 5 or 6 years old. I ask them if they want a 5-year-old to be making decisions about how to handle their lives. For some it is the first time they realize that they are acting from the past, and it no longer serves them to do so.

I have found the most successful approach to helping clients under-stand and manage their anger is first to teach them body awareness, so that they can track the way in which they experience anger in their bodies and learn to take time-outs and step out of the situation to experience the opportunity to make a choice as to how they want to handle their response to their anger. I also teach them when they maintain their dignity under all circumstances, the likelihood of their being understood and taken seriously is much more likely than if they rage or become intimidating.

It is also understood that the first rule in anger management is to agree to keep yourself safe. Exploring what are safe and unsafe situations is an important part of the work. For people who have grown up in abusive homes, there is often difficulty in even distinguishing abuse from normal behavior. It is important for them to experience a feeling of relaxed resourcefulness. It does not matter how much a person has intellectualized his or her behavior; until that person is able to experience and identify the feelings in his or her body, the person will not be able to effectively deal with his or her anger. Because our feelings are experienced in our bodies, having the ability to change our physiology is the path to controlling our emotions.

PEOPLE'S ALTERNATIVE TO VIOLENCE

I am the director of the People's Alternatives to Violence program (PAV) in Mendocino, California. PAV is a 52-week, court-certified anger management program. The program began under the name Men's Alternatives to Violence over 25 years ago. It was developed as a treatment program for men who were being identified as perpetrators but had no place to go to resolve their issues.

About 20 years ago, I was asked to take over the program, and because it seemed to me that there was also a need for women to deal with their violence, I renamed the program the People's Alternatives to Violence and included women in our groups. When the law was changed many years later, we were no longer able to treat men and women together, even though the mixed gender program was successful, and we never had any violence or threats as a result of the work that was done. (In fact, many of the couples we treated are still together and give credit to PAV for learning how to resolve their issues without violence.) Thus, now we conduct separate groups for men and women.

Because I live in a rural part of northern California, and our systems are both underfunded and understaffed, I often receive referrals through a brief phone call from a Child Protective Services worker or a form from the probation department. Most communication involves whether the client is coming to meetings and whether they are participating.

Although my men's programs are often full, there are usually only six to eight women in a women's group. The group dynamics change from week to week, depending on what is going on. Everyone checks in and discusses their time-outs or issues they have encountered the past week.

One of the issues might present a great opportunity for role-playing. I use traditional psychodrama tools that allow all members in the group to participate by playing various parts in the client's life or by doubling (standing behind the client or protagonist and acting as an alter ego; Yablonsky, 1976). At the end of the role-play, each participant shares what it felt like to be playing a certain part. This gives all the clients the opportunity to experience themselves from different perspectives. This is much easier to do when one is playing a role in someone else's life. Dealing with a situation that is not exactly like yours, but very similar, provides an opportunity to experience without resistance that people come from different stories.

Role-playing is followed by a discussion of the physical sensations that were experienced by participants and observers. With whom did they identify? With whom did they feel angry or fearful? Every week we do some kind of body work, which I describe later in the chapter.

Most of my clients also keep a personal journal. For some this may be a way of tracking mood swings or being aware of any medication they are taking. Some find writing cathartic and use their journals to chart their progress. However, when clients are illiterate or do not write easily, written assignments can be embarrassing and remind them of times in school where they were humiliated.

The first and most important commitment that members of PAV make each week before we leave is to keep ourselves safe. That means it is each person's responsibility to stay out of situations where violence may occur or police may be called. Anything that could land them back in jail is a violation of that commitment. From this point of view, it does not matter whose fault it is or how crazy the other person is. It also keeps the focus on the client's choices and not other people's problems. If a person makes foolish choices and puts oneself in harm's way, there is no one else to blame. Awareness always triumphs over fear and anger.

Because I have been fortunate to have many extraordinary teachers, my work is always different and thus always exciting and interesting, even after 28 years of practice.

CASE STUDY: JENNIFER

Jennifer was referred to me and the PAV program by both Adult Proba-tion and Child Protective Services. When Jennifer began the program, she was age 19 and the mother of a 2-year-old son named Jason. She was separated from her boyfriend Frank, who was the father of her child. Jennifer had been found guilty of attacking his car and threatening to hit him with a baseball bat when she discovered he was having sexual relations with another woman.

Jennifer had purchased the vehicle with her own money so that Frank could find work. She had put the title in his name so that she would not be responsible for the insurance or damage that he might cause, given that he used alcohol and drugs. Although she felt she had a perfect right to damage the car, the court felt otherwise, and she had spent 30 days in jail before coming to my class.

Jennifer first showed up to group therapy wearing a low-cut tank top and low-riding tight jeans. Jennifer is approximately 5 feet, 5 inches, tall and at that time weighed about 180 pounds. She was smacking her gum as she looked at me and said, "I have to do 52 weeks of this f—k—g class, and the bastard that sent me here is off doing drugs with his friends." In spite of her foul language and rough appearance, it was clear to me that she was intelligent. Along with her problem of impulse control, she was suffering from immaturity and low self-esteem.

Jennifer had a history of fighting in school and physically attacking her mother. She was from a middle-class family. Her mother, who was Native American, was a nurse and an alcoholic. She divorced Jennifer's father when Jennifer was 8 years old. The mother had a multitude of boyfriends and came in and out of Jennifer's life. Jennifer's father was the primary parent and for the most part was hardworking but emotionally uninvolved. Jennifer became sexually active at age 14 and began using marijuana and alcohol about the same time.

Jennifer said that she was physically violent in most of her romantic relationships and that most of the violence was mutual. When she was beaten up by a boyfriend, she said she usually initiated the violence. She was not going to let anyone push her around. She was proud of the fact that by middle school, she could beat up any boy or girl who challenged her.

Frank

Although Jennifer had thrown things at Frank and hit him, Frank had never physically assaulted her. However, he did everything else he could to emotionally wound her: he consistently lied to her, he was unfaithful, and he demeaned her. He was very handsome but was clearly psychopathic and manipulative in his behavior toward others. Although he looked like a choir boy, his rap sheet was astonishing: He had started out with petty crimes and then moved on to auto theft, drug dealing, and assault, including domestic violence. (Interestingly, about 4 years before this, Frank had completed my men's program. Although I could do nothing about his character disorder, he had stayed violence-free and had kept himself out of jail.)

At the time I began seeing Jennifer, Frank was still on parole for assaulting a police officer and was very aware that he was subject to the three strikes rule. He had been incarcerated for 10 of his 28 years and did not want to return to prison. He also had issued a restraining order against her.

I asked Jennifer how it happened that she was here and not her boyfriend if it was "all his fault." She replied, "Frank still really loves me, and I know we will end up together, but he keeps cheating on me, and he doesn't get how it's hurting his son. I know that he wants to be a good dad and that I'm the only one he's ever been able to talk to." I said, "How do you handle the fact that he is with other women? Did you hit his car because you were jealous or hurt?" Jennifer said, "I have my own friends to be with if I need to get laid. Let him be jealous for once."

Jason

In spite of the fact that Jennifer's choices were questionable, to say the least, she was very serious about raising her son Jason in a safe and appropriate home. She lived with her sister, who watched Jason when Jennifer was at work. However, when Jennifer returned home, she played with him and read to him. She made a clear distinction between her behavior when she was with her son and her behavior when she was off with her friends.

When Frank moved in with another woman and sued for custody of their son, Jennifer began to seriously look at her situation. It was very hard for her to see Frank clearly. He had spent very little time with Jason and did not show any affection for him. It was apparent that he did not want to pay child support, and he would use his new girlfriend to take care of Jason when he had visitation. The possibility that Jennifer could lose custody of Jason provided the opportunity to take a good look at herself and the life she was leading. I made it clear that the court would be scrutinizing her behavior, and it was up to her to decide what her priorities were.

I have discovered that women will often make positive changes in their lives only when they realize their children are at risk. It was clear that Frank, who continued to use drugs (medical marijuana), was not going to keep their son safe. Having known Frank and his attitude toward women, I did not consider it likely that he was going to fulfill Jennifer's dreams; this clearly was not a safe relationship for Jennifer or her son. However, I believe people need to find the inner resources to let go of the illusions to which they are attached. One needs to develop the psychic muscles to be able to stay aware even when things seem difficult or unfair (Ram Dass, 1977).

TREATMENT

The Group

The other women in the group included a woman who had just been released from prison for child abuse; another woman who went into jealous rages and had been arrested many times for violence with various men; a woman who had been diagnosed with Huntington's disease and took her rage out on her child; and a heroin addict who was missing most of her teeth and who had been arrested for brawling in the street with her boyfriend. Another woman was an alcoholic, violent with her children, and 5 months pregnant with a fourth child.

I want to give a sense of the composition of the group because it does not matter with whom you are working; every person has something to give and can discover both support and self-esteem within a group setting. That is why it is much more useful to work with violent people in a group. Both individual and couples therapy can certainly be beneficial, but a group provides a context where real situations are shared and discussed in a way that takes away the shame and gives the participants the opportunity to both identify and objectify their behavior with much less resistance. The bonds and trust that they build over time are often the very things that most support their changes. When group members challenge one another on their choices, it is not coming from an authority figure, but from one of their own. The support and help they offer gives the facilitator the opportunity to point out the value of their comments and compliment them on their insight, thus building self-esteem.

In group the women role-played provocative situations that ordinarily would cause an angry reaction and practiced expressing themselves in positive ways, both by setting boundaries and by expressing themselves without blaming others. In one session, I asked each participant to name the person with whom she had the most difficulty setting boundaries. They each chose someone in the group who most reminded them of that person. They described the situation and then modeled how the problem person reacted when confronted with the problem. The person chosen to play the role of the difficult person would then, as verbatim as possible, recite back to the group member what they portrayed. We took turns playing the different roles until we were satisfied that we had the inner and outer demeanor to state a boundary, specify what would happen if the boundary was violated, and follow through with actions we knew we could perform. We also had special sessions on how to recognize and use both verbal and physical feedback as a way to empower oneself in various contingencies (Bandler & Grinder, 1979).

The Medicine Wheel

Because many of the people I work with are from Native American backgrounds, and I have found it very useful as a tool, I chose to use the Native American medicine wheel to help clients gain both insight into and objectivity around their problems. I have worked with several wonderful Native American medicine teachers. They have taught me about the medicine circle and how it helps one establish a sense of balance and honesty in one's life.

The circle has four directions. The North is the place of the mind, the rules and laws and philosophies of a society. It is balanced by the South, the place of trust and innocence, the place of the child, creativity, and spontaneity. The West is a place of the material world, the physical body, the accumulation of worldly goods and security, ego, and construction of self as an individual. This is balanced by the East, the place of spirituality, letting go, unconditional love, and death (Swiftdeer, 1994).

I asked each one of my clients to look at their problem from the point of view of the medicine wheel. What do the rules and laws say about their choices? From the North, they can ask themselves, are they acting in an ethical manner? Do their actions place them in jeopardy with the justice system? It was difficult for Jennifer to own her own inner authority. Because she had never been well supervised as a child, she did not like to look at her behavior from an adult point of view. The very fact that she was attracted to Frank, who was so antisocial, was clearly a way to act out her own dislike of any limitations on her behavior. She was uncomfortable with questions such as "Is it worth the risk? How will it affect others and your child?"

With no regard for authority, the place of the North, it was equally difficult for Jennifer to have a clear vision of herself from the South, the place of vulnerability. Jennifer could not see that she was not keeping herself safe. Although she was exposing herself to harmful situations, she was unable to recognize the danger. One day she showed up with fake bullet-hole decals all over her car. I was horrified. Although I stress leaving judgment at the door, knowing that she was involved in a custody case, I tried to convince her that this was a really bad idea. A social worker might not find humor in a car full of bullet holes, fake or not, when she was driving around her 2-year-old son. She was argumentative and assured me that "everyone thought they were hysterical."

When Jennifer looked at the world from the West, she was able to be more positive about her ability to provide for herself and her son. She had been successful at her job and was planning on going back to school someday in the future. Although she did not rely on others to take care of her, she had to think about the threat to her emotional survival if she really had to give up this relationship.

The East is the place of spirituality, where one discovers the sacredness of all life; it is here that the most important work is accomplished. I have never asked people to believe in anything but to go out in nature and experience the wonder and beauty of life everywhere. When people give to one another, when they share with honesty and respect, something happens. People develop the ability to shift from thinking only about oneself, from defending one's position, to showing the willingness to look at other possibilities, other choices. Jennifer had a kind and loving heart. She was generous with her time and support for the other women in the group. I believe that when she realized that from the inside out, she was a woman deserving of respect and love, her self-esteem and behavior began to change profoundly. She began to let go of wanting things to be different and accepting her life for what it was.

Family History

One of the problems that I faced with Jennifer was her inability to recognize or react to abuse in an effective way. She was unable and unwilling to believe that Frank would really do anything to hurt her. She would tell the stories of his abuse and, like many other victims, then defend him when others in the group became angry upon hearing about the things that he did to her. They would tell her that he was no good and that she should get rid of him, but to no avail. It was interesting how reactive they were to each other, but they did not see the danger in their own situations.

As earlier, this is the evidence of numbing or minimizing abuse from childhood. This does not necessarily stop when one reaches maturity. Jennifer's mother was herself immature and often left her children alone to run off with a new boyfriend. After a few days, the children would call their father, and he would come and pick them up. Her mother made promises that she seldom kept. As an adult, Jennifer chose a partner who abandoned her, who made promises and lied to her. Because she had always physically and verbally defended herself, she thought herself invincible. As any competent therapist knows, you cannot talk a person out of his or her commitment to a belief, especially if that person has made a huge emotional investment.

When doing her work with the medicine wheel, Jennifer was connecting with herself as a young child. She started to feel uncomfortable when Frank would call and threaten her or put her down, but she believed that she could stay calm and avoid losing her temper whenever she had to deal with him. I still believed that it would be safer if Jennifer did not see Frank at all. I tried to convince her that it would be better to have Frank pick Jason up at the police station or a public place. She insisted that she was fine. And for a while she was. Even when Frank tried to provoke her, Jennifer used the tools she had learned in group. She took time-outs and began to practice breathing exercises three times a day to relax. She used her journal to write about her fear of abandonment and how it related to her anger.

When Jennifer role-played herself as a child, she remembered her mother leaving her to go out with a new boyfriend. Jennifer was 8 or 9 years old. She ate crackers and peanut butter because there was nothing else in the house to eat. Two days later, when her mother returned and saw that the house was not cleaned up as she had required, she beat Jennifer, and when Jennifer tried to hit her back, her mother told her she hated her and called her father to take Jennifer back to his house. She sobbed as she remembered how scared she was. It was then that she realized that her mother had not loved her and that her father had not kept her safe. She was able to see that even though her mother no longer drank alcohol and had changed her life significantly, Jennifer still resented her and did not trust her. In fact, she said that she really did not trust anyone. The women in the group offered support, at the same time sharing that they did not trust anyone either. In spite of themselves, the bonds and trust grew, both in the group and between our weekly sessions.

Voice Dialogue

During some of our sessions, I introduced the work of Hal and Sidra Stone, who created "voice dialogue" (Stone & Stone, 1998). It is a therapy like Gestalt and psychodrama that gives voice to personalities that live within us. It is possible to hear the 4- or 5-year-old that lives behind the scenes but is still making decisions for us. Or we can listen to the voice of the critic who has nothing good to say and in some cases can be deadly. It is possible for a client to move from one sub-personality to another and then release them all and see them from a place of an "aware ego."

This is similar to work with the medicine wheel. It is more important to teach people how to release beliefs and stories that limit them than for them to parrot back social theories that tend only to explain behavior and have very little power to change it. However, if one can see that in one's own life, choosing power and control is the best alternative to love and approval, it is then possible to begin to appreciate the power that can come from self-approval and self-respect. It is easier to deal with a world that is often unfair and rejecting if we have the courage to accept ourselves and others for who we are and if we can clearly understand that denial equals helplessness.

"Body Scan"

Jon Kabat-Zinn (1990), an important figure in the world of stress management, has written many books on how to center one's mind and improve both one's physical and mental well-being. One of his exercises that I used with Jennifer was the "body scan." This process can be done sitting down, but it is best done lying down on one's back. The process can take up to an hour and brings awareness from the feet up through the body. There is nothing asked of the client except to notice where there is tension and where there is pain. The mind stays with the body and allows each person to become more and more aware of what is actually going on in his or her body. As is often the case with people who are overweight or unhappy with their body image, this is a difficult exercise to do. It is also difficult for people who have cancer or other ailments that they would rather ignore. What happens, almost magically, is that when one trains oneself to observe one's body without judgment, compassion seems to fill the void. Jennifer discovered that she could face her most frightening feelings; she could accept herself for who she was and did not need to allow fear and fantasy to run her life.

The Turning Point

After 6 months, Jennifer was feeling better about herself, but she still could not completely let go of her hope that Frank would wake up and become the man she knew that he could be. She still believed that he really loved her because she was the only person who had truly cared about him. The thought that Frank might really obtain custody of Jason was inconceivable to her. Because of her arrest and conviction, Frank was having visitation on weekends. Jason was coming back dirty and seemed to be frightened. The restraining order had been lifted, and Frank would come by Jennifer's to pick up Jason. Again I told Jennifer that I felt this was not a safe situation for her. When I spoke with social services, they said there was nothing they could do.

One day, when picking up Jason, Frank told Jennifer that he was going to get custody of their son, and she was never going to get him to pay child support. He yelled at her and backed her up against the wall. Out of fear and anger, she punched him as hard as she could in the face. He began to laugh as he wiped the blood with one hand and made a 911 call with the other. Jennifer was arrested and put in jail for 2 weeks. The courts gave custody of Jason to Frank. This was the turning point for Jennifer. She had to finally accept Frank for what he was and change her behavior if she was ever going to get her son back.

For the first time, Jennifer began to really question the choices she was making. The illusion was broken. She removed the fake bullet holes from the car and began dressing in clothes that were flattering and much less revealing. By her 9th month in the group, she was truly finished with her fantasy of Frank. Because of her obvious changes in behavior and her careful reporting of Frank's consistent poor parenting, she was able to win back full custody of Jason.

OUTCOMES AND CONCLUSION

Three years after our therapy ended, I sat across from Jennifer. She was smiling and seemed glad to see me. I had asked her if she would come and talk to me about her experience in the group and how it had affected her life. She told me that the one thing that kept her together when things were difficult was remembering my face and how much I really believed in her. She said that nobody had ever treated her with real respect. Her eyes were brimming over with tears. "I always thought

I was smart, but I had never been anywhere or seen anything. I am starting back to school as soon as this fall. I am in a wonderful relationship with a man who is kind to me. When I look back at who I was and how I acted, I can't believe I was that person. I heard that Frank has had two other children with that woman he was with. He still is doing drugs and living off of her welfare money." I smiled and asked, "Have you forgiven yourself for wanting love from the wrong person?" She answered, "I pretty much have, but I still get freaked out when I think that I could have lost Jason. I did learn that it was up to me to take care of myself. I'll never give that away to anyone as long as I can help it." "What do you want to do when you finally graduate from college?" I asked. "Maybe do what you do. Help crazy women learn how fabulous we are." We both laughed. "I hope you do. What a wonderful role model you are."

REFERENCES

Bandler, R., & Grinder, J. (1979). *Frogs into princes: Neuro-linguistic programming.* Boulder, CO: Real People Press.

Kabat-Zinn, J. (1990). *Full catastrophe living: Using the wisdom of your body and mind to face stress, pain, and illness.* New York: Dell.

Lang, R. D. (1985). *Theoretical and practical aspects of psychotherapy.* Presentation at the Evolution of Psychotherapy Conference, the Milton H. Erickson Foundation, Phoenix, AZ.

Ram Dass. (1977). *Grist for the mill.* Santa Cruz, CA: Unity Press.

Stone, H., & Stone, S. (1998). *Embracing ourselves: The voice dialogue manual.* Novato, CA: New World Library.

Swiftdeer, H. R. (1994). *Shamanic wheels and keys: "The green manual," an introduction to ancient wisdom.* Scottsdale, AZ: Deer Tribe Metis Medicine Society.

Yablonsky, L. (1976). *Psychodrama: Resolving emotional problems through role playing.* New York: Basic Books.

RECOMMENDED READINGS

Arrien, A. (2005). *The second half of life: Opening the eight gates of wisdom.* Boulder, CO: Sounds True.

Crum, T. (1988). *The magic of conflict.* New York: Touchstone Books.

Eddy, W. A. (2003). *High conflict personalities: Understanding and resolving their costly disputes.* San Diego, CA: William A. Eddy.

Kornfield, J. (1993). *A path with heart.* New York: Bantam Books.

Madanes, C. (1981). *Strategic family therapy.* San Francisco: Jossey-Bass.

Middelton-Moz, J. (2002). *Bullies—From the playground to the boardroom: Strategies for survival.* Deerfield Beach, FL: Health Communications.

Miller, A. (1986). *Thou shalt not be aware: Society's betrayal of the child.* New York: New American Library.

Sun Bear & Wabun. (1980). *The medicine wheel: Earth astrology.* Spokane, WA: Bear Tribe.

QUESTIONS FOR REFLECTION AND DISCUSSION

1 The author emphasizes the importance of violent clients learning to keep themselves safe. How does Jennifer's case illustrate this point?

2 What does the author mean when she says that in abusive intimate relationships, "it does not matter whose fault it is"? Do you agree or disagree?

3 Explain the function of the medicine wheel as an assessment and motivational tool. Why was it useful in Jennifer's case? How successful would a more confrontational approach have been?

4 The author indicates that there are some advantages of group therapy over couples or individual therapy. What are the advantages that she cites? Do you agree?

5 Helping Jennifer let go of her reunification fantasy with Frank was one of the author's primary treatment goals. What was the correlation, if any, between her emotional dependency on Frank and how she was raised as a child? What was the relevance of this work to Jennifer's problem with anger and violence?

15

Therapeutic Interventions to Domestic Violence With Immigrant Couples

MIRNA E. CARRANZA

In this chapter I present a case vignette that took place in a community agency, K-W Counseling, located in Kitchener, Ontario, Canada. This agency provides individual, couples, and family counseling. In addition this agency provides psychoeducational and therapeutic groups for men, women, and children. Some of the programs include employee assistance programs (EAPs), career and financial counseling, family life education, a family violence program, and specific services to immigrant families. The agency also acts as a training institute for future social workers and marriage and family therapists.

My practice focuses mainly in working with immigrants and refugee families who have settled in this specific geographic location. Posttraumatic stress disorders (PTSDs), acculturative stress, grief, parent–child conflict, and couple conflict resulting from acculturation are among some of the substantive presenting problems that I have dealt with on a consistent basis.

My preferred theoretical orientations relate to critical theories (Almeida, 1999) and therapeutic narrative (Freedman & Combs, 1996). Within these frameworks it is important to start the therapeutic process where the client is rather than immediately following my own agenda or a specific theoretical protocol. At the same time it is important not to shy away from the issue at hand, that is, domestic violence. More often than not, I follow Jenkins's approach (1990) when working with men who abuse their partners.

In the next section I draw from my clinical notes and observations as well as from audiotapes used in the session. The sessions were audiotaped with the clients' consent. Some of the audiotapes have been used for teaching purposes. Biographical information has been changed in order to protect the anonymity of the clients. The case vignette presented here highlights the complex dynamics of domestic violence.

CASE STUDY: NADINE AND NOAH

The couple, Nadine and Noah, came voluntarily. They were referred by a settlement counselor, whose role is to assist and support new Canadians in their process of adaptation to their new country. Among other services, settlement counselors provide support with language interpretation, subsidized housing, child care, employment, English as a second language schools, and so on. In working with Nadine and Noah, the counselor had become aware of issues concerning domestic violence. A child protection worker was already involved with the family because of reports of corporal punishment toward the children. Noah had confided in her that "things were rough at home" and that he had, in the worker's words, "slapped his wife across the face because she wouldn't listen to him."

The couple, who were originally from the Sudan, had been apart for 5 years. Noah had been in Canada 2 years before the rest of the family joined him; now they were in the process of readjusting to each other. They were also going through their own individual acculturation stress (Berry, 1991) and process; however, Noah had had a little more time to adjust to the changes in his cultural milieu.

Assessment

The assessment lasted approximately 2 hours. Both clients were in their late 20s and spoke English fluently. Noah was a tall and slim Black man, at least 6 feet tall. He appeared resistant to the idea of attending couples counseling. Nadine, a Black woman, was also tall. She appeared shy and even fearful at the beginning of the first session. Both of them towered over me—I am a short Latina woman (not even 5 feet!).

After shaking hands, we entered the counseling room, and I invited them to sit down. At this point, with Nadine standing beside him, Noah looked down at me and defiantly said, "I want you to know that in Africa we beat our women and children. We've always done it. There is nothing that you can say or do that will make me change my mind."

The dynamics had been set! Noah was in charge of the sessions. Needless to say, I stood in shock, without knowing what to say. Eventually, I responded with, "I understand. I read in the intake that you beat your wife, and that is the reason you both are here. Is it OK to ask you some questions about what happened, and then you can tell me about how couples relate in your country?" He nodded in agreement, and I proceeded to listen. I also took notes, but not until asking for his permission, blaming the need to do so on my poor memory. This allowed me to obtain a sociocultural-historical-political genogram (McGoldrick & Gerson, 1999). In this process I learned several things. Noah had hit and pushed his partner when arguing about how to discipline their three children. This had taken place several times over the course of their family reunification. Noah thought Nadine was too hard on the kids and that she tended to their misbehaviors in an overly punitive manner. Nadine tended to use name calling and at times resorted to corporal punishment.

Their domestic disputes usually took place when Noah intervened in an argument between Nadine and their oldest daughter. One day, in an angry moment, Nadine accused Noah of abandoning the family. She resented that she had been responsible for looking after them during all the years that he was gone. Noah slapped Nadine several times and pushed her on their matrimonial bed. He stated in the session that he had become very angry when he heard how his wife perceived his migration to Canada. He added that his trip to Canada had been harsh and that many times, he thought he would be killed by the smugglers along the way. He stated that he thought that their situation with Family and Children Services would worsen because she had agreed, in a previous meeting, that she would stop hitting the children, but she had not stopped.

Family History

Noah's migration to Canada was a 5-year process. It took him about a year to travel from the Sudan to Italy, where he lived in a refugee camp for 2 years. Then Noah entered Canada as a refugee. As soon as he arrived, he secured full-time employment as a factory worker. His family joined him 2 years later.

Noah had endured multiple losses. Noah was the third of 12 children; his father and three other siblings had been killed in the war. His mother remarried. He grew up in poverty. This along with the economic and social chaos (e.g., destruction of the infrastructure, including schools) created by the civil war in the Sudan did not allow him to continue his formal education beyond grade 3. He began working at the age of 10 in order to help his mother raise his other siblings. In his adult years, he had grown disconnected from his siblings because of the chaos of the war, as they each sought shelter in different African countries. He did, however, remain close to his mother. It is important to note that Noah stated, with great pride, that he was well liked by all community members because of his helpfulness in time of need and his generosity toward others. He grew up surrounded by many single women raising their children (most men had left to join the war or had been killed). As a young man he helped community members in performing menial tasks such as fixing things around other people's houses, carrying water to those who could not because of physical frailties, and so on.

Throughout Noah's narrative, I learned that he was beaten as a child by his father and stepfather. He also witnessed violent incidents between his stepfather and his mother. We discussed how these kinds of experiences tend to help us normalize the violence occurring within the family household. I also learned that Noah had resisted fighting in the war. He managed to move his family across the country every time there was a threat of recruitment in the surrounding villages. Noah exhibited a high level of adaptability as well as a strong commitment toward his nuclear and extended family and resilience to adverse circumstances and his migration journey.

Nadine was the youngest of four siblings. She never knew her father, who died shortly after her birth. She was raised by her older siblings, uncles, cousins, aunts, and other community members close to the family. They, more often than not, used corporal punishment as a disciplining method during her childhood and teenage years. Her family and Noah's family were neighbors. They became boyfriend and girlfriend at a young age: Noah was 15 years old, and Nadine was 13.

It is important to note that in the first session most of the interactions that took place were between Noah and me. The initial assessment revealed that the abuse was not severe and that Nadine was not in any immediate danger. Therefore, I felt comfortable with continuing the process in the same manner. Although I attempted several times to draw Nadine into participation in the sessions, she always declined. She smiled and said,

> It's OK. You talk. I like listening to the stories that Noah tells. I did not know so many things about him. It is like I'm getting to know him all over again. There isn't much to tell about me. I am the youngest of my four sisters. I went to live with Noah when I was 14 because I got pregnant. I have been living with his family ever since.

In my own internal dialogue I wondered about a few things. Was Nadine so overpowered by Noah that she was not aware of her own need to talk about the violence that was happening within the household? What happened to make her lose her voice? Was she just shy and not feeling comfortable talking to a stranger about intimate things, or was this shyness part of her cultural transition into Canadian society? I also wondered if the domestic violence had been part of their shared history in their country of origin. As the internal dialogue continued, I also wondered about possible interventions: whether I should attempt to see her alone so that I could fully assess the intensity of the abuse and educate her about the dynamics of woman abuse or whether I should begin with asking specific questions about the violence that was occurring at home. Either way, I also considered the consequences that any of my actions would entail—that the violence could increase, and we had not yet developed enough rapport or a nonviolence contract. I worried about putting her at a higher risk and causing the therapeutic process to end prematurely.

Although I continued to always ask at the end of each meeting if they wanted to schedule another visit and keep our conversation going, by the second meeting I had created an informal and warmer environment. I selected a counseling room that felt like someone's living room rather than a clinical setting. I brought a warm pot of coffee and cookies. As time progressed, however, Noah offered to bring the cookies himself.

TREATMENT

We met a second time without having yet developed treatment goals or a treatment plan. All they had agreed on was to tell me more about life in their country of origin; hence at the beginning of our second session, I asked if it was OK to present to them the information that I had collected from a genogram during our first meeting. Noah and Nadine sat and listened in a very attentive manner. I drew pictures depicting his network—that is, his extended family and close friends—in his country of origin and in the settlement country and pictures of Nadine's involvement within the household, raising their daughters while he searched for a better life overseas. I emphasized the pressures and challenges of parenting alone, especially when the partner has immigrated to another country, and the difficulties of maintaining a relationship across borders. I highlighted Nadine's dedication, survival, and commitment and the many sacrifices that she endured for the well-being of the family (e.g., starvation when there was not enough food for the four of them).

The genogram highlighted Noah's helping nature and his concern for his other co-ethnics and people in general. It highlighted his resilience and his commitment to his family in Canada and abroad. Noah's and Nadine's eyes watered several times as I proceeded to retell the story that I had heard from him, especially regarding the childhood beatings and being separated from his mother. However, I still had some questions, more specifically about the contradiction of not fully endorsing corporal punishment toward his children, when at the beginning of the first session, he had said loud and clear, "in Africa we beat women." Hence, at the end of the session, I said, "Noah, I am confused. I am confused because you said before that it is OK to beat women in Africa. You both were beaten as children, yet you're against beating your own kids. What is this about?" Nadine smiled and interjected, "I don't know."

Therapist: Is it okay if I ask you to think about this?
Noah: I guess so.
Therapist: It's a deal then. This is your homework.

Noah looked at me in a serious and pensive mode. I gathered he was deciding whether to challenge me. He said, "OK." At this point I knew that he had become invested in the treatment process.

Third Session

In our third interview Noah talked about how hard it had been for him when his father and stepfather physically abused him. He stated that he did not want his daughters to feel the same way that he felt as a child. Noah knew firsthand the sadness and despair that a child feels when he or she is being beaten. He disclosed that he had learned that children were not beaten in Canada and that it was against the law. He proceeded to say,

> I always thought that kids were beaten everywhere. That was the way life was. It was shocking for me to learn that they were not in Canada. I couldn't understand why. I still can't, but I think it is nice that children are protected here. My daughters are in Canada now, so I think that they should have the same treatment that other Canadian kids get. . . . We do not have these laws in the Sudan. It gave me great sadness when I first learned about this. I wish my father would have known.

The rest of the session was dedicated to processing Noah's grief about the abuse that he had endured as a child. Nadine shed some tears as she proceeded to console him. At the end of the session, I asked, "Noah do you know what happens here to the men who beat their wives?" He responded, "No." I said, "That's your homework then. I'd like you to do some research. I'd like you to ask other people in your community and in other communities about it." He and Nadine smiled.

Fourth Session

Noah was very anxious at the beginning of our fourth session. He immediately started saying, "I know. I know what happens to men when they beat their wives. I didn't know, I didn't know," he said repeatedly. "I am sorry, I am sorry," he said to Nadine.

Therapist: Should we talk about the violence happening at home then?
Noah: It has not happened for a while.
Nadine: Since we began to see you, actually.
Therapist: I think it is important that we develop a nonviolence contract. This would give us the opportunity to develop other alternatives. More specifically, it may give Nadine the opportunity to talk about what it has been like for her. Should we do this all together, or should Nadine and I meet alone? What is your preference?

They both paused for a moment, and Nadine answered this time: "I don't know."

Therapist: To tell you the truth, I'd feel a bit nervous if Noah is present because I do not know if his presence may put you [Nadine] more at risk. I mean, what if you [Nadine] say something that you [the thera-pist looks at Noah] don't like? Would this mean that you'll get angry and physically assault her when you get home? Therefore, I'd need to be assured that the violence will not increase after the sessions. It would be absolutely necessary that Nadine [looking at Noah] learn about some community resources that are available to her should the violence reoccur. Is this OK?

In this session we developed a nonviolence contract, a crisis plan, and a safety plan. Parallel to attending weekly sessions, Noah agreed to attend psychoeducational groups focusing on anger management and a second group for male perpetrators of abuse. The latter was a legally mandated intervention in Ontario through Ontario's Partner Assault Response program (PAR). These groups act to "promote attitude change among men and support and reparation for women victims" (Baobaid, 2007b, p. 1). In addition, Noah attended several lectures regarding the oppression that is endured by women and children in a patriarchal society.

Meanwhile, in our counseling sessions, Nadine was slowly challenging Noah's authority and lack thereof with the children. She thought that Noah was "too permissive" with the children. She was afraid that they were going to fall into drug and alcohol use. We discussed at length how she was responsible for their parenting while he was away working all day and how by challenging her role he undermined her authority in front of the children. We developed a contract of nonviolence toward the children on Nadine's part. We developed rules for fair fighting should arguments occur. If Noah disagreed with something, he would talk to her away from their children. They were going to make all decisions affecting the children together. They both attended a parenting group, Raising Children Between Two Worlds, specifically designed to address the parenting needs and concerns of immigrant parents and their children.

Remaining Sessions

We met once a month for the remaining five sessions. I became the cultural broker; that is, my role was to be their sounding board as they both struggled to make sense of the laws in their new country. For example, Noah complained that the psychoeducational groups that he was attending did not meet his needs and the needs of the other immigrant men in the group. He stated that there was no space to talk about their migration. There was not enough emphasis on the importance of family and community. Moreover, he believed that the group was aimed only at serving the needs of North American men who endorsed individualist values (Baobaid, 2007a). Noah began to explore other ways of relating to his partner. He ceased his dominating behavior, to the point where he eventually became a leader and strong advocate of women's and children's rights in the Sudanese community. Nadine, on the other hand, found it difficult to relate to such a different man, who swore not to beat his wife again. She stated that she missed the man in charge who used to order her around. They eventually decided to separate. The time away from each other as a result of Noah's migration had made them grow apart, and they had become two different people who wanted different things. Nadine left their three daughters under Noah's care and went to live in a different province. They continued to be good friends and to be supportive of one another.

NEW CASE: NOAH AND ANNA

Three years after his separation from Nadine, Noah remarried, once again to a Sudanese woman. Soon after their marriage, Anna, Noah's new wife, began to physically assault him. It was at this point that I realized that domestic violence is a multifaceted phenomenon in which men and women and parents and children can in due course become perpetrators or victims (Hamel, 2007).

Noah and his new wife Anna came to see me at the same agency in which Noah and I had previously met. They each had a different agenda in mind. Soon after our initial introductions, Anna stated that Noah needed help in becoming a "real Sudanese man." According to Anna, he did not behave like "other" Sudanese men did; that is, she wanted a strong man that took control of the household and the wife and kids. Anna was raised in Canada. She appeared to be comfortable with her own power. Moreover, she appeared to possess some *agentic* traits; that is, she was aggressive in the manner in which she talked with Noah (Archer, 2006). In her frustration Anna had begun to hit Noah, expecting that he would hit her back. Anna came across as an assertive and demanding woman. Noah had become a gentle and soft-spoken man. Noah wished the violence to stop.

Given that this time around, Noah had come on his own accord, and they were both familiar with Canadian laws, I proceeded to develop a nonviolence contract. Anna left the counseling room upset, stating that she did not come for this reason. I proceeded to explain to her what would happen to Noah if he physically assaulted her and conducted an assessment to determine if Noah might still be engaging in nonphysical abusive and controlling behaviors, such as emotional abuse, financial control, and such (Almeida, 1999). The assessment revealed that Noah had learned to be an egalitarian man who did his share of household chores—cooking, cleaning, and laundry, for example—and took most of the responsibility for driving the children around and helping them with their homework. In Anna's presence, Noah stated that he had attempted several times to include Anna and teach her about the household budget, but Anna always responded, "I am not interested in that." Anna worked part-time and also attended school part-time. Anna's income was used to pay for her tuition, books, and transportation. I asked Anna what her thoughts were about Noah doing laundry and cooking. She responded as follows:

Anna: I don't like it. I feel like he is not a real man. I feel like I married another woman. I asked other men at school if they do what he does in the house, and they respond, "No, I think you married a sissy," and they laughed at me. I get mad, so if he is going to behave like a woman, he might as well.

Therapist: What do you mean?

Anna: Well, women get beat, so maybe if he gets treated like one, he'll grab his balls and remind himself that he is a man and hit me back.

She proceeded to verbally abuse him in front of me. Hence, I had to intervene by establishing some rules. Anna perhaps endorsed the belief that Noah deserved to be ridiculed because of his lack of masculinity (George, 1994). On the other hand, Noah was acting under his new belief that men are not supposed to hit women.

Noah: I told you that I will never hit you. I am not like that anymore. It doesn't matter what you do or say to me. I swore to myself that I would never hit a woman for the rest of my life, and I never will. I will do anything and everything within my power to support and help women to get out of that situation and to help other men see that hitting women is not acceptable.

Anna: See, this is why other people make fun of me and him. They say that he is acting like a White man rescuing women.

Therapist: White men also abuse women, Anna. It seems that you're trying to control his behaviors by hitting, ridiculing, and verbally abusing him. These behaviors are not acceptable. You need to stop. I understand your frustrations. I wonder if you're feeling neglected. If you are, we should talk about it because if you keep hitting Noah, you could be charged and put in prison.

Anna: No, I won't. The police have come to our house before, and they laughed at Noah when he told them that I had thrown a chair at him and left.

The lack of police intervention had affirmed Anna's abusive behaviors toward Noah. She denied feeling neglected. She hesitantly agreed to a nonviolence contract in between sessions. Several sessions were scheduled and missed following our last session. One day I received an urgent call from the police asking me to vouch for Noah. Anna had stabbed Noah three times, and he was being rushed to the hospital. Anna had broken our nonviolence contract.

Noah spent a couple of days in intensive care because of the seriousness of his wounds and loss of blood, followed by a couple of weeks recuperating in the hospital. Through the apologetic account of a police officer, I learned that the neighbors had called the police because of a domestic dispute. The police came and dismissed, once again, Noah's concerns about being the victim of a spousal assault. Later on the same day, Noah's three daughters had taken refuge at the neighbor's house, stating that Anna was chasing their father in the house with a knife. One of the neighbors called the police again. The police came to their house, and upon seeing a Black man with blood on his shirt and a woman with blood on her clothing, they automatically threw Noah on the ground and proceeded to handcuff him. Noah tried to explain, but the police refused to listen to him. His daughters came out of the neighbor's house, saying, "What are you doing? He didn't do anything!" It was at this point that the police took the appointment card out of his back pocket and saw that he and his wife had been attending couples counseling. They took the handcuffs off and then realized that he was wounded and had lost a lot of blood. He was rushed to the hospital.

Anna was charged with assault with a weapon. Pregnant at the time, she was released on bail with the help of some community members. She was placed under house arrest under the supervision of her uncle. A restraining order was also put in place.

I continued to work with Anna individually. We focused on behavior modification. Anna also processed some unresolved childhood traumas stemming from having witnessed horrible events during the war and from enduring childhood physical abuse. She attended anger management community groups. She was referred to her family physician and a psychiatrist in order to further assess her mental health needs. Anna was found competent and was given a clean bill of health.

Noah paid Anna's legal fees and continued to financially provide for her and their newborn son. However, Anna verbally and physically attacked Noah again when he was picking up their son at a supervised parent–child place, this time in the presence of child protection workers. Her rationale was that he had arrived before her just to make her look bad in front of the workers—that he knew that she was always late and that he therefore should have arrived late himself. Noah sued and obtained full custody of their then-toddler son.

The couple eventually divorced. I continued to work with Noah and his daughters in order to process the violence they had witnessed and their grief resulting from the separation. Noah continued to work in the community supporting and educating his co-ethnics about the impact of domestic violence. His oldest daughter is currently pursuing a degree in social work.

OUTCOMES AND CONCLUSION

If my involvement with the family had stopped when Noah separated from Nadine, my theoretical stance would have continued to be rooted primarily in the belief that domestic violence always occurs as the result of women's oppression in the patriarchal societies in which they live. This belief was challenged when I met Noah a second time, after he remarried. My work with Noah and Anna taught me that violence is a complex social phenomenon that, at times, involves more than gender inequalities. It challenged my belief that when women engage in violent behaviors, they do so in self-defense (Hamel, 2007; Strauss, 2006). Although I do not diminish the roles of patriarchal factors, I am no longer oblivious to the idea that women are also perpetrators of abuse. They too engage in physical, verbal, and emotional abuse as a means to control their partners. I learned a hard lesson; that is, for many men institutionalized power may not translate to personal power (Felson, 2002).

My involvement in this case served as a catalyst for some organizational changes and program delivery. I brought up this case in peer supervision, and it turned out other therapists in the agency had encountered this phenomenon as well. We sought funding to develop and implement gender-inclusive therapy and psychoeducational groups. In addition, a grassroots initiative emerged aiming to support men who were victims of spousal abuse.

Additional research that examines how family members negotiate their individual changes, as a result of acculturation, in the context of their family would enhance our understanding about how immigrant couples deal with family violence and might provide insights for mental health professionals and others who work with these populations (Carranza, 2007).

REFERENCES

Almeida, R. (1999). The cultural context model: Therapy for couples with domestic violence. *Journal of Marital and Family Therapy, 25*(3), 313–324.

Archer, J. (2006). Cross-cultural differences in physical aggression between partners: A social role analysis. *Personality and Social Psychology Review, 10*(2), 133–153.

Baobaid, M. (2007a). *Attitudes of Muslim men toward domestic violence against women and children: An exploratory study.* Unpublished paper available from the author at mbaobaid@uwo.ca

Baobaid, M. (2007b). *Culturally appropriate interventions for Muslim and Arab men who have been abusive toward their intimate partners and their children.* Unpublished paper available from the author at mbaobaid@uwo.ca

Berry, J. W. (1991). Refugee adaptation in settlement countries: An overview with emphasis in primary prevention. In F. L. Ahearn & J. L. Athey (Eds.), *Refugee children: Theory, research, and services* (pp. 20–38). Baltimore: Johns Hopkins University Press.

Carranza, M. E. (2007). *Salvadorian mothers and their daughters navigating the hazards of acculturation in the Canadian context.* Unpublished doctoral dissertation, University of Guelph, Ontario, Canada.

Felson, R. (2002). *Violence & gender reexamined.* Washington, DC: American Psychological Association.

Freedman, J. R., & Combs, G. (1996). *Narrative therapy.* New York: Norton.

George, M. J. (1994). Riding the donkey backwards: Men as the unacceptable victims of marital violence. *The Journal of Men Studies, 3,* 137–159.

Hamel, J. (2007). Domestic violence: A gender-inclusive conception. In J. Hamel & T. Nicholls (Eds.), *Family interventions in domestic violence: A handbook of gender-inclusive theory and treatment* (pp. 3–26). New York: Springer Publishing.

Jenkins, A. (1990). *Invitations to responsibility: The therapeutic engagement of men who are violent and abusive.* Adelaide, South Australia: Dulwich Centre.

McGoldrick, M., & Gerson, R. (1999). *Genograms in family assessments.* New York: Norton.

Straus, M. A. (2006). *Dominance and symmetry in partner violence by male and female university students in 32 nations.* Paper presented at Conference on Trends in Intimate Violence Intervention, University of Haifa and New York University, New York.

QUESTIONS FOR REFLECTION AND DISCUSSION

1   How did the author's use of narrative therapy help Noah andNadine focus on their issues?

2   This case illustrates how family violence can take many forms. Is it possible to say which was the "primary" problem—Nadine's abuse of the children or Noah's abuse of Nadine? Who is typically most at risk in abusive families? Does this depend on the characteristics of each particular family?

3   As a result of working with Noah and his family, the author completely reevaluated her theoretical orientation to family violence, changing from the traditional patriarchal paradigm (men as batterers, women as victims) to a gender-inclusive one. Why do you think the patriarchal paradigm persists, despite its limitations? How well does this case show that patriarchal factors, more relevant in non-Western cultures, negatively affect both men and women?

16

Unresolved Family Violence: The Samaras

JODI KLUGMAN-RABB

In my private practice in Marin County, a wealthy suburban area north of San Francisco, I help clients with a variety of issues, including grief and loss, trauma, life transitions, and parenting. My primary area of expertise, however, is anger management. Some of my clients seek help on a voluntary basis and come from the general public and community mental health agencies; others are referred by the courts, probation, or Child Protective Services. My cases range from benign road rage to violent crime and include escalated interpersonal violence such as sexual and physical abuse, otherwise known as domestic violence or intimate partner violence, and in their more severe manifestations as intimate terrorism. In my view, successful treatment of anger problems and domestic violence must take into account both the client's deficits in managing his or her anger and backgrounds of abuse (Kemp, 1998) and is best approached using a comprehensive lens, examining environment, culture, socioeconomic factors, and—foremost in my experience—intergenerational family systems.

This chapter addresses the unique intergenerational effects of unresolved violence on a family I met early in my practice, one with enormous cultural and age differences. The case will illustrate the undeniable, practical utility of the cognitive behavioral approach in addressing everyday problems of communication and anger, as well as the benefits of the family systems model in allowing me to address the long-standing negative patterns of anger in families where traumas have not been adequately addressed. I have found the marriage of these two orientations to be highly effective when dealing with family systems and especially useful when brief treatment is required, as is so often the case nowadays.

In my practice, I work within several treatment modalities, from individual, couple, and family to multifamily groups. Although it is the modality that is least frequently used, family work offers the richest environment from which to effect healthy change. Family systems are the perfect vessels from which unhealthy patterns, traumas, and anger are transmitted down generational paths; family members who are by themselves unable to overcome unhealthy, deeply entrenched behavior patterns, despite their damaging effects, can be helped to change when they are seen as a system. My anger management work draws heavily from the research and clinical work of Ronald Potter-Efron (Potter-Efron & Potter-Efron, 1995), who has blended emotional management with family systems theory. Based on his ideas, I have created a curriculum for a successful family anger-management group program, in which the legal problems of adolescent offenders can be addressed in the context of their families, where there is the greatest opportunity for change. This highly structured yet loving framework creates a safe context for adolescents to express anger in appropriate ways and thrive within the new, consistent boundaries their parents are helped to establish. Built into the curriculum are concrete, practical parenting skills from the highly successful Parent Project™.

Although anger is part of the fight/flight instinct present in all animals, its expression is also a learned behavior that can be controlled to fit within a culture's laws and norms of acceptable behavior (Klugman-Rabb, 2001). Regardless of how it is defined or adjudicated, anger is a healthy and normal emotion. Rooted partly in survival instincts from human prehistory, anger continues to serve important interpersonal functions; it provides the motivation to confront what is threatening, unpleasant, or disruptive, and without this healthy compass, mankind would not have survived this long (Potter-Efron & Potter-Efron, 1995). However, demographic variables such as economic status, culture, religion, and gender strongly influence how anger is expressed within a given society. In families, learned anger responses are in turn passed down through the generations and then acted out by the identified patient (IP), prompting a major shift in that system.

This chapter explores the complex nature of family violence by il-lustrating the effects of demographic variables, unresolved intergenera-tional trauma, and adolescent misconduct. It demonstrates how consis-tent structure and positive reinforcement can help families overcome problems of abuse and violence in a system beleaguered with unresolved intergenerational anger.

CASE STUDY: THE SAMARAS

As is typical of families arriving at their first therapy session, the Samara family entered the office with composure, each member poised and pre-senting as if to suggest that nothing was wrong. Barbara, a 44-year-old Swedish immigrant, had been married to Isaac, a 61-year-old Armenian immigrant, for 21 years. Barbara had initially called, seeking counseling services because of the escalating emotional and sometimes physical vio-lence between her husband and her eldest son, Joel, 17 years old. Joel, who was expelled from mainstream high school 3 months prior to treat-ment, was also fighting outside the family with peers and was assigned a juvenile probation officer after being arrested on an assault and battery charge. The second son, 15-year-old Michael, said that he did not have an anger problem and expressed displeasure at having to participate in therapy, wanting to "stay out of it." All family members were intelligent, educated, well spoken, and groomed. Aside from Isaac's diagnosis of ADD, there was no history of mental illness. Isaac had recently experi-enced some cardiac-related scares but was the only one to present any medical issues.

I explained to all of them that their best chance at solving their prob-lems and bringing about a positive change in their situation was for ev-eryone to participate in family therapy together and to do so on a regular basis. Both parents were on board, and the two boys agreed to "go along for the ride." All four family members would attend 21 sessions, missing only two appointments in a year's time.

ASSESSMENT

During the initial assessment process, which took place during the first two sessions, the family's presenting concerns were identified, and the following family goals were agreed upon: reduce conflict in the home, establish harmony, and successfully get Joel back in school and off probation. A mental status exam completed in the first session provided a broad overview of their general functioning, but it was from a genogram (see Figure 16.1) that I was able to obtain the most useful and pertinent information with which to properly treat this family. Through the use of a genogram, therapists can identify old patterns of behavior, beliefs, myths, and assumptions passed from one generation to another and can forecast their effects on the current family system. A genogram can help the therapist discern who relates well or poorly to one another and how substance use, mental illness, and culture impact multiple generations of individuals who never knew one another.

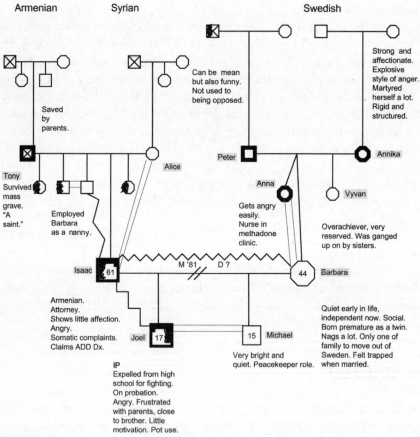

Figure 16.1 Genogram.

In family systems theory, restoration of the parental hierarchy is crucial when there has been discord and conflict among individual family members, and with the Samaras this was an important treatment goal. I also added communication proficiency training to the treatment plan to reduce anger reactions and provide family members the tools with which to appropriately assert themselves. Focusing on the family and restructuring hierarchies does not directly address peer fighting. There is a presumption, however, based on the strategic family systems work of Salvadore Minuchin (1974), that if the family can be induced to become harmonious and supportive of all its members, aggression is likely to also diminish elsewhere.

Isaac was visibly nervous for the first several sessions. He tried to explain this anxiety as related to his ADD, but it may have also been connected to what was going on in the therapy sessions—for example, Barbara's tendency to contradict him, which triggered embarrassment and quiet disapproval in him and palpable tension for the boys. Joel had trouble articulating the reasons for his overall angry feelings, but as the second and third sessions unfolded, he identified his mom's nagging and his parents' constant verbal fighting as triggers. According to Minuchin (1974), children of all ages will act out their pain within their family system until someone pays attention, and their needs are addressed. I believe Joel was unaware of this process until the third session. Barbara, however, was well aware of her nagging but felt she knew no other way in which to reach her son, whom she experienced as out of control and somewhat like his father.

Michael continued to lobby for his dismissal up to five sessions into treatment because of his compliant behaviors, which told me the family was pulling for homeostasis. Homeostasis is the common phenomenon that leads clients to revert back to old patterns because of their familiarity and "safety" despite negative outcomes. Through the fourth session, Joel predictably continued to act out against his parents through "calling them out" in session on what they were not addressing directly: The underlying marital discord and Isaac's abuse became the core issues of focus after the genogram was completed. Isaac used a deliberate style of anger (Potter-Efron & Potter-Efron, 1995) to wield control in his family. When Joel challenged him, Isaac escalated to physical violence (e.g., pushing and holding Joel up against a wall) but was able to keep it down to verbal abuse with Barbara. Michael stated he was not abused by anyone. It became clear that Joel's probation and expulsion from school were merely symptoms of the deeper issues no one wanted to face.

Family History

The genogram produced an immense amount of background information and history from both sides of the family. The most significant event was the genocide witnessed by Isaac's father, Tony, who was able to survive the forcible expulsion of Armenians from Turkey. Tony, a young boy at the time, was buried alive, naked and covered in gasoline, with neighbors and other members of his family (except his younger brother, whom their mother was able to hide) and ultimately climbed out of the mass grave. With nowhere to go, he met up with Arab Bedouins, who took him in as a shepherd until his 16th birthday. Through happenstance, Tony met up with the aforementioned younger brother in Jerusalem. After the expulsion and genocide, the brother had studied with Christian Dior, and he assisted Isaac in becoming a custom dressmaker like he had. In the first few sessions, Isaac described his father only in positive terms, always as a "good guy" and even a "saint." In later sessions, Isaac finally felt comfortable disclosing that his father was also withdrawn and moody. It took Isaac a long time to feel comfortable with me because his cultural norms prevented him from disclosing his true feelings to me so quickly.

Tony's marriage to Isaac's mother was arranged, lasting until Tony's death in the early 1990s, and Isaac had little to say about the quality of their marriage. Isaac was the fourth out of five children, all born in Lebanon, where their parents had settled. During Isaac's high school years the family moved to New York and eventually settled in California, where Isaac began to enjoy positive relationships with most of his siblings. Three of his siblings had a mental health diagnosis—a brother with depression, another brother with generalized anxiety disorder, and a sister with bipolar disorder. All entered professional careers and lived financially secure lifestyles. Isaac chose to be an attorney, and I wondered out loud to him if his championing the rights of others was more than a coincidence, given his family's history. Isaac shrugged and gave a detached laugh, as was his manner of dealing with the reflections I offered.

Isaac's mother, Alice, was the disciplinarian in his family of origin and had become a "preoccupation" in Barbara's experience. Isaac slept at his mother's home several nights a week, citing the proximity to his office, but Barbara felt this served only to keep them apart and spend less time together as a family. This issue was glossed over by the family and carried a greater weight than they recognized. This was evidence the nuclear family had become fragmented by the abuse and communication problems and left them feeling they were less important than the extended family. Recognizing the need to first build rapport, I decided to wait until the later stages of treatment to approach this issue, including the priority of the immediate family as manifested in quality time among it members.

Barbara described her family of origin as loving and nurturing, with no unspeakable traumas in its history like those of her husband's family, only a robust and healthy expression of anger. Anger was displayed openly and nonaggressively, allowing her to internalize it as a normal emotion. Barbara was one of three siblings and an identical twin who enjoyed strong positive relationships with all her family members. Her parents, she said, had a long-standing, "good" marriage and were professional, driven, and strict people, but she also revealed that her relatives from earlier generations were typically explosive, rigid, and intolerant of opposing points of view.

The most pressing therapeutic issue for Barbara was her experience of her husband trying to control her through arguments or manipulation. Attributing nearly all the blame to their cultural differences, they never considered the 16-year age difference to have an impact on their situation. Through the genogram, I learned how they met—Barbara had been the nanny to Isaac's brother's family. Again, the family minimized this fact, but I recognized its importance in setting up the structure for the marital roles. Barbara's experience of being controlled was very real and began as early as their first meeting, when she was introduced to him as "the help." A level of rejection and degradation had thus been quickly established, and this subtle pattern of abuse (Kemp, 1998) became a part of their relationship dynamic. By the time of our fourth session, the marital discord had become more apparent as Barbara took advantage of the safe environment therapy offered. She displayed her repressed criticism and argued in session, allowing me to witness firsthand the abusive, sneaky family dynamics.

There was no doubt that unresolved anger and trauma were influencing this family to act out upon each other aggressively. The extent of the aggression was fully revealed when Joel later disclosed the physical fighting between him and his father. Barbara acknowledged that and disclosed her own victimization by Isaac, characterizing the abuse as purely emotional through the controlling behaviors and attacks on her character. Michael had maintained his innocence from these problems, remaining a passive figure in the room, until the seventh session, when he began to acknowledge that he was more affected by the fighting than he had realized and began to champion the treatment, thus triggering the last remaining shift required to promote change.

TREATMENT

With the history completed, it was now appropriate to discuss the psychological role of anger. Anger is a motivating emotion, intrinsic to our psyche, part of the fight/flight response instinctual to all animals. We use anger as a catalyst to change what we have identified as not working for, or hurting, us. It is important to understand then that anger is a normal and healthy emotion, which can be used as a positive tool for expressing needs, as well as something that can be used inappropriately or downright cruelly.

Patterns of anger are repeated in family systems intergenerationally until a catastrophe or the IP brings the family in for treatment. Individuals misread anger cues, become defensive, and find it difficult to express and control this emotion appropriately as it spreads like the flu, catching from person to person. Joel was the IP in this case because of his involvement in the judicial system, but it quickly came to light that everyone was unhappy. Michael's decision to engage in treatment presented a major turning point in treatment because Isaac could no longer deny the realities of the family dynamics. The family's anger revolved around Isaac's misuse of anger. Kemp (1998) cites the ecological model for understanding psychological maltreatment when examining the effects of abuse on children. Within a family context, "parental activities" beget a "child's personal characteristics," begetting a "child's behaviors and other manifestations of the self," begetting "parents' personal characteristics and perceptions of the child" (Kemp, p. 86). Isaac was unable to see the vast implication of his anger for the family because of his preoccupation with his own relationship with his father.

I have focused thus far on the fascinating history of the family, and now it is important to explain the assessment of abuse as indicated by Joel and Barbara.

Juvenile probation and the school district were already involved with the family as a result of Joel's acting-out behavior, as was Child Protective Services (CPS) because of Isaac's violence against his minor son. This placed a predictable, troubling strain on the therapeutic relationship with Isaac, undermining the rapport that we had established.

CPS can be a difficult agency to work with because it is experienced as intrusive, even bullying, by families. I try to counteract this reaction by emphasizing the positive side of its involvement: despite the often embarrassing and seemingly endless questions, CPS is there to provide support and resources when parents are incapable of changing themselves. When the circumstances require it, there can be legal action taken against the parents, yet I still urge my clients to cooperate and adjust their expectations to allow for support rather than intrusion. Whenever possible, I make sure that I place calls to CPS while in the session with the family. The parents have the benefit of hearing everything in real time, eliminating the selective hearing and misinterpretation that occurs through third parties. The intake staff can then speak with the parents directly as well, helping to reduce their fear of the unknown. I always offer my full support in the process, and when approached this way, families generally cooperate and have a successful experience. In this case, CPS decided not to investigate because of Joel being almost 18 years old. With a report on file, the treatment was free to move forward, and I was able to reengage Isaac because of the support I had offered in dealing with CPS.

In general, treatment goals are designed to move the client away from harmful habits and toward healthy, sustainable self-actualization. Cases involving violence or abuse must prioritize client safety as the initial treatment goal—in the Samaras' case, reduction of emotional abuse and elimination of any physical harm prior to any other cognitive or emotional work. In conjunction with the CPS intervention, I notified the family that if I was told of any further violence, or if I saw physical evidence of violence on any of the family members, I would call the authorities to create safety. The family was asked to sign a no-violence contract that spelled out a protocol for dealing with escalated temperaments and identified myself and two other "safe people" to call when anyone felt an argument was getting out of control. They were also advised to call the police if they were threatened with immediate harm between sessions. Interventions for safety can be significant roadblocks to rapport and therefore treatment success. Although Isaac remained reluctant to contact any authorities because of his involvement with probation and CPS, my experience has taught me that people in similar situations recognize they are out of control and welcome intervention when needed.

Remaining treatment goals were identified in order for the family to understand the roots of the dysfunction and included the following: increase parental unification and hierarchy, teach appropriate disciplinary methods, increase consistent positive parenting, reduce marital tension, and increase assertive communication techniques. All treatment goals were conducted within family systems and cognitive-behavioral orientations and remained unchanged throughout treatment. I relied heavily on the genogram to successfully attain these goals.

The Genogram

The genogram is compiled over several sessions explicitly to involve family members in describing how they inherited their patterns, as well as to motivate them to adopt an internal locus of control. Until threaded together through a genogram, patterns often go unaccounted for. Initially, Isaac found it "impossible" that he was expressing anger learned from his father and that Joel was learning the same lesson. Ultimately, the genogram worked as an intermediary, providing Isaac with sufficient distance to accept responsibility for the mistreatment of his family and see that he was not the bad person he feared therapy would expose him as being.

In the first phase of treatment, Isaac had been resistant, concerned that he was being labeled a "bad guy" or a "child abuser." Ultimately, the genogram helped Isaac reframe his experience—how he needed for his father to be a "saint" and that they were both good people making bad choices. Throughout his life, Isaac had defined himself in harsh terms, never feeling that he "measured up." This internal dialogue held him back from practicing patience with himself and others. The genogram helped him to internalize a broader definition of himself, one that included "bad choices made by a good and sensitive man," thus helping him change his internal dialogue and therefore the family dynamic.

Another layer of the genogram included cultural considerations, composed not only of ethnic origin and practices but also of socioeconomic and age factors. The Scandinavian culture taught Barbara to be compliant and supportive, as she described it, despite the emotional abuse she would eventually endure. Therefore, Barbara felt an internal struggle between those cultural norms and the sense of individual safety and self-esteem she had acquired from her adopted American culture. Barbara's nuclear family was rigid and strict, yet she did not feel abused by them in any way, and her personality allowed her to feel supported in this environment. Her life with Isaac was different in that he controlled the finances and restricted her emotional expression. Life in American culture opened her eyes to the possibility of self-expression, something she had never been aware of in her family of origin in Sweden. Conversely, Isaac was struggling with tendencies to control and with demonstrative expressions of emotion inherent to the Armenian/Middle Eastern culture, immediately placing him at odds with American values. The boys, who had three cultural norms to choose from, identified with the dominant, peer-based American values.

Cultural examination requires sensitivity, so I approached this issue with the goal of fostering acceptance. In one session, I asked each family member to identify the three most valuable aspects of the three cultures and then the three least valuable characteristics. This exercise provided a "cobweb" type of diagram concerning the commonalities among the family members. Barbara valued honesty and education but shunned total materialism, inequality of gender roles, and teenagers' narcissistic self-preoccupation in the States. Isaac valued structure and respect and disliked what he termed "therapy culture," rudeness, and teenage narcissism. Both Isaac and Barbara identified the priority placed on family by their respective cultures, so we focused on this common valued goal. Michael identified strongly with socialization, money, and work, and Joel stated freedom, music, and friends. Both boys agreed parental controls, greed, and crime were the downfalls of American culture. All these cultural characteristics are common complaints and benefits of the American, Swedish, and Middle Eastern cultures they blended. With this common foundation clearly in place, I asked them to prioritize the important qualities and exclude the lesser ones, thereby creating a harmony for the family designed specifically for them, by them. Immediately, a collective sigh of relief was experienced, and the parents unified around a new common goal: family harmony expressed in quality time together and successfully launching the boys.

Although Isaac's legal practice generated a comfortable living for the family, a considerable amount of the money was tied up into Barbara's pursuit of a bachelor's degree. This contributed to many financial arguments. Because of the level of emotional separation in the family, I asked the parents to postpone worrying about superfluous needs they or the boys may have and helped them establish priorities that would reflect the importance of the family over things. Using the genogram to explore Isaac's control over money yielded both expected and surprising results. Middle Eastern culture demands that men be in control, yet he had not considered the generational impact of his father's poor Bedouin shepherd's need to save, which he equated with survival. Sometimes, the simple act of shining a light on the darkest corners of a client's life can produce enough insight to dramatically shift how they view these experiences.

In a subsequent session I changed my focus and asked the family to create significant and consistent family time each week in order to facilitate more positive attention. The boys expressed concern that dedicated family time would detract from their social schedules. My response was to redirect their attention on what will help rather than what will prohibit the goal of family unity. Family mealtimes remain the most effective way to keep family members supporting one another emotionally and cognitively, by stimulating conversation and promoting intellectual growth through problem solving and discussion, to keep kids invested in the family and using good judgment (Gallup, Syracuse, & Oliveri, 2003). "All of the research points to the fact that eating family meals together influences family communications. . . . development of family traditions . . . and character and social development, while building and strengthening family bonds" (Gallup et al.). Other benefits include consuming a better overall diet, increasing vocabulary in toddlers, decreasing risk for eating disorders in girls, increasing academic performance, and reducing likelihood of smoking, drinking, and drug use in teens (Lamb, 2007). Structured family time offers kids a great sense of security that sets up a strong foundation for later life skills.

Cognitive-Behavioral Therapy

Once the interpersonal work from the genogram had been completed, I shifted my attention to the goals of parenting and communication, using a cognitive-behavioral approach. In this type of work, the initial focus is on identifying the family members' self-statements, some of which are functional and some of which are detrimental. Isaac held and acted on numerous damaging beliefs ("I am not good enough and haven't lived through enough to be of value"), all stemming from his father's traumatic origins, which he then translated into beliefs about himself. Barbara's self-statement was more productive—"I am good enough on my own"—but clashed with her husband. The boys alternated between "Why am I surrounded by trouble?" and "I can be successful and happy." In these sessions, I felt like an archeologist at an excavation site, having to dig through the layers of a family's past until I reached a foundational level from which to rebuild a functional, supported structure. The "dig" can encounter resistance or even sabotage depending on the entrenched belief statements and patterns. This was the case with the Samaras, at first with Michael presenting resistance and ultimately with Isaac, who insisted that the family dynamic was not a big problem throughout the early treatment—both pulls toward homeostasis. Ultimately, however, Isaac was able to let go of his irrational beliefs and ascribe them to his father, thus freeing him to formulate his own positive thoughts and take responsibility for them.

Anger management therapy also has a cognitive-behavioral component and goes hand-in-hand with parenting and communication skills training. The course of anger management treatment begins with identification of triggers and cues and is completed when assertive tools have been learned and practiced. The thermometer exercise (Potter-Efron & Potter-Efron, 1995) is the first anger management tool in my practice. Drawn from the analogy of a thermometer, the client is asked to view his or her anger as low (level 1), mid (level 2), or high (level 3) in range and then describe those levels using the terms provided (see Figure 16.2). Clients typically describe "frustration" as level 1 anger, whereas "ballistic" or "furious" is associated with level 3. Primarily the thermometer is used by a client as an internal assessment to prevent anger from escalating; however, its secondary function is to reduce miscommunication among family members by acknowledging differing perspectives in language (e.g., Isaac labeled "frustration" as level 2, yet Joel labeled it level 1). Automatic escalations occur in these situations when families incorrectly identify thermometer levels. For example, Joel would often incorrectly judge his father to be at level 1 when Isaac used the term "frustration" because he attributed it to his own thermometer, instead of the actual level 2 Isaac experienced. If individuals consistently attend beyond level 2, the limbic brain takes over, and the use of assertiveness tools is minimal at best.

I asked the Samara family members to become familiar with the results of each other's thermometer exercise in order to reduce miscommunication and unnecessary conflict and redistribute the control Isaac had become accustomed to wielding. Anger management succeeds when individual clients are able to identify appropriate means of self-control and expression, but it excels when whole families learn the styles of their members. When the thermometer exercise is accompanied with body cues, where somatic manifestations of anger are identified, a comprehensive assessment tool is always at the family's disposal, beginning with the individual and culminating with the collective dynamic. Joel and Michael's results were typical of the adolescent males in my practice in

Acrimony Affront Agitated Angry Animosity
Annoyed Antagonized Ballistic Blow Up Bothered Bugged
Chagrin Choler Conniption Cross Dander Disapprobation
Dislike Displeased Distemper Disturbed Enmity Exasperated
Frustrated Fuming Furious Gall Grouchy Hatred Huff
Ill Humored/Tempered Impatient Indignation Infuriated Insulted
Ire Irked Irritated Mad Miffed Offended Outraged Peeved
Piqued Pissed Off Provoked Rage Rankled Resentment Riled Up
Snappy Snarly Sore Stew Sulky Ticked Off Tiff Troubled
Umbrage Upset Vexed Violent

Figure 16.2 Thermometer exercise.

that they experienced a lot of sensation in their hands, which would ball into fists. Barbara was more cerebral and quiet, so her cues manifested in the tightening of her jaw with eventual headaches—both effects of passive, unresolved anger. Finally, Isaac manifested in the chest and abdominal regions, contributing to his cardiac issues mentioned earlier along with irritable bowel issues.

The Value Shield

The next crucial tool in building communication is the value shield (Potter-Efron & Potter-Efron, 1995), another internal anger management tool used to develop a deeper understanding of core beliefs and what triggers anger (see Figure 16.3). The premise of this exercise is that an individual's core values will trigger anger when his or her needs are not being met. For example, a value of honesty triggers anger when lying occurs.

Instructions: On the shield below, indicate the six most important values in life for you. Make a red square around the one that is most important to you.

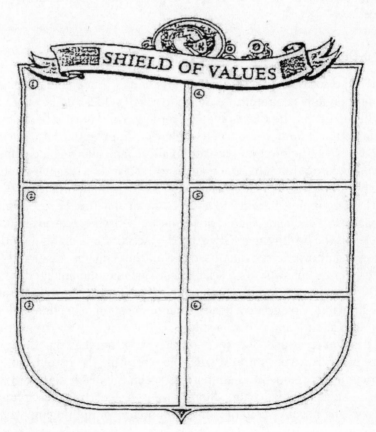

Figure 16.3 Shield of values.

In order to break through the initial resistance to this intervention, the client is asked to think about what is most important to him or her, in a stream-of-consciousness fashion, and then to reduce the list down to his or her top six core values, such as honesty or responsibility. I then work with each member to backtrack to triggers from recent experiences of anger. Both Joel and Michael identified the value of freedom, whereas their parents identified respect. Initially Joel identified cars as a value and later redefined the importance in the freedom a car afforded him by processing what would anger him about not having a car. The Samara family yielded results expected of most families—different values identified by parents compared to the children and adolescents. These results are typical because values are fluid, changing over time with developmental stages and new experiences. Through the mutual values identified in this exercise, I was able to reframe the communication problems they were experiencing as errors in their presentation and established another common goal: respect for the parents and individuality for the teens.

Time-Outs and "I" Statements

Next we discussed the use of time-outs and "I" statements, necessary to appropriately communicate their identified values and level of anger established from the thermometer exercise. Time-outs are effective in setting strict boundaries on one's behavior, interrupting disagreement and disrespect before they escalate to abuse, and allowing a cooling-off period before attempting once again to resolve the issue. I asked the family to practice "I" statements (e.g., "I feel unimportant when you don't listen to me") in order to address the dual nature of responsibility in anger and reducing shame or blame by behaving assertively. Assertiveness is the healthy anger style, used to accept the feelings underlying anger (e.g., powerlessness and sadness in the Samaras' case) and label the triggering behavior (e.g., Isaac did not listen or manipulated for control). The combination of "I" statements and time-outs reduces anger and ultimately violence to a healthy communication of needs and desires inherit to all functional relationships.

I taught Isaac and Barbara parenting skills, emphasizing the importance of structure in contrast to discipline by using the Parent Project™ curriculum, developed to help parents specifically with destructive and abusive adolescent behaviors. Many parents are fearful of discipline because of the negative connotations from their own upbringing, whereas structure also implies consistency, a key to parenting and without which boundary testing or acting out is sure to follow. Highly demanding of parents, this parenting protocol calls for them to overcome any remaining disagreements and join in a strong alliance, difficult for Isaac and Barbara to attain. They learned to formulate plans before addressing the boys with structure in order to join forces and prepare for escalation. Ultimately successful, Isaac and Barbara realigned the family hierarchy and bolstered boundaries also described as house rules by redefining grounding, planning discussions ahead of time, and using more positive reinforcement.

The two cornerstone interventions include highly structured grounding for misbehavior and positive reinforcement for good behavior. Like traditional grounding, the child is confined for a week's time period, but the removal of all desired privileges is enforced to closer resemble the consequences of an adult's world. It is a lengthy program best summarized for this chapter's purposes as teaching parents how not to argue with defiant, violent, or willful children while they *also* show them they are loved through positive reinforcement. Praise was absent in the Samara household, so it felt foreign to Isaac, who found some difficulty with the assignment because his parents did not model that in his childhood. Barbara, on the other hand, was naturally adept at praise because of her more sensitive nature but lacked the consistency required to impose consequences. This far into treatment, they were able to focus on using their respective strengths to bolster the hierarchy and back one another up, and the parenting tools in turn became another common goal that served to bolster the marriage, in that Isaac and Barbara rallied around the tools. Both had become accustomed to focusing on the negatives about each other and the family. The new parenting tools became common goals because they served to unify them and gave them something to work for together.

OUTCOMES AND CONCLUSION

One year after treatment, the Samaras terminated, ready to apply the tools learned as a family. The combination of family history, communication, and parenting skills interventions allowed for nonviolent communication and an increase in family harmony.

Ultimately, Isaac released the grip of power he held over the family and redistributed it to his wife, promoting partnership. He addressed the emotional pain learned from his father in the form of damaging self-statements and redirected it to the appropriate owner, thereby reducing negative cognitions contributing to poor parenting and the unraveling of his marriage. Barbara learned how to apply communication skills to further her ability to communicate without nagging and foster mutual respect in her marriage based on a balance of power. Most importantly, violence was eliminated from the repertoire, including emotional and financial control.

The change toward positive, consistent parenting provided Joel a safe container to stop acting out, and the boys began to trust their parents more now that Isaac and Barbara were working toward a unified parental hierarchy. Both Joel and Michael were able to address untapped thoughts and feelings regarding their family and enjoyed a greater range of personal satisfaction in all areas of life, including personal interests and employment. For Michael especially, given his initial resistance, family anger management provided him with confidence to directly address a previously unknown need for more visibility in the family. Michael began therapy believing he had no problem in asserting himself but left understanding that he was really trying to keep the peace by remaining quiet. Joel successfully enrolled back in the high school of his choice and reported a greater sense of confidence.

Some years after termination, I met Joel again and learned that Barbara had decided to leave the marriage, believing she "grew" beyond the capacity of Joel's father. Although the abuse had stopped, the limits Barbara still faced in the marriage appeared contrary to her emotional growth. Treatment may not always accomplish 100% of its goals, as evidenced by Barbara and Isaac's eventual divorce. However, given the enormous differences this family faced with culture, age, and intergenerational transmission of trauma, a different perspective suggests their success was in allowing each other to be who they needed to be as individuals without violence.

REFERENCES

Gallup, S., Syracuse, C. J., & Oliveri, C. (2003). What the research tells us about family meals. *Family tapestries packet.* Columbus: Ohio State University Extension.

Kemp, A. (1998). *Abuse in the family: An introduction.* Pacific Grove, CA: Brooks/Cole.

Klugman-Rabb, J. (2001). *Multi-family anger management group curriculum.* Unpublished manual.

Lamb, M. (2007, August). Happy meals! How to make family dinners easy, sane and fun for all. *Parenting*, 77–80.

Minuchin, S. (1974). *Families and family therapy*. Cambridge, MA: Harvard University Press.

Potter-Efron, P., & Potter-Efron, R. (1995). *Letting go of anger: The 10 most common anger styles and what to do about them*. Berkeley, CA: New Harbinger.

QUESTIONS FOR REFLECTION AND DISCUSSION

1   The author asserts that "family work offers the richest environment from which to effect healthy change." To what extent does her work with the Samaras support or fail to support this point of view?

2   What was the relevance of Isaac's family of origin to how he expressed his anger around Barbara and the boys? What irrational beliefs did he need to overcome in order to stop his abusive behavior?

3   In what ways was the genogram helpful in getting Isaac to reframe his experiences and thus become motivated to take more responsibility for his actions?

4   Describe the value shield and its application to anger management. How did the author use it to help members of this family reduce the conflict among one another?

17

Addressing Family Systems Issues in a Psychoeducational Group Setting

DARLENE PRATT

As a marriage and family therapist and certified domestic violence counselor, I work with many issues, including anger, family violence, sexual addiction, and codependency. I serve a socioeconomically and ethnically diverse population. My agency in Walnut Creek, California, is certified in three counties to provide batterers' intervention programs for men and women. Referrals for groups come from criminal courts, Children and Family Services, Family Court Services, and other agencies. Some group clients are self-referred. I also conduct mixed-gender anger management and couples groups and a 52-week family violence/high-conflict parenting program.

My treatment approach is eclectic; I believe that therapy ought to begin where the client is, and I choose interventions based on a thorough assessment of the client's needs. I view most issues through the family systems lens but often use cognitive behavioral and psychoeducational techniques—especially in group work. Family-of-origin issues, trauma and attachment theories, and the intergenerational transmission of violence inform my work. With individuals and children, I use eye movement desensitization reprocessing (EMDR) when trauma is hindering growth and change.

Intimate partner violence usually involves mutual abuse (Morse, 1995; Straus, 1993), and even when a perpetrator and a victim can clearly be designated, family systems can be an effective model through which

307

to view marital conflict. From this perspective, problematic behavior is seen as an outcome of family interactions and not exclusively as an individual problem or deficit. In a systems context, causality is circular or reciprocal, and problems, including interpersonal violence and child abuse, may be manifested in family organizational structure and development (Hamel & Nicholls, 2007). According to Michael E. Kerr (1981), "Conflict in the marriage often provides an amazingly stable 'solution' to the relationship dilemma of the need for emotional closeness on the one hand and the allergy of too much closeness on the other" (p. 243). Both the personal and the family emotional system operate as if governed by the interplay of two counterbalancing forces—individuality and togetherness.

Family conflict can sometimes reflect the push–pull for change and homeostasis. If one considers the nuclear family as an emotional system, there may be four options in responding to acute or chronic relationship tension: distance, conflict, compromise of individual functioning, or banding together on a common issue—often a concern over a child. When these options fail to restore equilibrium, or conflicts become too intense, the distress may spill over into other parts of the system—for example, to children or extended family in the form of triangles or out into the larger system, which is where therapists, courts, agencies, and lawyers become involved. In working with couples or individuals, educating the clients about how family emotional systems work can be an important aspect of the early stage of treatment. This can give a better understanding of beliefs, themes, roles, and patterns that are systemic. Systems perspective allows a way to reframe the presenting problem from one of individual failure and defectiveness to one that relates to family patterns. Client motivation and hope are increased when the client understands that family patterns may be more easily shifted than individual failures or flaws can be changed.

A systems approach can blend well with cognitive-behavioral work as the clients grasp that emotional reactivity must be lowered in order to change roles, restructure hierarchy, repair developmental gaps, create new patterns of behavior, and better adapt to life cycle changes. The emphasis on thinking, rather than being emotionally reactive, maximizes the possibility for change.

CASE STUDY: CARMELLA

Carmella, a petite, dark-haired 39-year-old architect, self-referred to our office because of increasing depression, rage, and dissatisfaction. Feeling powerless to control her destructive behavior, she wondered if her anger outbursts were adversely affecting her daughters, ages 3 and 9. The daughter of Hawaiian-Japanese immigrants, Carmella had married a White man 12 years before. She characterized their relationship as having been "okay prior to the birth of our youngest daughter," Solana, age 3, but admitted that her rage had escalated in the last year, and she experienced bouts of screaming, yelling, and destroying property. She was verbally and emotionally abusive to her eldest daughter, Sarah, as well as to her husband, screaming, criticizing, and belittling. On occasion she pushed, shoved, and slapped her husband.

Although there were periods of mutual aggression, Carmella could admit that she was the primary aggressor. Her husband, Kevin, referred himself to our program after he had thrown a dish at her for berating him as he cleaned the kitchen. He was appalled by his behavior and knew the parental discord was affecting their children. He joined a 52-week men's anger management/domestic violence group and was near completion when his wife decided to seek help.

Carmella admitted, "He has changed dramatically, so our old patterns are not there." Yet she experienced his refusal to engage as unwillingness to support and reassure her, and this further enraged her. When she began one of her rage attacks now, he often left the house with the children so that they could escape the tirade. She interpreted his new behavior as a sign of weakness.

Carmella confessed to using alcohol as a way to deal with her feelings of boredom and disappointment with her husband, a feeling of emptiness within herself, and her worries over the things she had not yet accomplished. Even though she loved her career, she remembers being happiest when she was in school. She complained that she felt like the "man of the house." She viewed her husband as too passive. Paradoxically, she also felt that it was his house and that he had made the kids too dependent on him: "The girls are too needy, always too dependent on Kevin." This was her perception because the girls seemed to look to Kevin for help and support and enjoyed spending time with him. I did not witness this dynamic, but Kevin's perception was that Carmella's erratic behavior made the girls anxious—they never knew when she would be able to give the safety and support they needed. I wondered if they were exhibiting the anxiety and regression that children in abusive families can experience.

One of Carmella's anger triggers was Kevin's inability to undertake major home repairs, even though they were both successful professionals who could afford competent services. It contributed to her view that he was "not a man."

Carmella admitted that she needed to have the "areas around me in perfect order to give me a sense of inner order." Sunday nights were a stressor as she tried to get the house organized for the workweek. She was usually disappointed in the weekend because either Kevin had failed to attempt home repairs or family outings were frustrating as a result of his "slowness in getting prepared." On Sunday evening, if she walked into the living room and found shoes and newspapers, she would scream and rage that "no one appreciates me, and I have to do everything" or that they were "lazy and incompetent." She sometimes threw items down the hall. When this happened, Kevin would alternate between becoming defensive and argumentative or silently putting things in order. The 3-year-old would cry, and Sarah would scoop up her toys and run to her room. None of these responses gave Carmella any relief.

Previously, they had tried couples counseling for 1 year through their insurance plan and later continued with another therapist for 6–8 months. "It was not productive; it just gave us a safe place to spar," Carmella said, so she was not open to trying marital therapy at this time. Carmella had also completed a brief 6-week anger management class and was currently on psychiatric medication for depression. Her husband was in individual therapy with one of my colleagues concurrent with his participation in our men's group. At the time of her intake at our office, she was willing to give the relationship "6 months."

Carmella was an outwardly anxious individual with a frustrated, hopeless attitude. She spoke of her extreme anger with her husband, whom she described as "indecisive and slow." She was attractive and well groomed and reported being successful in her profession; she was an architect in a large, long-established firm.

Carmella was enmeshed with her family of origin. Because she had complained to them regularly about all of Kevin's faults, they had taken her side and were thus unable to be supportive of any family repair attempts. Her father was an alcoholic who raged at his family and demanded allegiance. She had several brothers and sisters and described family gatherings as being "loud and sometimes angry."

Carmella had also complained to her friends about Kevin. Some of them sided with her, yet she had alienated others who knew him and did not hold her view. She also admitted she had lost some friends "because I can't commit; I often cancel our plans at the last minute." She reported she had some minor difficulties at work because of her frustration and perfectionism but had no major outbursts in that setting.

Kevin was deliberate and thoughtful with a less forceful manner. Age 41, he was slim, and he wore glasses and dressed in low-key professional attire. He was quite successful in his career as a computer expert in an engineering firm. He had an MBA as well as a master's degree in computer science. An only child, he reported that he felt close to his father, who was ailing, but was unable to spend much time with him because of Carmella's objections. His mother had died when he was 3. He described his father as "a quiet man who reasoned with me rather than spank." Kevin shared that he had few male friends; he preferred activities with his wife and children. He talked of his daughters fondly and talked also of his attempts to protect them from his wife's nagging, put-downs, and rage attacks. He felt his wife was not setting appropriate boundaries with their youngest child, who still slept in their bed and did not have a reasonable bedtime. This difference was another source of conflict between the couple.

ASSESSMENT

A thorough psychosocial history was conducted with Carmella. Her parents immigrated to California from Honolulu shortly before her birth. Based on her descriptions, I determined the family to be enmeshed in the dimension of family cohesion and rigid on the dimension of family change and adaptability. Her father demanded loyalty to the family, was dismissive of personal separateness, and allowed for little personal space. Family obligation was paramount. Members were extremely emotionally reactive to each other. When she was growing up, her father exercised an authoritarian style of parenting: Rules were strictly enforced, and violations were met with physical and verbal abuse, including shaming. Some of Carmella's family-of-origin dynamics can be attributed to her cultural heritage in which the father is the leader of the family, family norms are rigidly proscribed, and family allegiance is expected. "Shame and shaming are the mechanisms that traditionally help reinforce societal expectations of proper behavior" (McGoldrick, Pearce, & Giordano, 1982).

Expecting perfection, Carmella's father raged over minor frustrations and disappointments and was sometimes physically abusive to his wife. When in a good mood, however, the father could be physically affectionate. Carmella's mother could be verbally abusive to the children but deferred to her husband on most issues. As an adolescent Carmella felt some disdain for her mother because she was "weak." Carmella's father had developed a coalition with her, his eldest daughter, yet he felt his eldest son was more important (in a cultural context, the eldest son is regarded as the most important offspring). However, when her father was angry with his wife or another child, he became more emotionally and physically affectionate with Carmella, sometimes buying her special gifts. He also expected her to side with him against her mother and brothers and sisters. Consequently, Carmella alternated between feeling special and feeling ashamed and disregarded.

As part of the assessment procedure, the Conflict Tactics Scale (CTS) was administered to both parents at the times of their intakes. There were only a few discrepancies in their self-reports, and Carmella identified 12–15 times in the past year in which she had thrown, "smashed, kicked, or hit something." However, she admitted to only 3 incidences of pushing, grabbing, or shoving her partner and said he had reciprocated the same amount. Kevin's CTS had Carmella perpetrating these behaviors at least 6–7 times in the past year whereas he admitted to 2, one of which he described as being "in self-defense." Neither reported any serious injuries. One of her triggers was "his lack of physical affection." As previously mentioned, Carmella stated that Kevin had changed his behavior dramatically because of his involvement in group and individual therapy.

Carmella filled out the Anger Styles Questionnaire (Potter-Efron & Potter-Efron, 1995) with high scores for numbers 5 and 6 relating to explosive anger; numbers 13 and 14 regarding the dimensions of shame-based anger; numbers 17 and 18, which indicate excitatory anger; and numbers 19 and 20, which measure habitual anger. Her scores on numbers 7 and 8 were also somewhat elevated, showing a tendency toward instrumental anger. Carmella scored over 300 on the Novaco Provocation Inventory, a general measure of anger, indicating a severe anger problem. Her level of functioning on the Relationship Functioning Self-Assessment (RFSA; Hamel, 2005) indicated she saw herself as "poor to fair" in the area of personal responsibility; she put herself in the "very poor" range in anger management. In the RFSA she admitted she was a "Type A personality, driven, a perfectionist who is unable to unwind and has no lifestyle balance." This indicated her inability to cope with stress. She also rated herself as "poor to fair" in the areas of communication, conflict resolution, and control, yet "fair to good" in the dimension of social support. Interestingly, she assumed an outer locus of control attitude in blaming her husband for her low level of functioning.

In the Experiences in Close Relationships Questionnaire, Carmella scored as "preoccupied" in Farley's four-category, two-dimensional model of attachment (see Hamel, 2005). John Bowlby (1973) theorized that interpersonal anger arose from thwarted attachment needs and was similar to the anxiety behaviors and protests infants engage in when attachment needs are not satisfied. Bartholomew, Henderson, and Dutton (2001) found in a review of studies on attachment and abusive relationships "that the associations between women's 'preoccupation' and their tendency to be dominating and isolating toward their partners was especially strong." Carmella exhibited a preoccupied response to Kevin's new behavior of leaving instead of engaging—the more he withdrew, the angrier and more desperate she became. His desire to stop the escalation seemed to be perceived by Carmella as further evidence of rejection and unresponsiveness to her needs.

The assessment indicated that Carmella had little ability to control her anger when she was triggered, including her inner feelings of shame and disappointment. This inability was having a profound impact on her immediate family—it helped to drive Kevin into treatment but was continuing to be stressful for the children. Because of Carmella's experiences in her own family, she often viewed anger and aggression as a normal part of family life, even a sign of love and connection. A family or cultural belief was that aggression was needed to shape compliance with established norms. Her view that the men in the family should be "strong" often led her to rage at Kevin for his "weakness," especially as he strove for a more egalitarian relationship.

In both Kevin's and Carmella's families, age-appropriate hierarchies were not well established. Because Kevin was the only child of a single father, they often operated as a dyad. Carmella was in a coalition with her father against her mother and, sometimes, the other siblings. She experienced jealousy toward her eldest brother, who held the family place of honor. Kevin appeared to have a somewhat higher level of differentiation than Carmella. However, he suffered some attachment deficits because of the loss of his mother at an early age. Boundaries were skewed in Carmella's home; the need for personal space was not valued. External boundaries were mainly focused inside the family, so they were not open to outside influences. Carmella's family appeared to have difficulty navigating life cycle changes; her family was interfering in her adult life. Her father maintained his role as the patriarch; loyalty to family was required, and holidays were to be spent with them. Kevin was criticized for time spent with his father. Carmella's parents seemed to have a control–compliance dynamic, whereas she and Kevin had a demand–withdraw dance (Hamel, 2005).

One of the ways skewed boundaries and coalitions carried over into Kevin and Carmella's family was in Carmella's relationship with their girls. Three-year-old Solana slept with the parents, which interfered with their intimacy and served as a source of conflict between Kevin and Carmella. Carmella attempted to infantilize Solana as well as to shape her as an ally against Kevin. She also raged against her elder daughter, Sarah, acting more like a jealous sibling than a parent. Sarah seemed to be more aligned with her father because he was available for comfort, and his responses were not reactive. Sarah's personality echoed Kevin's; she was thoughtful and methodical, which seemed to annoy Carmella. Her mother's rage was causing Sarah to become even more quiet and withdrawn. As Kevin changed his conflict responses, removing the girls to protect them from Carmella's rages, he may have inadvertently been building a coalition with them "against" their mother.

Carmella's rage attacks were interfering with normal family functioning and impeding the development of effective co-parenting strategies. Her behavior also inhibited Sarah's ability to have friends visit and the couple's ability to have a satisfactory social life. Carmella complained to their friends about Kevin, criticized him in front of others, and canceled plans when she was upset. Her complaints to her family about Kevin made visits uncomfortable for him because they sided with Carmella. Their disparaging remarks about Kevin also had a negative effect on Sarah and Solana. Kevin's father was seldom able to join with the family because of Carmella's objections. She was jealous of the time Kevin or the girls would spend with him. Kevin's father's illness stoked further conflict as Kevin attempted to spend more time with him.

Carmella's extreme reactivity made discussions and problem-solving attempts impossible. Through his involvement in group and individual therapy, Kevin had lessened his own reactivity, learned new communication skills, and attempted to be positively assertive. However, Carmella could not always respond in ways that enabled them to feel safe or to discuss issues. When questioned about her alcohol use, she admitted that two or three times a month she would drink a bottle of wine when she was feeling anxious and empty. She did not believe it increased her anger outbursts because, she said, "I usually do this when I am alone."

TREATMENT

The family systems lens was helpful to me as I formulated my treatment. This couple certainly had issues with individuality, togetherness, and self-differentiation. Power imbalances in family organization were apparent: Carmella had a shifting coalition with Solana, yet Carmella, Kevin, and the girls were triangulated. The coalition was evident because Carmella was usually more verbally and physically affectionate with Solana and would often give in to her whining—for example, Solana's earlier upsets when asked to sleep in her own room. Carmella seemed to identify more with Solana and supported her occasional outburst at her father or sister. However, when Carmella was in a rage, even Solana was at risk for verbal attacks. The parental hierarchy was not well defined. Short-term problem solving seemed impossible. Emotional reactivity was evident in all the members—there were reciprocal extremes of behavior with no model of normalcy. Not knowing what normal is, Carmella was driving for perfection. The family was experiencing some life cycle changes—Kevin's aging and ailing father, Carmella's midlife crisis, and Solana's need to individuate—yet development was blocked.

Regardless of the lens or treatment approach, it is always important to assess and monitor for safety in working with family aggression. Kevin had a clear understanding of safety issues—these had been discussed in his men's group. He was also doing extensive work with his individual therapist relating to self-differentiation, boundary and limit setting, and safety for himself and the children. Because of his group and individual treatment, Kevin was less reactive to Carmella and understood the necessity of time-outs, reflective listening, preparing for provocation, stress management, and other anger management tools. As previously mentioned, these behaviors often further triggered Carmella's anxiety, but as Kevin became more alert to destructive cycles, he was able to get himself and the children to safety. He did not return until a phone call indicated that Carmella was no longer volatile. At some point she seemed desperate for the return of the family to momentarily satisfy her need for love and security. Through treatment, he was more open to calling the police if Carmella's abuse should become more severe. His original objections to doing so echoed some common gender biases: "I could not have the mother of my children arrested; she can't hurt me, and I would be considered weak if I complained about being hit by a woman." He now understood that escalating family violence was having a detrimental effect on the children, no matter who the primary aggressor was.

Carmella was not interested in pursuing couples counseling because that approach had been unsuccessful. It did seem apparent that couples counseling could not be helpful until her anger and reactivity issues were addressed. We discussed the option of individual therapy or joining my mixed-gender anger management group, or both. My clinical opinion was that she could benefit most from a combination of individual and group therapy. Attachment issues could be more easily addressed in individual work. For Carmella the perception that Kevin was emotionally unresponsive drove her to demanding, petulant behaviors that increased the marital conflict. In turn, the conflict further eroded the ability of the relationship to be a secure base for either partner. Individual therapy would be a helpful modality to address this attachment anxiety and to better understand mutual needs for security and closeness. Exploring the differing family-of-origin approaches to family cohesion could help Carmella understand that Kevin's reactions were not a sign of rejection.

Even though Carmella was depressed and dissatisfied, she was not yet motivated to enter into individual therapy. She did not accept that her anger could have long-term effects on the children, and she blamed Kevin for her disappointment and unhappiness. Her stated reason for settling on group therapy was to ease the tension in the household while she decided whether she wanted to remain in the marriage. Carmella was somewhat ambivalent about lessening her reactivity, which she considered normal, but she was willing to try a group and hoped the support would be helpful. She was particularly interested in learning how other people handled their anger and relationship issues. Her previous short-term group was primarily educational, and she felt she would have gained from the experiences and sharing of other group members. The anger management group I facilitated was both didactive and supportive.

In my view, Carmella was in the contemplation stage of change—ambivalent, simultaneously seeing reasons to change and reasons not to change (Eckhardt & Utschig, 2007). Compliance with change strategies can be enhanced with client choice, and joining the group was her current choice of treatment. Because motivation can be influenced by social interactions, I wondered if the group members' influence could assist in moving Carmella to the preparation and action stages. Community support has been shown to influence an individual's motivation for change. The group process is also a venue for personal, individualized feedback from the facilitator and other members. Feedback and gentle advice can enhance motivation for change.

In the group we are able to have a preliminary discussion of anger and aggression from a social learning and family systems perspective. Topics covered include the feelings under anger, defensive reactions to "triggers," self-soothing techniques, and cognitive distortions. For someone such as Carmella, this type of exploration is needed in addition to standard anger management and stress reduction techniques and communication skills building.

The initial treatment goals for Carmella were the elimination of violence and a reduction in emotional abuse. Social support, anger management skill building, education about family systems, linking childhood wounds to reactivity, cognitive distortions, and the detrimental effects of family violence on children were treatment interventions that could be undertaken in a group setting. A secondary goal for Carmella was to decrease her sense of fear, shame, and isolation and to increase her sense of self-efficacy. I also recommended that Carmella educate herself about the effects of alcohol on moods. We discussed the circular effect alcohol can have in our lives, using it to cover problems while actually exacerbating them.

I knew that not all these goals could be met through the group process. However, I was hopeful that group participation could be a step toward the preparation and action stages and would encourage Carmella to undertake individual therapy later on.

Concurrent with Carmella's involvement in group, Kevin and his therapist were utilizing a reinforcement approach. They decided that one of the consequences for Carmella's rage attack would be for Kevin to purchase an item he wanted or needed and charge it to Carmella's account. As mentioned, he was refusing to engage in abusive conflicts and would withdraw from the scene when he sensed that things were getting out of control. At family gatherings, he would take a time-out if he became the object of criticism from Carmella or her family. He began to calmly assert his need to visit his father and did so at least weekly.

OUTCOMES AND CONCLUSION

Carmella initially agreed to enter the group for a minimum of 20 weeks. Unfortunately, she dropped out after 15. She did not give the recommended 4 weeks notice for termination. (We suggest this to help clients learn to facilitate healthy relationship closure, to enable other group members to deal with possible feelings of failure and abandonment, to allow for feedback about the readiness of the client to leave treatment, and to allow the terminating client to articulate how the process was or was not helpful to him or her.) A follow-up phone call to Carmella brought the "I don't have time" rationale; she stated she wanted to take a night class. She also felt she had achieved some of her goals because her behavior had improved. She stated that her main goal now was to decide whether to remain in the marriage.

Carmella had made progress in some areas but, in my opinion, was not ready to terminate. According to her self-reports in class, she was having less frequent anger outbursts. On Sunday nights, she was able to utilize stress reduction techniques she had learned in group: stretching exercises, progressive relaxation, and guided meditation. She often spent an hour at the gym late Sunday afternoon, following the group's recommendation that she learn to take care of some of her own needs. This enabled her to ask for help in ways that were constructive and productive and allowed everyone to begin the next week with less anxiety and stress. (Because of his participation in therapy, Kevin was more proactive in the Sunday night cleanup and was teaching the girls how to help.)

Carmella had not engaged in property destruction for the last 10 weeks. Carmella discovered that a trigger for her destructive behavior was her feeling dissatisfied with Kevin and with herself; she was able to identify the "feelings under anger." She was learning to change her inner dialogue and to also contemplate consequences: destruction left her with a mess to clean up and allowed Kevin to spend her money on items for himself! It also left her feeling exhausted, ashamed, and unloved. It did nothing to improve her need for support and reassurance. She also reported progress in her communication with Sarah. She criticized less and was finally able to apologize to Sarah for her occasional bad behavior—letting the child know it was not her fault. Carmella felt the group process had been helpful in her understanding of the effects of family violence on children. Even though she continued to inwardly blame Kevin for many of her negative feelings, she was less likely to verbalize this to the children.

One success the couple achieved together was in getting Solana to sleep in a bed of her own. Kevin purchased a beautiful bed after Solana told them how she wanted it to look. Kevin was able to paint and paper the room, and Carmella was pleased that he had undertaken a "manly" act. They agreed on a bedtime, even though Carmella was still leaving the routine up to him. She was not yet able to resist Solana's demands to stay up later. Without the child in their bed, the couple was attempting to increase their physical and emotional intimacy. One of Carmella's complaints had been Kevin's lack of affection, even though her desire to sleep with Solana had contributed to the problem.

Carmella's frustration with Kevin's slowness and deliberation remained, but she was making attempts not to criticize him in front of their friends. She called her family less frequently with her list of laments, but they continued to call her for information, updates, and admonitions that she should leave.

Through the group process, Carmella made some progress in anger management and stress reduction and decreased the intensity and frequency of her outbursts. She gained some short-term social support and better understood the effects of her anger on her children. She gained a rudimentary understanding of the intergenerational transmission of violence but little awareness of the family as a system. By the time she left group, Carmella had a preliminary awareness of cognitive distortions and self-talk and how they can contribute to reactivity; when feeling unloved, she could occasionally remind herself that she was treading in "wound territory." However, her cognitive-affective representational structure still resulted in a predominately "automatic" processing of information.

Carmella did not decrease her overall level of fear, shame, and isolation. She was often disappointed and hopeless and maintained an outer locus of control. My fear was that Carmella's progress might be short-lived as a result of her fear and blame as well as the loss of group support and feedback. I encouraged Carmella to return for treatment if she found it difficult to maintain the progress she had made. I also suggested that she explore other avenues for support and feedback and that she continue to visit her psychiatrist on a regular basis. I offered referrals, but she insisted she had gone as far as she could go while staying in this relationship.

My fears proved well founded. About 1 year after her termination from our program, we received a call—Carmella had been arrested for spousal abuse and was now mandated to a 52-week batterers' intervention program. Because we did not have a group schedule that could work for her, she chose another program.

As a therapist, I find it helpful to review and think about those cases in which treatment has fallen short. In reviewing the treatment plan, I realized that Carmella did in fact meet her preliminary goal: the elimination of physical violence and a reduction in emotional and verbal abuse. Without the 4-week termination, there was no way to help her assess her ability to maintain that goal. I struggled with the fact that I had not met all my goals for her. I wondered if, in my initial work with Carmella, I could have more strongly emphasized the need for long-term support or for individual treatment while respecting where she was in the change process. In retrospect, had I been more cognizant of her concerns or fears about change, I would have made a greater effort in helping her explore the pros and cons of behavior change while normalizing her ambivalence about change.

REFERENCES

Bartholomew, K., Henderson, A., & Dutton, D. (2001). Insecure attachment and abusive intimate relationships. In C. Culow (Ed.), *Adult attachment and couple psychotherapy* (pp. 43–61). New York: Brunner-Routledge.

Bowlby, J. (1973). *Attachment and loss: Vol. 2. Separation: Anxiety and anger.* London: Hogarth Press.

Eckhardt, C., & Utschig, A. (2007). Assessing readiness to change among perpetrators of intimate partner violence: Analysis of two self-report measures. *Journal of Family Violence, 22,* 319–330.

Hamel, J. (2005). *Gender-inclusive treatment of intimate partner abuse: A comprehensive approach.* New York: Springer Publishing.

Hamel, J., & Nicholls, T. (2007). *Family interventions in domestic violence: A handbook of gender-inclusive theory and treatment.* New York: Springer Publishing.

Kerr, M. E. (1981). Family systems theory and therapy. In A. S. Gurman & D. P. Kniskern (Eds.), *Handbook of family therapy* (Vol. 1, pp. 226–264). New York: Brunner/Mazel.

McGoldrick, M., Pearce, J. K., & Giordano, J. (1982). *Ethnicity and family therapy.* New York: Guilford Press.

Morse, B. (1995). Beyond the Conflicts Tactics Scale: Assessing gender differences in partner violence. *Violence and Victims, 10*(4), 251–269.

Potter-Efron, R., & Potter-Efron, P. (1995). *Letting go of anger.* Oakland, CA: New Harbinger.

Straus, M. (1993). Physical assaults by wives: A major social problem. In R. Gelles & D. Loseky (Eds.), *Current controversies on family violence* (pp. 67–87). Newbury Park, CA: Sage.

QUESTIONS FOR REFLECTION AND DISCUSSION

1   How was violence and abuse transmitted intergenerationally in Carmella's family? What else was transmitted?

2   How did Carmella's internalized conflict of pride and shame play itself out in her relationship with her husband, Kevin?

3   What is the connection between Carmella's personal character-istics, including the need to dominate and her insecure attach-ment style, and the structural problems of the family?

4   The author states that family violence and dysfunction work in a circular and reciprocal manner. Describe at least one circular dynamic in this particular family.

5   The author identifies as one of her key principles of treatment that one should "begin where the client is." In this case, the au-thor respected Carmella's decision to join a group in an attempt to engage her in treatment and motivate her to move forward in the change process. In the end, the author suggests that she could have been more successful had she pushed for a more in-tensive, personal form of therapy, such as individual work. What do you think? Were her initial goals reasonable and appropriate? How much of any treatment success is dependent on the thera-pists' skills, and how much on a client's willingness to change?

I Learned to Think for Myself: A Solution-Focused Approach to Domestic Violence Therapy

MARTIN SÖDERQUIST AND BO GUNNEHILL

In Sweden, couples counseling has traditionally had special status in the mental health field. Except for child abuse and neglect, couples counselors have less obligation to report to social agencies and no obligation to provide written documentation of therapy sessions. Couples can therefore participate in therapy anonymously. For many years domestic violence was not taken seriously, and when it was, couples counselors regarded the problem as a matter for law enforcement, social agencies, and child protection services. They were of course criticized by social workers and feminists for not doing their part in addressing this issue.

More recently, however, because of the efforts of social workers and others, domestic violence has become a matter of public concern, perhaps the family problem most often talked about and most likely to be mentioned in the press. Numerous public policy and intervention efforts have focused on families affected by domestic violence, including the establishment of crisis centers for women and children as well as for men, and a variety of changes have been instituted in the criminal justice system. And an increasing number of couples counselors are now working with domestic violence cases.

As part of an independent and private team of six therapists, we work for three communes in the northwest of Skåne, the most southern part of Sweden, and provide counseling services to couples and families with a multitude of problems—infidelity, sexual problems, conflicts, separation, and divorce. We are not restricted by the communes to meet only with couples who have relational problems but can also meet families in which the parents present with concerns about their children. Often, we begin couples therapy by seeing the individual partners for separate sessions and then bring them together in later sessions. Every year we take on approximately 600 new couples and families, most of them self-referred. In addition, the female therapists in our team have for many years run groups for physically abused women. These groups, known as "Johanna groups" and consisting of eight women, meet for 10 weekly group sessions. They are facilitated by two therapists, who work with the women in addressing such topics as expectations and goals, domestic violence, everyday psychology, gender issues, and living in violent contexts.

As we began to see more and more families affected by domestic violence, we realized that we had to start discussing our methods and therapy models for working with this population. In Sweden, it is not common for therapists to work integratively with the whole family or the couple together in the same session. Most of the programs provide services to either women and their children *or* men; women in high-conflict and abusive relationships have traditionally been seen in individual sessions without their male partners, who are not invited to participate or else are unable to be reached. As family therapists, we wanted to develop ways to work with the entire family system and not be limited to helping the women in individual or group formats.

The authors of this chapter are both trained and experienced family therapists and also work as family therapy supervisors. Bo has been conducting couples therapy for many years and has a special interest in finding solutions to difficult case problems. In his work he aims to create dialogue instead of giving lectures, debating, or engaging in techniques that clients may find manipulative. Martin has conducted family therapy sessions in the field of child and adolescent psychiatry and with drug addicts. Between 1985 and 2000 he worked with child sexual abuse cases from a family therapy and solution-focused perspective. Among his areas of special interest are how to work collaboratively with clients (Bergmark & Söderquist, 2002; Söderquist, Clas, & Sundelin, 2002) and developing a solution-focused model for doing family assessments (Söderquist, 2002.)

THEORETICAL AND PRACTICAL ORIENTATION

We define domestic violence, like Vetere and Cooper (2001) and the Council of Europe (1986), as "any act or omission committed within the framework of the family, by one of its members that undermines the life, the body or psychological integrity, or the liberty of another member of the same family, or that seriously harms the development of his or her personality" (Vetere & Cooper, 2001, p. 378). We see domestic violence as a relational problem that concerns the whole family. Everyone in a family is influenced by what happens in the family, directly or indirectly, and all its members have their reasons for wanting to contribute to end the violence. We see all family members as resources and helpers in finding ways to create safety for everyone involved. The abuser is of course responsible for ending his or her violence, but other family members are also responsible for their own behavior.

As family therapists we have been trained to help our clients stop destructive patterns and to find new behavioral alternatives. We do not spend a lot of time trying to find the causes to the problems; instead we use words and narrative language in helping people create new and more constructive stories of their lives (Ziegler & Hiller, 2001). Following are some ideas we have picked up from others and from our own experience that have guided us when working with domestically violent families.

Secrecy

As with families where there has been incest, there is a tendency in domestically violent families to keep the abuse and other problems a secret to outsiders. Its members dare not reveal what goes on in the family, knowing that if they do, they will be blamed for all its problems by the abuser and other family members and relatives or else get punished and further abused. Secrecy has very destructive consequences, not just for the family but also for the therapist or social worker involved in the case. Therapists who bring up what family members do not want to talk about must be prepared for a range of negative reactions, from disappointment to rage and aggressiveness. "If you name it," observed Tilman Furniss, "you get blamed for it" (1991). Addressing problems such as physical, sexual, and verbal abuse and not accepting destructive behavior while at the same time accepting all the family as persons worthy of regard is a challenge and can at times feel like walking on eggshells.

Focus on Responsibility and Collaboration

Very much linked to secrecy, shame, and guilt is the tendency for the abuser to deny or minimize what he or she has done to his or her partner or children. We regard this as a context-dependent behavior rather than a personal trait. Abusers know that if they admit to the abuse, they will be punished and possibly sentenced to jail by the criminal justice system, an outcome that they naturally try to avoid. It sometimes takes an abuser a lot of thinking and talking before he or she is willing to take responsibility. The social worker or therapist can further this process by inviting abusers to discuss their situation and figure out on their own what they can to do help themselves and the other family members. We have found Jenkins's book *Invitation to Responsibility* (1990) very helpful in this regard, as well as *Working With "Denied" Child Abuse* (Turnell & Essex, 2006), which offers an excellent program for working with families, their relatives, and professional networks in cases where denial is a significant therapeutic obstacle.

Vetere and Cooper's concept of the "stable third" has also been very useful (2001). The stable third is any person who knows the family, such as a doctor, social worker, member of the clergy, or respected extended family member, who can corroborate for the professional team whether the violence has ceased. This person helps the therapists in providing alternative perspectives and acts as a whistle-blower when necessary. In domestic violence cases, a certain degree of statutory, mandatory force is often necessary, but professional collaboration is crucial—domestic violence is a matter for the police (it is a crime), for child and protection services (protection), and for therapists (treatment).

Resistance and Coping

Resisting is a natural reaction to oppression and abuse and, most importantly, is a way to protect and preserve one's own integrity. In some dangerous situations, the resistant behavior may have to be very subtle, such as cautiously looking away or dissociating. People in shock or with symptoms of posttraumatic stress syndrome (PTSD) often forget what they did in previous abusive situations to preserve their integrity. In therapy a focus on the client's resistance behavior can be of the utmost importance in building up self-confidence and constructively coping with the consequences of being abused. Highly recommended is the article by Allan Wade in which he describes in detail how he works with victims of abuse and what they did to preserve their integrity (1997).

Collaboration and Focusing on Clients' Goals, Exceptions, and Competencies

Research indicates that client factors and the client–therapist relationship are the two most important factors contributing to a positive treatment outcome (Miller, Hubble, & Duncan, 1996). A focus on client competence, client goals, and a therapist stance of gently "leading from behind," a term coined by Peter Cantwell (Cantwell & Holmes, 1994), is in congruence with this research and a cornerstone of our team's solution-focused brief therapy model. Although it seems simple, this model is in fact very difficult to learn and to practice. For some therapists, constantly focusing on the client's competence and goals and not allowing themselves to be the expert that solves all the problems can be very demanding and poses a challenge to long-standing beliefs and assumptions rooted in other therapeutic models. Kim Berg has written several books on doing solution-focused work in child protective services cases (Berg & Kelly, 2000). Lee, Sebold, and Uken (2003) use a solution-focused model, consisting of eight 1-hour sessions, in conducting group therapy with 88 court-mandated domestic violence offenders at the PLUMAS project, with a focus on the group participants' personal goals. Ziegler and Hiller (2001) combine solution-focused therapy with narrative therapy in working with couples. Recognizing that safety is often a prerequisite for being able to reach individual and personal goals, the authors focus on both safety and clients' goals when working with domestic violence cases.

Position and Role of Therapist

Working within a solution-focused family therapy model, the therapist asks for and encourages multiple and various perspectives from the clients and seeks to understand the positions taken by all of the family members. We use the term "position" as Andrew Turnell does: "by the term position we mean strongly held values, beliefs and meanings that individuals express through their stories" (Turnell & Edwards, 1999, p. 50). The role of the therapist is to help each family member describe specifically what has previously happened and, most of all, how they want things to be different. The therapist, working collaboratively and in dialogue, tries to understand the positions taken by all the family members with respect to their problems and goals, past and future. The therapist is neither a judge nor the one who knows everything.

Research

Alasdair Macdonald's book (2007) provides a comprehensive summary of current research on the development and effectiveness of the solution-focused model. The best summary can be found on the Web site of Wally Gingerich (www.gingerich.net), who has identified several studies supporting the effectiveness of solution-focused brief therapy. In one Swedish study, for example, prisoners were randomly assigned to five solution-focused treatment sessions or a control group (no therapy session). At a 16-month follow-up, the treatment group reported a lesser number of total offenses and drug offenses than the control group (Lindforss & Magnusson, 1997). Lee, Uken, and Sebold (2007) in the PLUMAS project found that specific, detailed client goals and agreement between client and therapist on those goals were important variables in predicting recidivism in domestic violence. Stith, Rosen, and McCollum (2004) compared multi-couples therapy with individual couples therapy and a no-treatment comparison group for couples that choose to stay together following mild-to-moderate violence. Multi-couples therapy was significantly more effective than individual couples therapy and the comparison group, as reflected in lower rates of recidivism 6 months after treatment and increased marital satisfaction.

CASE STUDY: KARIN AND LARS

Karin, mother of two sons—Lars, age 18, and Emil, age 12—was very worried about her oldest son because of his shouting, throwing things, and occasional physical aggression toward her and his girlfriend. She contacted our team, and Martin met Karin and Lars in January 2007 for the first session.

The Family

Karin was a middle-aged woman who had been through rough times in relations with men, including the fathers of her two sons. She was a warm and caring person who wanted her sons to respect and value her; when under stress, however, she would nag them and raise her voice and would not stop talking. In the therapy sessions she oscillated between being very serious and being humorous. The two boys had different fathers. Lars had not seen his father since he was 2 years old, and Emil had been seeing his father occasionally since Karin had separated from him a few years before. "It wasn't my idea to come here," a reluctant Lars announced in typical teenage fashion at the beginning of the first session. When engaged he had a lot to say and was in one respect very much like his mother—a caring person. However, when frustrated he could easily lose control of his temper and act impulsively.

First Session

Martin asked them to briefly describe themselves. Karin began by talking about her drinking problem and the constant fighting (verbal and physical) between Lars and her. She admitted to having hit Lars and also recounted how both she and Lars had previously been verbally and physically assaulted by Emil's father. We never explored in detail Karin's alcohol abuse, but it was clear that it had caused the family a lot of trouble. Reports had been made to child protection service as a result of Karin leaving the boys alone in the house without supervision while she went out drinking with her friends, and there had been numerous incidents of shouting and ongoing conflicts among all the family members.

Karin and her sons had been assessed and provided counseling on several previous occasions at the local hospital's department of child and adolescent psychiatry and at child protection services. In addition, Karin had attended Johanna groups (mentioned earlier), and Emil had been in a group for teenagers. Initially, Lars said that it was his mother's idea to come to us and that he was not motivated to attend therapy sessions. He agreed with his mother's description of their fighting but insisted that the home situation had improved over the last 2 weeks. Furthermore, he and his girlfriend had started breaking up and were seeing each other only occasionally. At their sessions with child protection services, Lars had learned to "think before, not after" and to express his feelings, and Karin had been advised to understand how her drinking was causing problems for her sons.

But Karin insisted on getting help, not just for her own sake but also for Lars and his girlfriend. She expressed concern that Lars would destroy his life and the lives of others if he did not change his ways. In response, Lars acknowledged, "I do not want to be like this—mean and angry," and agreed with his mother that the sessions with our team might help them improve their communication and help him overcome his aggressive behavior.

Prompted by Martin to say more about the improvement Lars claimed had occurred, mother and son described the previous 2 weeks in the same manner—less fighting, with mother not allowing arguments to escalate and son doing a better job of managing his anger. They both agreed that Lars had been listening to her and had been more thoughtful too. When asked to explain Lars's improved behavior, they agreed that Karin had found ways to calm herself and to back off from confrontations. Martin then asked each of them to imagine what it would be like if this more constructive way of relating were to continue for several more weeks. Karin pictured a positive atmosphere, the two of them engaged in adult discussions and Lars listening carefully when she would address him. She also imagined Lars spending more time with her and his brother, Emil. Lars imagined that things would be calmer, with his mother not nagging him so much and both of them expressing their feelings to one another without escalating conflict. When asked to describe how satisfied she felt about the relationship on a scale of 1 to 10 (10 representing how she might feel if everything she pictured about their relationship ideally were to come true), Karin gave herself an 8. When asked the same question, Lars gave himself a 6. Both said that they were at an 80 on a confidence scale in which 100 meant that they were totally convinced they were going to solve their problems. "We have to get over it," they said. "We do care about each other."

After a short reflection break, Martin ended the first session with the following summary: "Things have improved for you the last weeks. I am impressed by your honesty and your efforts to do things differently from what you have done before. Most of all I see how much you care about each other. You, Karin, talked about 'breaking the power of history' and changing a long-standing pattern of abuse in your family, and you are convinced this is possible. You, Lars, really don't want to be negative and destructive—you want to change this." When asked if they would like to schedule another session, Karin and Lars indicated that they would, and Martin continued: "I have a suggestion for you: Between now and the next time we meet, carefully observe the positive ways that you relate to one another, and how you imagine you will keep doing this when your problems are solved." A second session was then scheduled for 2 weeks later.

Before moving on to a discussion of the second session, we would like to offer some observations about the first session:

1   Session 1 was structured like most other first sessions of solution-focused therapy, with clients giving a brief presentation and problem description; describing their hopes for the current session and future hopes; explaining what they have already been doing that reflects where they want to be; and using "scaling" techniques to determine their satisfaction with the current situation and confidence in achieving their goals. The session ended with the therapist's summary of the session after a short reflection break.

2   Clients' descriptions of their problems are important, but even more important are their goals, aspirations, and dreams. Many of the therapist's questions were therefore oriented to the future (e.g., "What are your hopes for this session and for the next few weeks?" "Where are you now in relation to where you want to be?") The miracle question is an option we find useful in generating client goals. The client is told, "A miracle happens while you are sleeping—and the miracle makes the problem that brought you here disappear. But this happens while you're sleeping, so you can't know it happened. How do you and people close to you discover this miracle happened?" (de Shazer & Dolan, 2007, p. 38). The therapist's exact phrasing and tone of voice is very important in creating an atmosphere in which all possibilities can be considered, so that therapist and clients can later collaborate in finding evidence of progress (miracles) in the client's real world. Focusing on hopes and goals lays the foundation for further sessions by giving the therapist clues about the direction clients are heading and where they want to be in the future. In this case, mother and son articulated their goals, or at least how they would like to proceed therapeutically, and Martin helped them move in that direction. In solution-focused therapy, the initial session is the most important; subsequent sessions are considered follow-ups to the first.

3   Martin followed the clients' leads and waited for an invitation to discuss what was important to them. When therapists are given this opportunity, they should encourage as detailed descriptions of goals and exceptions as possible, including what the clients are already doing in their everyday life that may be advancing those goals. When, in response to Lars mentioning the improvements

made over the previous 2 weeks, Karin talked about improving the communication in her relationship with Lars, Martin considered this an invitation to further explore the clients' goals and expectations.

4   In our approach the assessment and the first therapy session are not separated; the first session is both assessment and therapy. We work with what the clients bring and usually do not depend on tests and formal protocols to understand their relationships and the problems they are struggling with.

5   Karin and Lars were able to describe in specific details their goals, and they were convinced they were going to make it. It was evident that they cared about each other, wished things to change, and were going to put in the effort to make this happen. They had already started to do things differently at home to stop fighting and create greater safety. Martin's final suggestion, that they observe their behavior in the following week, is a standardized first-session task and useful for getting more descriptions of the good aspects of their relationship.

Second Session (2 Weeks Later)

Karin and Lars started the session by telling Martin that things had gotten worse over the weekend and that Karin had had to call for help, but that things were already starting to get better again. Over the weekend, Karin had come home drunk late at night with some friends. Very upset and disappointed, Lars shouted and spit at Karin and threw and broke a glass and his cell phone. Karin yelled back, trying to explain herself but without much success. Although Lars refrained from hitting his mother, he was so angry and volatile that Karin decided to seek help. Only then did the two of them manage to cool down.

Sitting in the therapy office a few days later, Karin confessed that she was ashamed about Lars's abusive behavior. "It is my fault," she said. "I have done wrong over the years." Still very disappointed with her, Lars responded by saying, "A mother should not be drunk at 8 o'clock in the morning. She is supposed to choose her children over others. You don't even remember what we talked about that night!" As mother and son talked about this incident, they also revealed to Martin more of the abuse and fighting that had been going on between them. Lars, for example, had previously kicked her and thrown things at her (oranges and shoes, as well as water in her face). It was also revealed that during many high-conflict situations with his mother, Lars had been able to calm down and not shout or engage in physical assaults but instead go out for a walk. Lars really had the capacity to control himself at least some of the times he would get upset and angry.

Two other events, both significant, also happened over that shameful and disappointing weekend: Lars and his girlfriend broke up for good, and Emil was attacked on his way home from school by three other boys. How, Karin asked, was she to cope with all these problems? Rather than simply give her advice, Martin asked Karin and Lars how things could be getting better, considering everything that had recently happened. Lars responded by saying that he still has friends, has started training at a gym, and is more confident. Karin said that it was calmer now at home and that they both try to help each other. Most importantly, she could see that Lars was very sad, something that was easier for her to cope with than the aggressiveness. Martin stressed the importance of avoiding abusive and aggressive situations and asked Karin and Lars what they thought they could do in this regard. Lars suggested that they both needed to listen to and respect each other. He asked that Karin listen to him and not just give him orders, considering that he was 18 years old and was now, in his mind, grown up. Lars went on to explain that when Karin nags and yells at him, he feels patronized.

He also stressed how much it helped when Karin talked to him in a calm and soft voice. It made him calmer and helped him feel accepted as a grown-up person. For her part, Karin agreed that she had made a serious mistake by bringing home her friends in the middle of the night and said that she could no longer allow herself to do things that hurt and disappointed her sons. She expressed hope that Lars would continue to find emotional stability by being with friends. Martin then asked each of them, "When in the future your conflicts escalate and you suspect that aggression is about to happen, how will you cope with that?" Karin said that she would walk away, calm herself down if necessary, and talk with Lars later. Lars agreed to put his feelings into words instead of acting out—for example, ask his mother that she listen and not order him around.

As with the first session, Martin ended session number 2 with a summary:

I am impressed by how observant you are and how much you influence each other. That tells me you are very important to each other. You, Karin, are very worried, and you, Lars, are very sad. These are indications of how much you care. It is very important for the two of you that you avoid destructive and abusive situations. It is important for Emil too, I think. Earlier you have told me you want to be able to discuss in an adult way, both of you being able to listen to each other and being able to express what you want without escalating to anger and conflict. To achieve this, you need to have alternative strategies for creating calmness and acceptance in your relationship. You have already presented some good ideas. I have two more suggestions that you might find helpful. One is paper therapy—if you want to say anything that might upset the other person, write it on a paper and just hand it over without saying a word. The other is strengths therapy: create a symbol or a metaphor for your strengths—this can be anything that represents your strengths, what you are good at or feel good about—and bring out the symbol when you begin to notice an increase in stress or when there is the possibility of aggression. I can not tell you what your own symbol should be, but others I have worked with have used an animal, a fantasy figure, or words from their grandmother like, "You know you can do it!" or "You are strong like me."

Comments

1   We do not see violence and abuse between parents and teenagers as merely one person abusing the other. We see two parts contributing to an abusive situation. The violence cannot be accepted, of course, but both mother and son are responsible for their own behavior. Mother and son are aware of that, and they realize how much they also need help from each other to create a calmer, nonabusive relationship. They have ideas, and they know what they need to do.

2   The suggestions from the therapist are just suggestions—if clients find them helpful, that is all for the good; if not, we can all simply forget them. It should be noted that in this case the suggestions offered by the therapist at the end of session 2 were spontaneous, not previously thought through. This might have been a mistake. Ideally, suggestions should match as much as possible the clients' own ideas and positions and should be considered in advance.

Third Session (2 Weeks Later)

In the past 2 weeks, interactions between Karin and Lars had been calmer, and in the session mother and son appeared quite relaxed. Lars said that he was still trying to get over the breakup with his girlfriend and that he had been having emotional ups and downs but was coping by spending time with friends and thinking of positive things.

Lars had also learned to stand up for himself around those who bully him. This was an issue Lars had not previously mentioned, and Martin asked Lars to elaborate. Lars said that some of the other students in his class, boys with delinquent tendencies, had tried to get him to hang out with them and to join them in various criminal activities. Although they kept teasing him for not wanting to join in, calling him a "coward," he had held his ground and made it clear to them that he was unwilling to become involved in things he did not want to be involved in. Lars reported that he had learned to also express to friends and family members what he thought was right for him; for example, wanting to be treated as a grown-up. From his mother he asked that she stop nagging, stop giving him orders, and talk to him calmly and in a lower tone of voice. Karin was still worried, but she could see that Lars was coping with his issues in a constructive way. They could even laugh together at home, as they did in the session.

Throughout the rest of the session, the discussion focused on Emil's situation, how he was doing after having been physically assaulted, and Karin's and Lars's concerns about him. Lars had talked to his brother, trying to lift his spirits. Martin told Karin and Lars a story about a teenage girl who had been raped and who as a result of this trauma could not express her feelings about what had happened or find out what she needed to do in order to cope. However, when she was given the opportunity to give advice to other teenage girls who had been similarly victimized, she was able to be very wise and thoughtful. The therapist asked Lars to think about what advice he might give his brother. Without hesitating, Lars offered three suggestions: (a) "Do not be afraid (or at least do not show it)"; (b) "Believe in yourself" (e.g., "you will make it"); and (c) "Think about good things." Karin and Lars then discussed with Martin how these various suggestions might be useful to Emil.

At the end of session 3, Martin offered the following summary: "I am impressed by you, Lars, how you have been coping—being able to calm down around your mother, how you have handled the separation from your girlfriend, and most of all your very wise advice to your brother." Martin turned to Karin and added, "You are very concerned and observant—you know your son, you notice his moods and temper, and you are aware of the positive things he does. Keep on doing what you are doing—you are on the right track."

Comments

Further progress was illuminated and reinforced in the session. The other family member not present (Emil) was talked about in a constructive way. The "advice to others" question gives the teenager an opportunity to express the wisdom of young people, helping him increase his own self-confidence.

Fourth Session (1 Month Later)

Since the last session Karin had had a cold and still was quite tired. She said she was pleased that Lars had been getting out of the house, enjoying the company of his friends. Lars had been busy and active; he had been with friends and enjoyed himself in ways that were positive for him. He said he felt good and had a lot of plans: planning university studies, getting a summer job, and looking forward to activities with friends and university studies in the fall. Most of all he was pleased to no longer be fighting with his mother. Lars still thought, however, that Karin had been too harsh with her rules. Karin disagreed. She admitted that she had been, in her own words, "kind of negative," by which she meant always expecting trouble and conflicts, nagging him, and expressing frustration sometimes in a very loud voice, but she also stressed that she had become more consistent in her limit setting. She had learned to calm herself down before talking to her son and enforcing rules they had previously agreed on. She had learned not to give in and change her mind as soon as someone had another opinion and instead held on to what she had decided. If she had decided it was important for Lars to be home at 11 o'clock at night because all family members needed to sleep to be able to go to school and work the day after, she did not change her mind or decision if Lars tried to prolong his stay out. This was good for her and her sons; the atmosphere at home was better and calmer, she thought.

As a way to evaluate how much progress mother and son had made in therapy, Martin introduced a new scale in which 1 represented where they were just before the first session, and 10 stood for when their therapeutic goals would be reached. Using this scale, Karin and Lars indicated that they were currently at around a 6, now that their fighting had diminished. They had moments when they were together and enjoyed each other's company and also enjoyed their time separately (Karin doing things by herself, Lars getting together with friends). For Lars it was very important that Karin believed him when he had been falsely accused of being drunk in public and arrested. Karin had stood up for him, believing his side of the story before she even talked to the police and before they admitted they had been in error.

What will it look like, Martin asked, when they have arrived at a 7? For Lars, a 7 would mean that they both are a little bit more understanding and positive toward each other. For Karin, a 7 would be when they are not grumpy and they could engage in pleasant conversations, sharing thoughts about events in their everyday life. Martin then asked Karin and Lars to imagine that they had already arrived at a 7 and had put this on videotape. If he, Martin, were to watch this videotape, what would he see that would show the difference between a 7 and a 6? In other words, what would have changed about their relationship? Together, they described the "7" video as follows: "The sun will be shining. You will see us doing things together, not fighting, and you will see us sitting down and discussing things. And when we discuss things, we allow ourselves to talk with and listen to each other."

A few minutes after this video discussion, Karin said something to Lars (when we discussed this later on, none of us could remember what she had said), and Lars reacted angrily. Somehow, they were able to work this out and laugh together instead of allowing the argument to escalate. Martin asked them to reflect on how they managed to handle the situation so constructively. At first they could not really say how, but with Martin's help they reconstructed the disagreement. Essentially, what happened was that Karin had said something that bothered Lars, and he had responded by saying, "I'm irritated." Karin accepted this and paused for a while, allowing him to feel heard. As a result, what might have turned into a small fight became an opportunity to talk in a more constructive way and even to laugh a little bit.

Martin concluded session 4 with the following summary:

Despite the fact that you both have had a cold and been very tired, you have managed to stay on the right track. You, Lars, have kept busy and active— that is good for you, I think. To you, Karin, I want to say that it was of the utmost importance that you believed in Lars and stood up for him. I also want to remind you about the end of the session when Lars got irritated. Instead of becoming verbally or physically aggressive, Lars expressed himself with words, and Karin accepted what he had to say instead of responding in an argumentative way. This was a very nice, effective strategy in coping with a possible "might be fight" situation, a situation that easily could have turned into a fight.

Comment

As in earlier sessions, the therapist conducted an ongoing progress evaluation and validated their progress by focusing on things the mother and son had done since last session to achieve their goals and on constructive coping.

Fifth Session (1 Month Later)

Karin arrived alone and announced to Martin that this would be her last session. Her relationship with Lars had, she said, remained calm, and they had a lot of things to plan and do—Karin had decided to move back to the part of Sweden she had come from, and Lars was planning to celebrate his high school graduation. He was also going to have to decide whether he would go on to a university or would start working. Lars said that he wanted to stay where he was, in the south of Sweden. He was determined to make it on his own, without having to be involved with social workers, therapists, or other authorities. He had had enough of counseling. Martin of course accepted this decision and framed it in a positive way, as a sign of progress. Everyone agreed that this would be the last session. Martin invited Karin and Lars to write an article or a book chapter on their work together.

Comments

A solution-focused therapist is always ready and prepared to terminate therapy when client goals are reached, the clients are close enough to their goals to be able to continue on their own, or they inform the therapist that it would be useless to continue.

Follow-up interviews and writing something collaboratively in a mutual summary can help therapist and clients learn more from each other, marking a shift from a client–therapist relationship to a coauthor relationship (Bergmark & Söderquist, 2002; Söderquist et al., 2002).

FOLLOW-UP INTERVIEW

You never know what question you asked until you hear the answer. Likewise, you can say that you never know what kind of therapy you collaborated in until the clients tell you afterward. Several months after the last session, Bo interviewed Karin and her therapist, Martin.

Bo, who had not been given any information about the previous sessions, began the interview by asking Karin to briefly say something about the reasons they came for therapy. Karin mentioned two reasons: first, the intense conflicts between her and Lars that they could not control and that from time to time ended in violence; and second, her worries about how Lars's behavior was affecting both his relationship with her and his ability to cope with others and life in general.

Bo asked what their situation was now. Karin replied that it was much improved; they no longer engaged in serious fights, and both had found ways to calm down and avoid threatening situations. There had not been any physical violence. Karin said that she had been keeping silent in situations where she might have previously reacted to Lars by getting angry or arguing. This did not mean that she would back down or deny herself the right to be heard; she knew she could continue the discussion at a later time. Karin had also come to understand that Lars had expressed anger at her not because she was a bad person, but because she was so important to him and that this was his way of trying to engage. She realized that she needed to be the adult in their relationship, rather than behave on the same childish level as Lars, the way it had been before therapy began.

Karin brought up an example of Lars coping in a more mature and considerate way. One day, not long before this session, Lars had been holding a glass of water as they argued, and he felt his anger rise. Instead of throwing the water in her face, something he had done in the past, he restrained himself and put the glass on the table. She did not know exactly how Lars managed, but she was convinced that he wants to cope with conflicts in a constructive way. Perhaps this was partly a result of her more consistent limit setting, as, for example, when she insisted that he accept the consequences of destroying his mobile phone—costly and a lot of trouble.

"In what way were the therapy sessions useful?" asked Bo. "How would you compare Martin with some of the other therapists you have seen?" Karin responded by saying that the people in child psychiatry told her it was her own fault and that after a while Lars refused to continue meeting with the therapists. The Johanna group was especially useful because of the opportunity to meet other women affected by family violence. Participating in this group made her feel that she was not alone. It was an entirely new experience to talk with people who understood her in a way that her friends could not. More recently, she had been seeing a therapist in individual sessions at an outpatient clinic for alcoholics. Many of their discussions, she said, focused on parent–child relations.

Karin went on to say that in sessions with Martin, she learned to think for herself. She came to understand that not everything was her fault and that it was possible to see and experience things differently. We discussed what it was about her sessions that might have helped her come to these realizations. Karin indicated that in collaboration with Martin, she found out how to better cope with her problems. Martin, she said, gave her and Lars good ideas on how to calm down when things got out if hand—for example, counting to 10 before doing something that she might regret afterward. But Martin pointed out that it was Lars, not he, who came up with this suggestion.

Bo continued the interview by asking Karin to imagine how Lars would have answered the questions he had been asking her. Karin did not know but was sure he would have said how much he appreciates their more peaceful and relaxed interactions. She also thought that if Lars were to get in trouble in the future, he would consider the possibility of seeking a therapist. He knew now how much this can help and no longer believed that it is strange for men to talk in that way.

"How do you see your future, and that of your son?" Bo asked. Mostly in positive terms, Karin replied. She would have liked to have continued meeting Martin for a few more sessions, but Lars thought it was enough. Still, Karin felt that they were now on solid enough ground to further build on their successes and further develop their relationship. Karin and Emil were definitely going to move to another part of Sweden, as she had been planning, and Lars had decided for now to stay where they had been living. Karin recognized that it would be risky for her and Lars to live together for a longer period. Lars was somewhat disappointed in her decision, at one point threatening to move to Australia. However, he had secured a job and intended to enroll into a university later on. Karin thought she could help him accept her decision and stay cool and behave in a mature and adult way. Karin also said that it was a good thing Lars and his former girlfriend broke up.

Bo next turned to Martin and asked him to describe the course of therapy. Very much happened in only a few sessions, Martin said, and he went on to describe how much Lars and Karin cared for each other and their determination to make things better. Their strong wills, which previously had led to conflict escalation and abuse, had become something they could now put to constructive use—such as moving on with their lives. Martin was not at all surprised to hear about Lars controlling himself and putting the glass of water down; Karin and Lars showed creativity and flexibility in the sessions and had come up with several ideas for how to handle high-conflict situations. Before they only had two options—fight or avoid each other. After therapy they had several options.

In Bo's last question for Martin, he asked what Karin and Lars had learned that would be most useful for Karin and Lars in the future. Their strong willpower and the new interpersonal skills they have in their repertoire, Martin said, were very important. Lars learned in the sessions to express himself with words rather than act out aggressively, and mother and son could now talk together calmly and productively. Lars had plans for the future, and Karin was more observant and wise about their relationship dynamics, with a good capacity to evaluate when to interfere and when to withdraw.

Bo ended the interview with asking if there was anything else to add. Karin responded immediately by saying, "Never give up—things can be better. I really want to be a resource in my children's lives. I want them to be able to discuss and talk with me—something I could never do with my parents."

Martin added that he will always remember what Karin said about thinking for oneself. That was very important. "That is what I try to do in therapy," he said, "what my goal is—help people find their own solutions."

OUTCOMES AND CONCLUSION

According to Karin, things were calmer, they fought verbally less often, the physical violence had ceased, and she was less worried. She also thought that the sessions had been a good experience for Lars. According to the therapists, mother and son had demonstrated after therapy the ability to engage in some constructive discussions and to make important decisions about their lives.

Was this enough? Is it possible to say that the therapy sessions were effective, based on what we know, or do we need more outside and objective criteria? From the clients' perspective we think it was enough. The problems that Karin and Lars brought to therapy no longer dominate their relationship, they are able to plan for the future, and they have good memories about the work we did together. From the team's perspective, we think it was enough, too. The feedback from the mother indicated success, and Martin was quite satisfied with the therapeutic process, both with the sessions that he conducted and with the follow-up collaborative session he did with Karin and Bo.

The follow-up session was conducted only a few months after the last meeting with Karin and Lars present. To know for sure whether the gains that the clients made are really long lasting, a longer period needs to go by to determine how well things are going—in this case, job and school progress, the mother–son relationship, no involvement with authorities, and so on. You never know what will happen in the future; health problems, accidents, and other life events can quickly change a person's life, and a few therapy sessions, no matter how successful, are no vaccination against future problems. Four or five therapy sessions do not guarantee anything, but sometimes they can be drawn upon in the future if and when the client encounters new problems or has to face difficult personal challenges.

Solution-Focused Family Therapy and Domestic Violence

Solution-focused family therapy is not designed to address one specific problem. It is a model for (or a map for) the therapist to collaborate with clients regardless of the problems presented. Through a focus on client goals, coping strategies, and what they have been doing to achieve their goals, the therapy sessions can help individuals redirect their lives, providing a clearer direction for how to proceed and giving them the confidence to cope with the present and the future.

Therapists working with domestic violence cases need to know a lot about abuse of all kinds. Relationship abuse and violence, whether mutual or directed by one person toward another, is more than disrespectful; it can pose a serious threat to physical safety as well as to personal integrity and emotional well-being, making individuals vulnerable for disrespect, humiliation, and being controlled by others. A consequence of this is that with abused individuals, the risk of "therapeutic abuse" is always present in the therapy sessions. By not listening to what a client says, refusing to take no for an answer, and forcing him or her to accept their point of view, therapists can contribute to or create an abusive-like situation in which the client feels intimidated and disrespected. However well intended a therapist's intentions may be, the value of a session can be determined only by the clients' reactions and the quality of their experiences.

In domestic violence cases, perhaps even more than in other cases, it is necessary to listen very carefully and proceed with every step of the therapeutic process in collaboration with the clients. Because clients affected by domestic violence are so often subjected to monologues and to being told what to do, it is of utmost importance that the therapist emphasize the opposite, specifically, collaboration and dialogue. Whom the therapist agrees to see in sessions and what modality he or she chooses should always depend on the risks and dangers involved. In domestic violence cases characterized by minor violence, individual, couples, and family sessions or a combination may all be appropriate options. In cases involving more serious and dangerous violence, a victim's safety should be considered primary, and individual and group sessions are the preferred modalities.

Not all clients, of course, benefit from solution-focused therapy. The therapeutic alliance, upon which the success of this type of approach depends, can be hindered by a client's expectations and beliefs, and likewise there may be a mismatch in the personalities of client and therapist. Aside from the more severe domestic violence cases just mentioned, we have found the solution-focused brief family therapy model very useful in all cases we have worked with, whatever the constellation of family members. The model is a non-iatrogenic model, doing no harm and giving clients a chance to direct their own lives.

REFERENCES

Berg, I. K., & Kelly, S. (2000). *Building solutions in child protective services.* New York: Norton.

Bergmark, A. K., & Söderquist, M. (2002). Fighting for freedom: A collaborative success story. *Journal of Family Therapy, 24*(2), 167–186.

Cantwell, P., & Holmes, S. (1994). Social construction: A paradigm shift for systemic therapy and training. *The Australian and New Zealand Journal of Family Therapy, 15,* 17–26.

Council of Europe. (1986). *Violence in the family* (Recommendation No. R(85)4, adopted on March 26, 1985, and explanatory memorandum). Strasbourg, France: Committee of Ministers of the Council of Europe.

de Shazer, S., & Dolan, Y. (2007). *More than miracles: The state of art of solution-focused brief therapy.* New York: Haworth Press.

Furniss, T. (1991). *The multi professional handbook of child sexual abuse: Integrated management, therapy & legal intervention.* London: Routledge.

Jenkins, A. (1990). *Invitations to responsibility: The therapeutic engagement of men who are violent and abusive.* Dulwich: Dulwich Centre.

Lee, M. Y., Sebold, J., & Uken, A. (2003). *Solution-focused treatment of domestic violence offenders: Accountability for change.* Oxford: Oxford University Press.

Lee, M. Y., Uken, A., & Sebold, J. (2007). Role of self-determined goals in predicting recidivism in domestic violence offenders. *Research on Social Work Practice, 17*(1), 30–41.

Lindforss, L., & Magnusson, D. (1997). Solution-focused therapy in prison. *Contemporary Family Therapy, 19*(1), 89–103.

MacDonald, A. (2007). *Solution-focused therapy: Theory, research & practice.* London: Sage.

Miller, S. D., Hubble, M. A., & Duncan, B. L. (1996). *Handbook of solution-focused brief therapy.* San Francisco: Jossey-Bass.

Söderquist, M. (2002). Goals, interactive play and golden moments. *Context, 64,* 3–8.

Söderquist, M., Clas, C., & Sundelin, J. (2002). Hold on to your goals: Clients and therapists commenting on videotaped SFT-sessions. *Journal of Systemic Therapies, 21*(4).

Stith, S., Rosen, K., & McCollum, E. (2004). Treating intimate partner violence within intact couples relationships: Outcomes of multi-couple versus individual couple therapy. *Journal of Marital and Family Therapy, 30*(6), 305–315.

Turnell, A., & Edwards, S. (1999). *Signs of safety: A solution and safety oriented approach to child protection casework.* New York: Norton.

Turnell, A., & Essex, S. (2006). *Working with "denied" child abuse: The resolutions approach.* Maidenhead, England: Open University Press.

Vetere, A., & Cooper, J. (2001). Working systemically with family violence: Risk, responsibility and collaboration. *Journal of Family Therapy, 23,* 378–396.

Wade, A. (1997). Small acts of living: Everyday resistance to violence and other forms of oppression. *Contemporary Family Therapy, 19*(1), 23–39.

Ziegler, P., & Hiller, T. (2001). *Recreating partnership: A solution-oriented collaborative approach to couples therapy.* New York: Norton.

QUESTIONS FOR REFLECTION AND DISCUSSION

1 Solution-focused therapy was highly effective with this family. Do you think it would have been as useful if mother and son did not already have a fairly good bond, if there had been more serious mental health issues or past trauma, or if there had been greater resistance to treatment? What aspects of solution-focused therapy do you think would be useful with *any* case of family violence?

2 How likely would Lars have been to abuse his mother if he had not observed his father doing the same? Would the problems between mother and son, such as her drinking and their conflictual communication, have gotten so far out of hand? Please explain the relationship between the distal factors (past abuse) and proximal factors (current problems and stress).

3 What did you think of the team's practice of having a second therapist interview clients and their previous therapist in a follow-up interview?

Supervision in Domestic Violence Casework

19

Supervision and Family Safety: Working With Domestic Violence

ARLENE VETERE AND JAN COOPER

We started the Reading Safer Families domestic violence service over 12 years ago, in the city of Reading, UK. We provide assessment and systemic integrative therapeutic services to individuals, couples, and family/kin systems and to both victims and perpetrators of domestic violence in a socially inclusive way. In addition, we consult legal and social care professional networks, helping to understand and resolve network difficulties in complex cases of family violence.

During this time, many individual practitioners and teams, in both our statutory and voluntary social and health care services, have approached us for supervision. As supervisees they have become worried about the levels of violence in their case loads, and they seek supervision from us in the context of our approach to safe practice, that is, our safety methodology. As part of our approach to supervision, we pay careful attention to the self of the therapist and the impact on practitioners of working in the field of family violence. It is of some interest to us that although there has been much written about working therapeutically with individuals, couples, and families where domestic violence has occurred, there is relatively little written about supervision practice in this area of work (Anderson & Goolishian, 1986). We agree with Sand-Pringle, Zarski, and Wendling (1995) that working with family violence provides a complex challenge to the supervision process and probably demands that supervisors become more active and directive in supervision than they otherwise would in their usual supervision practice.

We have written extensively elsewhere of our approach to safety in therapeutic work where domestic violence is known or suspected (Cooper & Vetere, 2005; Vetere & Cooper, 2007). We shall briefly outline our safety methodology here, to set the scene in this chapter for our approach to supervision of others' practice, but it is important to say at the outset that it is our approach to safety that usually initiates the request for supervision from us, and it is this methodology that guides our supervision practice. This chapter is more concerned with the supervision of qualified-level practice, although the approach outlined here can be adapted for prequalification supervision, where arrangements for clinical responsibility and accountability differ.

RISK, RESPONSIBILITY, AND COLLABORATION

We put safety first in all aspects of our work, assessment, therapy, consultation, and supervision (Vetere & Cooper, 2001). We use a minimum of six sessions to assess for safety, before we undertake couples work or family reunification work, for example.

Risk

We distinguish between the management of risk and the assessment of risk. We assume that none of our work is without risk. We manage risk by ensuring we always work alongside a "stable third," both to help manage processes of anxiety in the family and professional system and to corroborate what we are being told by the family members with respect to safety. The stable third may be our referrer or may be a trusted member of the community, such as a grandparent, a faith leader, a community worker, a health visitor, and so on. If children are involved, it is essential the stable third knows the children and has access to the home. We establish a no-violence contract and develop a safety plan in our first meeting, with the knowledge and support of the stable third. We consider it our responsibility to help the family members keep to the safety plan. We hold regular reviews with the family and the stable third to check that the safety plan is working and to adapt it as appropriate.

We assess for risk by asking about repeat violence, the contexts in which violence takes place, the family members' ability to manage anger and other upsetting feelings, empathy for the victim of violence and assault, the ability to reflect on and learn from experience, and internal motivation for change.

Responsibility

We agree with Goldner, Penn, Sheinberg, and Walker (1990) that it is essential to distinguish between responsibility for violence on the one hand and explanation for how violence is enacted on the other. If we do not hold these two discourses in mind at the same time, we risk losing sight of responsibility in our search for therapeutic understanding. We are prepared for signs of responsibility to grow and develop during the work, and we encourage people to develop responsibility for their own and others' safety. We do this by seeking some acknowledgement that there is a problem and some recognition of the relational aspects and consequences of domestic violence. We do not meet the children in the company of the parents or caregivers until we are sure the parents can take responsibility for safety in the family. We ask parents about the impact of their violence on their children's well-being and development. We discourage the minimization or denial of violence by paying careful attention to how people talk about their own and others' violent behavior.

Collaboration

We try to work collaboratively in a working context of social and legal control. We do this by being transparent about our own moral position in relation to safety and violence. We work together in the room with couples, families, and teams and use systemic reflecting processes to make our thinking and responding as clear as possible. We do not offer confidentiality; rather, we negotiate what information can be kept confidential, if it has no bearing on safety and risk. We assess family members' ability to cooperate with other professionals and to see professionals as potentially helpful.

Our approach to safety, outlined previously, directly informs our supervision work. When considering the formative and educative function of supervision, we instruct supervisees in our approach to safety and help them adapt it to the needs of their clients, their agency, and the professional network. This activity makes us more active and directive and emphasizes our role in helping our supervisees develop their skills, understanding, and abilities in relation to safety and risk.

We have been influenced by the guidelines developed by Sand-Pringle et al. (1995) for the supervision of therapeutic work with family violence. According to them, supervision is helpfully structured according to the assessed level of violence in the family system. This helps prioritize safety and determine when to access the help and support of other professional workers. The history of violence and the potential for future violence influences the short- and long-term goals for supervision. Sand-Pringle et al. try to make the covert overt. They inquire around the existence of family secrets and recognize processes of minimization and the impact of the work on the supervisee. In addition, they are alert for processes of mirroring between the workers and the family, where patterns of interaction within professional systems can increasingly reflect patterns of interaction within family systems in unhelpful ways to both. They respond to crisis with crisis-intervention advice and support the recognition of emergent signs of safety. They explore maneuverability on behalf of the supervisee, such as flexible responding and best use of available resources, and pay attention to problems of interprofessional network functioning. They use systemic working hypotheses and reflective practice to aid the development of a meta-perspective for their work.

ASSESSING THE CHILD'S SAFETY

Sometimes we supervise practitioners working in schools and other community settings where domestic violence is suspected. In these cases, we ensure our supervisee pays attention to the safety of child by developing a safety plan with the child that reflects the child's age and understanding: identifying a safe place for the child to go, or a person he or she can go to if necessary, and making sure the child knows how to contact emergency services and that it is neither safe nor the child's responsibility to intervene to try to protect his or her parents (Hester, Pearson, & Harwin, 2000). In assessing the child's safety, we advise supervisees to ask questions about the most recent incident of violence, whether weapons were used, whether substance use was involved, and what happened. In addition, they should inquire about the frequency of these incidents and whether the police or others have been involved at any time. It is important to find out what the child did and whether the child tried to intervene and to ask about siblings and what they were doing at the time. Questions can be tailored to the child's understanding in terms of asking what happens when the child's parents or caregivers disagree or get angry, or whether the child has ever seen a family member hurting another family member. Asking the child whom they talk to and what makes them frightened, angry, upset, and worried, and especially who the child is worried about, helps explore the child's coping responses (Hester et al., 2000).

THE SUPERVISION CONTRACT

We hold ourselves accountable to our supervisees through our clear articulation of safety in practice, our theory base, and our respective responsibilities, negotiated through our supervisory contract.

Upon meeting individual practitioners and teams for the first time, we like to explore their preferred ideas about safety, risk, responsibility, and collaborative practice. We ask a number of questions as we get to know them and their agency context, including their agency policy toward violence, such as the following:

1   What theoretical ideas and practices are supervisees firmly wedded to, and what are the implications for safe practice?
2   What theoretical ideas and practices do supervisees occasionally draw upon, and what are the implications for safe practice?
3   What theoretical ideas and practices are supervisees less attracted to, and what are the implications for safe practice?

We explore how our relationships with particular schools of thought may either constrain or support safe practice. Over time, we identify with supervisees how they may need to challenge or experiment with their preferred theoretical ideas in order to develop safety in their practice and in their supervision of trainees and to aid their further understanding of themselves in relation to their preferred ideas. This understanding informs how we might adapt our safety methodology, given that we supervise practitioners trained in different psychotherapeutic disciplines and orientations.

Similarly, we explore their common and not-so-common dilemmas in their work with couple and family violence. For example, we find that practitioners report getting overloaded with information about a family from multiple sources, without finding any clarity for subsequent action. Supervisees speak to us about holding the tension of constantly being asked to judge and make predictions about possibly unpredictable be-havior. They sometimes describe feeling isolated because they cannot al-ways easily share their concerns with others. This can result in increasing preoccupation with the couple or family or in seeking simplistic solutions, which can then lead the practitioners to lose sight of their competence and resilience and even to patterns of overempathizing with the victims of violence. All of this can result in mirroring victim or rescuer positions with the resultant anger and frustration with their agency's responses and service or management decisions.

RESPONSIBILITIES OF THE SUPERVISOR

When supervising therapeutic work with couple and family violence, we have learned to adapt our supervision style and approach to take account of the following responsibilities. We believe it is helpful for supervisors to share with their supervisee some ideas about their style of supervision and their supervisory role and about how that is adapted when super-vising work with domestic violence. It is then possible to discuss and continue to review what are the acceptable and collaborative parameters for such a process.

   We strive to create a safe space for thinking, within a trusting and collaborative relationship, where indecision, reflectivity, and action will be held in equal regard. We are clear about accountability and our re-spective responsibilities. We allow tension and anxiety to be expressed and contained in such a way that creative thinking and responses are not stifled. We think it is always helpful to tell supervisees that we will *always* ask about their personal safety because we think it needs to be a natural part of the ebb and flow of the supervisory conversation. If their personal safety is mentioned for the first time in the context of a particular piece of therapeutic work, it can have the effect of unhelpfully raising anxiety rather than acknowledging the safety, risk, and threat that runs through such work. We pay attention to the emotional well-being of supervisees and the effects this work has on them (discussed further as this chapter continues). There may be moments when their work triggers unexpected memories and feelings that take everyone by surprise. We are straight-forward about our willingness to be supportive within the supervisory relationship and to offer appropriate comfort, advice, and referral for personal work, as appropriate. We believe that self-reflexive monitoring of these boundaries is the responsibility of the supervisor also, given that personal issues have the potential to impact on their supervisory work. In this respect we hold a commitment to trying to maintain a balance between getting overwhelmed (or frozen) and being underwhelmed and potentially unresponsive. We believe in supervision for supervisors as a necessary part of a balancing and rebalancing process.

Working in the Territory: Stress, Distress, Resilience, and Resources

> We are open to absorbing profound loss, hurt and mistrust from our clients but also to the stimulation of these human states, present in us all. (Berger, 2001, p. 189)

In the supervision of therapeutic work with family violence, the restorative and supportive functions of the supervisor process are often in the forefront. We provide a space for thinking and for the illumination of feelings where our supervisees' responses can be explored to help throw light on what is happening in the therapeutic or rehabilitation work. We explore systemic patterns and political and economic processes in their organizational context and within the professional network that both supports and constrains their practice. If our goal is to help them be more effective in their therapeutic work, we need to pay very careful attention to the balance in our work between the supportive, educational, and managerial functions of supervision.

Stress for our supervisees stems from many aspects of their practice, including the following:

- Hearing grueling accounts of physical, emotional, and sexual cruelty and the concomitant risks of secondary traumatization
- Their disappointment when violence continues despite their best efforts in therapy or rehabilitation work
- Powerful feelings evoked in them, that if left unexamined, can get in the way of their therapeutic and collegial relationships
- Risks to them of carrying an inflated sense of responsibility around their work, particularly when they work in unsupported ways, in the absence of agency policy around responses to couple violence, and without support from a stable third person
- Tensions around introducing psychotherapeutic ideas into a conservative legal system with little tradition of acknowledging the role of emotion and passion in people's thinking and behavior

- A high case load where violence is the issue
- The recognition of societal patterns that foster abuse, marginalization, and social exclusion, such as institutional racism and sexism

The supervisory relationship can provide a secure base and a holding environment within which difficult feelings of uncertainty, helplessness, ignorance, and incompetence can be tolerated. Similarly, it is a place where strengths, resources, and resilient responding can be encouraged and supported. We encourage supervisees to reflect on their strategies of coping, both individually and collectively—for example, encouraging self-care and maintaining consensually appropriate emotional and behavioral boundaries—by developing realistic expectations of themselves and others, by acknowledging our commonly held wish for denial, and by a developed awareness of countertransference processes and symptoms of secondary trauma, for themselves and for others. We maintain our curiosity about social support and balance in their lives, we encourage them to engage in teaching and learning for professional development, and we support collaborative projects and actively seek opportunities for them to engage in prevention work. Sometimes we support time-outs from therapy, and we always pay attention to their personal safety in the work.

CASE STUDY: DAWN

In this section, we describe our supervision of a small team of social workers who were asked to manage a complex process of assessment for rehabilitation work with a woman (we call her Dawn) and her four children. She had been a victim of repeated violence from all of the four men she had lived with, and the children had witnessed violence to their mother from their own father and a succession of stepfathers. The mother used amphetamines to help her cope. The care of the children had been sorely neglected, as Dawn struggled increasingly to look after her children and manage the household. The case was described to us as "sex, lies, and drugs." It appeared that Dawn had lied to social workers about her drug taking and could not keep her repeated promises to break her habit. In addition, Dawn had agreed with social services to stop seeing her former partners as a way of showing that she was able to look after her children and keep them safe. However, she was unable to prevent the men from coming to the house and did not tell the social workers for fear she would not get her children back. Thus, neither Dawn nor the social workers trusted one another.

The following description of our work with the social services team focuses on a number of specific supervision tasks. The social services team had asked us for supervision a number of times previously and knew us well. They called saying that they urgently needed support for a problematic new case. They had not yet met with any members of the family but were feeling caught in a web of interagency communications. Dawn and her children had been living in an adjoining county and had moved to their county recently. However, the family's previous social worker had contacted them by telephone and by letter outlining her extreme concerns about the family and defensively listing all the opportunities and help that her department had offered to Dawn without success. The children's names had all been put on the child protection register. After receiving such a welter of negative information, the team and the designated social worker, JB, were trying to find a way to position themselves so that they would not either overreact or underreact in a way that was not helpful either to the family or to the agency. JB told us she felt overwhelmed by the complexity of the issues in the case and did not want to be prejudiced against Dawn before she had even met her.

Family History

The family consisted of a single parent—mother Dawn—and her four children: two older boys, Jason, 13, and Sam, 11, and two girls, Denise, 8, and Susie, 4. All the children had different birth fathers and had experienced the other fathers as stepfathers or potential co-caregivers with their mother. There was no information about the fathers or their whereabouts in any of the files or court papers. At the time of her move to her new address, Dawn was not in a relationship. She had moved her residence a number of times over the years to escape the violence, and the children had a fragmented school experience, with limited opportunity to make and keep friends.

Dawn had been in the care system herself from 12 years old. Her father had been repeatedly violent to her mother, her four siblings, and her. At the age of 12, she harmed herself in a dramatic way, in order to bring the attention of the authorities on her family. The investigation at that time resulted in the imprisonment of her father and led to the placement of her and her siblings in the care system, but all living separately. Dawn had hoped she and her siblings would be placed together, and in her disappointment, she vowed that if she ever had children, she would help them grow up together to have strong sibling bonds. Alcohol abuse had been part of Dawn's life for some time, but drug abuse was linked to her relationships and in particular to one partner who had introduced her to amphetamine use. Dawn found that amphetamines helped her cope with the effects of the violence, and they also led to her developing an inflated sense of her competence and ability to cope and look after her children, when it was clear to the social workers that the children were neglected and emotionally abused; for example, the children did not sleep or eat regularly or well, they had repeated absences from school, and they were often unsupervised—in addition, they were exposed to the fathers' violence to their mother and were fearful for her, for themselves, and for each other.

Dawn was difficult to engage, and her previous social worker had found her untrustworthy in that she could not believe her. The children had rather fragmented school attendance and were very wary of strangers but intensely loyal to their mother. JB was interested to note that there were no details or information about any of the fathers, partners, or potential co-caregivers in the accompanying documentation. It was just as if they had been written out! Even Dawn did not know how to contact the men, it seemed, and was unable to predict when they would show up at her front door. This unpredictability left her in a state of fear that led to her increased use of alcohol and amphetamines and led the previous social workers to think she was lying to them.

Assessment

At our first supervision meeting with JB and the team together, we identified three overlapping systems that the team needed to pay attention to: (a) the family first of all, which included the "missing" men; (b) then their own team; and (c) the influence of the referring team and the impact of their negative views about the family. These views needed to inform JB and her colleagues but not limit their responses at the present time.

During our initial meeting and in subsequent supervision meetings, we framed our conversation with our supervisees with the aid of the following prompts. We explored multiple viewpoints by asking them to describe the case from the family members' point of view and then from their agency's point of view. We asked what other descriptions of the family the team and the professional network wanted us to know about. We wished to know if there were rumors and secrets within the system about the family that contributed to the family's reputation and that implicitly influenced decision making. We asked what the supervisees wanted from us in terms of supervision goals. We wanted to know what the mother and the family were doing right—we explored the potential for taking responsibility for safety and asked about signs of safety. We tracked the history of domestic violence, checked what action had been taken in the past, and challenged the apparent invisibility of the men in the case. We asked whether our supervisees and the team/professional network agreed about the level of risk and action that needed to be taken. We wanted to know what, if the mother and the family had been able to listen to our conversation, they might say.

Before our second supervision session with JB and the team, there had been a violent and dangerous situation during the night when a previous partner of Dawn's, the father of the youngest girl, had forcibly tried to gain entry to the house and had been abusive to Dawn with the intention of abducting his birth daughter. The police became involved, and the children were placed temporarily in foster homes. The team was then asked to do a formal assessment, and care proceedings were started. From the point of view of JB and the team, the safety of the children was paramount, as was the safety of the mother, but because they had been overloaded with information from their colleague, they wanted to have a plan for this assessment that would help them find some clarity. They did not want to seek simplistic solutions in a situation of complex family relationships, nor did they want to be so weighed down by negatives that they lost sight of potential competencies and resilience in the mother and children. They were also aware, as are many other workers making assessments, of the tension and uncertainty when constantly being asked to judge unpredictable behavior in potentially volatile situations. They were interested in thinking about this case in a way that would help them with future cases.

In a risk assessment we think that uncertainty is the range of behaviors or outcomes that are possible, given the existence of risk; and chance is the influenced or uninfluenced possibility of change in the context of the assessment and during the time of the assessment. Together we devised a set of questions that would help JB achieve the following goals: (a) access the management of risk during the assessment, (b) develop an understanding of Dawn's potential for change, (c) develop an understanding of Dawn's ability to keep herself and her children safe, and (d) explore and support the resources and circumstances that would allow them all to flourish as a family. This assessment involved sessions with the children individually and as a sibling group, sessions with the children and their foster caregivers, sessions with the children and their mother individually and as a sibling group with their mother, a meeting with one grandmother who was in touch, and a meeting with the original social worker. We advised JB to try to track down the fathers who seemed so invisible, who were not taking responsibility for their behavior, and who were not being held accountable within the professional network. JB was able to arrange an interview at her office with the father who had broken into the house. None of the other fathers were interviewed, nor did they come forward to take up their responsibilities. At the very least, the fathers, their actions, and their responsibility could be written back into the documents.

Initially we focused on JB's meetings with Dawn and how Dawn could be given the best opportunity to tell her story and create opportunities for her to work collaboratively with JB and the agency. Together with JB and her colleagues we devised the following list of questions that we hoped would both promote and assess Dawn's competence. As the work progressed, JB gave us feedback as to how the questions helped to keep her focused on the assessment but also gave her an opportunity to hear from Dawn the reality of her own story in her own words. It also addressed the important influences of Dawn's relationships with her partners and what they had meant to her and gave her an opportunity to own her experience as she understood it.

These questions, probes, and points of view were created to promote Dawn's sense of competence, assertiveness, self-esteem, and authoritative parenting as well as to provide a framework for JB's assessment:

- Stressing the importance for Dawn of cooperation and developing competence in working with social services and those caring for her children
- As a woman acknowledging her need for change and challenging her feelings of failure
- Increasing her self-worth by emphasizing achievement and competence
- Unpacking ideas about telling the truth
- Empowering Dawn when she told about her lived experience
- Asking her about her relationships with her children and what she wanted for them in the future
- Inquiring how she managed to develop such a sense of loyalty and family in her children and their feelings about their family

- Listening when Dawn talked about poverty, living on benefits, often moving because of domestic violence, and not really trusting professionals
- Seeing drug taking in her adult life and domestic violence in her childhood and adult life as distinct but overlapping
- Emphasizing Dawn's right to safety
- Asking her to reflect and predict about herself and her children into the future
- Helping her to refuse to accept the invisibility of her partners and expecting them to have shown responsibility toward her and their children
- Asking her to talk legitimately about her relationships with her partners and how these relationships developed and what decisions were made together
- Getting her to differentiate between her ideas about being a victim and being a survivor emotionally and within the wider system
- Encouraging her to talk about relational aspects of herself as opposed to her overwhelming sense of individual responsibility

OUTCOMES AND CONCLUSION

JB and her colleagues concluded their assessment by arguing that Dawn needed to commit to residential drug rehabilitation before she could care for her children again. The children remained in the care of the local authority. Dawn herself emerged from the assessment with renewed feelings of self-respect and a strong sense of entitlement to her own and her children's safety. The court gave Dawn access to her children, and she was able to develop cooperative relationships with the new caregivers of her children. In the longer term, Dawn became drug- and alcohol-free.

In conclusion, we hope we have shown how supervision of therapeutic and assessment work in the context of domestic violence demands certain changes in the style and approach of supervision. We think it is possible to focus on safety while maintaining a committed therapeutic stance that emphasizes resources, resilience, and competence, both for families and for the supervisees. As in therapeutic work with issues of family violence, supervision practice also makes emotional and practical demands on the supervisor, with the concomitant need for occasional supervision of our supervision. We hope this chapter goes some way toward raising the profile of the importance of active and directive supervision in the context of family violence.

REFERENCES

Anderson, H., & Goolishian, H. (1986). Systemic consultation with agencies dealing with domestic violence. In L. Wynne, S. McDaniel, & T. Weber (Eds.), *Systems consultation: A new perspective for family therapy.* New York: Guilford.

Berger, H. (2001). Trauma and the therapist. In T. Speirs (Ed.), *Trauma: A practitioner's guide to counselling* (pp. 189–212). Hove, England: Brunner-Routledge.

Cooper, J., & Vetere, A. (2005). *Domestic violence and family safety: A systemic approach to working with violence in families.* Chichester, England: Whurr/Wiley.

Goldner, V., Penn, P., Sheinberg, M., & Walker, G. (1990). Love and violence: Gender paradoxes in volatile attachments. *Family Process, 29,* 343–364.

Hester, M., Pearson, C., & Harwin, N. (2000). *Making an impact: Children and domestic violence.* London: Jessica Kingsley.

Sand-Pringle, C., Zarski, J., & Wendling, K. (1995). Swords into ploughshares: Supervisory issues with violent families. *Journal of Systemic Therapies, 14,* 34, 46.

Vetere, A., & Cooper, J. (2001). Working systemically with family violence: Risk, responsibility and collaboration. *Journal of Family Therapy, 23,* 378–396.

Vetere, A., & Cooper, J. (2007). Couple violence and couple safety: A systemic and attachment oriented approach to working with complexity and uncertainty. In J. Hamel and T. Nicholls (Eds.), *Family interventions in domestic violence.* New York: Springer Publishing.

Index

Abandonment, 51, 253
Abuse. *See also* Child abuse; Elder
    abuse; Sexual abuse
  child, 141–142, 334
  children as more reliable source of
    information about, 15
  emotional, 67, 73, 263
  as form of connection, 238
  inability to recognize, 267
  minimized childhood, 267–268
  physical, 63–64
  politics of, 3–15
  primary predictor of, 238
  three-phase cycle of, 8, 12
  verbal, 73, 126, 282
  warning signs of, 30, 34
  witnesses of, 231
Abused aggressor, 60
Abusive-behavior checklist, 119
ADD. *See* ADHD
ADHD, 50, 56, 141, 218, 291
Adolescence, 247
Adolescent offenders, 288
Adoption, 218
Adult attachment, 16
Adult Protective Services (APS), 240
Affective involvement, 80
Affective responsiveness
  anger highlighted in, 88
  in PCSTF, 80
Africa, 274–275
Agentic traits, 281
Aggression, distance complementing,
  221
Al-Anon, 122, 123–124, 192
Alcohol, 309, 314
  abuse, 329
  blame for marital problems on, 179,
    190

drinking habits of, 82–83
increased violence and, 49–50, 204
owning responsibility and, 53–54
reduced use of, 122
Alcoholics Anonymous, 129, 180
Alienation, 231
Alternative therapies, for domestic
    violence, 3–18
  current models and, 15–16
  politics of abuse and, 3–15
Amphetamines, 356
Anger
  acknowledgment of, 148
  affective responsiveness highlighting,
    88
  awareness of, 84
  curves, 84
  demographic variables influencing
    expression of, 288
  intimate partner, 10
  learned responses of, 288
  managing, 165
  psychological role of, 294
  rage *v.*, 63
  reactive, 202
  women and, 62–63
Anger management therapy
  case study, 262–271
  cognitive-behavioral component in,
    299
  experiential approaches in, 259–271
  family history and, 267–268
  keeping oneself safe as first rule of,
    261
  medicine wheel in, 266–267
  outcomes and, 270–271
  PAV and, 261–262
  treatment and, 259–270
Anger Styles Questionnaire, 312

361